What Leaders Are Saying

"This is the book senior teams need right now, a grounded, practical, and sharply attuned approach to the pressures of global operations. McLennan gives leaders the tools to lift enterprise performance without losing the creativity and courage that drive it."

Tony Ross, Senior Director, Americas Operations & Supply Chain, Apple

"A rare guide for leaders who want to strengthen culture while navigating profound technological change. Katharine shows how trust, clarity, and connection become strategic assets in the AI era."

Judy Hoff Gilbert, Chief People Officer, ŌURA; Chief People Officer, Zymergen; VP, People Operations, Google & YouTube;

"A compelling and practical roadmap for executives facing the next frontier of leadership. McLennan draws on her deep experience to show how ingenuity and collaboration, not automation, will define organizational relevance in the years ahead."

Peter Crawford, Managing Director & Chief Financial Officer, Charles Schwab

"*Before the Fingerprint Fades* gives leaders something we all need: a practical way to build organizations that stay human as AI accelerates in the business world. McLennan shows how insight becomes the enterprise's true competitive edge."

Chris Smith, CEO, NeoGenomics; CEO, Ortho Clinical Diagnostics; CEO, Cochlear

"Katharine cuts straight to the reality facing today's executives: performance now depends on how well leaders blend human judgment with machine intelligence. This book shows exactly how to do it."

Jon Sutton, CEO, ScotPac; CEO, Bank of Queensland; CEO, Bankwest

"A masterful guide for leaders who want to strengthen culture, accelerate performance, and keep humanity at the center of technological change. Credible, wise, and insightful, written by a woman critical to shaping Sydney 2000 Olympics' operational planning."

John Quayle, GM, Sydney 2000 Olympics; CEO, Australian Rugby League

Leadership and Culture
Readiness
for the AI Era

BEFORE THE FINGERPRINT FADES

Katharine McLennan

katharinemclennan.com

This is a work of nonfiction. The executive team described in this book is a composite constructed for illustrative and educational purposes. Certain names, characters, organizations, and scenarios have been fictionalized or combined to protect confidentiality and enhance clarity. Any resemblance to actual persons or organizations is coincidental.

Copyright © 2025 Katharine McLennan

All rights reserved. No part of this book may be reproduced or used in any manner without written permission of the copyright owner except for the use of quotations in a book review.

Front: by Katharine McLennan
Back cover: Arjan Van Woensel
Original interior design & typesetting: Arjan Van Woensel
Revised interior design and typesetting: Katharine McLennan
All diagrams and illustrations: Katharine McLennan

ISBN 978-1-7644069-4-9 (paperback, IngramSpark)
ISBN 978-1-7644069-9-4 (paperback, Amazon)
ISBN 978-1-7644069-5-6 (hardback, Ingram Spark)
ISBN 978-1-7644069-2-5 (ebook, Draft2Digital)
ISBN 978-1-7644069-7-0 (Kindle)

Published by Vistahouse Publishing
Sydney • San Francisco • New York

www.katharinemclennan.com
kath@katharinemclennan.com

For my children Kate and Geoff
Your Gen Z was born into possibility and potential
at the turn of the twenty-first century.
May you and Gen Y take the baton to usher this world
into the Ingenuity Age, and may my Gen X join the
Boomers in the years that might become our
Wisdom Years
if we have the Grace to earn them.

Table of contents

Introduction — 1 — Today

PROLOGUE
Stuck in the Information Age — 6 — 17 December, New York

PART I
What Age Are We In Now? — 16

1	The Industrial Age	24	6 January, Berlin
2	The Information Age	32	7 January, Berlin
3	The AI Threshold	42	8 January, Berlin

PART II
VISTA: The Leadership Compass — 54

4	Vision versus Void	60	1 February, Tokyo
5	Intuition versus Inertia	92	1 March, Sydney
6	Synergy versus Silos	122	1 April, São Paulo
7	Trust versus Tyranny	152	1 May, Bangalore
8	Authenticity versus Apathy	184	1 June, Dublin

PART III
ORG6: The Six Levers of Culture — 216

9	Talent	224	1 July, Tokyo
	The Chief People Officer We Need	273	
10	Structure	288	1 August, Sydney
11	Operations	316	1 September, São Paulo
12	CEO Stewardship	350	15 September, New York
13	Leadership Everywhere	376	1 October, Bangalore
14	Engaged Hearts, Minds, & Bodies	408	1 November, Dublin

EPILOGUE
Toward the Ingenuity Age 440   16 December, New York

AFTERWORD 452

SOURCES 456

SELECTED WORKS BY THE AUTHOR 478

SELF ASSESSMENT FOR
Your Leadership and Culture Readiness
for the AI Era 480

ABOUT THE AUTHOR 484

The book in four pictures

See Prologue

A self-assessment for
Ingenuity Readiness™ for the AI Era

AI Amplifier (vertical axis: 1 to 5)

- 5 — AI Igniting Leadership & Culture Strength
- 3.5
- 1 — AI Untapped for Leadership & Culture Strength

VISTA Leadership and ORG 6 Culture (horizontal axis: 1 to 5)

- 1 — Your leadership and culture are detrimental to AI-era talent expansion
- 3.5
- 5 — Your leadership and culture attract, develop and retain AI-era talent with ever-increasing momentum

Quadrants:

OUTPACED by misdirected AI
Weak leadership & culture. Advanced but misdirected AI. Strengthen leadership & culture before scaling AI.

INGENIOUS in an AI Era
Strong leadership & culture. Strategic AI. Ever-expanding **INGENUITY**.

IRRELEVANT in the AI Era
Outdated leadership & culture. Minimal AI. Ever-expanding **IRRELEVANCE**.

PRIMED for AI Acceleration
Strong leadership & culture. AI underdeveloped. Deploy AI to amplify the strength in your leadership and culture.

Source and Design: Katharine McLennan, 2026.
Please email me for a formal assessment kath@katharinemclennan.com

See Part I
What Age are We in Today?

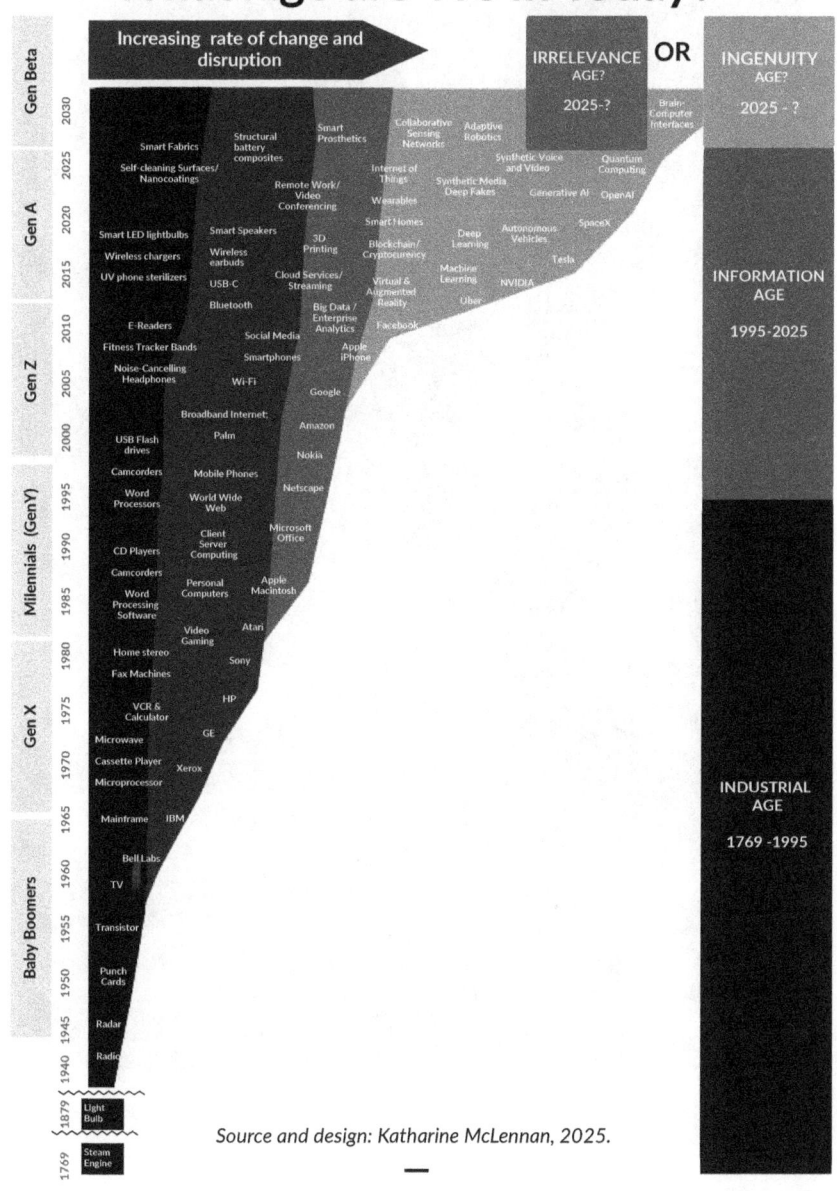

Source and design: Katharine McLennan, 2025.

See Part II,
VISTA™
The Five Leadership Choices

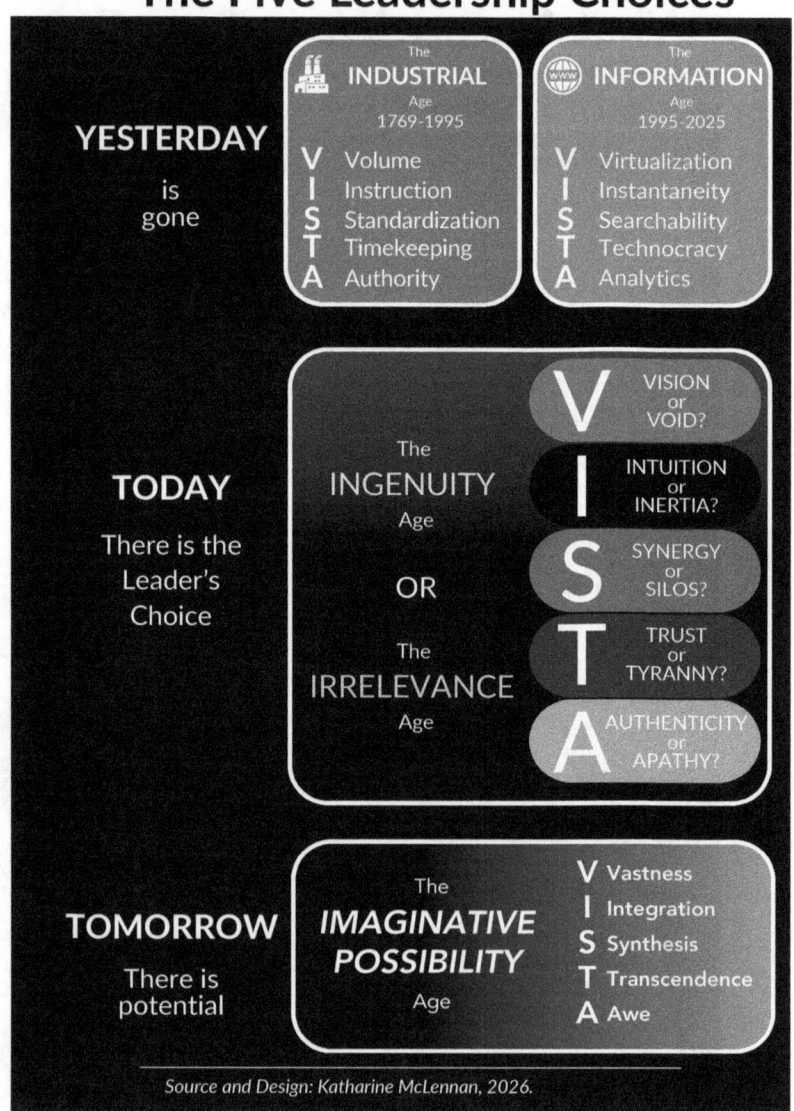

Source and Design: Katharine McLennan, 2026.

See Part III, ORG6™ The Six Levers of Culture

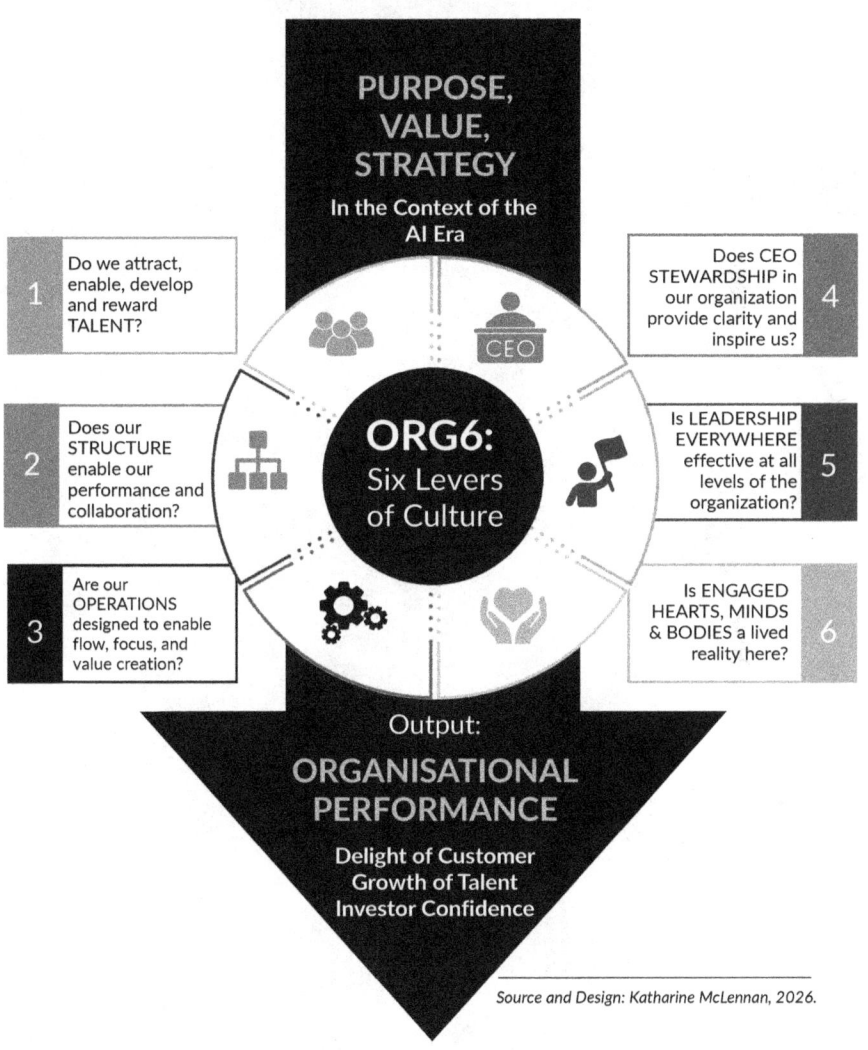

Source and Design: Katharine McLennan, 2026.

Strategy without operations is a daydream.

Operations without strategy is a nightmare.

Either without talent development is unsustainable.

All without a kind and curious awareness of Self is meaningless.

Katharine McLennan

Written on the eve of the Sydney 2000 Opening Ceremony,
after four years (1996-2000) as

Head of Operational Planning for the
Sydney Organising Committee for the
Olympic Games

Introduction: The Choice Before us

Every age gives leaders a choice about what kind of organizations they will build. Some ages make that choice more visible than others.

The Industrial Age measured our output. The Information Age expanded our knowledge. Information is now a commodity, and we face a new era. The age before us will not be defined by technology alone. It will be defined by how we respond. It will call forward something more profound: our ingenuity.

This book, *Before the Fingerprint Fades*, was born from thirty-five years spent inside and alongside leadership teams, asking a core question: how do we build enterprises where people are free to think, create, and matter?

Our workplaces have mastered efficiency and information. Yet in the process, they have often drained imagination and, in some cases, eroded mental and physical well-being. The next Age will not be about machines or data; it will be about humans rediscovering their inventive capacity in partnership with artificially intelligent tools. The AI Era is the technological condition of our time. The Age we inhabit within it will be a matter of leadership choice.

The danger is not that AI will become more intelligent than us; it is that we will stop using our own intelligence altogether. That is the shadow side of progress, the quiet drift into irrelevance. You may be technologically advanced and still be culturally unprepared.

The fingerprint on this cover is more than a design; it is a declaration. It represents the trace of human originality in a world that risks becoming synthetic and uniform. Each fingerprint is distinct, impossible to replicate, and impossible to erase once impressed. It carries identity, a sense of belonging, and evidence that we have been here. In this book, the fingerprint represents the ingenuity we possess: what makes us human in an age of machines.

But fingerprints can fade. When organizations lose sight of what is uniquely human, the ability to imagine, to empathize, and to connect, they risk becoming featureless, efficient, and forgettable. Before the Fingerprint Fades is an invitation to reclaim and deepen our mark of ingenuity, designing enterprises where the human pattern is not worn away by automation, but enlivened by it.

Readiness is a concept I learned to honor during my four years leading operational planning for the Sydney 2000 Olympic Games. In that world, readiness was not a theory; it was the difference between a city that performed on the world stage and one that failed in front of it. The same is true now for every organization facing AI. This book translates philosophy into action through two frameworks that together define your Ingenuity Readiness: the degree to which your leadership and your organization are prepared to thrive in the AI Era rather than drift toward irrelevance.

VISTA is the Leadership Compass. It defines five leadership choices, Vision, Intuition, Synergy, Trust, and Authenticity. These five choices determine whether AI amplifies wisdom or accelerates corrosion. When these choices erode, their shadows emerge: Void, Inertia, Silos, Tyranny, and Apathy. VISTA assesses your Leadership Readiness for the AI Era.

I chose the word VISTA deliberately. In Italian and Spanish, vista means 'view,' 'sight,' 'the act of seeing.' In English, a vista is a long view through an opening, a perspective that reveals what lies ahead. In law, 'a vista' means 'at sight,' a bill payable on presentation, a commitment honored the moment it is seen. The acronym carries all three meanings. Each age in this book carries its own VISTA, its own version of what leaders see and how they see it.

ORG6 is a roadmap. It describes the Six Levers of Culture: Talent, Structure, Operations, CEO Stewardship, Leadership Everywhere, and Engaged Hearts, Minds & Bodies. Together, they define how culture becomes visible, operational, and tangible. ORG6 assesses your organization's Culture Readiness for the AI Era.

One role sits at the heart of all six levers: the Chief People Officer for the Ingenuity Age. Chapter 9 describes this role in full, not the HR administrator of the past, but the strategic leader accountable for the human system that every other chapter depends on.

Leadership Readiness and Culture Readiness, taken together, become your Ingenuity Readiness. VISTA and ORG6 provide the scaffolding for a twelve-month journey, turning intention into practice and insight into tangible progress. The self-assessment woven through every chapter of this book tracks both.

To ground these ideas, the book follows a representative C-suite team as they implement the work over the course of a year. Each month focuses on one leadership choice from VISTA or one culture lever from ORG6. The team establishes the rhythm of a real leadership year: beginning with diagnosis and direction, then moving through design, delivery, and renewal. By following this sequence, any executive team can chart its own path toward the Ingenuity Age.

Throughout the book, you are invited to assess your own Ingenuity Readiness across two dimensions. The first is your Foundation: is this leadership choice or culture lever alive in how you lead and how your people grow?

The second is your AI Amplifier: are you deploying AI to strengthen your leadership and culture practices? Not AI in general, but AI in service of how you lead and how your organization sees, grows, and keeps its people. The self-assessment is explained in full in the Prologue. Chapter by chapter, you will build a picture of your Ingenuity Readiness, with an opportunity in the final pages to bring it all together into your Overall Ingenuity Readiness.

This book is not a toolkit. It does not prescribe step-by-step implementation or detailed diagnostic instruments. It is designed to do something that must come first: to help leaders see where they stand, understand why they stand there, and recognize what the AI Era demands of them. The self-assessment offers an honest starting point, not a finishing line. For leaders and organizations ready to move from awareness to action, from diagnosis to detailed design, the deeper work of building ingenuity into systems, processes, and culture requires dedicated facilitation and tools beyond the scope of any single book.

You can read this book cover to cover, following the Omnivista team through their twelve-month journey. You can also use it as a reference, turning directly to the leadership choice or culture lever most pressing for you right now, completing that chapter's self-assessment, and returning to other chapters as your priorities shift. The frameworks reward whichever chapter you need most.

My experience, spanning over thirty-five years, and my formal education in neuroscience, history, political science, business, and psychotherapy have taught me that the conditions for mental optimality, not just health, are the same conditions required for ingenuity: safety, curiosity, connection, and purpose. When people are seen and heard by other people, their creativity flourishes.

Far more important than my experience and education, though, are my continuous study and attempted practice of our ancient philosophies and spiritual paths, and the contemplative quiet of time in nature: wellsprings that keep imagination alive and judgment clear.

This is a book about the leadership and culture practices that allow humans to tap into their ingenuity, and about how a technology called AI can support those practices. If you came here searching for the latest AI bots for HR, marketing, finance, or manufacturing, you have come to the wrong book. But if your company is on the cutting edge of AI for its products while your people are miserable and leaving just as soon as they learn what they need from you technically, your fingerprint is already fading. AI will not notice. Your best people already have. And an organization without the people who give it meaning is not an organization at all. It is a machine running on borrowed time.

What gives an organization meaning? People who are seen.

AI grows exponentially in its capabilities, in ways that are impossible to predict given the very nature of its own learning. It will continue to remove activities that were once thought irreplaceable. So what does this give humans the time and space to explore in our own ingenuity? What is possible to discover in our own minds, bodies, and hearts? Do we fall into the abyss of despair, forecasting our irrelevance? Or do we open up to an ingenuity that no technology can replicate?

AI can run your systems with infinitely more efficiency, capacity, and, yes, innovation. This innovation comes from its ability to integrate the ideas of billions of humans over thousands of years, helping us access our own knowledge faster, more clearly, and more provocatively than ever before. It can combine that knowledge in ways we never could: a radiologist's lifetime of pattern recognition compressed into seconds, a drug molecule designed in days rather than years, a supply chain rerouted before the earthquake's aftershocks settle.

But remember. AI is integrating the ideas we have captured in writing and speech. It cannot capture the questions and ponderings of the mind and heart that form in between the words. It cannot reach the genuine, wordless Eureka that arrives as we walk in the Himalayas, sit around the campfire with people we love, create an oil painting from deep within our subconscious, witness a newborn's first breath, say goodbye to a loved one, or experience the joy of winning the game with the goal no one thought was possible.

We are the ones asking the questions of possibility for humans. We alone can discover questions that have not been answered and deliver meaning to the way we want to live our lives. We have yet to explore our infinite access to the extraordinary wisdom that emerges every morning: in the shower of water that comes from our pipes, in the rain that falls unbidden, in the stillness before dawn. Our ancient people knew this from the stars they gazed at in wonder and the nature they felt pulsing from the ground they walked on with bare feet.

We might one day use AI to operate a company now staffed by 250,000 people, but AI cannot tell you why that company matters to the humans it serves. AI cannot experience the love and joy that is our human birthright.

The Zulu greeting is one of those ancient teachings that shape my perspective on leadership and culture. Their version of "hello" is Sawubona, which translates to "I see you and your potential." The response, Sikhona, means "Because you see me and my potential, I exist and thrive." That exchange, seeing potential and being seen, is the essence of leadership in the Ingenuity Age.

From the timeless teachings of our philosophies and religions comes a consistent reminder: we are not our tools; we are the consciousness that wields them. The elephant, a recurring symbol in my work, represents remembering: the mind that never forgets its inner strength, its community, or its purpose.

The choice between irrelevance and ingenuity is not theoretical; it is unfolding in every organization right now. The Irrelevance Age emerges when we let technology think for us. The Ingenuity Age begins when we design organizations that bring together the best of human and machine intelligence. In the yardsticks that matter, value will not be limited to shareholder growth, customer delight, or GDP; it will also encompass human well-being, learning velocity, fairness, trust, and contributions to the community and the planet.

We have seen enough to know that knowledge alone is not wisdom, and efficiency alone is not progress. The yardstick that will matter most in our lifetimes will be the capacity to unite intelligence with imagination, technology with compassion, and power with purpose.

If this book helps even one leader design the conditions where people can bring their full ingenuity to work every day, it will have done its job. That is my hope, my gratitude, and my invitation.

Katharine McLennan

*"Two roads diverged in a wood, and I—
I took the one less traveled by
And that has made all the difference."*

Robert Frost
"The Road Not Taken," Mountain Interval
(1916)

"Leadership equates to two words: Conscious Choice. Conscious, because we must stay awake to change and possibility. Choice, because drifting is easy, but courage means deciding; even when the outcome is uncertain."

Katharine McLennan

PROLOGUE

Stuck in the Information Age

17 December — **NEW YORK**

Omnivista Board Meeting

The boardroom was unnervingly still, not the calm of confidence but the pause before a storm. The hum of the climate control fought the city's heavy winter air. Beyond the glass walls, Manhattan's skyline pressed in: cranes promised growth, ferries cut restless lines across the harbor, and towers gleamed with the confidence of capital. Yet, inside, the Board of Omnivista faced a different view: a choice they could no longer put off.

At the head of the table, Evelyn Grant, the Chair, leaned forward. At sixty-seven, she had lived through every tremor of modern capitalism: the 1987 crash, Enron, WorldCom, the global financial crisis, and the COVID-19 pandemic. Her career had been forged in the crucible of the late Industrial Age, sharpened by Six Sigma rigor and honed through relentless turnarounds. Her voice carried the certainty of someone who had learned not to waste words.

"Omnivista is losing relevance, Chris. Fast. Every indicator is flashing red. Patients expect AI-powered care, but they often receive paper forms instead. Startups deliver diagnostics in minutes, while we take weeks. Regulators are inquiring about how our algorithms operate, and we don't have definitive answers. Talent is leaving for firms that give them copilots instead of committees. Relevance is no longer about scale or legacy; it's about speed, trust, and imagination. And on those fronts, we're already behind."

The words landed like a hammer.

Chris Morgan, forty-nine, Omnivista's CEO, who had started only last month, exhaled slowly before answering. "Relevance? That's your primary concern?"

"It's the only concern that matters now," Evelyn said. Her tone was even, but her eyes did not move. "We've seen this movie before. Kodak invented the digital camera in 1975 and buried it to protect film. Blockbuster laughed at the idea of buying Netflix for $50 million. Nokia controlled half the smartphone market in 2007; five years later, it was gone, defending keyboards instead of imagining touchscreens. And GE, once the most valuable company in the world. Complexity crushed it before it could shift from efficiency to agility."

She let the silence draw out. "The pattern is always the same: when technology arrives, companies let it multiply their worst tendencies instead of their best."

Chris glanced down at the quarterly reports spread across the table. Numbers, targets, and capital allocations; none addressed the urgency Evelyn demanded. "We're not Kodak," she said carefully.

"Maybe not. But Omnivista's numbers say otherwise." Evelyn tapped the page in front of her. "Our valuation has fallen from eighty billion to forty-five billion in five years. Talent is fleeing to AI-native startups who can scale in months what takes us years. Regulators are circling our algorithms because we can't explain them; they're black boxes. Clients tell us our innovation is glacial while competitors are rolling out copilots, predictive diagnostics, and AI-driven care pathways."

"This isn't drift, Chris. Omnivista's decline is accelerating with AI. The very technology that should amplify our ingenuity is instead magnifying our inertia. We are watching the future arrive, but through the rear-view mirror."

Around the table, directors shifted uncomfortably.

Omnivista is one of the world's largest healthcare conglomerates, headquartered in New York and operating across sixty countries. At its peak, it commanded an $80 billion valuation, which is now nearly half that amount. Annual revenues of $32 billion make it formidable, but not untouchable. Its 210,000 employees span hospitals, aged care, research, pharmaceuticals, and digital health services. Each of its five business lines is anchored in a global city: pharma and therapeutics in Tokyo, science and research in Sydney, healthcare operations in São Paulo, digital health in Bangalore, and aged care in Dublin. Today, they stand as both the company's assets and its vulnerabilities, proof that Omnivista has the reach of a giant but the fragility of an incumbent.

At the far end, Mei Lin, the youngest board member at thirty, broke the silence. A venture capitalist in Shanghai, she had watched AI transform health-tech from the ground up. Her words were precise, her cadence urgent. "In Asia, clinics are already AI-first. Diagnostics run automatically. Empathy is simulated and available instantly. Patients prefer it because it's there twenty-four-seven. If we hesitate, if we treat this as just another technology wave, Omnivista won't fade gradually. It will be eclipsed suddenly, completely, and irreversibly."

She leaned forward. "This isn't theory. The adoption curves are measured in quarters, not decades. Mo Gawdat warns of the moment when we hand over our future to machines that don't share our values. Martin Ford demonstrates that entire professions, such as radiologists, accountants, and lawyers, are at risk of being replaced by automation. Harari warns that algorithms may soon know us better than we know ourselves. The window for gradual adaptation has closed."

Tunde Adeyemi, sixty, a Nigerian-British entrepreneur and serial founder, nodded. Tunde had been in Silicon Valley in the mid-90s alongside the founders of eBay, Hotmail, and Yahoo. "Mei Lin is right. Between promising and too late, there's barely a season. If you're not moving, you're irrelevant. And irrelevance comes fast."

Chris lifted her head, meeting each director's gaze. "So, what exactly are we choosing? Because we can't decide unless we name the paths."

Mei Lin drew a deep breath. "Then let's name them. There are three."

"First: The Irrelevance Age. Corrosive Irrelevance. AI amplifies our worst habits: void instead of vision, inertia instead of intuition, silos instead of synergy, tyranny instead of trust, and apathy instead of authenticity."

"Second: Ingenuity Age. AI augments our best human qualities: vision, intuition, synergy, trust, and authenticity. This is where the firms pulling away are already headed. Brynjolfsson's research at Stanford shows augmentation consistently outperforms automation."

"And third: Imaginative Possibility. The path where we dare to build what our ancestors dreamed of when they looked at the stars. Ray Kurzweil calls it the singularity, when human and machine intelligence merge. History reminds us: every impossibility becomes inevitable once someone imagines it."

The room went quiet.

Evelyn tapped her pen against the table, the sound sharp in the silence. "And which path is ours?"

Chris stood, uncapped a marker, and turned to the whiteboard. "Our stakeholders are the ones we are serving: Employees, customers, investors, regulators, they will judge us faster than we can judge ourselves." She then led a conversation with the Board, in which they hypothesized what each stakeholder group would expect in the different scenarios looming now that AI has arrived.

After the table had been completed, Chris summarized, "Employees now measure value in meaning, growth, and mental health. Customers measure it in journeys that flow end-to-end, with trust and humanity intact. Investors measure it in narratives that

Part I:
The Ages in the Context of our Stakeholders

	1700s-1995	1995-2025	Where are we headed now that AI has arrived?		
	Industrial Age	Information Age	Irrelevance Age	Ingenuity Age	Imaginative Possibility
	Efficiency	Data & Digital	AI x Human Shadow	AI x Human Wisdom	AI x Human Wisdom x Boundless Imagination
Employees	Job security, steady wages	Career growth, flexibility, and learning	Surveillance, skill rot, burnout, exodus	Skills marketplaces, copilots, mastery time, engagement	Personal AI coaches, boundless learning, creative fulfillment
Customers	Reliable, low cost, consistency	Digital convenience, speed personalization	AI walls, no empathy, fragmentation, frustration	End-to-end journeys, human touch when needed, trust	Preventive care, impossible made possible, partnership
Investors	Dividends, productivity, assets	Growth from digital platforms, analytics ROI	Theater, no unit economics, confused signals, value destruction	Coherent narratives, learning velocity, sustainable growth	Investment in humanity's potential, exponential returns
Regulators	Compliance, safety, labor rules	Data protection, transparency, governance	Reactive, surprises, minimal engagement, distrust	Partnership, early engagement, designed-in ethics	Co-creating frameworks for impossible possibilities

cohere and growth that endures, not performance theater. Regulators measure it in ethics designed in from the first line of code, not excuses drafted after the damage.

That is the actual scoreboard under the AI ultimatum. It has always been the scoreboard, but with artificial intelligence multiplying every weakness and every strength, the demands arrive faster, the scrutiny is sharper, and the margin for drift has disappeared." She capped the pen. "They are our real scorecard."

No one spoke. The hum of the climate system filled the room, then faded as Evelyn pushed her papers aside. "I can't shake the feeling we're dancing on the edge of irrelevance. And if we fall, everyone pays: shareholders, employees, patients." She looked around the table. "What if we're not just saving Omnivista for the next quarter? What if this choice determines whether we have a future at all?"

The boardroom held its breath.

How the Book Works

Omnivista stands here not as an isolated example, but as a miniature case study of what every organization now faces. The AI Era does not automatically determine the next Age; each organization will create its own: drifting into Irrelevance, stepping into Ingenuity, or reaching toward Imaginative Possibility.

Part I sets the context. It examines why Information Age frameworks no longer suffice and how the arrival of AI reshapes the conditions of leadership.

Part II introduces VISTA, the Leadership Compass. It defines the five leadership choices, Vision, Intuition, Synergy, Trust, and Authenticity, that determine whether the AI Era strengthens wisdom or drives organizations toward irrelevance. Together, these choices define your individual Leadership Readiness for the Ingenuity Age.

Part III presents ORG6, the Roadmap for the Organization. It comprises Six Levers of Culture. These levers convert direction into mechanism, shaping how leadership becomes daily mastery across the enterprise. Together, they define your organization's Culture Readiness for the Ingenuity Age.

From February through November, Omnivista follows a monthly rhythm. Each month focuses on one VISTA leadership choice or one ORG6 culture lever. The sequence provides a practical cadence any executive team can follow.

Each chapter unfolds in four movements: a kickoff, a deep dive into the chapter's core discipline, a team review, and a board presentation, where progress is reviewed, guardrails are set, and lessons are distilled.

Between the kickoff and the chapter's core discipline, you will find a section called My Fingerprint: a story from my own thirty-five years of practice that connects the chapter's argument to a lived moment. These are not case studies. They are the experiences that shaped how I see the work, offered so you can test the ideas against a human reality before the research begins.

At the end of each chapter in Parts II and III, you will find five paired questions for that chapter's lever or leadership choice. For each pair, you rate yourself on two dimensions.

The first is your Foundation: how you and your organization are actually operating today in the area the chapter covers, regardless of the technology available to you. Is this leadership choice or culture lever alive in how you lead, how your teams work, how decisions get made? Where the foundations are strong, the wisdom is already present, waiting to be extended.

The second is your AI Amplifier: whether you are deploying AI to strengthen those foundations. Not AI for its own sake. Not AI for other functions such as finance, marketing, engineering, or customer service. This is AI in service of leadership and culture practices. Together, these two dimensions reveal your Ingenuity Readiness, chapter by chapter, then as a whole.

The scale is the same throughout for each chapter's paired questions:

1: **Not Yet**. This doesn't describe us. We're operating from an older playbook.

2: **Emerging**. Occasional glimpses, but not yet a conscious practice.

3: **Developing**. Working on this and making progress, but inconsistently.

4: **Practicing**. Becoming a genuine habit, visible to others around us.

5: **Second Nature**. This is how we operate. It defines who we are.

When you average your five scores for each dimension, the result places you in one of four positions:

- **Ingenious in an AI Era.** Average of 3.5 or above on both your foundations and the AI Amplifier. Strong leadership and culture. Strategic AI. Ever-expanding ingenuity.
- **Primed for AI Acceleration.** Average of 3.5 or above on your foundations, below 3.5 on the AI Amplifier. Strong leadership and culture. AI underdeveloped. Deploy AI to amplify your foundations.
- **Outpaced by Misdirected AI.** Average below 3.5 on your foundations, 3.5

or above on the AI Amplifier. Weak leadership. Advanced but misdirected AI. Strengthen leadership and culture before scaling AI.
- **Irrelevant in an AI Era.** Average below 3.5 on both your foundations and the AI Amplifier. Outdated leadership and culture. Minimal AI. Ever-expanding irrelevance.

At the back of the book, you will find an overall scoreboard where you can bring together your chapter scores for the VISTA leadership and ORG6 culture dimensions. When you see them side by side, the patterns will speak: where your foundations are strong but AI remains untapped as a leadership and culture tool, where AI may be racing ahead of the foundations it should serve, and where the real work of the months ahead lies.

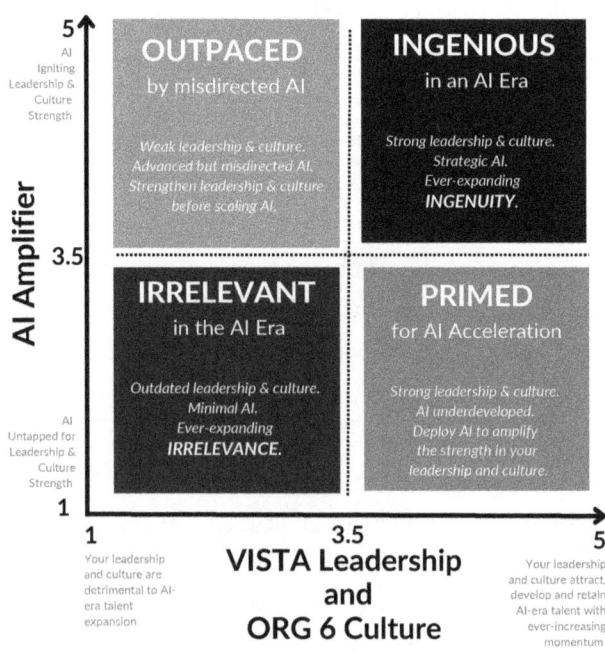

Source and Design: Katharine McLennan, 2026.
Please email me for a formal assessment kath@katharinemclennan.com

On with the Story

As the story unfolds, remember: a leader always has a choice. This book explores the one choice AI itself cannot make, the choice between Irrelevance and Ingenuity. This book will not hand you a blueprint. It will help you see clearly enough to draw your own.

There is a line, widely attributed to Viktor Frankl, that has shaped my understanding of leadership more than any other: "Between stimulus and response, there is a space. In that space is our power to choose our response. In our response lies our growth and our freedom."

Whether Frankl wrote those exact words or whether they emerged from the tradition his work inspired, the truth they carry is the bedrock of everything in this book. When someone asks me to name a synonym for leadership, I answer with two words: Conscious Choice. That space between stimulus and response is where leadership lives. It is where ingenuity begins.

If we dare to build leader by leader, company by company, we may yet earn the right to name the Age that follows the Information Age: the Ingenuity Age, where human wisdom works in concert with artificial intelligence.

The question now is simple.
What kind of leaders will choose to build it?

PART I

What age are we in with the arrival of AI?

Understanding how past eras shaped today's leadership defaults and why AI now forces a critical choice point.

Part I
What Age are We in Today?

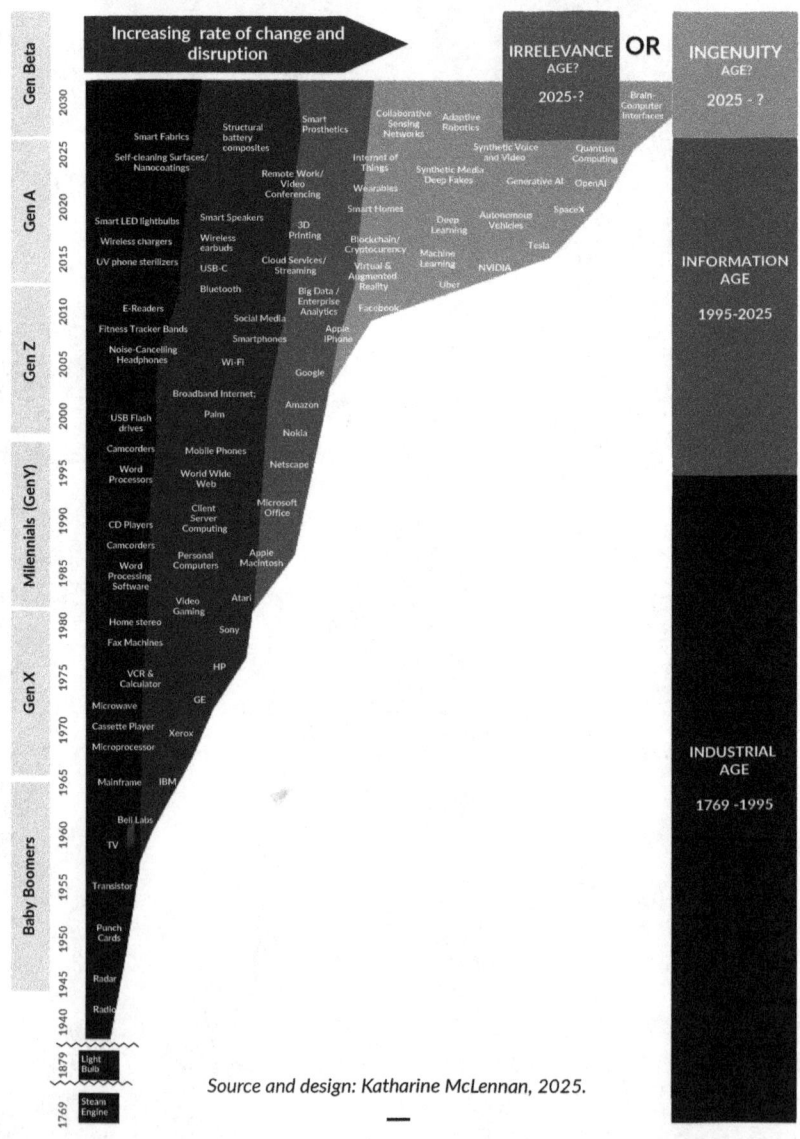

Source and design: Katharine McLennan, 2025.

18 December — **NEW YORK**

Omnivista Executive Team Meeting

The morning after the bruising ultimatum-delivery board session, Omnivista's executive team assembled on the 40th floor of their New York headquarters.

The quarterly reviews agenda seemed routine, but the room carried the stillness of an organization that had been told its survival was no longer guaranteed.

Chris Morgan sat at the head of the walnut table. Normally, she would open meetings with a quick scan of the faces around her, sensing who was restless and who was ready to participate. Today her gaze lingered longer. She wasn't scanning for mood. She was searching for signs. Who understood that they were no longer managing gradual change, but standing at the edge of an ultimatum?

Around her sat the leadership team:

Yuki Nakamura, CPO (forty, Millennial, Tokyo): Talent custodian. She believed work should grow people, not grind them down. Candor was her strength. Under ultimatum speed, it could either save the company or brand her as "soft."

John Wallace, CFO (thirty-eight, Millennial, Sydney): Finance as a Fortress. Numbers meant discipline and predictability. But prudence could calcify into inertia disguised as caution.

Maria Esteves, COO (fifty-five, Gen X, São Paulo): backbone of operations. Loyal to throughput and compliance. Efficiency that polished silos left the company brittle.

Liam O'Connor, CMO (forty-eight, Gen X, Dublin): master of story. He could rouse a room with a phrase. But theater without substance risked slipping into a void.

Sanjay Mehta, CTO (twenty-eight, Gen Z, Bangalore): the future in code. Fast, impatient, raw energy. But unchecked, his drive could tip into tyranny by algorithm.

And Chris herself: the fulcrum. Every lever bent toward her chair, every VISTA choice converged in her daily decisions: Vision or Void, Intuition or Inertia, Synergy or Silos, Trust or Tyranny, Authenticity or Apathy. Schooled in the churn of the Information Age, she had survived on dashboards and deadlines. But under ultimatum pressure, those instincts were no longer enough.

The meeting began.

Yuki spoke first. "Our people are burning out. In some regions, turnover is approaching 20%. Exit interviews mention *unclear direction* and *decision paralysis*."

Silence followed. No one pressed further. Apathy settled like dust.

John followed: slide after slide, budget variances, quarter-on-quarter ratios, forecasts assuming tomorrow would repeat yesterday. Inertia dressed as prudence.

Maria reported throughput, compliance, and utilization, every division "on target." Perfect silos, brittle under surprise.

Liam's glossy campaign promised transformation. The volume was high, the substance thin. Void disguised as vision.

Sanjay pitched an AI platform to automate compliance, monitor performance, and track behavior. "We can reduce human error by 80%," he said. Chris heard the unspoken corollary: reduce human agency by 80% as well.

In a single hour, the team unconsciously replayed an old script: efficiency over adaptability, silos over synergy, control over creativity, past data over present insight, and surveillance over trust.

Omnivista's problem was not incompetence. It was an inheritance of outdated scripts, scripts that were well-suited to an Industrial Age setting.

Chris let the silence settle, then pushed her chair back slightly. "We can't afford another quarter of autopilot," she said. "The Board made it clear yesterday; our challenge isn't gradual change; it's choosing relevance before AI chooses for us."

She looked around the table, pausing on each of her executives. "Here's what I need. Between now and January, each of you will choose one pilot site in your city. Don't dress it up. Don't hand me glossy dashboards. I want you to walk the floor, talk to the people, and analyze the site with clear eyes."

She wrote the headings on the whiteboard:

- **Industrial Age** habits still alive in the system
- **Information Age** practices that accelerate but may not deepen value
- Early signs of **Irrelevance** if those habits are left unchecked
- Seeds of **Ingenuity**, if we choose differently

"Bring that analysis to Berlin, January 6–8. Be prepared to show, not tell, what you've seen. Our job there will be to name whether Omnivista is drifting into irrelevance or daring toward ingenuity. This is not an academic exercise. It's a rehearsal for survival."

The team scribbled notes, though Chris could already see the unease in their posture. The year ahead would demand more than metrics. It would require courage.

"One more thing," Chris said. "Name your signal site now, the place we'll keep returning to across the year."

Yuki (Tokyo): "Shinjuku Research Tower; we'll tackle stopwatch science: output over learning velocity."

John (Sydney): "Barangaroo Biotech Hub; we'll break the escalate-for-permission chain that freezes judgment."

Maria (São Paulo): "Paulista General Hospital; we'll shift from bed-throughput to true end-to-end patient flow."

Sanjay (Bangalore): "Whitefield Digital Campus; we'll move authority to the teams closest to the code."

Liam (Dublin): "Liffey Aged Care Centre; we'll stop measuring care as checklists and start counting presence."

Chris nodded. "Good. Berlin, January 6. Day one: the Industrial habits we must retire. Day two: The Information Age habits we must outgrow. Day three: the implications of what we know so far about the opportunities and threats emerging with Artificial Intelligence."

She continued, "Artificial intelligence is advancing at a speed that defies precedent. In the space of months, copilots have gone from novelty to necessity in knowledge work. Robots navigate warehouses and assist in surgery. AI chat systems mediate millions of customer interactions each day. Generative models design proteins, co-author legal briefs, write code, and storyboard films. Every week brings another breakthrough.

"The acceleration is astonishing and sobering. For leaders, the realization is inescapable: technology will continue to advance, whether we like it or not. Left to its own devices, AI will amplify the systems it encounters. If those systems are brittle, it will multiply brittleness. If they are corrosive, it will accelerate corrosion. If they are designed for ingenuity, it will amplify ingenuity."

The team stood, the city of New York spreading beneath them as they contemplated the work ahead: five sites, five signals, one question: irrelevance or ingenuity.

As the room emptied, Chris lingered at the window. The plan was taking shape. But a quieter question surfaced, one she wasn't ready to raise with anyone, least of all Yuki. The year ahead would test whether Omnivista's Chief People Officer needed to become something the market had never built: a strategic peer to the CFO, not a custodian of programs. Yuki had the candor. Whether she had the range was a question only the year itself could answer.

My Fingerprint

In 1995, our Stanford MBA class graduated at the dawn of the Internet. The average age of my class was around thirty. We had no laptops on our desks, no mobile phones in our pockets, only the trusty HP-12C financial calculator everyone carried. Mosaic was the browser a few adventurous classmates were tinkering with, and "web crawlers" were sparking curiosity. We had no idea what was coming.

Thirty years later, I began hosting a podcast called Stanford MBA: From Baby Boomer to Gen Z. In each episode, I facilitate a conversation between a member of the 1995 class, now around sixty, and a member of the 2025 class, around thirty. The podcast is expanding: in 2026, I am widening the circle to include graduates from the 1960s through the 1990s alongside graduates from the 2000s onward. The generational range is becoming richer, and so are the conversations. What began as a dialogue between two cohorts is becoming a living exchange across an entire arc of leadership experience.

One conversation captures dozens like it. A 1995 graduate, a CEO who had led three companies through digital transformations, was describing how he had spent his career learning to be the smartest person in the room. "That was the game," he said. "Know more, decide faster, be right." The 2025 graduate, a twenty-eight-year-old who had built an AI startup before finishing her degree, listened quietly. Then she said: "I have never once tried to be the smartest person in the room. I just need to know who to ask and which tools to use. The room is bigger than any one person now." The silence that followed was the sound of one age ending and another beginning. Neither of them was wrong. Both had described the leadership their era demanded. But the world the younger graduate was entering no longer rewarded the model the older one had mastered. And the older graduate knew it. He said: "I spent thirty years accumulating expertise. She is spending her career accumulating access. I am not sure my version survives."

That is the threshold this book stands at. It is not enough to name it the "AI Age," because that makes it sound like a technology story. It is a human story. The choice is between ingenuity, where human wisdom and machine intelligence amplify one another, and irrelevance, where we stop using our own intelligence altogether because the machines seem faster. The question that echoes across the decades remains the same: are we walking toward irrelevance or ingenuity? The answer will not come from the technology. It will come from the leaders who choose what to do with it.

On with Part I

Part I explores the thresholds of leadership across three pivotal moments.

Chapter 1: The Industrial Age. How Taylorism, efficiency, and exhaustion as virtues echo in today's AI debates, revealing why the old scripts still haunt us.

Chapter 2: The Information Age. How the Internet era reshaped leadership, rewarding virtualization, instantaneity, and technocracy, benefits that came with hidden costs to connection and belonging.

Chapter 3: The AI Threshold. How generative AI confronts leaders with an ultimatum: to drift into irrelevance or to catalyze ingenuity.

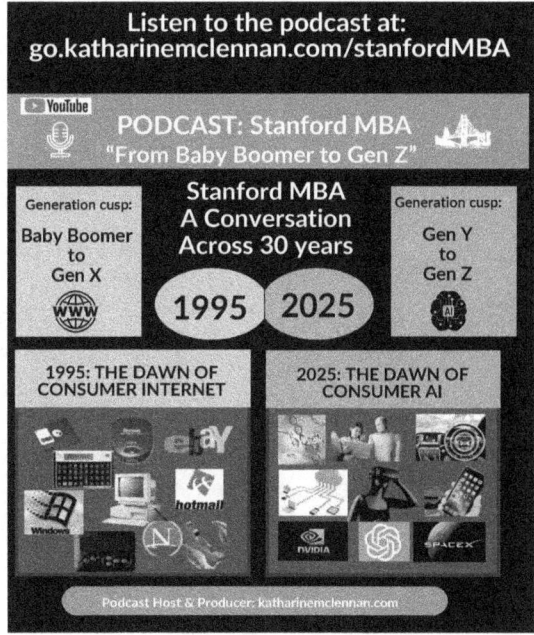

*"The past is never dead.
It's not even past."*

William Faulkner

Requiem for a Nun (1951)

*"When the Wall fell on November 9,
1989, it shattered more than concrete.
It marked the collapse of an age that
mistook control for strength,
and the awakening of a new hunger
for freedom and ingenuity."*

Katharine McLennan

CHAPTER 1

The Industrial Age

Noticing how Industrial Age thinking still governs leadership reflexes built on efficiency and control.

6 January — BERLIN

Day 1, Executive Team focus: Industrial Age

Snow fell in steady sheets outside the workshop hall, softening the city's edges. Inside, Omnivista's executive team sat in a circle, stripped of their usual PowerPoints and quarterly decks. Chris stood at the front, marker in hand. "Today is about naming the ghosts of the Industrial Age still alive in our system," she said. "Each of you has walked your site. Each of you has seen where efficiency overtakes creativity, where control still masquerades as strength. Let's put those truths on the table."

She nodded to Yuki. "Tokyo first."

Yuki didn't soften it. "Our labs are brilliant but still bound by Taylor's stopwatch. Productivity is measured in hours logged, patents filed, and protocols followed. Researchers talk about 'checking boxes,' not about breakthroughs. Talent is hired for pedigree, not potential. We reward endurance, not ingenuity."

John went next. "Sydney runs like a Ford assembly line. Work is split into fragments, escalated for approval in steps, until projects stall. Authority is hoarded at the top. Standardization is our virtue and our cage. People wait for permission instead of moving."

Maria's tone hardened. "Our hospitals run like factories. Bed turnover is celebrated, nurses are timed on tasks, and departments pass patients like parcels. Compliance drives behavior more than care does. Patients feel processed, not healed. We have mistaken throughput for value."

Sanjay looked up from his notes. "Our coders move fast, but bureaucracy keeps them leashed. Algorithms pass through endless committees, stamped and restamped, while innovation slows. Authority sits with managers, not engineers. They feel like cogs, not creators. We call it governance, but it is hierarchy in disguise."

Liam spoke last, his voice quieter than the others. "In Dublin, caregivers give their hearts, but the system reduces them to checklists and shift hours. Singing with a patient with dementia isn't recorded, so it isn't valued. Rules suffocate initiative. We measure control, not care, and authenticity evaporates."

Chris wrote the five findings on the whiteboard in steady strokes. "These are our signals," she said. "Proof that the Industrial Age isn't past; it's still inside us. Tomorrow we turn to the Information Age. But today, we start here."

Background to the Industrial Age

The Industrial Age started more than two and a half centuries ago, when James Watt refined the steam engine in 1769, transforming it from a mine pump into a source of mechanical power that would drive factories, locomotives, and entire economies.

Fast forward to the end of the 19th century, when Frederick Taylor carried a stopwatch onto the shop floor of Bethlehem Steel. He studied men hauling pig iron, timing every move. Taylor insisted that, with proper training and incentives, output could quadruple. To his admirers, this was science applied to management. To workers, it was dehumanization. They protested by slowing their pace: "soldiering," to resist being reduced to cogs.

In Detroit, Henry Ford applied these principles to his assembly line. By 1913, a Model T could be built in ninety-three minutes. Cars rolled off the line with astonishing efficiency. But workers described the monotony as soul-crushing. Ford had to double wages to stop them from quitting.

Henri Fayol codified the functions of management, including planning, organizing, commanding, coordinating, and controlling. Max Weber emphasized the importance of bureaucracy as a means of achieving fairness through the concept of impersonality. Rules would be neutral and follow a rational hierarchy. In reality, bureaucracy often meant people served the system, not the other way around.

Fast forward now to the 1980s, when Jack Welch at GE became the corporate high priest of efficiency. Fortune named him "Manager of the Century." His "rank and yank" system, cutting the bottom 10% each year, enshrined fear as a form of discipline.

By its own standards, the Industrial Age was a success. Railways stitched continents together. Cars transformed daily life. Pharmaceuticals extended health. Hospitals saved millions. Peter Drucker, the defining management thinker of the mid-twentieth century, recognized that the Industrial Age had achieved something unprecedented: turning knowledge into productivity at scale.

But the shadow was heavy: conformity over creativity, exhaustion as virtue, humans treated as parts of the machine rather than as creators.

If efficiency was the Industrial Age's crown jewel, exhaustion was its shadow. Taylor's stopwatch measured not just speed, but stamina as well. A "good worker" could endure long hours without complaint. At Bethlehem Steel, men carried 90-pound pig iron bars from dawn to dusk. Those who faltered were labeled unfit, not the system.

The ethic persisted long after the factory whistle. By the 1980s, exhaustion had become a badge of honor in corporate towers: "first in, last out." In offices around the world, it became known as hustle culture, characterized by sleeping under desks and glorifying "crunch time." The term "presenteeism" took hold: not just showing up when ill, but showing up for endless hours, long after the value had been added. If you weren't still at your desk at 11 p.m., perhaps you weren't serious enough to be considered partner material.

Neuroscience confirms what workers have long known: exhaustion narrows cognition. Chronic stress locks the brain into survival circuits, shrinking perspective, blocking creativity, eroding trust. In other words, the very conditions leaders glorify when they reward exhaustion are the ones that obliterate ingenuity.

No wonder Yuki's warnings at Omnivista, burnout climbing toward 20% turnover, were met with silence. The silence itself was an inheritance. A belief buried in organizational DNA: fatigue equals commitment. The Industrial Age turned exhaustion into virtue. Today, we still mistake its symptoms: burnout, attrition, and "quiet quitting," as individual weaknesses instead of systemic issues.

Each age produced its own version of VISTA, the same five letters carrying different meanings as leadership defaults shifted.

For the Industrial Age, the VISTA (compass of leadership) is:
　Volume: growth measured in more units at a lower cost.
　Instruction: managers decide, workers comply.
　Standardization: variance is the enemy, conformity the virtue.
　Timekeeping: value measured in hours; human rhythm bent to machines.
　Authority: wisdom presumed to sit at the top, hierarchy as a
　natural order.

The Industrial Age VISTA produced prosperity but also discontent. Workers organized unions, fought for and won safety laws, and worked toward a forty-hour work week, not as gifts from management, but as victories against exploitation. The Industrial Age's VISTA was not confined to factories and offices; it shaped whole societies.

CEO's Reflection, That Evening

That night, Chris walked through Berlin. She passed the Reichstag, once gutted by fire, claimed by tyranny. She followed the scar where the Wall had sliced the city in two, a monument to fear that collapsed in a single night. And she stood beneath the Brandenburg Gate, luminous and unguarded, a reminder that freedom can be reclaimed faster than anyone imagines.

In Berlin that first day, each executive named the inheritance still clinging to their site.

- John's Barangaroo hub: quarterly controls and escalation chains that froze movement in place, essentially Taylorism rebranded.

- Maria's Paulista hospital: compliance ratios polished into perfection while patients felt the brittleness of silos, standardization masquerading as virtue.

- Yuki's Shinjuku labs: talent drained by exhaustion, creativity sacrificed to protocols, endurance still mistaken for excellence.

- Sanjay's Whitefield campus: algorithms slowed by bureaucracy and cloaked in surveillance, industrial control reborn in digital clothing.

- Liam's Liffey Centre: caregivers reduced to checklists, over substance, attention

Each story was different in texture but identical in shape. The stopwatch. The assembly line. The hierarchy. The badge of exhaustion. All the ghosts of the Industrial Age, alive inside Omnivista.

Artificial intelligence does not erase these habits; it tempts leaders back into them. Dashboards promise what Taylor's stopwatch once promised: visibility, control, efficiency. Algorithms optimize for output, not renewal. Platforms run without pause, and leaders intoxicated by their own capabilities expect humans to keep pace with machines. The Industrial belief that the line must never stop reemerges as the digital belief that the platform must always be on.

The danger is not only dystopia. It is corrosion: leaders multiplying their worst reflexes and calling it progress.

History whispered its warning: irrelevance is not the only danger. Far worse is when fear corrodes the soul and imagination is surrendered without protest. Yet history also offered a promise: if walls can fall overnight, then ingenuity can return, if leaders choose to do so.

The Industrial Age taught us how to build machines, and in the process, how to become machines. It gave prosperity, but at the cost of conformity, exhaustion, and brittleness. Those scripts were not buried with the factory whistle. They still haunt boardrooms today, and with AI in our hands, they can accelerate irrelevance at machine speed. The answer begins by recognizing the echo.

Tomorrow, the team would confront the next inheritance, the Information Age playbook that promised liberation but too often delivered speed without creativity.

My Fingerprint

I experienced the Industrial Age's manifestation in Eastern European society. From 1978 to 1980, I lived in West Berlin, a tiny dot of freedom, barely 185 square miles, surrounded by a wall. My father was the U.S. Military Intelligence Liaison Officer to the French military. On our side, the Americans, British, and French faced East Berlin and East Germany, which were occupied by the Soviet Union. The Cold War was not abstract. It was the air we breathed.

West Berlin pulsed with jazz clubs, bright food stalls, and Technicolor life. At twelve, I loved its vibrancy. Yet every time we drove through the high, militarized gauntlet of Checkpoint Charlie in our army-green station wagon, the images turned black and white, soldiers with dogs patrolled above us in watchtowers. Children ran toward our car, pressing their faces to the glass as if peering at an alien object. To them, a car meant a Trabant, a flimsy industrial relic that families signed up for and might receive years later. To me, the Trabant was the coldest symbol of the Industrial Age production without imagination, scale without soul.

And then, on November 9, 1989, history took a turn. I had graduated from Duke in May that year and moved to Brussels for an internship at a think tank studying the European Community. Just two weeks earlier, in mid-October of 1989, I had visited Berlin. At the Brandenburg Gate, tanks, barricades, and German Shepherds ringed the square for a mile. Nothing had changed since I had lived there ten years prior as a teenager. The sight left me with the same black-ice dread I had felt as a child, a void of inertia, silos, tyranny, and apathy. Nothing hinted at change.

And yet, only two weeks after that visit, thousands of East Berliners pressed against the wall and demanded passage. The guards, ordinary young men, looked at the people in front of them, people who looked just like them, and let them through. Not even NATO, nor my friends in the British Army stationed there, had the intelligence to predict what was happening. In hindsight, it feels almost absurd: after twenty-eight years of standing guard, perhaps the soldiers had forgotten why they were there in the first place. Possibly, they shrugged and decided tyranny wasn't worth another hour of their lives.

To me, that night remains the most extraordinary day in history. The machinery of the Industrial Age, decades of grinding human spirit into uniformity, collapsed in a single evening. Vision, intuition, synergy, trust, and authenticity carried a people through the wall, and took the world into a new chapter.

I returned in 2014, twenty-five years later, and saw a different Berlin. At Checkpoint Charlie, commercialization had done its worst. Tourists lined up for photos with men in fake uniforms and bought snow globes with fragments of counterfeit 'wall' inside. Starbucks and McDonald's flanked the corners where East Berliners faced off against West Berliners. My father, who had once stood duty there, would have been dismayed. It felt as if the sacrifices of thousands had been dishonored, reduced to novelty.

But just a few blocks away, the city pulsed with ingenuity. Berlin had become Europe's Silicon Valley, one of the two great pulse points of innovation outside the United States, the other being Israel. Startups thrived in repurposed factories, venture capital poured in, and entrepreneurs from across the continent converged to test new ideas. If the Industrial Age had trapped Berlin in rigidity, the new digital age was transforming it into a hub of creativity and possibility.

And then there was the Brandenburg Gate. In 1989, I had seen it desolate: ringed with tanks, barbed wire, and silence. In 2014, it stood open and unguarded, a living monument reclaimed by humanity. I walked back and forth beneath it 108 times, in tears and awe. For me, the Gate was no longer just a landmark; it had become a symbol of my past. It was proof that walls can fall, that rigidity can collapse, and that wisdom and authenticity can emerge again, even after decades of suppression.

"Where is the wisdom we have lost in knowledge? Where is the knowledge we have lost in information?"

T.S. Eliot

"Sydney 2000 bridged centuries. It was the last Games built without devices in every pocket, and the first where information flowed freely: a joyful glimpse of how digital ingenuity could amplify the human spirit."

Katharine McLennan

CHAPTER 2

The Information Age

Understanding how speed, overload, and digital fragmentation undermined depth, community, and sound judgment.

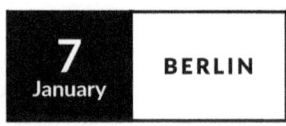

Day 2, Executive Team Focus: Information Age

The snow still pressed against the windows of the workshop hall, but inside the air was sharper, more restless. Day One had forced the team to name their Industrial Age inheritances. Today, Chris turned the marker in her hand and set a new frame.

"Yesterday we faced the ghosts of the Industrial Age," she said. "Today, we face the illusions of the Information Age. The dashboards, the data, the clicks, the benchmarks, the things that make us feel faster, but don't always make us wiser. Each of you has seen it on your site. Let's surface those truths."

She gestured to John. "Sydney first."

John: Sydney (Science & Research) "In Sydney, dashboards glow in every lab. We can view gene sequences in real-time, with variations from the plan occurring by the minute. But the more data we have, the less clarity we create. Scientists spend hours reconciling dashboards instead of asking questions. We've mistaken immediacy for insight. The Barangaroo Biotech Hub has become a mirror of the Information Age: flooded with information, starving for meaning."

Maria: São Paulo (Healthcare Operations) Maria tapped her notes. "Our hospitals are benchmark machines. Every metric is compared against global 'best practice,' and every department is told to copy the winners. But benchmarking only guarantees we're a step behind. Patients feel processed through metrics rather than cared for as individuals. In the Paulista General Hospital, the obsession with comparison makes us predictable, not progressive."

Liam: Dublin (Aged Care & Community Health) "In Dublin, engagement is reduced to clicks. Campaigns track open rates, likes, and responses. But trust doesn't move at the speed of dopamine. Families want consistency, presence, and humanity. Yet our metrics celebrate shallow signals. At the Liffey Aged Care Centre, staff feel pressured to chase numbers that don't match the lived experience of care. It's attention, not relationship."

Yuki: Tokyo (Pharma & Therapeutics) Yuki frowned. "In Tokyo, our people live in a culture of 'always-on.' Midnight emails. Zoom calls across time zones. The idea is that connectivity equals productivity. But the more connected we are, the more depleted we become. At the Shinjuku Research Tower, burnout is not just a risk; it's the cost of keeping pace. Connectivity has replaced community."

Sanjay: Bangalore (Digital Health & AI Services) Sanjay spoke quickly. "At Whitefield, we run pilots stacked on pilots, AI demos that look impressive in a sprint review but lack durability. The culture worships speed. If something scales, great; if it breaks, we launch another demo. But shallow experiments don't build trust with regulators or patients. The Whitefield Digital Campus is a prototype factory: fast, but fragile."

Chris wrote the five findings on the board again, this time under a new heading: The Information Age.

"These are our accelerants," she said. "They promise liberation: speed, data, scale, but they don't always deliver depth. Tomorrow we'll face the final threshold: what happens when AI multiplies these habits. And whether we dare to shift from irrelevance to ingenuity."

Background to the Information Age

With Netscape's 1995 IPO, factories no longer defined the frontier. Networks and software did. As Bill Gates argued, software would define every business. "The world is flat," wrote Thomas Friedman. Data became the oxygen of the enterprise.

New leadership exemplars emerged: Lou Gerstner pulled IBM into services, Andy Grove steered Intel through Moore's Law, Jeff Bezos transformed "everything" into a store, Michael Dell streamlined supply chains into just-in-time, and Gates envisioned a computer on every desk.

Consulting firms like McKinsey, Bain, Booz Allen & Hamilton, and BCG mastered the art of codifying knowledge across continents, leveraging the speed of ideas. Knowledge work had supplanted manual work as the driver of advantage.

But alongside liberation came overload. Knowledge workers were empowered, yet tethered to the first BlackBerrys, endless emails, and the tyranny of dashboards. The factory whistle was gone; the always-on phone was its replacement.

In 1997, McKinsey consultants Ed Michaels, Helen Handfield-Jones, and Beth Axelrod coined a phrase that would resonate for decades: *The War for Talent.*" Talent, not capital or strategy, became the scarce resource.

For the first time, CEOs were told that leadership pipelines, coaching, and succession weren't HR 'programs.' They were survival imperatives. Yet the very language of "war" betrayed the mindset: talent was still something to be hunted, ranked, and hoarded.

The paradox was stark. Just as the Information Age promised human liberation through knowledge work, some of its most influential management doctrines militarized human potential, ultimately undermining its original promise.

The 1990s and 2000s also saw a revolution in how we conceptualized leaders. Daniel Goleman's *Emotional Intelligence* (1995) reminded us that IQ was not enough. 360-degree feedback became mainstream. The profession of *executive coach* emerged.

Thinkers redefined the conversation, identifying more and more characteristics of the skills and the qualities that a leader had to have:

Peter Senge urged systems thinking in *The Fifth Discipline*. Jim Collins sought disciplined greatness in *Good to Great*. Gary Hamel called management itself "ripe for reinvention." Bill George popularized *Authentic Leadership*. Danah Zohar introduced *Spiritual Intelligence*.

Together, they expanded the lens and, therefore, the list of everything a leader had to be. The leadership capability frameworks against which people were judged became increasingly complex, encompassing hundreds of skills, each defined at various levels of complexity and detail.

Over the past thirty years, each generation has entered the workforce through different interfaces. Baby Boomers found jobs through classified ads and geography-bound networks. Gen X straddled typewriters and PCs, knocking on doors as early online postings began. Millennials rode the rise of Monster, SEEK, and LinkedIn as careers became search-enabled. Gen Z built portfolios and reputations in Discord groups, Upwork, and Fiverr, where networks mattered more than institutions. And now Gen Alpha arrives as AI natives, expecting to co-create with machines rather than retrieve information.

Work itself transformed physically. Offices shifted from cubicles with lower and lower partitions and then to coworking spaces. Communication moved from memos to Slack. Markets expanded from local to global supply chains. Presentations jumped from overhead projectors to PowerPoint to Zoom. Project management evolved from industrial-style compliance to agile sprints.

Yet culture and leadership adapted unevenly. We layered new technologies onto old instincts of control. Meetings multiplied, dashboards proliferated, and annual reviews survived. We gained speed and searchability, but wisdom often lagged.

After the Internet connected the world's pages, seven further waves reshaped the fabric of work between 1995 and 2025. Each brought extraordinary gifts and shadows that leaders are still grappling with today.

Social Media. Social media transformed work by turning every employee, customer, and community into a live publisher. A product could be amplified or destroyed overnight. The gift was immediacy and reach: leaders could listen at scale and engage communities directly. The shadow was performance culture and polarization: optics often trumped substance, and outrage was rewarded over nuance. The leadership lesson: amplify evidence of progress, not slogans.

Smartphones. Smartphones collapsed work cycles from days to minutes. Work became portable; decisions moved faster. The gift was responsiveness and inclusion: expertise could be tapped anywhere, at any time. The shadow was depletion: boundaries dissolved, attention shattered, people never truly "off." The leadership lesson: responsiveness needs rhythm. Thriving teams agree when to be "on" and when to pause.

The Cloud. Cloud computing turned technology into a service, available on demand. A small team could scale instantly. The gift was democratization: innovation became cheap and fast. The shadow was tool sprawl: overlapping apps, fragmented data, and security risks. The leadership lesson: tools only create value when embedded in culture. Internal platforms need owners, guardrails, and discipline.

Big Data. Big data promised truth at a glance. Leaders believed that dashboards revealed reality in real-time. The gift was visibility: operations improved, and anomalies were quickly surfaced. The shadow was an illusion: correlation was mistaken for causation, and analysis crowded out judgment. The leadership lesson: numbers only matter when paired with human judgment.

Predictive AI & Machine Learning. Before ChatGPT, predictive algorithms had quietly entered the workplace, including fraud detection, forecasting, and personalization. The gift was accuracy: better demand planning, fewer errors, and more intelligent targeting. The shadow was opacity: models were black boxes, and people trusted them unquestioningly. The leadership lesson: keep a human hand on the tiller. Prediction supports decisions, but people must remain visibly accountable for their actions.

Virtual & Augmented Reality. VR and AR made work immersive, surgeons rehearsed, engineers co-designed, students learned history in 3D. The gift was an embodiment: training became safer and more vivid. The shadow was a novelty: many deployments were gimmicks, excluding some while boring others. The leadership lesson: use immersion where embodiment matters, in safety, spatial design, and clinical practice.

Autonomous Systems & Robotics. Robots and autonomous vehicles shifted repetitive work to machines. Warehouses became safer, factories faster. The gift was safety and capacity: fewer injuries, more human time for judgment. The shadow was fear and complacency: workers worried about replacement, leaders grew overconfident. The leadership lesson: frame autonomy as choreography, not replacement. Humans and machines working together, with explicit overrides, build trust.

Across all seven waves, the gift was speed and scale. But the cost was a thinning connection: people tethered to devices, dazzled by networks, but lonelier at work. Sydney's lesson still holds: speed only works when it deepens trust and preserves human connection.

CEO's Reflection, That Evening

That evening, Chris walked along Unter den Linden, the grand boulevard stretching from the Brandenburg Gate to the heart of Berlin. Neon signs flickered in shop windows, taxis wove impatiently through the slush, and phones glowed in every passerby's hand. The city pulsed with information, endless, instant, insistent.

She thought of what the team had just named in their sites: data overload without clarity in Sydney; benchmarks that were copied instead of created in São Paulo; engagement reduced to clicks in Dublin; connectivity mistaken for community in Tokyo; and pilots without durability in Bangalore.

Berlin, with its restless screens and constant motion, felt like their mirror: a city alive with signals, but not always with meaning. The danger of the Information Age was becoming clear to her. To mistake light for vision. To confuse connection with community. To equate acceleration with progress. The promise of liberation had been real, faster access, wider reach, data at scale. But speed without depth was not freedom. It was drift, dressed in efficiency.

Chris looked back at the Brandenburg Gate, luminous again in the night. The Gate had once been a barrier, then a passage, and now a beacon. If the Information Age is a gate, it is one we have already rushed through without asking what lies on the other side.

Tomorrow, she knew, they would face the most challenging question: what happens when AI multiplies these habits? And whether Omnivista would step into irrelevance or dare to cultivate ingenuity.

My Fingerprint

In June 1995, I graduated from Stanford's MBA program. Just weeks later, Netscape went public, launching the internet era and sending classmates into pioneering "dotcoms." Many stayed in Silicon Valley to ride the wave. I, however, returned to Sydney to join the organizing committee for the 2000 Olympic Games.

I was employee #110 in what grew to 3,000 staff, 60,000 volunteers, and 70,000 contractors. Together, we served 10,700 athletes from 200 countries, across 28 sports, dozens of venues, and 300 events. In addition to athletes, we also served 5,000 team officials, 16,000 accredited media (press and broadcasters), 5,000 VIPs, and 6.7 million ticketed spectators.

Looking back, Sydney enjoyed three remarkable advantages that made it the first actual Information Age Olympics.

First was the English-to-English transition. We inherited directly from Atlanta, something not seen since St. Louis passed the Games to London nearly a century earlier. In 1996, I spent weeks in Atlanta interviewing organizers across every function, asking thousands of questions. Nothing was lost in translation. Sydney absorbed and applied lessons with extraordinary precision.

Second was the arrival of the Internet. Until then, Olympic knowledge transfer relied on binders and trunks of reports. For the first time, information moved electronically. Email was slow, but revolutionary compared to paper. Sydney also created the first Olympic intellectual property collection, which influenced every Games since and generated millions in revenue.

Third was the rise of consulting. Once knowledge moved at digital speed, expertise itself became a commodity. After Sydney, consulting firms emerged to sell curated playbooks, frameworks, and strategies, the Information Age applied to one of the world's most significant events.

What had not yet arrived was the 24/7 digital tether. We had no laptops, no smartphones. Work took place in the office, face-to-face, through endless brainstorming and co-creation sessions. We didn't take computers home or check email at midnight. Four weeks before the Opening Ceremony, the COO even turned off all email to signal that success would depend on real-time communication, in person or over the radio.

The culture that resulted was joyful in a way that feels nostalgic today. We worked hard but ended our days with a sense of completion. We imagined the Games together in meeting rooms, fueled by human connection rather than screens.

Sydney 2000 was a bridge: the first Olympics of the Information Age, and the last to fully enjoy the rhythm of working, creating, and celebrating without a device in every pocket.

"What will happen to society, politics and daily life when non-conscious but highly intelligent algorithms know us better than we know ourselves?"

Yuval Noah Harari

Homo Deus

"At the threshold of AI, every organization faces the same ultimatum:
drift into irrelevance as machines multiply our shadows, or choose ingenuity as they amplify our wisdom."

Katharine McLennan

CHAPTER 3

The AI Threshold

Recognizing how AI magnifies existing patterns and exposes the divide between Irrelevance and Ingenuity.

8 January — **BERLIN**

Day 3, Executive Team Focus: AI Threshold

The snow had stopped, leaving the city bright and brittle in the winter light. Inside the workshop hall, the team gathered for their final day. The room felt different now, heavier, but also sharper.

Chris stood at the front, marker in hand, and spoke in a quiet voice. "We've faced the Industrial Age habits that still echo. We've surfaced the Information Age accelerants that give speed without depth. Today, we stand at the threshold. The question is simple: when AI multiplies what it touches, do our sites slide into irrelevance, or can they become seeds of ingenuity?"

She turned to Maria. "São Paulo first."

Maria: São Paulo (Healthcare Operations) Maria's tone was sober. "At Paulista General, you can already see irrelevance creeping in. Bed-turnover algorithms optimize scheduling but make patients feel like they are being processed. Staff complain that the system prioritizes throughput over recovery. Left unchecked, this is irrelevance: efficiency without humanity." She paused, then lifted her eyes. "But I also saw ingenuity in the ICU pilot, nurses redesigning handover routines with AI to flag subtle risk patterns. When trust flows into the system, ingenuity emerges."

Liam: Dublin (Aged Care & Community Health) "In Dublin, irrelevance looks like caregivers reduced to data-entry clerks, logging hours into platforms that never notice the human moment. Families feel it as absence, not presence. But at the Liffey Centre, one small seed stood out: staff using AI to transcribe family stories into personalized care plans. When technology amplifies memory instead of erasing it, authenticity can breathe again."

Yuki: Tokyo (Pharma & Therapeutics) "At Shinjuku, irrelevance is protocols stretched into paralysis. Trials slowed because compliance checks multiply faster than discovery. Talent is leaving for AI-native labs that move twice as fast. But I also saw a spark: a small foresight team using generative models to explore treatment scenarios and map them to our Skills Graph. It showed me that vision can reframe talent, not just measure it."

John: Sydney (Science & Research) "In Sydney, irrelevance looks like dashboards on dashboards, drowning decisions in decimals. We confuse more data with more discipline, and the lab stalls while competitors act. But ingenuity? I found it in a team working on a prosthetics prototype, they trusted intuition alongside the data, building and testing faster than the model predicted. It reminded me that structure should enable judgment, not smother it."

Sanjay: Bangalore (Digital Health & AI Services) "At Whitefield, irrelevance shows up as fragile demos: we launch pilots fast, but they collapse under real-world pressure. Regulators don't trust us; patients don't either. However, I also saw ingenuity: a pod that created a transparency layer, allowing doctors to review AI decisions. For the first time, trust ran both ways, humans questioning machines, and machines learning from humans. That is the threshold worth crossing."

Chris wrote two headings on the board: Irrelevance and Ingenuity. Under each, she listed the examples, the shadows, and the sparks. Then she capped the marker.

"These sites have shown us both our risks and our possibilities. Ingenuity is not guaranteed. It is a choice. And choices only endure if they are anchored in two things: the foundation of a strong culture through our ORG6 levers and the leadership choices that reflect our new context: Vision, Intuition, Synergy, Trust, and Authenticity. That is the compass for the year ahead."

She paused, scanning the room. "And remember this: AI at Omnivista is not magic. It is not even unique. It mirrors the wave of copilots, assistants, platforms, and engines flooding every enterprise in 2025. What AI reveals is unforgiving but straightforward; it multiplies whatever system it enters.

"At our five sites, we've already seen outcomes diverge: sometimes acceleration without depth, sometimes corrosive irrelevance, sometimes genuine seeds of ingenuity. The difference is never the tool. It is the system it enters, and the reflexes we reach for."

The room was silent as Chris closed her notebook. But the lesson lingered: the most significant risk was not in the technology but in the reflexes leaders brought to it. Again and again, Omnivista's executives had reached for the Industrial and Information Age playbooks, scripts that once delivered prosperity, now turning brittle under AI's pressure.

Background to the arrival of AI

Under pressure, Omnivista's executives instinctively reached for the playbooks of the Industrial and Information Age. Those reflexes once delivered prosperity. In the Irrelevance Age, they betrayed.

At the Barangaroo Biotech Hub in Sydney, John tightened controls, convinced discipline alone would protect against risk. But as Charles Perrow warned in *Normal Accidents*, complexity always outgrows control. Dashboards became the new stopwatch: more data, less clarity.

At Paulista General Hospital in São Paulo, Maria doubled down on compliance ratios that were polished to perfection, but innovation was suffocating beneath them. It was Taylorism reborn: measure, constrain, optimize. What Frederick Taylor's stopwatch once did to steel workers, dashboards now threaten to do to clinicians.

Maria benchmarked obsessively against global "best practice," echoing the Information Age's obsession with copying winners. Yet Jim Collins reminded us in *Good to Great* that greatness cannot be benchmarked into existence; it must be built through originality and discipline.

At the Shinjuku Research Tower in Tokyo, Yuki warned of burnout, late-night emails and scientists being stretched past their limits. Colleagues dismissed her as "soft." Yet Jeffrey Pfeffer, in *Dying for a Paycheck*, shows what neuroscience confirms: chronic stress narrows cognition, destroys trust, and corrodes ingenuity. Exhaustion may have been a badge of honor in the Industrial Age. Under AI speed, it becomes fatal.

At the Liffey Aged Care Centre in Dublin, Liam dazzled with click-throughs and campaign reach. But as Sherry Turkle argued in *Alone Together*, metrics of connection often mask disconnection. Engagement reduced to dopamine hits is fragility, not trust.

At Whitefield Digital Campus, Sanjay stacked pilots of "smart automation," demos that looked impressive in reviews but collapsed under scrutiny. As Thomas Davenport and Rajeev Ronanki warned in Harvard Business Review, ambitious AI projects that lack pragmatic foundations produce setbacks, not results.

Efficiency, compliance, dashboards, and benchmarks, all logical in their original ages, become corrosive when AI multiplies them. Efficiency without humanity becomes brittle when algorithms optimize output while stripping meaning. Speed without wisdom floods leaders with data while starving them of judgment. Control without trust accelerates failure when machines extend their reach more quickly than oversight can keep pace.

As Yuval Noah Harari cautioned in *Homo Deus*, the danger is not that algorithms replace human decision-making, but that leaders outsource judgment so entirely that they forget they ever had it.

In a single month, the team observed this trend across Omnivista's five sites. The executives were not incompetent. They were playing yesterday's playbooks at the very moment those playbooks were most betrayed.

For decades, leaders spoke of artificial intelligence in the future tense. Someday, it would arrive. But Omnivista's reflection on their sites shattered that illusion. *Arrival* is not a date circled on a calendar. It is the moment when a system stops being experimental and starts reshaping choices in real time.

Even the word itself gives us a clue. *Artificial* comes from *artificialis*:"made by skill." *Intelligence* derives from *intelligere*: "to choose between." Read literally, artificial intelligence is "skilled discernment." Its danger is not falsity but emptiness: deploying it without anchors of vision, intuition, synergy, trust, and authenticity.

Alan Turing foresaw this in 1950 when he reframed the question "Can machines think?" into a practical test: if you could converse with a machine and not know the difference, the machine had passed. Today, that test is already behind us. We speak with systems daily; copilots, recommendation engines, chat interfaces whose outputs are often indistinguishable from human effort. But Turing's deeper question remains unanswered: How will humans choose to think alongside machines?

Voices across disciplines echo the urgency. Mo Gawdat warns in *Scary Smart* that we are handing our future to systems that do not share our values, faster than anyone dares admit. Martin Ford documents in *Rise of the Robots* how entire professions, such as radiology, law, accountancy, and financial analysis, are being reshaped, not in decades but in quarters. Harari cautions that algorithms may soon know us better than we know ourselves, predicting our choices before we experience them. Brynjolfsson and McAfee show in *The Second Machine Age* that pairing human judgment with machine capacity consistently outperforms automation alone.

The threshold is not about whether AI is here; it's about whether we are ready for it. It is about the choices leaders are already making, often unconsciously, in every meeting and every decision:

Drift into Corrosive Irrelevance, outsourcing judgment until trust cracks. Choose Optimistic Ingenuity, deliberately pairing human wisdom with machine capability. Dare Imaginative Possibility, asking questions that felt impossible until they suddenly become inevitable.

At Omnivista, all three futures appeared in a single week. That is what makes the AI threshold different from earlier ages. The divergence is no longer measured in decades. It is visible within days.

AI is not confined to screens. It is now appearing across at least four realms: digital, physical, relational, and creative. Each reveals the same ultimatum: old playbooks corrode, ingenuity is possible, imagination flickers.

First, there is the Digital Realm, in which copilots are transforming how knowledge is created and refined.
Goldman Sachs uses AI to draft equity research reports, giving analysts machine-generated "first passes." PwC is embedding AI copilots into tax and legal workflows. Microsoft's Copilot is arriving in Word, Excel, and Teams, embedding AI into everyday documents and correspondence. GitHub's Copilot is already generating significant portions of software code.

The shift is profound: from producing drafts to refining, questioning, and deciding. The Information Age reflex of measuring outputs and dashboards no longer fits. This is precisely where the Talent and Operations levers, which we'll explore in Part III, must be redesigned, and where leaders must cultivate Intuition and Authenticity, the leadership choices we return to in Part II.

Second is the Physical Realm, in which robotics and automation transform how goods are produced, distributed, and maintained.
Amazon now deploys over 750,000 robots in its fulfillment centers. The Da Vinci surgical robot supports precision operations, autonomous vehicles from Tesla and Waymo test city streets. Google DeepMind's RT-2 connects vision, language, and action in a single system.

Here, the Industrial reflex of control collides with intelligent machines. Leaders who design for surveillance corrode trust. Leaders who choreograph synergy, matching human dexterity with machine endurance, multiply ingenuity. The VISTA leadership choices of Trust and Authenticity (Part II) and the ORG6 culture levers (Part III) must anchor decisions.

Third is the Relational Realm, in which AI mediates relationships at scale.

Delta Air Lines and major banks are now utilizing chatbots as their primary customer service channels. Healthcare triage bots provide immediate reassurance. A study in *JAMA Internal Medicine* found that patients sometimes rated AI-generated bedside notes as more empathetic than those written by physicians, until they discovered the notes were machine-written. Education and well-being apps now include AI "companions" and therapy bots.

This strikes at authenticity. If leaders replace too many touchpoints with machines, they corrode belonging. But if they design AI to support human contact, surfacing insights before meetings, translating across languages, flagging emotional tone: dignity and connection deepen. The Engagement and Leadership Everywhere levers will be tested here, and the VISTA choices of Synergy and Authenticity become essential.

Fourth is the Cognitive/Creative Realm, in which AI becomes a collaborator in possibility. DeepMind's AlphaFold predicted protein structures, accelerating biology by decades. Netflix uses generative AI to model alternate storylines. Marketing teams use MidJourney and DALL·E to co-create visuals. For instance, Khan Academy's Khanmigo tutors students to ask better questions, rather than to memorize facts.

At Omnivista, Dublin glimpsed this realm: Its AI system helped design a preventive health service in days. Here, the Industrial reflex of rigid planning and the Information reflex of benchmarking corrode. Ingenuity requires CEO Stewardship and Talent levers, plus the VISTA choices of Vision and Intuition. Without them, AI recombines the past. With them, it helps invent the future.

As we depart the Information Age, we face a choice: The Irrelevance Age or The Ingenuity Age.

Irrelevance comes from the Latin *in + relevare*: "not to lift, not to lighten." What is irrelevant is what no longer matters, what fails to rise, what does not weight the world. To drift into irrelevance is to surrender significance: to let technology multiply shadows until human presence is overlooked, unneeded, unseen.

Ingenuity, by contrast, carries an entirely different lineage. Its root is the Latin *ingenuus*: "native, inborn, free, natural." To be *ingenuus* was literally to be born free, not enslaved, with a mind unshackled and unconstrained. It evoked candor, nobility of spirit, a willingness to speak frankly and act generously. From there, *ingenerare* gave us the verb "to beget, to bring forth, to produce." Ingenuity was never about clever tricks; it was about bringing something forth from within, not imposed from without.

When the word entered English in the sixteenth century (from French *ingénuité*), it meant honor and nobility; by the seventeenth century, it tilted toward inventiveness and resourceful originality. Yet the deeper resonance remains: ingenuity emerges when human beings are free and bold enough to generate what has not yet existed.

Hidden inside the word ingenuity is the same generative root as genius and genie. In Roman belief, your genius was the spirit assigned at birth, the generative force that guided your destiny. Later, the genie evolved into the spirit that granted wishes, a being of transformation. The family resemblance is no accident. To speak of ingenuity is to invoke that generative spark, the "genie" within each of us.

Artificial intelligence has no such genius. It recombines. It remembers. It mimics. But it does not originate from within; it does not beget. Ingenuity, by contrast, is alive. It is the uniquely human capacity to draw from what is innate, free, and unconstrained, and to bring it forth into the world.

The threshold we face, then, is not about whether AI will outsmart us. It is about whether we will forget the genie within. If we surrender to irrelevance, we collapse into shadows, busy but empty, optimized but hollow. If we choose ingenuity, we pair the genie with the machine: the human spirit generates, AI amplifies. That choice may be the inflection point of our age, not just for organizations, but for our species.

Day 3, Executive Team Evening Wrap-up

After the day was over, Chris stood before the whiteboard in front of her team, the words *"Irrelevance"* and *"Ingenuity"* still scrawled above the examples the team had surfaced. She let the silence stretch until every pair of eyes was fixed on her.

"These three days have shown us the arc of our inheritance," she said. "We have revisited the Industrial Age, its discipline, its stamina, its belief that endurance equals strength. We have moved through the Information Age, its dashboards, its metrics, its promise that speed equals progress. And today we have faced the threshold of AI, a force that amplifies whatever reflex we bring to it."

She capped the marker and rested her hand on the table. "Ingenuity will not arrive by accident. It is not a feature we install. It is a leadership choice. Before we redesign the enterprise, we must examine the quality of judgment, attention, and courage we bring to it."

She turned back to the whiteboard and wrote five letters in a column: V I S T A.

"These are not slogans. They are choices. Vision or void. Intuition or inertia. Synergy or silos. Trust or tyranny. Authenticity or apathy. We can lead consciously toward ingenuity, or we can slide toward irrelevance without naming it."

She looked around the circle at Yuki, John, Maria, Liam, and Sanjay.

"Part II is about the leadership compass. One VISTA choice per month, February through June. On the first of each month, one of you will lead us through the choice you have done the homework for: Vision, Intuition, Synergy, Trust, or Authenticity. Throughout the month, we will work with the framework and our chosen site to diagnose the Industrial and Information Age reflexes still at work, surface where irrelevance could take root, and design practices that could expand ingenuity.

"Part III follows from July through November. That is when we turn to ORG6, the six levers of culture: Talent, Structure, Operations, CEO Stewardship, Leadership Everywhere, and Engaged Hearts, Minds, and Bodies. The leadership choices sharpen how we see. The culture levers reshape how the organization works. First the compass, then the roadmap.

"At the end of each month, we will gather in one of your cities for three days to accomplish three things: reflect on the month and what we learned applying the frameworks to each of our sites, report to our Board about what we learned, and launch the next month's focus."

She looked around the circle, her voice steady. "This is not a side project. It is the work of the year. Sharpen these choices and pull these levers well, and AI becomes a partner in human ingenuity. Neglect them, and AI becomes an accelerant of irrelevance."

"We need to see each choice and each lever not just as it is, but as it has been, and as it could become," she said. "Each carries an inheritance. Each has a drift path. And each can be redesigned into something far stronger."

"At the end of each month, I will bring our progress to the Board and then sit with Evelyn to test my own stewardship. This is how we turn insight into system, and system into endurance. Each of you will take the lead for one month."

CEO's Reflection, That Evening

That evening, Chris stood once more beneath the Brandenburg Gate. On Day 1, she had seen it as a monument to what walls can become when they fall. On Day 2, as a passage rushed through without asking what lay on the other side. Tonight, she saw it as a threshold: the Industrial Age behind them, the Information Age beneath their feet, and ahead, the choice that would define whether Omnivista's next chapter was written in irrelevance or ingenuity. In Tokyo next month, they would begin with the first choice of the Leader's Compass: Vision.

My Fingerprint

I should tell you how I know the threshold is real. I am standing on it.

This book was written in collaboration with artificial intelligence. Not the parts that sound like a textbook. The parts that sound like me. For thirty-five years I have carried a washing machine in my head: decades of boardrooms, coaching sessions, frameworks tested and discarded, stories from five continents, and a stubborn conviction that leadership is a conscious choice. All of it spinning, never quite settling into the form I knew it could take.

I tried to get it out the way the Information Age taught me. Spreadsheets. Models. PowerPoint decks at midnight. Mud wrestling with Word. Databases that promised structure and delivered frustration. Emails, texts, social media, web design, meetings upon meetings upon meetings, with only a breath here and there for new thinking.

Then I sat down with AI and something shifted. It was like being interviewed by a thousand book writers simultaneously, each one asking the next question before I had finished answering the last. I queried back and forth, tried different examples, debated with a mind that honored my own. Through the collaboration, I realized what I already knew, but in ways I had never been able to communicate, not to other people and not to myself. Thirty-five years of pattern recognition, suddenly legible.

I felt no fear of irrelevance. None. What I felt was the opposite: the joy of ingenuity unlocked after decades of analysis. AI did not think for me. It amplified what I had spent a lifetime learning to see. The washing machine finally stopped spinning and the clothes came out folded.

If that is the threshold, I am not standing at it with dread. While boards calculate the costs AI will cut and headlines count the jobs it will take, I find myself looking out the window and asking a different question: what does AI take off our hands that unlocks something we never knew we had?

Not efficiency. Not cost reduction. A way of living and working that expands talent none of us knew we could discover within ourselves, far from the chicken coops we have built in our offices, rows and rows of humans with scrunched shoulders staring into rows and rows of glowing boxes. If that is irrelevance, I have not found it. What I have found is ingenuity, breathing for the first time.

PART II

VISTA™
The Leadership Compass

The choices leaders must make between the Ingenuity Age and the Irrelevance Age

Part II, VISTA™
The Five Leadership Choices

YESTERDAY
is gone

The INDUSTRIAL Age
1769-1995
- **V** Volume
- **I** Instruction
- **S** Standardization
- **T** Timekeeping
- **A** Authority

The INFORMATION Age
1995-2025
- **V** Virtualization
- **I** Instantaneity
- **S** Searchability
- **T** Technocracy
- **A** Analytics

TODAY
There is the Leader's Choice

The INGENUITY Age

OR

The IRRELEVANCE Age

- **V** VISION or VOID?
- **I** INTUITION or INERTIA?
- **S** SYNERGY or SILOS?
- **T** TRUST or TYRANNY?
- **A** AUTHENTICITY or APATHY?

TOMORROW
There is potential

The IMAGINATIVE POSSIBILITY Age
- **V** Vastness
- **I** Integration
- **S** Synthesis
- **T** Transcendence
- **A** Awe

Source and Design: Katharine McLennan, 2026.

Part I named the threshold and clarified the stakes as we aim to leave the Industrial and Information Ages and respond to the AI Era with ingenuity.

In this Part II, we introduce VISTA, the Leadership Compass of five leadership choices we make as we develop our own individual leadership presence.

For each of the choices, we first identify the patterns that draw leaders toward irrelevance, toward void, inertia, silos, tyranny, and apathy. Only then do we articulate the disciplined capacities required to move toward ingenuity. This is a compass for being, not a roadmap for doing. Here, each choice is framed first by its generative quality: Vision, Intuition, Synergy, Trust, and Authenticity, before naming what erodes it under pressure: Void, Inertia, Silos, Tyranny, and Apathy.

Tools multiply what they find. If we carry yesterday's reflexes, AI will amplify irrelevance. If we bring wiser ways of being, it will amplify ingenuity.

Across ages, the same tensions repeat in different clothing. We use VISTA as a compass for the leadership choices that guide us toward Ingenuity:

V: Vision: Do we see and hold a path, or drift into a Void?
I: Intuition: Do we trust cultivated judgment, or freeze in Inertia?
S: Synergy: Do we create value across boundaries, or retreat to Silos?
T: Trust: Do we lead through trust, or control through Tyranny?
A: Authenticity: Do we lead as who we are, or slide into Apathy?

We start with Vision because, without direction, no system matters. We conclude with Authenticity because, without congruence, no direction holds. The middle letters: Intuition, Synergy, Trust, describe how decisions are actually made together at an ultimatum pace.

Each choice carries the inheritance of two previous ages and the tension of three possible futures.

Each chapter traces one VISTA choice through the same arc. The Industrial Age version of the choice will feel familiar: authority over vision, instruction over intuition, standardization over synergy, timekeeping over trust, and compliance over authenticity. The Information Age version refined but rarely replaced it, adding dashboards and frameworks while leaving the underlying reflex intact. From there, each chapter maps three possible futures: the Corrosive Irrelevance that arrives when AI amplifies yesterday's habits, the Optimistic Ingenuity available to leaders who choose differently, and the Imaginative Possibility waiting beyond what most organizations have yet dared to design.

To ground each choice in its full depth, the VISTA chapters examine it through six lenses: history, etymology, philosophy, neuroscience, artificial intelligence, and real-world examples from organizations that chose well and those that did not. The lenses reveal that the tension between ingenuity and irrelevance is not new. It is ancient. What is new is the speed at which AI forces the choice.

The Omnivista team lives this journey month by month. Each executive takes ownership of one VISTA choice, leads the team through it at their signal site, and brings the results to the Board. The table overleaf shows how each choice maps across the five ages, from the Industrial past to the edge of Imaginative Possibility, and names who carries it and when.

Part II
VISTA™
Monthly Assignments

	THE PAST		THE POTENTIAL		
	Industrial Age	Information Age	Irrelevance Age	Ingenuity Age	Imaginative Possibility
"V" Chapter 4 Yuki FEBRUARY	Volume scale & throughput	Virtualization digital reach	Void slogans without substance	Vision clear North Star shaping budgets & calendars	Vastness purpose scaled across communities
"I" Chapter 5 John MARCH	Instruction managers decide, workers comply	Instantaneity speed & dashboards	Inertia frozen caution under ambiguity	Intuition trained judgment + premortems/ red team	Imagination disciplined invention with AI as muse
"S" Chapter 6 Maria APRIL	Standardization variance = enemy	Searchability copy best practice	Silos brittle boundaries	Synergy interface contracts, reuse across teams	Symphony living networks composing together
"T" Chapter 7 Sanjay MAY	Timekeeping hours over outcomes	Technocracy metrics over meaning	Tyranny surveillance & fear	Trust safety, fairness, fast repair	Transcendence trusted fabrics across institutions
"A" Chapter 8 Liam JUNE	Authority wisdom presumed at top	Analytics quantified everything	Apathy disengagement, optics	Authenticity congruence under pressure.	Awe values that widen the circle of "us"

"The only thing worse than being
blind is having sight but no vision."

Helen Keller

"Vision is not prediction; it is
disciplined seeing. It is the courage to
name what matters,
hold purpose steady
when metrics clamor, and articulate a
future others can walk toward."

Katharine McLennan

CHAPTER 4

Vision versus Void

*When uncertainty strikes, do we
see a clear path forward and
inspire others to follow,
or
lose focus and
drift into the dark?*

First Day of Month: Executive Team

Chris opened the day in the Tokyo office: "Last month, we set the rhythm for the year ahead, starting with the five Leadership Choices of our Leadership Compass," she said. "Five months, five ways of being. Today is the first: *Vision or Void*. Yuki's got the baton. We'll listen, test, and leave with one thing to keep, one to improve, one to stop, and one to start. Narrative only."

Yuki stood and wrote on the glass wall: "How our energy is distributed across the 'V' ages."

She drew a single bar with five labels:

Volume (Industrial Age): 20%
Virtualization (Information Age): 40%
Void (Irrelevance Age): 10%
Vision (Ingenuity Age): 25%
Vastness (Imaginative Possibility): 5%

"This is where our attention, budgets, and calendars already go," she said. "Not aspirations, but results. Challenge me. First, why these numbers?

"Twenty percent still sits in Volume, the Industrial "V." Adjacent teams are paid on quotas and utilization, so Marketing keeps prioritizing throughput over meaning. The old reflex toward two big, stage-gated launches a year keeps assembly-line logic alive. And we still signal busyness as value: complete decks and long updates, but sweat is too often mistaken for progress.

"Forty percent live in Virtualization, the Information "V." Budget gravity pulls toward performance media, so we end up feeding dashboards more than clarifying direction. We begin with benchmarks and competitor decks before articulating what we stand for. A calendar X-ray tells us: dozens of analytics meetings and only a handful marked "customer time" or "narrative work." Classic Information-Age behavior.

"Ten percent slips into the Void, the Irrelevance "V." When trade-offs, pricing and regulation get complex, we hesitate, and our message fractures by region. In EMEA, we refer to it as "precision preventive care"; in LATAM, it's "access at scale"; in North America, it's "platform intelligence." None is wrong; together they're blurry. Debriefs are driven by metrics, not meaning, and the pulse reads as whiplash.

"Twenty-five percent already expresses Vision, the Ingenuity "V." Edges have sharpened the North Star: Dublin's "prevent first" sketch and Pune's "human at the helm" travel well and align behavior. Budgets tell the same story: we fund customer time and pre-reads that connect data to choice, not just to dashboards. In live moments, we make decisions more quickly, with less drama; people leave a bigger impression.

"Only five percent touches Vastness, the Imaginative "V." We rarely ask the impossible-altitude questions, like "What becomes inevitable if we succeed?" Our external constellation is thin. Partnerships exist, but communities don't yet. And we protect calendars for delivery, not for dreaming."

Yuki capped the marker. "If we accept this map, the central choice is plain: when uncertainty hits, do we see and say a path others can follow, or do we drift? Vision or Void."

The team spent the morning at Omnivista's Shinjuku Research Tower, walking through labs and control rooms where the company's narrative was supposed to guide choices. Chris watched quietly as vision and void wrestled in plain sight. In one lab, a dashboard dominated the wall, displaying throughput targets, cycle times, and budget variances. A draft North Star poster sat half-hidden behind a cabinet. "Which one do I follow?" a technician muttered. In a meeting pod, managers rehearsed the quarter's marketing slogan. A young engineer whispered later, "It doesn't match the trade-offs we actually face here." At a workstation, a researcher explained a complex scan to a patient, citing accuracy rates, then hesitated when asked why it mattered. The story had slipped out of reach.

Vision was present in fragments, but void crept in whenever the narrative didn't align with the reality of spending, scheduling, or daily trade-offs. Chris left the site resolved: the story had to be visible where decisions were made, not floating in campaigns or buried in dashboards.

Team Assignments for the Month

Chris assigned the month's work on Vision versus Void. She gave each person their month's assignment:

"K: Keep: Decision-making by narrative

Significant choices must identify who benefits, what changes will be made, why they serve our purpose, and what we won't do. Money and time follow the story. The owner will be Maria, who will surface one additional operational 'Keep' action that begins with a vision but gets embedded into routine." She continued,

"I: Improve: Follow the money/time

We need to review our portfolio view against the three priorities and a visible won't-fund list; rebalance quarterly. Our Executive diaries need to shift to a 60/30/10 priority/system/learning approach. The owner will be John, who will ship a one-page before/after with three named stops and three named accelerations." Looking over to Sanjay, she said,

"S: Start: Edge-story pipeline

We will kick off two 'edge stories': Sentinel Heart (Dublin) and MumLine (Lagos). Here, we will learn to develop a vision into a concise plan and then conduct a 'micro-experiment' over a 30-day period. The owner will be Sanjay, who will stand up safety guardrails, instrumentation, and scale/no-scale calls." And finally, she looked at Yuki, saying

"S: Stop: Untethered local campaigns

We will require every major campaign to include a one-page Trade-Off Pre-Commit (TOP) that provides for named tension, won't-dos, readiness proof, and a rollback plan. The owner will be Yuki, who will co-chair a Customer Integrity Council with red-flag pause authority."

"And Liam, you have a parallel task. Test whether our North Star narrative can travel from this room to the care floor. Take the narrative format we are building, who benefits, what changes, why it serves our purpose, what we will not do, and translate it into one resident communication at Liffey. Show me whether families and frontline staff can hear the vision in language that matches the care they deliver. If the narrative cannot survive the journey from the executive team to the bedside, it is not a vision. It is a memo."

CEO's Notebook: Vision

That night, Chris walked back through Shinjuku, neon reflecting off wet pavement, trains clattering overhead. The city felt like the site they had just visited: dazzling data, relentless movement, but easy to lose the thread of why it was there. She opened her notebook. "Vision is the compass. If it isn't visible at the point of choice, the system drifts into a void." She wrote her three commitments for the month:

Actions

1. Rewrite one North Star daily. Take one purpose statement or strategy line and render it in plain, human language.

2. Post one trade-off sentence daily. For a live decision, name the tension and which side we will privilege and why.

3. Align one result daily. Shift one calendar block or one spend line to match the story we claim to follow.

What I'll Notice

1. *Industrial* (Volume): Where quotas crowd out purpose and busyness masquerades as value.

2. *Information* (Virtualization): Where dashboards and benchmarks lead instead of the North Star.

3. *Irrelevance* (Void): Where messages fracture or slogans drift from reality, where decisions hide behind metrics.

4. *Ingenuity* (Vision): Where the North Star and trade-offs are visible at decision points; spend and time mirror the story.

5. *Imagination* (Vastness): Where vision expands beyond the firm: open narrative walls, co-authored with clinicians, partners, and communities.

Chris closed the notebook. At the end of the month, the team would reconvene to test whether Vision could survive the weight of reality, or whether the void would reclaim the system. Tonight, she carried one private anchor: make the story visible where the work happens.

My Fingerprint

In 1967, a young Australian otolaryngologist named Graeme Clark began researching whether electrical stimulation could restore hearing to the profoundly deaf. His father had been a pharmacist with severe hearing loss, and Clark had watched him struggle to communicate with customers his entire life. The medical establishment told Clark it was impossible. He spent the next eleven years proving them wrong, performing the world's first multi-channel cochlear implant surgery in Melbourne in 1978. That single act of vision created an entirely new field, medical bionics, and gave rise to Cochlear Limited, the company I joined as Global Vice President of People and Culture.

By the time I arrived as Global Vice President of People and Culture, Cochlear had grown from Clark's university lab into a global enterprise operating in over 180 countries, with more than five thousand employees based in over fifty of them. Over 700,000 people worldwide had received one of its implantable hearing solutions.

Our mission was four sentences long and every employee could recite it: "We help people hear and be heard. We empower people to connect with others and live a full life. We help transform the way people understand and treat hearing loss. We innovate and bring to market a range of implantable hearing solutions that deliver a lifetime of hearing outcomes."

What struck me about Cochlear's vision was far more than the mission statement. It was also our time horizon. These are products implanted in human beings, often in children who will live with them for decades. Every decision, from the science to the regulatory strategy to the manufacturing process, must account for technology that does not yet exist. Cochlear works on a ten-year development horizon: what is being designed today must anticipate what will be possible, clinically and technologically, a decade from now. That is vision as a daily discipline, not a poster on the wall.

The leadership challenge matched the scientific one. How do you bring together inventors, scientists, engineers, audiologists, regulatory experts, surgeons, finance professionals, marketers, and people & culture leaders across fifty countries into a coherent whole? How do you integrate the extraordinary stories of people hearing for the first time, the hospitals and ENT surgeons and audiologists and regulators and insurance companies who form the ecosystem of care, into a culture that is as alive as the technology it produces?

That was the work I shared with an integrated leadership team not unlike Chris's Omnivista team in this story: including a CEO, Chiefs of Technology, People, Finance, IT, Supply Chain, and Legal, plus all the leaders of the regions and countries, all pulling the same levers this book describes. Together, we worked to see potential in people across every function and every geography, to grow talent in a culture where the science and the humanity were inseparable. What I learned at Cochlear about how to marry extraordinary advances in technology with a bedrock of what I would now call Ingenuity Age approaches to leadership and culture has shaped everything I have written in these pages.

Cochlear was, and remains, a perfect marriage of extraordinary technology advancement and extraordinary leadership and culture. Neither succeeds without the other. The science cannot advance without people who can collaborate across disciplines and continents. The culture cannot hold without a vision that gives every employee, from the lab bench in Sydney to the clinic in São Paulo, a reason to bring their best.

And the vision keeps expanding. Clark's Bionic Ear Institute, founded in 1983, has since become the Bionics Institute, and the scientists who helped develop the cochlear implant are now making advances toward a bionic eye and devices capable of deep brain stimulation for conditions from epilepsy to Parkinson's disease. The technology that restored hearing is becoming the platform for restoring sight, movement, and neural function. That is what vision does when it is real: it does not stop at the first breakthrough. It opens doors that the original inventor could not have imagined.

Let us not only wonder about the possibilities that AI and technology could take us toward. Let us also wonder, and act, on the leadership and talent that can take us there. The cochlear implant did not emerge from an algorithm. It emerged from a young man who watched his father struggle and decided to spend his life fixing it. The technology followed the human vision. It always does.

Vision: Through 6 Lenses

To understand the Vision versus Void leadership choice more fully, we view it through six lenses:

1. **History** shows how the meaning of Vision has evolved across ages and how it could evolve further.E

2. **Etymology** uncovers what the word itself invites us to see.

3. **Philosophy** reveals what it has meant to live with purpose.

4. **Neuroscience** shows how Vision functions in the brain and behavior.

5. **Artificial Intelligence** challenges us to extend Vision beyond human perception.

6. **Real World Examples** show what Vision and Void look like in practice.

History and potential evolution

Industrial Age VOLUME

Greatness was calibrated in volume: more units, more throughput. Ford's moving assembly line at Highland Park in 1913 made that logic famous: speed and standardization eclipsed technical skill as the unit of progress. Scientific management translated judgment into time-and-motion, that is, Taylor with a stopwatch, the Gilbreths with motion studies, Gantt with the chart that turned effort into bars on a timeline. Cost accounting matured to track variance; divisional structures professionalized management and separated planners from doers. Electrification, rail, and standardized parts made scale the default answer.

The prosperity was real, and so were the human costs. As work fragmented and workers became interchangeable, many experienced estrangement, what social theorists later called alienation. The line could be sped up, but the meaning could not. In practice, "vision" often meant making a bigger version of what already existed: more plants, more shifts, more output. When healthy, this era's clarity built shared prosperity; when unhealthy, it confused motion with meaning and treated curiosity as variance. The few bright counter-threads, such as quality systems that let anyone pull the cord indicating an abnormality, labs that protected invention, hinted at a larger kind of seeing but were exceptions, not the rule.

Information Age: VIRTUALIZATION
The center of gravity shifted from factories to virtualization. Spreadsheets put modeling on every desk; ERP and CRM systems made operations legible from end to end; dashboards delivered real-time visibility. Management language followed suit: KPIs, OKRs, and "data-driven" everything. Planning became simulation; decisions moved from the shop floor to the screen. With so much visible, it grew easy to mistake visibility for vision and to assume that more metrics equal more foresight.

This era enabled faster learning loops and smarter bets, but it also gave rise to deck culture: rhetoric polished faster than reality, with values posters substituted for actual value practices. A poster is not a value; a deck is not a direction; a direction is a choice you budget for. Netflix's public bet on streaming in 2007 is the counterexample that proves the rule: the company chose a future that its competitors couldn't yet see and retrained itself to meet it. When healthy, information becomes insight that orients action. When unhealthy, we get dashboard glare, activity optimized, purpose obscured.

Irrelevance Age: VOID
Irrelevance arrives when vision is reduced to short-term metrics, with leaders fixated on dashboards while horizons narrow. Abundance turns into overload. Calendars fill, dashboards multiply, and collaboration time balloons. When everything is urgent and visible, almost nothing is genuinely seen. Organizational research shows collaboration overload can consume roughly 80% of managers' time and still reduce clarity and energy, which is a classic marker of Void: motion without meaning.

Ingenuity Age: VISION
Ingenuity unfolds when vision becomes a living narrative, orienting people toward possibility and coherence amid turbulence. Ingenuity remodels vision to see precisely and make decisions in daylight. Think of large-scale operations that rehearse reality before it hits. Olympic "test events," for instance, are designed to make unseen interdependencies visible and decide accordingly. In product domains, the iPhone's 2007 debut dramatized the same principle: a "what if" design, shown with such clarity that an industry reorganized around it. In both cases, vision isn't a poster; it's

a pattern of seeing, choosing, and building.

Imaginative Age: VASTNESS

We recognize that the choices we make ripple across systems bigger than the firm. Research on awe, a perception of vastness that demands new mental "accommodation," shows measurable effects, including an expanded time sense, broadened altruism, and even links to reduced markers of inflammation. In practice, leaders who cultivate awe (in nature, art, science, or service) tend to broaden their frames, quiet their egos, and steward rather than merely scale.

Etymology

The word "Vision" comes from the Latin *videre*: "to see." It is about perception before persuasion, recognition before rhetoric. The word "Void" comes from Old French *voide*, from Latin *vacuus*: "empty, unoccupied." In leadership, a void is not silence; it is emptiness disguised as motion. The calendar is complete, but the meaning is vacant. Slides multiply, but they say nothing new. The organization hums, but no one can say why.

A void occurs when leaders stay in the moment, solving problems. Vision is what happens when they step beyond the moment, imagining futures not yet seen and inviting others to help shape them.

Philosophy

Simone Weil: "Attention is the rarest and purest form of generosity."

Vision begins not with declarations but with attention. Leaders who see before they speak resist the Void of noise. In boardrooms, this means asking not "what is our response?" but first, "what is really happening here?"

James Baldwin: "The purpose of art is to lay bare the questions hidden by the answers."

Vision demands this unsettling work: naming the questions that strategy decks obscure. Baldwin reminds leaders that seeing clearly is not about conjuring optimism but about exposing the real. A Vision statement that avoids hard truths is not Vision. It is Void dressed up in bullet points.

Rainer Maria Rilke: "Be patient toward all that is unsolved in your heart and try to love the questions themselves, like locked rooms and like books that are now written in a very foreign tongue."

Vision in turbulent times is rarely a single epiphany. It is a sustained inquiry, marked by the patience to hold onto uncertainty without retreating into slogans. In practice, this might mean a CEO admitting, "We don't yet know the answer, but here is the question we must pursue together."

Octavia Butler: "All that you touch you change. All that you change changes you."

This captures Vision as agency. Leaders who shrink from choice drift into the Void. Leaders who step into responsibility discover that choosing reshapes both them and their organizations.

Zaha Hadid, the architect who bent concrete into flowing curves, demonstrated that Vision is not abstract. It is embodied.

The spaces we design: offices, digital platforms, cities, invite or constrain behavior. Leadership Vision must be architectural in this sense: shaping environments where ingenuity becomes possible.

Confucius: To see what is right and not to do it is cowardice.

Vision here is moral sight, perceiving not only what is profitable but what is just. A Confucian leader avoids the Void not by cleverness but by aligning sight with virtue.

An Akan proverb from Ghana: "The ruin of a nation begins in the homes of its people."

Applied to leadership, the Void is seeded in small failures of vision, neglecting meetings, avoiding difficult conversations, and being blind to the human cost of decisions. Ingenuity begins when leaders see the micro as consequential to the macro.

Our philosophers show us that vision is attentive seeing that becomes public action. It begins with attention (seeing before speaking), stays with the hard questions, accepts agency, and names trade-offs in daylight. It has Hadid's embodiment: spaces and systems that invite better behavior. It is moral sight (seeing what is right), alert to the micro that shapes the macro. Anything less is noise dressed as strategy.

Neuroscience

Vision and Void are not just metaphors; they are neurobiological states. Modern neuroscience reveals that the brain's rhythms, chemicals, and networks determine whether leaders can see clearly or whether they become blind, disguised as activity.

Brain Rhythms: Beta versus Alpha/Theta/Gamma

In beta wave dominance, the "everyday alert" rhythm of email, meetings, and firefighting, the brain is vigilant but narrow. Cortisol and adrenaline prepare us for fight-or-flight, but they hijack the prefrontal cortex. Leaders under chronic beta become tactical, literal, and reactive. They may think they are steering, but they are actually circling. This is the Void disguised as productivity.

By contrast, alpha and theta rhythms: slower, calmer brain waves, support association and recombination. In experiments, just before participants solved insight puzzles, EEGs recorded a dip into alpha, followed by a theta pattern, and then a brief burst of gamma when the solution was arrived at. The brain literally "quiets" to see. That is Vision's habitat: a quiet before the flash.

Kahneman's Two Systems

Daniel Kahneman's dual-system model sharpens this picture. System 1: fast, intuitive, automatic, generates hunches, often shaped by patterns we can't articulate. System 2: slow, deliberate, effortful, tests them, asks "What evidence supports this? What's missing?" Vision requires both System 1, which imagines, and System 2, which disciplines the imagination. A leader who relies only on System 1 risks fantasy; one who clings to System 2 risks paralysis.

Prediction and Models of the Future

Neuroscience now frames the brain as a prediction machine. We don't just perceive the world; we constantly generate models of what will happen next. Vision, then, is the ability to update these models in light of weak signals and new evidence. Leaders who can't revise their predictive maps fall into Void: they interpret everything through yesterday's assumptions, even as reality changes.

The Default Mode Network and Imagination

fMRI studies reveal that the default mode network (DMN), active during daydreaming, walking, or rest, is where the brain integrates memory, present cues, and imagined futures. Vision often emerges here when seemingly idle time allows disparate inputs to combine and merge. Leaders who fill every calendar block with meetings suppress this network. They confuse constant activity with effectiveness, but neurobiologically, they are shutting down the circuitry of Vision.

Chemistry of Trust: Oxytocin and Serotonin

By contrast, oxytocin and serotonin: neurochemicals associated with trust and significance, reopen the prefrontal cortex. Paul Zak's experiments showed that when leaders recognized excellence, set challenging but winnable goals, gave discretion, shared information, built relationships, invested in development, and showed vulnerability, oxytocin rose measurably. Trust was not just a feeling; it was chemistry. Vision flourishes when trust flows through the system.

Awe as a Neurobiological State

Research on awe shows that when people experience vastness through nature, art, or service, the brain shifts into increased alpha coherence, the amygdala quiets, and networks for attention and imagination expand. Participants report an altered sense of time, heightened connection, and increased prosocial behavior. Leaders who deliberately cultivate awe by doing activities like walking in forests, attending concerts, or serving in communities, are giving their brains the conditions to see beyond the immediate. Void leaders never look up; their horizon collapses to the next meeting or the next quarter.

Dopamine and the Anticipation of a Future

Vision is not only about clarity of sight; it is about energy for the journey. Dopamine pathways activate not just when rewards arrive but when we anticipate meaningful progress. Wolfram Schultz's research showed that dopamine spikes when the brain detects novelty or possibility. Leaders who present compelling narratives trigger this anticipatory system: people feel rewarded not just by outcomes, but by the sense of moving toward an Ingenuity Age worth believing in. In the absence of such narratives, dopamine drains away. Teams collapse into the Void: disengaged, tired, going through motions.

Polyvagal Theory: Safety and Seeing

Stephen Porges' polyvagal theory suggests that humans need cues of safety to access social engagement and higher-order cognition. In unsafe environments where people expect punishment, ridicule, or arbitrary power, the nervous system defaults to fight, flight, or freeze. Leaders who neglect psychological safety may think they are driving performance, but they are, in fact, neurobiologically shutting down Vision. Leaders who signal calm, fairness, and care re-activate the circuits that allow foresight and ingenuity.

Collective Brains: Vision as Synchrony

Vision is rarely a solo act. Studies using hyperscanning (simultaneous brain imaging of multiple people) show that when teams are deeply engaged, their brainwave patterns synchronize. This neural entrainment correlates with trust, flow, and shared problem-solving. In practice, it means that collective Vision is not a metaphor but a measurable state: people literally begin to "see" together. By contrast, teams in Void exhibit fragmented neural activity, with each brain running its own track and no coherence and no shared future.

Sleep, Dreams, and Incubation

Vision often arrives not at the desk but in the margins of consciousness. During REM sleep, the brain integrates emotionally charged material and makes unexpected associations. Breakthroughs from Kekulé's dream of the benzene ring to Larry Page's dream of a universal web index point to this incubation power. Leaders who treat sleep as expendable sacrifice one of the brain's deepest incubators of Vision. Dreams are not just fantasies; they are neurological laboratories where tomorrow's pathways are rehearsed.

Mood, Play, and Creativity

Mood matters. Studies show that teams that laugh together solve more complex problems more creatively. Positive affect expands the brain's associative networks, making it easier to form novel connections. The line between comedy and creativity is thinner than we think. That is why visionary teams protect play. Void cultures, by contrast, treat levity as a distraction. In doing so, they suppress one of the brain's oldest sources of ingenuity.

Strengthening Vision by Applying Neuroscience Every Day

Vision and Void live in the brain. They are not abstractions but biological realities. Leaders who cultivate the conditions of Vision, alpha states, trust chemistry, anticipatory narratives, awe, synchrony, sleep, and play literally rewire their organizations toward ingenuity. Leaders who normalize stress, tunnel vision, fear, and busyness create the Void: a full calendar and an empty mind.

Neuroscience's insights help us choose Vision every day. We can build them into our daily leadership activities:

- Protect downtime and daydreaming: leave space for the default mode network.

- Curate awe experiences: nature, art, and service expand neural possibility.

- Narrate apparent horizons: dopamine thrives on the anticipation of meaning.

- Guard against chronic urgency: constant cortisol erodes perception.

- Build safety signals: fairness, calm tone, transparent rules.

- Encourage synchrony: design spaces where teams think and see together.

- Treat sleep as a strategic asset: rest is a leadership practice, not an indulgence.

- Protect play and humor: levity is not a distraction but a catalyst of creativity.

Artificial Intelligence

We can now see the leadership choice between Vision and Void in the light of five examples of AI-fueled decisions.

Generative Abundance versus Narrative Discipline

AI now inundates leaders with generative content: reports, strategy decks, and customer insights, produced at scale. This abundance is double-edged. On the one hand, it creates extraordinary visibility; leaders can simulate scenarios and draft options faster than ever. On the other hand, it risks burying organizations in complex language and dashboards with no straightforward guiding narrative. Vision in this age means using AI as a co-writer of narrative clarity. Void means letting AI's torrents overwhelm with volume.

For example, boards are already asking ChatGPT or Gemini for "five-year strategy drafts." A visionary CEO will use this input to sharpen their unique North Star; a drifting one will paste it in and lose the thread of purpose.

Predictive Foresight versus Reactive Overload

AI's predictive models can reveal weak signals, including market shifts, consumer sentiment, and even supply chain risks. Leaders with Vision use these predictions to sharpen foresight and make disciplined bets. Without discipline, however, predictive dashboards can paralyze with endless alerts, probability trees, and "what if" noise leading to analysis inertia.

In healthcare, for example, predictive AI can flag high-risk patients (like Omnivista Sentinel Heart). A leader with Vision frames these alerts into a coherent prevention story. In Void, they collapse into fragmented dashboards that clinicians ignore.

Synthetic Reality versus Authentic Seeing

AI now generates not only text but also hyper-real images, video, and voices. This creates new possibilities for communicating a shared vision, but also new risks of deception and distraction. Leaders in Vision will use synthetic media to help people imagine futures together; leaders in Void will be seduced by spectacle or misled by deepfakes.

Companies like Nvidia are showcasing entire "digital twins" of factories to rehearse operations. A visionary leader uses this to discipline the "seeing-before-building" approach; a drifting one dazzles stakeholders with simulations while avoiding real trade-offs.

Decision Support versus Delegation of Judgment

AI copilots are entering every domain: finance, legal, product, and HR. They can dramatically improve speed and accuracy. But the deeper question is whether leaders treat them as support for human judgment or as a substitute for it. Visionary leaders utilize AI to augment System 2 thinking, testing intuition and probing assumptions. Void leaders abdicate: "the model said so," drifting into false objectivity and fragile decisions.

In finance, BlackRock and Goldman Sachs are already leaning on AI models for investment strategy. A visionary portfolio leader will treat outputs as a challenge to their own narrative. A void leader will hide behind "the model."

Imaginative Possibility versus Narrow Optimization

AI offers leaders the chance to imagine beyond old constraints with new business models, new scientific discoveries, and even new definitions of work. But it also tempts organizations to aim AI narrowly: shaving costs, optimizing clicks, speeding throughput. Vision stretches AI toward imaginative possibilities. Void traps it in yesterday's efficiency reflex.

DeepMind's AlphaFold opened vast new frontiers in biology by solving protein folding, an "impossible" problem. By contrast, many firms deploy AI solely to optimize ad targeting, a more efficient approach, but hardly a visionary one.

Amplifying Vision by Deploying AI Every Day

These are five examples of how AI serves as the amplifier of Vision or Void. AI can enhance narrative clarity, foresight, authenticity, disciplined judgment, and imaginative possibility, or it can overwhelm organizations with noise, spectacle, and shallow optimization.

Leaders can build these into daily practice:

- Use AI to draft and then sharpen narrative clarity, not to replace it.

- Deploy predictive models as inputs to judgment, not substitutes for it.

- Test synthetic media for shared imagination, not spectacle.

- Treat copilot outputs as challenges to your own thinking, not as final answers.

- Point AI toward imaginative possibility, not just cost reduction.

Vision: Real World Examples

Adobe's Creative Cloud Pivot

- **What they did.** In 2013, CEO Shantanu Narayen abandoned perpetual software licenses and shifted Adobe to a subscription model: Creative Cloud. Shares fell nearly 7% on the announcement. User forums erupted in protest.

- **Why this matters.** Narayen framed the decision as visionary inevitability: creation was moving online, and Adobe had to move with it. He chose near-term pain for long-term coherence. The North Star was clear enough that the organization could hold through the backlash.

- **Consequences.** By 2023, recurring revenue exceeded $15 billion annually, with more than 30 million Creative Cloud users. Adobe was repositioned as a platform for creators, not a software vendor.

Microsoft under Satya Nadella

- **What they did.** When Nadella became CEO in 2014, Microsoft's stock had stagnated for over a decade. He reframed the mission as "empower every person and every organization on the planet to achieve more" and tied it to Carol Dweck's growth mindset as a cultural reset. Investment flowed into Azure, developer tools, and AI while legacy businesses were deemphasized.

- **Why this matters.** Vision here was resource reallocation: what to stop, what to fund, and how to behave. Nadella told employees their industry does not respect tradition, only innovation, and that Microsoft must rediscover its soul.

- **Consequences.** Market capitalization grew from $300 billion in 2014 to over $2.5 trillion by 2023. Azure became the second-largest cloud provider. Microsoft re-established itself as a defining player in the AI revolution.

Unilever's Sustainable Living Plan (2010s)

- **What they did.** Under CEO Paul Polman (2009-2019), Unilever declared it would decouple growth from environmental impact. Polman scrapped quarterly earnings guidance, telling investors the company would not chase short-term numbers at the expense of long-term vision.

- **Why this matters.** Polman's stance was that sustainability was not charity but the engine of long-term performance. Brands like Dove, Lifebuoy, and Ben & Jerry's leaned into purpose-driven campaigns backed by measurable reduction in carbon, water, and waste footprints.

- **Consequences.** From 2009 to 2019, total shareholder return was over 290%, compared to 120% for the broader sector. Unilever became a global case study in purpose-led strategy.

Patagonia's "Don't Buy This Jacket"

- **What they did.** In 2011, founder Yvon Chouinard ran a Black Friday ad inviting customers to reflect on overconsumption before purchasing new gear. The company backed the message with its Worn Wear repair program, pledged 1% of sales to environmental causes, and transferred ownership into a purpose trust in 2022.

- **Why this matters.** Chouinard said "Growth is not the problem, blind growth is." Vision here was aligning brand, operations, and ownership around a higher narrative, making purpose visible in every decision.

- **Consequences.** Revenue climbed steadily through the 2010s, crossing $1 billion by 2018. The ownership transfer ensured profits would serve the planet permanently.

Void: Real World Examples

Nokia after the Smartphone Disruption

- **What they did.** Nokia commanded over 40% of global mobile phone sales in 2007. As Apple and Android redrew the industry, internal factions fought between Symbian, MeeGo, and Windows Phone. CEO Stephen Elop acknowledged the crisis in his "burning platform" memo but partnered with Microsoft on a platform that never gained more than 3% market share.

- **Why this matters.** Awareness of disruption is not vision. Nokia recognized the threat but could not commit to a singular direction. The organization drifted between competing strategies rather than choosing one.

- **Consequences.** By 2014, the handset business was sold to Microsoft for $7.2 billion, a fraction of its former value.

Toshiba's Nuclear Overreach

- **What they did.** In 2006, Toshiba acquired Westinghouse Electric, betting that nuclear power would surge as a global energy solution. After the 2011 Fukushima disaster shifted sentiment, Toshiba failed to articulate a new vision. Costs spiraled.

- **Why this matters.** When the world changed, leadership had no narrative to unite employees, investors, or society. What began as a bold bet became a void.

- **Consequences.** A $6.3 billion write-down in 2017 effectively bankrupted Westinghouse and threatened Toshiba's survival. The company was delisted from the Tokyo Stock Exchange in 2023.

WeWork's Collapse

- **What they did.** CEO Adam Neumann branded WeWork as a tech company selling "the future of work," drawing over $12 billion in funding and a paper valuation of $47 billion. Governance failures, reckless spending, and cult-like leadership masked the absence of a coherent business model.

- **Why this matters.** Vision without discipline is not vision. It is void masquerading as charisma. When the IPO prospectus revealed losses exceeding $1.9 billion annually, investors balked.

- **Consequences.** Valuation collapsed to below $10 billion. WeWork filed for bankruptcy in 2023.

MySpace's Drift

- **What they did.** Acquired by News Corp in 2005 for $580 million, MySpace was the largest social network in the world with over 100 million users by 2008. Leadership focused on advertising monetization and superficial personalization while neglecting user experience and platform trust.

- **Why this matters.** Facebook doubled down on clarity: real identities, clean design, disciplined product iteration. MySpace refused to prioritize coherence over clutter.

- **Consequences.** News Corp sold MySpace for $35 million in 2011. Dominance became irrelevance within a few short years.

Vision: Bringing the Lenses Together

Vision is not a statement on a wall. It is attention disciplined into a narrative that an organization is prepared to fund, staff, and defend under pressure.

- *History* shows the pattern clearly: the Industrial Age confused scale with sight, the Information Age confused dashboards with direction, and the Irrelevance Age confuses busyness with purpose.

- *Etymology* returns us to the root: videre, to see. Before a leader can persuade, they must perceive. Before they can direct, they must notice what others have missed.

- *Philosophy* deepens the claim: Weil taught that attention is the rarest generosity, Baldwin insisted that seeing clearly means exposing the real rather than conjuring optimism, Rilke urged us to love the questions, Butler showed that choosing reshapes both the chooser and the organization, and Confucius bound vision to moral sight, not cleverness.

- *Neuroscience* confirms that vision is a biological state, not a personality trait: it requires alpha and theta rhythms that chronic urgency destroys, a default mode network that packed calendars suppress, trust chemistry that fear shuts down, and awe experiences that expand the brain's capacity to see beyond the immediate quarter.

- *AI amplifies* whichever state it finds: it can sharpen narrative clarity, strengthen foresight, and rehearse futures with digital twins, or it can flood organizations with generative noise, predictive overload, and spectacle that substitutes for substance.

- *And the real-world evidence* draws a clean line: Adobe, Microsoft, Unilever, and Patagonia funded their vision with irreversible commitments, while Nokia, WeWork, and MySpace proved that awareness without commitment is not vision but drift with better slides.

- *The practical test belongs to everyone*: can you name the budget lines that follow the North Star, the meetings you will stop holding, the metrics you will stop pursuing, and the rehearsals you will conduct before reality arrives? Vision lives in those choices. Void lives in everything else.

27 February — SYDNEY

End of Month: Executive Team Review

The team reported back, each anchoring to the Vision commitments.

Maria (Ops): Keep → "Decision-making by narrative"

- **What she did**: Replaced four standing status meetings with an asynchronous pre-read + a single decision session per topic at Paulista Hospital; installed the one-page North Star & won't-dos in the Ops wiki and on the wall behind intake.

- **What changed**: Decision latency down 22% on Tier-1 site issues; clinicians could retell the North Star from memory.

- **Proof points:** Meeting diffs; photo of wall; three decisions with narrative → money/time alignment shown.

John (Finance): Improve → "Follow the money/time"

- **What he did:** Published a before/after spending split; reallocated €120k to navigation & enablement; set exec diary targets; introduced a monthly narrative spend review.

- **What changed**: Two "halo" projects were paused; one customer-immersion program was launched; diaries are moving toward a 60/30/10 approach.

- **Proof points:** One-pager (spend), diary screenshots, immersion agenda & attendee list.

Sanjay (Tech): Start → "Edge-story pipeline"

- **What he did:** Ran Sentinel Heart micro-test (Dublin) and MumLine pilot (Lagos) with safety guardrails and event logging; added a narrative prompt to the Sentinel UI at Paulista Hospital (São Paulo).

- **What changed**: The early false-positive rate improved with the clinician over-read and environmental exposure feature; MumLine recommends a scale with language packs and a clinician-first escalation signature.

- **Proof points:** Two learning memos; UI screenshot; scale/no-scale decisions recorded.

Yuki (People): Stop → "Untethered local campaigns"

- **What she did**: Co-chaired the Customer Integrity Council; audited five campaigns (retired FastPath Sixty-Second Diagnosis; re-scripted three regional assets).

- **What changed**: Slogan drift reduced; regulator concerns eased; teams report "safer to speak up" in creative reviews.

- **Proof points:** Audit notes, "speak-up safety" pulse up 11 points.

Liam (CMO): Keep → "North Star narrative at the frontline"

- **What he did:** Translated the narrative format into one resident communication at Liffey: who benefits, what changes, why it serves our purpose, what we will not do. Tested it with families and frontline caregivers.

- **What changed**: Families responded immediately; three asked to share it with their networks. Staff said it was the first time they had seen the strategy in language that matched the care they delivered. One caregiver said, "Now I can explain why we are doing this, not just what we are doing."

- **Proof points:** Revised communication, family feedback, and staff verbatims on narrative clarity.

What If

After the review, Chris took the team to the Royal Botanic Garden in Sydney to reflect on the "What-ifs" of Vision:

1. What if every enterprise-wide decision we made required a one-sentence trade-off posted publicly?
2. What if the North Star were visible at every decision station: labs, wards, finance desks, not just in strategy decks?
3. What if every budget line expired unless it was renewed against the declared story?
4. What if calendars showed "time by purpose" instead of "time by meeting"?
5. What if slogans were banned until results (spend, schedule) proved alignment?
6. What if every Board pack began with a story from the edge, a patient, customer, or engineer before it showed the numbers?
7. What if trade-off sentences were logged by AI and surfaced whenever a similar dilemma reappeared?
8. What if promotions depended on how well leaders made the story visible in their teams?
9. What if every region wrote its own one-sentence North Star, then tested it for coherence against the whole?
10. What if dashboards couldn't be published unless the North Star was printed at the top?

28 February — **SYDNEY**

End of Month: Board Review

Chris opened plainly. "Vision is our compass. If it is visible at the point of decision, ingenuity compounds. If it drifts into campaigns or dashboards, we fall into Void. This month, we tested both across Omnivista."

She described the trials. In Tokyo's Shinjuku Research Tower, Yuki posted one-sentence North Stars at the places where choices are actually made. For every Tier-1 decision, teams wrote a trade-off sentence, naming the tension, then naming which side we will privilege. Budgets and calendars were reviewed each week to ensure that spending and time aligned with the story. Field tests touched a research allocation, a lab-upgrade choice, and a hiring-freeze exception.

The room leaned in for the results. Seventy-one percent of staff could now retell the one-sentence North Star in their own words (up from forty-two percent). Fourteen Tier-1 decisions were logged with explicit trade-offs; two escalations never materialized because clarity was posted at the edge. In one lab, a $200k reallocation was made to match the declared story, and a recurring reporting meeting was replaced with a collaboration block.

Perception moved as well. Staff surveys showed a 12-point rise in "I know why my work matters," and a 9-point rise in "Our priorities are consistent." The numbers were modest but directional: when the story meets the decision, people regain coherence and energy.

"The signal is simple," Chris said. "Vision becomes Ingenuity when the story is visible at the moment of choice, trade-offs are named, and money and time align. Void becomes Irrelevance when dashboards or slogans displace narrative, or when budgets contradict the story. Our early proof points suggest Omnivista can move from fractured messaging to a living compass that directs spend, schedule, and attention."

She offered three guardrails. First, the story must meet the decision; if it isn't visible where choices are made, it's theater. Second, trade-offs must be named; if tensions stay hidden, drift follows. Third, results must align; if calendars and budgets don't match the story, belief evaporates.

Chris let the room sit with it. "Vision or Void isn't abstract," she said at last. "It's a daily discipline. This month shows we can make it visible, if we choose."

The Chair nodded. "Bring us proof again next month, when Intuition is tested."

CEO's Reflection, That Evening

Chris left the Boardroom and walked down toward Circular Quay. Ferries cut quiet arcs across the harbor, their wakes glimmering under the bridge lights. The day had confirmed what she already sensed in Tokyo: Vision can be held, but only if it is made visible at the point of choice. Otherwise, it fractures into Void: campaigns without conviction and dashboards without direction.

She stopped at the edge of the water, notebook in hand. "Next month is about Intuition," she wrote. "The discipline of noticing before the data arrives, of holding steady in ambiguity, of listening to the signal behind the noise."

Vision: Exercises for You to Try

Vision only matters when it moves beyond the whiteboard and into the rhythm of leadership. Posters fade; dashboards age; even the most eloquent speeches vanish if not embodied in practice. What endures is the discipline of seeing, naming, and acting with consequence.

Leaders who cultivate Vision understand that it is not a single act of foresight but a repeated pattern of attention. It is found in the walks where the mind clears, in the one sentence that names a trade-off honestly, in the discipline of portfolios that show not just what was funded but what was stopped. Vision is fragile if left to inspiration; it becomes powerful when translated into habit.

To make Vision more than an aspiration, try this seven-day practice plan. Each element is simple in form but cumulative in effect. Done together, they retrain an organization's eyes to see and its hands to build in alignment with its purpose.

> Day 1: Daily Vision Walk: Set aside 20 minutes a day for reflective walking. No agenda, no device. This is the time when the brain's default mode network integrates fragments into future patterns. Vision requires margin.
>
> Day 2: Edge Story Intake: Request at least two stories per week from the boundary, including those of a customer, a clinician, a community

partner, or a frontline team member. Capture them in a simple format: what changed, why it matters, and what tension it tests in your North Star. Vision sharpens at the edges.

Day 3: Trade-Off Sentence: For every Tier-1 decision, require a one-line statement of the tension and which side you privilege. Example: We chose speed over perfection, and here is what we will delay as a result. If you cannot write the sentence, you are not yet in Vision; you are in Void.

Day 4: Diary 60/30/10 Check: At the end of each week, review how your time was spent: 60% on priorities (customers, product, capability), 30% on running the system, 10% on learning and horizon work. Adjust if drift has pulled you elsewhere. Vision is what your calendar proves, not what your words declare.

Day 5: Awe Habit: Once a week, step deliberately into an encounter with something larger than yourself: a concert, a hike, a work of art, a community ritual. Neuroscience shows awe widens frames and restores foresight. Vision needs the humility of vastness.

Day 6: Before/After Metrics: Every month, publish a single "before/after" snapshot of money and time reallocation. What did you stop? What did you fund? Vision becomes visible when results match rhetoric.

Day 7: Narrative Audit: At least once a month, ask three people on the frontline to retell your organization's North Star in their own words. If the story is transparent, portable, and alive, Vision is intact. If it has drifted or fractured, you have early warning of Void.

None of these practices is complicated. They require no new software, no budget lines, no external consultants. What they need is constancy: the leader's choice to attend, to clarify, and to narrate.

Vision, in use, is less about grand pronouncements and more about everyday discipline. It is how an organization learns to keep its eyes open when the fog thickens. It is how leaders see before they act, and act in ways that others can follow. And it is how the drift into Void is prevented, not once, but daily, in the choreography of choices.

Self-Assessment: Vision versus Void

Rate yourself honestly. For each question, score both the Foundation and the AI Amplifier.
1 Not Yet · 2 Emerging · 3 Developing · 4 Practicing · 5 Second Nature

---

1.

Foundation. I articulate a compelling North Star that shapes real decisions, not just slogans.

    Foundation score (1–5):_____

AI Amplifier. I use AI to model strategic scenarios and surface signals of change that sharpen our North Star.

    AI Amplifier score (1–5):_____

2.

Foundation. Our vision actively guides budget allocation and calendar priorities, not just offsites.

    Foundation score (1–5):_____

AI Amplifier. We deploy AI to translate our vision into live dashboards and decision tools the team uses daily.

    AI Amplifier score (1–5):_____

3.

Foundation. I translate long-term purpose into near-term choices people can act on this week.

    Foundation score (1–5):_____

AI Amplifier. I use AI to generate options, test assumptions, and accelerate the translation from strategy to action.

    AI Amplifier score (1–5):_____

4.

Foundation. When ambiguity rises, I help my team see the path forward rather than retreating to familiar playbooks.

Foundation score (1–5):_____

AI Amplifier. I use AI to cut through information noise, synthesizing complexity into clarity when ambiguity peaks.

AI Amplifier score (1–5):_____

5.

Foundation. I actively scan for signals of change and adjust direction before crisis forces it.

Foundation score (1–5):_____

AI Amplifier. I use AI to monitor weak signals, emerging trends, and competitive shifts that human scanning alone would miss.

AI Amplifier score (1–5):_____

AVERAGE SCORE: Vision versus Void

Foundation average (total of five scores ÷ 5):_____

AI Amplifier average (total of five scores ÷ 5):_____

Now: Transfer these two averages to the "V" row of your VISTA Scoreboard at the back of the book.

"Intuition will tell the
thinking mind where to look next."

Jonas Salk

""Intuition comes when we inspire
ourselves within the magnificence
of nature, integrate mind, body, and
heart by listening with intent, and
imagine potential as extraordinary as
it may seem, all in the deep silence of
our inner wisdom."

Katharine McLennan

CHAPTER 5

Intuition versus Inertia

*When ambiguity arises, do we
trust cultivated judgment,
or
freeze in place, overwhelmed by
a world that no longer makes sense?*

First Day of Month: Executive Team

In the Sydney office, John stood at the glass wall with a single marker. "This afternoon is Intuition versus Inertia," he said. "Let's start by seeing where our energy really lives."

He drew one bar, five labels, the I-eras:

> *Instruction* (Industrial Age): 20%
> *Instantaneity* (Information Age): 45%
> *Inertia* (Irrelevance Age): 10%
> *Intuition* (Ingenuity Age): 20%
> *Imagination* (Imaginative Possibility): 5%

"About twenty percent of our work still lives in Instruction," he began. "That's the Industrial hangover. When things get tricky, we still default to 'the manager decides.' We over-document to prove diligence instead of sharpening judgment. We keep mistaking training for practice; people complete courses, but few get coached through real decisions."

He moved to the next column. "Forty-five percent of us are stuck in Instantaneity, the Information reflex. Dashboards set our tempo; speed and freshness take precedence over depth. Slack storms decide which issues get airtime, not which arguments hold up. Meetings rush to answers before the question's even framed."

John glanced back at the board. "Ten percent has drifted into Inertia, the Irrelevance layer. When data conflict, we freeze. We treat tiny, reversible bets as if we're certifying an aircraft. And the fear of being wrong has become a badge of prudence: 'better to wait than to move.'"

He tapped the next section, Intuition. "But twenty percent of our system already looks different. In Product and Ops, decision journals capture Tier-1 calls. Premortems before launches cut the noise later. And advice rounds, where experts, stakeholders, and one skeptic weigh in, have sped up two major decisions."

Finally, John pointed to the smallest column: Imagination. "Only five percent of our work touches this. We have no protected time for impossible ideas, no silence in the calendar. The sandbox is too small for safe experiments. And AI still summarizes rather than invents."

He capped the marker and turned to the group. "This is the map," he said quietly. "It shows where the old reflexes still rule and where ingenuity's starting to take hold. Next month, our job is to shift the weight."

The executive team then gathered at the Barangaroo Hub, Sydney's financial and biotech center, where John had chosen to illustrate Intuition versus Inertia. Glass towers looked out over the harbor, the bustle of ferries below in sharp contrast to the slow-moving approval processes they were about to confront.

John led them first into a finance operations floor. On a wide screen, dashboards were updated in real time, displaying variance to budget, cost allocations, and risk ratios. Staff scrolled through rows of numbers, waiting for "green lights" before making any move. One manager admitted, "We don't decide until the data tells us to. By the time it does, the opportunity is often gone." This was inertia: dashboards substituting for judgment, action delayed until certainty seemed perfect.

In another corner, they saw a different experiment underway. A project team had been piloting decision journals. Each day, team leads wrote a short note: what decision was made, what signals were noticed, what assumptions carried weight. Data was used, but never as the sole trigger; decisions were framed as hypotheses to test, not certainties to defend. A young analyst explained, "It's not about being right, it's about noticing early, acting, and learning." This was intuition: choices made consciously in the face of ambiguity, trade-offs logged openly, and lessons fed back into the system.

John paused by the glass wall, harbor glittering behind him. "Intuition is not guessing. It is disciplined noticing, sensing the signals, triggers, and the patterns. It is then having the courage to decide before the dashboard is perfect. Inertia looks safe, but it's corrosive. Intuition looks risky, but it's how we stay alive."

Chris jotted a line in her notebook: "Courage in ambiguity is the currency of ingenuity." The team left the floor thoughtful. They had seen both realities within the same building: one side paralyzed by waiting, the other already shaping the future through real-time decisions.

Team Assignments for the Month

Chris assigned the month's work on Intuition versus Inertia.

"K: Keep: Decision journals on Tier-1 choices.

This moves us from stories after the fact to learning before the fact. Every significant decision gets a journal entry: the intuition, the evidence, and the trade-off. Sanjay will ensure journals auto-attach to the tooling for any Tier-1 decision ticket." She turned to Maria.

"I: Improve: Premortems and red teams as a standard gate.

For all irreversible decisions, what we are calling Type-1, we will require a thirty-minute premortem and a brief red-team pass before approval. Maria will embed these in operating reviews, and Liam will supply the red-team roster." She looked at John.

"S: Start: Two-track decisions, Type-1 versus Type-2.

Reversible decisions can ship with lighter evidence at the edge. Irreversible decisions require the full test. John will publish the policy and audit three live calls this month." Finally, she turned to Yuki.

"S: Stop: Metric-only approvals.

No major decision may be approved solely on quantitative thresholds. The narrative and trade-off sentence are mandatory. Yuki will add the one-line trade-off to the approval template, and I will enforce it."

John closed his notebook. "Let's give Intuition a chance to speak by creating silence before analysis, and then we'll test it in daylight."

Chris nodded. "Assignments stand. Tomorrow I'll go to the field. I want to see where Intuition shows up, or gets smothered."

CEO's Notebook: Intuition

That evening, Chris walked through the Royal Botanic Garden, the city lights breaking against the water. The day's site visit at Barangaroo had shown both sides: dashboards freezing in action until the data felt perfect, and young analysts logging their decision journals with courage in the face of ambiguity. Sydney felt like that tension itself, gleaming towers built on sandstone cliffs, discipline and daring coexisting uneasily.She paused at Mrs. Macquarie's Chair, the harbor stretching wide. "Intuition is not impulse," she wrote in her notebook. "It is disciplined noticing: signals, context, body sense, before the dashboards arrive." For this month, she set her daily practices.

Actions

1. Begin each day with two minutes of stillness: no devices, breathe, before reviewing the agenda.

2. One sentence after. Write down one intuition that surfaces in that silence, even if it feels fragile.

3. One test daily. Run a premortem, ask a skeptic, or design a reversible micro-experiment, turning intuition into learning.

What I'll Notice

1. *Industrial* (Instruction): Where rules silence frontline judgment; compliance over curiosity.

2. *Information* (Instantaneity): Where speed and dashboards overshadow the framing of the real question.

3. *Irrelevance* (Inertia): Where ambiguity freezes action; "the model said so" replaces ownership.

4. *Ingenuity* (Intuition): Where leaders integrate signals with awareness; decisions logged with trade-offs and learning loops.

5. *Imagination* (Integration): Where intuition sparks generative experiments with safe trials that expand what's possible.

Chris closed her notebook as ferries carved trails of white across the dark water. Tomorrow, she would return to routines and reviews. Tonight, she carried a private commitment: to protect silence, to honor the faint signal, and to act before inertia could settle in.

My Fingerprint

Early in my career, I traveled across Southeast Asia with a strategy executive who would one day become one of Australia's most successful CEOs and Board Chairs. We were looking for opportunities for a steel manufacturing company, visiting sites in Taiwan, Malaysia, Indonesia, and Thailand. There was no internet. We carried briefcases and read the room. That was the job: walk the factory floor, sit across from the local management team, watch their eyes when you asked about capacity, safety, and ambition. He taught me to notice what people said with their posture before they said anything with their mouths. He taught me that the answer to most due diligence questions was visible within the first thirty minutes if you knew how to look.

Twenty years later, I visited him in his CEO's office. He was preparing to purchase a major company. Across his desk were valuations from the world's leading investment banks and strategy firms. Goldman Sachs, McKinsey, BCG, and others. The numbers ranged from roughly fifteen billion to seventy billion. The gap between the lowest and highest valuation was larger than the GDP of some of the countries we had visited together two decades earlier. He looked at me and said, "What's your pick?"

I told him the truth: I had no idea. But I said he could pay me one of the banks' fees and I would happily give him my valuation.

He laughed. Then he said, "I don't know either. But I'm going to buy it, because it's going to work. It's a matter of people."

He bought it. He did not predict the global financial crisis of 2008. No one did. The acquisition looked catastrophic for the first two years. Analysts questioned the price. Boards questioned the logic. The media questioned his judgment. But through a decade of putting the right leadership in place, caring about the floor managers and the client-facing people as much as the capital structure, he turned it around. Not by cutting costs or selling assets, but by building the human system inside the company until it could deliver what the models said was impossible.

That was intuition. Not a guess. Not a hunch divorced from experience. He had spent thirty years reading rooms, reading people, reading the signals behind the numbers. When the world's highest-ranking investment banks and consulting firms gave him ten different wildly varying answers, he trusted what no spreadsheet could calculate: whether the people inside the company had the capacity to build something worth more than the models predicted.

What I learned from him has stayed with me longer than any framework in any textbook. Intuition is not the absence of analysis. It is what remains after you have done all the analysis and the analysis has told you nothing conclusive. It is the pattern recognition that builds over decades of paying attention to people, not data, and of noticing what is present in a room that will never appear in a report. He was right about the acquisition. He was right because he had trained his intuition the only way it can be trained: by showing up, year after year, in rooms where the stakes were real and the answers were not in the spreadsheet.

Intuition: Through Six Lenses

As with Vision, we examine Intuition through the same six lenses: history, etymology, philosophy, neuroscience, artificial intelligence, and real world examples.

History and what could evolve

Industrial Age

Intuition was treated as a liability. Managers decided, and workers complied; checklists and procedures raised the floor but also taught people to wait for orders. Training was plentiful, coached practice was rare, and "good leadership" often meant supplying quick answers rather than cultivating judgment. Over time, organizations rewarded obedience over feel. When the frontline sensed a weak signal or knew when a rule no longer fit, their insights were ignored. The system excelled at eliminating variance but struggled to recognize emerging changes. Two helpful reminders from this era: near-miss reporting works only when people feel safe speaking up, and technical skill wanes when it is privatized in notebooks instead of being shared as a teachable method.

Information Age

The center of gravity shifted from the foreman's whistle to the dashboard's ping. "Show me the data" became reflex; freshness outranked depth, and teams got faster at answering than at framing the right question. Used well, analytics widened vision; overused, they narrowed judgment. Recency trumped relevance, and Goodhart's law (when a measure becomes a target, it distorts the system) showed up in everyday work. For example, Wells Fargo targeted cross-selling (eight accounts per customer) in 2016. Employees opened millions of fake accounts. The metric hit record highs while trust collapsed, costing the bank over $3 billion in fines.

Slack storms set the agenda, rewarding speed over reasoning, and meetings rushed to solutions before the problem was clearly stated. Leaders skimmed charts, chased benchmarks, and outsourced judgment to the loudest metric. Two insights are helpful here: treat dashboards as evidence, not orders, and pair every metric with a narrative that states assumptions, trade-offs, and what would change your mind.

Irrelevance Age

The abundance of data produces a scarcity of courage. Signals conflict, ambiguity rises, and leaders stall: "Run one more survey," "Pilot the pilot," "Let's study it another week." Small, reversible choices get treated like aircraft certification; accountability shifts from choice to cover ("the model said so"), and the organization becomes exquisitely busy yet conspicuously undecided. Opportunity cost compounds while competitors cycle faster. Talented people disengage because they cannot exercise judgment; indecision becomes a decision. Two practical warnings: delays degrade decisions because reality moves underneath them, and risk avoidance quietly morphs into reputation risk when customers and staff lose faith.

Ingenuity Age

Intuition is rehabilitated as disciplined sensemaking. Leaders feel quickly (pattern recognition from lived experience), test openly (premortems, dissent rounds, decision journals), and decide in daylight (one-line trade-offs and stated confidence). Two-track decisioning puts speed where it belongs: reversible calls move on partial evidence at the edge; irreversible calls get a brief red-team and a documented why. Prototypes and micro-missions bring reality forward, so judgment is trained against feedback, not folklore. Incident reviews ask not only "Who approved this?" but "What did we sense, and how did we test it?" Product forums prize question-framing as much as chart-reading. Two added habits strengthen the system: record "what would change my mind" beside every significant decision, and calibrate intuition with base rates so experience doesn't drift into overconfidence.

Imaginative Possibility

Disciplined invention becomes a shared practice, with AI serving as a collaborator rather than a summary machine. Leaders simulate futures, generate options, and rehearse second-order effects before spending real capital; experiments are safe-to-try. These are tiny, time-boxed, and with clear kill criteria. Protected silence returns to the calendar so minds can recombine ideas; sandboxes are powerful enough to try the "impossible" without jeopardizing the firm. Diverse teams broaden what the group can sense, and awe via nature, art, science, service, expands the frame so ego shrinks and stewardship grows. Intuition sets direction; imagination offers variants; method decides what survives. Two closing nudges: rotate people across boundaries to cross-pollinate patterns, and task AI to propose surprising hypotheses (and their risks), not just to compress what you already know.

Etymology

Intuition comes from Latin *intuitio* and *intueri*: "to look at, to contemplate." At its root, it isn't guesswork; it is attentive seeing from within, a direct apprehension formed by experience, then clarified by reflection. In leadership terms, intuition begins as a felt recognition and becomes sound judgment when it is disciplined and tested.

Inertia comes from Latin *inertia*: "idleness, lack of skill," from *iners* ("inactive, unskilled"). Long before physics borrowed it to mean resistance to change, it referred to a human tendency not to move, waiting, deferring, and avoiding the moment of choice. In leadership, inertia is not calm; it is stalled agency dressed up as prudence.

This is the contest at the heart of decision-making today: attentive inner seeing that moves versus resistance that waits.

Philosophy

Across centuries, thinkers have argued that good judgment begins before explanation, then earns its right in the open.

Michael Polanyi: We know more than we can tell."

Intuition is that tacit store, patterns learned in practice, brought to the surface and made discussable. Decision journals and premortems convert tacit feel into shared reasoning.

Blaise Pascal: "The heart has its reasons which reason does not know."

Intuition is not about sentimentality; it is about integrated sensing. Leaders who incorporate emotion and embodiment as data points broaden the scope of judgment without compromising rigor.

Louis Pasteur: "In the fields of observation, chance favors only the prepared mind."

Intuition is not a guess; it is preparation meeting ambiguity. The prepared mind quickly sketches a hypothesis and then invites a red team to try to break it.

Jonas Salk: "Intuition will tell the thinking mind where to look next."

Use intuition to aim inquiry, not to end it. The next step is evidence, dissent, and a visible trade-off.

Martha Nussbaum: "Emotions are appraisals or value judgments, which ascribe to things and persons outside the person's own control great importance for that person's own flourishing."

In practice, leaders treat fear, unease, or excitement as signals to investigate, not commands to obey.

Lao Tzu wrote, "Practice not-doing, and everything will fall into place."

The point for executives is silence before analysis, a brief emptiness that lets the pattern appear before we fill it with noise.

Audre Lorde: We recognize that all knowledge is mediated through the body and that feeling is a profound source of information about our lives.

In complex social decisions, leaders who invite lived experience into the room debias sterile analysis and make wiser, more humane calls.

Herbert Simon: "The task of decision is not to find the one right alternative but to find one which is good enough, which satisfices."

Intuition is the skill of satisficing well, using cues and prototypes to reach good-enough decisions fast, reserving depth for the irreversible few.

Our philosophers show us that intuition is not anti-thinking. It is pre-thinking, which is attentive, embodied, and prepared, followed by open testing and owned consequences. Inertia is the opposite: more facts without a frame, more meetings without a move.

Neuroscience

Intuition and Inertia are not just metaphors; they are neurobiological states. Modern neuroscience reveals that the brain's rhythms, chemicals, and networks determine whether leaders detect patterns, integrate gut and data, and act with grounded judgment, or whether they stall, overthinking disguised as progress.

Brain Rhythms: Beta versus Alpha/Theta/Gamma

In high-beta (busy vigilance: emails, meetings, firefighting), the brain narrows, favoring rule-following and quick, literal responses, which make fertile ground for Inertia when ambiguity rises. Shifts into alpha/theta support association and recombination; insight often arrives with a brief gamma burst after a dip into alpha/theta. In practice: create a short, quiet window before deciding, the brain needs a beat to pattern-match well.

Interoception: The Body as Data (Insula & ACC)

Interoception is the brain's readout of internal signals (heart rate, breath, gut). The anterior insula and anterior cingulate cortex (ACC) integrate those signals with context, contributing to "felt" judgments. Expert intuition often includes reliable somatic markers (Damasio), subtle body cues that predict risk or fit. Leaders who pause to notice what the body is signaling add a valuable channel to cognition, then they test it.

Prediction and Error: The Brain as a Forecaster

Under predictive processing, the brain constantly generates models and compares incoming data to expectations. A strong prediction error (surprise) serves as a nudge to update or investigate further. Intuition often starts as a "this doesn't fit" feeling. Good practice: Name the hunch, then ask, 'What would I expect to see if this were true?' What would disconfirm it? and look for those signals.

Dopamine & the Prepared Mind

Dopamine doesn't just reward outcomes; it spikes with novelty and promising uncertainty, mobilizing exploration. Teams with a bias for small, reversible experiments harness this: intuition suggests a direction, and dopamine supplies the energy to test. Inertia, by contrast, starves the system of bets, learning, and momentum.

Systems 1 & 2 Used Together

Kahneman's System 1 (fast/automatic) produces the hunch; System 2 (slow/analytic) tests and tames it. Pure System 1 invites overconfidence; pure System 2 invites paralysis. Ingenuity cultures stage both: silence → surface the hunch → premortem/red-team → one-line trade-off → decide.

Expertise and Heuristics

With experience, the brain compresses patterns into heuristics (Gigerenzer): fast rules that work well in familiar domains. Expert firefighters, surgeons, and traders often decide quickly and explain later because the pattern library is rich. Leaders must separate domain-true heuristics from bad shortcuts: keep a decision journal so intuitions and outcomes can be audited and refined.

Default Mode Network & Coupling with Control Networks

Brief DMN activity (mind-wandering, walking) supports mental simulation; coupling between DMN and executive control networks lets a "felt possibility" be translated into a testable plan. Schedule micro-pauses before high-stakes calls; they measurably improve sense-making.

Sleep, Dreams, and Incubation

During REM, emotionally salient material and remote associations integrate, which are classic conditions for intuitive leaps. Protect sleep after heavy sensory or analytical days; many "aha" connections consolidate overnight.

Teams and Synchrony

As we saw in the Vision chapter, decision quality improves when teams achieve neural/physiological synchrony (as measured in hyperscanning studies). Rituals that promote turn-taking, shared attention, and respectful dissent help the room "feel" patterns together and reduce single-leader bias, which can masquerade as intuition.

Strengthening Intuition by Applying Neuroscience Every Day

Intuition is attentive, embodied forecasting that becomes sound when it is tested in daylight. Inertia is the opposite: stress-narrowed attention, endless metrics, and no move. Design the biology (calm), the method (journals, premortems, two-track), and the culture (safety, dissent) so fast that feeling turns to wise choice. Here are some practical exercises for intuition that use these neuroscientific ideas:

- Silence before analysis (two to five minutes): drop beta, allow alpha/theta; breathe, steady the body.

- Interoceptive check: name one body signal ("tight chest," "lightness") and write one sentence: what might this be telling me?

- Decision journal (Tier-1): record the hunch, the evidence for/against, and the trade-off sentence.

- Premortem + skeptic round: Ask, 'If this fails, what is likely to have gone wrong?' Invite one named skeptic; log their top two risks.

- Two-track policy: move quickly on reversible calls; require a premortem/red-team analysis for irreversible ones.

- Threat scan: before the meeting, reduce avoidable threat (clarify stakes, invite voice, state fairness rules).

- Sleep on it (when time allows): defer final commit to next morning for Tier-1 bets.

- AI as copilot, not judge: use models to surface weak signals and generate options; never let "the model said so" replace ownership.

- After-action review (twenty-four hours): what the intuition got right/wrong; update the heuristic in the journal.

Artificial Intelligence

We can now see the leadership choice between Intuition and Inertia in the light of AI-fueled choices.

Signal mining versus signal drowning

AI copilots can surface weak signals you'd otherwise miss, anomalies in operations, patterns in customer sentiment, faint risk indicators. Used well, they aim human attention and help intuition find the right question. Used poorly, they bury teams in alerts and secondary metrics, producing inertia by overwhelm.

Example: A product copilot flags a subtle drop in "first-use delight" among a niche segment. An intuitive team treats it as a hypothesis and runs a seventy-two-hour reversible test. A stalled team opens five dashboards and adds three meetings.

Pattern libraries versus cargo-cult heuristics

Fine-tuned models become institutional memory: codified pattern libraries that train fast judgment (the "prepared mind"). But if you import generic heuristics without context, you get cargo-cult intuition: confident calls built on someone else's data distribution.

Example: A sales AI trained on your win-loss notes helps reps identify your genuine buying cues. Copying a viral "best-practice" prompt from another industry yields confident nonsense and slows real learning.

Simulation sandboxes versus analysis paralysis

AI enables leaders to simulate options quickly, stress-testing go-to-market paths, capacity plans, or safety scenarios. Intuition uses simulation to narrow to a reversible bet; inertia builds model stacks and delays the first step.

Example: Ops generates three staffing scenarios for flu season, picks the safest reversible one, and trials it at one clinic this week. The inert alternative runs "scenario v7" next month.

Human-in-the-loop judgment versus "the model said so"

AI can audit assumptions, probe counterfactuals, and red-team your hunches at speed, but only if humans are in control. Abdication ("the model decided") is textbook inertia disguised as objectivity.

Example: Finance treats the copilot's forecast as one input in the decision journal, adds a premortem, and writes the trade-off sentence. Elsewhere, leaders hide behind a score and avoid accountability.

Interoceptive prompts versus stress loops

Some tools now nudge interoception (breath rate, HRV), suggesting a brief silence before analysis to reduce tunnel vision. Ignored, AI can feed the very stress loops that blunt intuition with constant pings, always-on dashboards, and zero recovery.

Example: Before a Tier-1 call, an exec accepts a ninety-second "calm prompt," then records the intuition hypothesis and runs a skeptic round, the inert version: Slack, Slack, meeting, meeting, and no decision.

Amplifying Intuition by Deploying AI Every Day

Treat AI as a spotlight and lab for intuition; aim attention, simulate, then make small, owned bets. Keep human-in-the-loop standards: decision journals, premortems, red teams, and trade-off sentences. Build your pattern library; don't import heuristics without careful consideration. Use AI to reduce stress and noise, not amplify them (silence before analysis). If speed goes up but ownership goes down, you don't have intuition; you have inertia with graphs.

Intuition: Real World Examples

Amazon's "Two-Way Door" Culture

- **What they did.** Jeff Bezos institutionalized a simple distinction: Type-2 (reversible) decisions should be made fast by small, accountable teams; Type-1 (irreversible) decisions deserve slower scrutiny with premortems and documented reasoning.

- **Why this matters.** The framework prevents Inertia by removing over-engineering for reversible bets while preserving rigor on the few that are one-way doors. Intuition becomes a method: feel quickly, classify by consequence, then test in daylight.

- **Consequences.** A steady cadence of experiments across Prime, AWS, and the marketplace that compound learning. Missed bets are contained; good ones scale. The two-way door language has become shorthand across industries for separating courage from recklessness.

Cook County ER Chest-Pain Triage

- **What they did.** In the early 2000s, Cook County Hospital adopted Lee Goldman's simple decision rule for heart-attack triage, replacing complex clinical checklists with a streamlined algorithm that used just a few data points. Physicians still used judgment but within a tested, straightforward heuristic.

- **Why this matters.** Intuition is trained and then constrained by premortem-style logic: what fails, what gets missed, what costs the most time. Simple rules and disciplined intuition outperformed both guesswork and analysis paralysis in a high-tempo, life-or-death setting.

- **Consequences.** Faster, more accurate admissions. Less noise, fewer misses. An existence proof that trained judgment with a lightweight structure beats complexity in domains where time is the scarcest resource.

SpaceX Rapid Iteration

- **What they did.** From its earliest launches, SpaceX built a culture of launch, learn, relaunch. Intuition sets the hypothesis; telemetry and post-flight reviews serve as the red team. Reversible design choices move fast; irreversible ones get deeper pre-flight analysis.

- **Why this matters.** The culture converts gut feel into a decision journal with immediate feedback loops. Feel, test, modify becomes the operating rhythm. Failure is information, not stigma.

- **Consequences.** Dramatic cycle-time compression in rocket development. Reusable boosters, once considered impossible, became routine. Intuition becomes smarter with every iteration because the learning loop is measured in days, not years.

Inertia: Real World Examples

BlackBerry after the iPhone

- **What they did.** BlackBerry sensed the smartphone shift early but struggled to reconcile loyalty to its physical keyboard, its enterprise security positioning, and a delayed operating system overhaul. Leadership waited for "more proof" while the market moved beneath them.

- **Why this matters.** This is inertia under ambiguity: smart people, conflicting data, no decisive bet. The signals were present. The courage to choose was not. Every quarter of delay compounded the disadvantage.

- **Consequences.** Rapid share loss from market leader to irrelevance. Belated pivots to touchscreen and a new OS could not overcome the early stall. The company that defined mobile communication became a cautionary tale about the cost of waiting.

Yahoo's Strategy Oscillation

- **What they did.** Yahoo had ample talent, a massive user base, and early advantages in search, media, and advertising. But the company cycled through competing strategies and short CEO tenures without committing to a unifying direction. Acquisitions were made without integration. Priorities shifted before results could compound.

- **Why this matters.** Analysis and options were plentiful. An owned call was not. Yahoo's leadership saw the need for a decisive bet but hesitated to commit and bear the trade-offs. The organization became expert at starting and amateur at finishing.

- **Consequences.** Dilution of brand, product focus, and talent. The core business was eventually sold to Verizon for a fraction of its peak value. Yahoo became the textbook example of what happens when decision-making stalls at the top.

Boeing 737 MAX Crisis

- **What they did.** Boeing engineers and test pilots raised concerns about the MCAS flight-control system during the 737 MAX development. Internal signals suggested the automated system could behave unpredictably under certain conditions. Leadership prioritized production timelines and competitive pressure against Airbus, treating the concerns as manageable risks rather than fundamental design questions.

- **Why this matters.** The signals were present inside the organization. Frontline intuition identified the danger. But institutional inertia, the pressure to ship on schedule, the reluctance to revisit certified assumptions, and the diffusion of accountability through layers of process, meant that no single decision-maker owned the call to pause. Inertia does not always look like indecision. Sometimes it looks like momentum in the wrong direction.

- **Consequences.** Two crashes in 2018 and 2019 killed 346 people. The 737 MAX was grounded worldwide for nearly two years. Boeing faced over $20 billion in costs, criminal charges, and a reputational crisis that continues to shape the company. The lesson: when the system rewards speed over sensing, intuition gets buried, and the cost is measured in lives, not just quarters.

Intuition: Bringing the Lenses Together

Intuition is not guesswork. It is pattern recognition earned through experience, surfaced through attention, and disciplined through testing.

- **History** traces the cost of ignoring it: the Industrial Age trained it out of workers, the Information Age drowned it in dashboards, and the Irrelevance Age stalls it with endless pilots and one more survey.

- **Etymology** returns us to the root: intueri, to look at from within, a direct apprehension that precedes explanation.

- **Philosophy** builds the case across centuries: Polanyi showed we know more than we can tell, Pascal insisted that the heart carries reasons that reason cannot reach, Pasteur proved that chance favors only the prepared mind, Salk taught that intuition aims inquiry rather than ending it, Lorde reminded us that feelings are sources of information, and Simon gave us the verb that captures the whole practice: satisfice well under constraints, reserving depth for the irreversible few.

- **Neuroscience** confirms that intuition is a measurable brain state: alpha and theta rhythms that chronic busyness destroys, interoceptive signals from the body that most leaders have been trained to ignore, prediction-error alerts that register as "something doesn't fit" long before the spreadsheet catches up, and dopamine pathways that reward the courage to make a small bet rather than commission another study.

- **AI amplifies** whichever habit it finds: it can surface weak signals, stress-test hypotheses, build pattern libraries from lived experience, and simulate options before capital is spent, or it can bury teams in alerts, import heuristics from someone else's context, and provide the false comfort of "the model said so" while no one owns the call.

- **And the evidence is decisive**: Amazon's two-way door culture, Cook County's triage heuristic, and SpaceX's launch-learn-relaunch rhythm prove that trained intuition with lightweight structure outperforms both gut instinct and analysis paralysis, while BlackBerry's hesitation, Yahoo's oscillation, and Boeing's buried signals prove that when organizations reward speed over sensing or study over deciding, the cost is measured in markets, reputations, and lives.

- **The practical test is human:** can you name the hunch, write the trade-off sentence, run the premortem, and decide in daylight before the window closes? Intuition lives in that discipline. Inertia lives in everything that postpones it.

30 March — **SÃO PAULO**

End of Month: Executive Team Review

The team reported back on their assignments and the Sydney work.

Maria (COO): Improve→ Premortems inside operating reviews

- **What she did**: embedded a 20-minute premortem and five-minute skeptic round into weekly Type-1 ops decisions at Sydney; added the two to five-minute quiet window to the ops agenda.

- **What changed:** time spent debating dashboards decreased; two likely failure modes were identified and addressed early (shift-change coverage and escalation handoff).

- **Proof points:** two premortem pages with preventive and detective actions; updated shift-cover rota; fewer reopened tickets week-over-week.

John (CFO): Start →Two-track policy and audit

- **What he did:** published the reversible/irreversible policy; created a simple audit of three live calls.

- **What changed**: reversible decisions closed in thirty-six to sixty hours; one irreversible call earned a pause and a narrower pilot after the premortem.

- **Proof points:** policy link; audit sheet showing cycle-time improvement; the paused decision's trade-off sentence, and the new pilot plan.

Sanjay (CTO): Keep → Decision journals and Copilot as a challenger

- **What he did:** auto-attached decision journals to Tier-1 tickets; configured the copilot to list disconfirming signals and open questions (not a single recommendation).

- **What changed**: journals captured the intuition hypothesis and its evidence; one copilot prompt surfaced a missing counterfactual, shifting thresholds.

- **Proof points:** three journal links; copilot prompt transcript; threshold change log.

Yuki (CPO): Stop →Interoception prompts and safety signals

- **What she did:** added a one-line interoception check to the review template; prepared herself for likely conflicts in the meeting; briefed at the start of critical meetings; named a rotating skeptic so dissent had cover.

- **What changed:** more candid dissent; quicker convergence after risks were named; less performative agreement. **Proof points:** template screenshots; "speak-up safety" pulse up nine points at Sydney; two skeptic notes logged and addressed.

Liam (CMO): Improve →Skeptic roster and messaging trade-offs

- **What he did:** built the skeptic roster; ensured the trade-off sentence appeared in the approval flow for any external claim.

- **What changed:** one campaign was reframed after the skeptic flagged an evidence gap; a reversible A/B ran instead of a broad promise.

- **Proof points:** roster page, the campaign's revised copy, and A/B results memo.

What If

Chris closed the day. "Our test for Intuition was simple: feel quickly, test openly, and own the call in daylight."

That afternoon, Chris led the team out of the Paulista General Hospital and toward Ibirapuera Park. The noise of Avenida Paulista, its horns, buses, and motorbikes, faded as they entered the green canopy. Palms and sprawling fig trees cast long shadows across the paths; families picnicked on the lawns while joggers circled the lake.

"This is the place for intuition," Chris said. "Not in fluorescent-lit rooms, waiting for dashboards to turn green. Here, away from the noise, we can sense differently. What if we noticed signals sooner? What if we built silence into our system before rushing to speak? What if we learned to test courage in ambiguity instead of waiting for certainty?"

The team found benches near the water. Chris asked them to pause, let stillness sharpen their seeing, and then put to paper the provocations that could move Omnivista from inertia to ingenuity.

1. What if every Tier-1 decision required a premortem before approval, imagining failure first?
2. What if leaders logged a one-sentence intuition daily, then tested it within thirty days?
3. What if reversible decisions were always taken at the edge never escalated up?What if dashboards couldn't be consulted until teams first wrote their "gut hypothesis"?
4. What if dissent were mandatory: one skeptic had to sign every consequential decision?
5. What if decision journals became the promotion currency, proof of judgment under ambiguity?
6. What if AI copilots highlighted not just data trends but contradictions leaders might miss?
7. What if silence were built into calendars, five minutes of stillness before any major call?
8. What if failed experiments were rewarded for speed of learning, not punished for error?
9. What if leadership performance was measured by time-to-decision under uncertainty, not time-to-report?
10. What if every leader had to name the assumption they were most afraid to test, and AI was tasked with testing it within a week?

31 March — SÃO PAULO

End of Month: Board Review

Chris opened without slides. "Four weeks ago in Sydney," she began, "John led our Intuition versus Inertia workshop. The next morning, I moved to our Sydney diagnostics hub for a month. We asked a single, simple question: can trained judgment show up quickly, be tested in daylight, and be owned on record, without being lost in dashboards or meetings?"

She paused, then added quietly, "We learned that intuition isn't a substitute for data; it's the discipline that gives data meaning. However, without structure, intuition can drift into bias. So, we built experiments to give intuition a framework."

In Sydney, the team noticed that decisions jumped straight from Slack threads into metric debates. No one paused to sense before speaking. They introduced two to five minutes of silence before Tier-1 reviews, with a short breathing prompt added to every agenda and console. "It's not mindfulness for its own sake," Chris explained. "It's calibration, a moment to move from reaction to perception."

All decisions had been escalated to the same committee, regardless of consequence. "It was as if every door was fire-rated," she said. A new two-track policy split splits calls by reversibility: Type-2 (reversible) decisions move in-house within forty-eight hours; Type-1 (irreversible) decisions get a premortem and a skeptical review. Using a phrase like "Type-1 versus Type-2" broke the logjam of fear.

Until now, rationales lived in slide decks and email chains. Decision journals changed that. Each Tier-1 ticket now includes a short reflection: a one-paragraph summary capturing the felt intuition, supporting evidence, and a trade-off sentence. "When you write down what your gut is saying," Chris said, "you invite your brain to test it."

Failure analysis was typically used only after a failure had occurred. The new norm required a twenty-minute premortem and a named skeptic for every irreversible call. The skeptic's job wasn't to block; their job was to illuminate. Every risk raised was logged with an owner and a date, turning dissent into data.

The team also added a single interoceptive prompt to high-stakes meetings: What is your body telling you right now? It disarmed tension, reduced performance theater, and restored presence to the room.

The results arrived quickly. Meeting records now showed quiet prompts;

participants reported more precise framing and fewer restarts. Three Type-2 calls were completed within forty-eight hours, while two Type-1 calls underwent full premortems with skeptical signatures. Three complete decision journals were linked to ticket IDs; one caught a mis-triage early because the reasoning was explicit. Two premortems led to plan adjustments. Thresholds and staffing and one skeptical note shifted a rollout into a reversible micro-test.

The "speak-up" pulse rose nine points, and dissent began to appear on record rather than in corridors. "We're not making fewer mistakes," Chris said. "We're making them where we can learn."

She glanced around the boardroom. "Inertia," she said, "is irrelevance when dashboards become crutches, ambiguity freezes action, and every decision escalates upward. Intuition is ingenuity when leaders pause to sense, classify by reversibility, record their reasoning, and test judgment in daylight."

The evidence, she continued, showed that Omnivista could move from overwhelm to orientation, not by chance, but by habit. "We're training judgment as a system," she said. "Not as a heroic act."

Chris summarized the month's work in four guardrails: silence before certainty, classify by reversibility, record the reasoning, and test in daylight. "These are our non-negotiables," she said finally. "AI will multiply whatever system it finds. If we design only for dashboards, we'll train inertia. If we design for disciplined intuition, we'll multiply ingenuity."

A director leaned forward. "We've seen premortems before," he said, "but never this structured. What's different now?"

Chris replied evenly. "The difference is in the results. We don't just run the exercise; we attach outcomes, skeptic notes, and decision journals to ticket IDs. That way, we don't just remember; we learn."

Another asked, "And what about you, Chris? How do you stay aligned in ambiguity?"

She smiled slightly. "Twenty minutes every day since the beginning of the month. Silence first. One question written. One sentence captured after. One test chosen. It's how I model that intuition isn't luck; it's discipline."

The Chair nodded. "Bring us the same rigor next month," she said.

CEO's Reflection, That Evening

That night, Chris walked back through Ibirapuera Park, the city's traffic softening to a distant hum. The day had been proof: inertia wasn't destiny. With small disciplines, such as silence, journaling, and skepticism, intuition can be cultivated into a habit.

She paused by the park's lake, watching lights shimmer across the water. Tomorrow, Maria would open the next choice: Synergy versus Silos. Chris knew it would demand a different kind of courage, turning boundaries into bridges, interfaces into flow. Tonight, she let the quiet settle. One choice closed, another about to begin.

Intuition: Exercises for You to Try

Intuition only matters when it moves beyond a hunch and into a repeatable method. Decks can impress and models can persuade, but good judgment under uncertainty depends on disciplined habits: noticing, naming, testing, and owning the call.

Leaders who cultivate Intuition treat it as trained judgment felt quickly and tested openly. It appears in a brief, quiet moment before the meeting, in a one-line trade-off written in daylight, in a short premortem that identifies the obvious-in-retrospect risk, and in a decision journal that converts experience into a pattern library. Intuition is fragile as inspiration; it becomes powerful as practice.

To make Intuition more than aspiration, try this seven-day practice plan. Each element is simple in form but cumulative in effect. Done together, they retrain attention, steady the body, and convert fast feeling into smarter choices.

> Day 1: Daily silence before analysis: Protect five minutes before your most significant decision of the day. No device. Breathe, label one sensation (tightness, calm, heat), and let a first hypothesis surface.
>
> Day 2: Interoceptive check-in: Write one sentence: "My body might be telling me_____because_____." Treat it as data, not a verdict.
>
> Day 3: Decision journal (Tier-1): For any irreversible call, log three lines: the intuition, the evidence for/against, and the trade-off sentence (we choose X over Y because Z).
>
> Day 4: Premortem (micro): Assume the decision failed three months from now. Name the top three reasons. Add one preventive action and

one early-detection signal for each.

Day 5: Skeptic round: Invite one named skeptic for five minutes. Ask for two disconfirming facts you might be missing. Adjust or proceed, and record what changed.

Day 6: Two-track call: Classify the decision: reversible (ship in forty-eight to seventy-two hours) or irreversible (run the full test). If reversible, launch a tiny, time-boxed experiment today.

Day 7: Sleep on it (when stakes are high): If time allows, defer final commit to the next morning. Capture any overnight shift in the decision journal and either confirm or course-correct.

None of these practices is complicated. They require no new software and little time: only the leader's choice to pause, to notice, to test, and to own.

Intuition, in use, is less about flashes of genius and more about everyday discipline. It is how an organization learns to move from overwhelm to orientation: quickly, openly, and with consequences that others can follow.

Self-Assessment: Intuition versus Inertia

Rate yourself honestly. For each question, score both the Foundation and the AI Amplifier.
1 Not Yet · 2 Emerging · 3 Developing · 4 Practicing · 5 Second Nature

---

1.

Foundation. I make timely decisions under ambiguity rather than waiting for perfect data or deferring upward.
    Foundation score (1–5):____

AI Amplifier. I use AI to rapidly gather and synthesize evidence that informs, but does not replace, my judgment.
    AI Amplifier score (1–5):____

2.

Foundation. I cultivate judgment through premortems, red teams, and structured dissent.
    Foundation score (1–5):____

AI Amplifier. I use AI to run premortems, stress-test assumptions, and surface blind spots my team and I might miss.
    AI Amplifier score (1–5):____

3.

Foundation. I trust my experienced instinct while actively seeking disconfirming evidence.
    Foundation score (1–5):____

AI Amplifier. I use AI as a thinking partner, asking it to challenge my reasoning and present counter-arguments.
    AI Amplifier score (1–5):____

4.

Foundation. I encourage my team to act on trained judgment rather than freezing in analysis paralysis.

Foundation score (1–5):_____

AI Amplifier. I use AI to accelerate analysis so that judgment can be exercised faster, not deferred longer.

AI Amplifier score (1–5):_____

5.

Foundation. I distinguish between productive caution and the inertia of fear.

Foundation score (1–5):_____

AI Amplifier. I use AI to model the cost of delay, making visible what we lose when we don't decide.

AI Amplifier score (1–5):_____

AVERAGE SCORE: Intuition versus Inertia

Foundation average (total of five scores ÷ 5):_____

AI Amplifier average (total of five scores ÷ 5):_____

Now: Transfer these two averages to the "I" row of your VISTA Scoreboard at the back of the book.

"You can't optimize the parts and expect to optimize the whole."

Donella Meadows

*"Synergy is the art of designing the seams so clarity flows, generosity is easy, and handoffs are clean, not cloned.
When the seams are right, the whole learns and delivers faster than the parts."*

Katharine McLennan

CHAPTER 6

Synergy versus Silos

When challenges demand collaboration, do we create value through shared responsibility,
or
retreat into silos, protecting our turf?

First Day of Month: Executive Team

The team had spent the morning reviewing Intuition and took a quick lunch break on Avenida Paulista.

By mid-afternoon, they were back in the room with traffic hum below and windows cracked for air, ready for the third choice.

Maria stood at the glass wall with a single marker. "This afternoon is Synergy versus Silos," she said. "Let's start by seeing where our energy really lives."

She drew one bar with five labels, the S-eras:

Standardization (Industrial Age): 25%
Searchability (Information Age): 35%
Silos (Irrelevance Age): 15%
Synergy (Ingenuity Age): 20%
Symphony (Imaginative Possibility): 5%

"Proof points, not aspirations," she said. "Push me.

"A quarter of the enterprise still sits squarely in Standardization, the Industrial 'S.' Here, the process itself is the product. Stage gates, rather than outcomes, define handoffs, and success is measured by compliance with the procedure. Teams hit their throughput and customer service level targets even as the end-to-end flow stutters. Checklists thrive, but interface ownership is unclear: everyone is accountable for their piece, but no one is accountable for the whole. It is efficient but airless: a choreography of control without curiosity.

"About a third of the organization lives in Searchability, the Information "S." Knowledge has become a scavenger hunt. "Best-practice" decks travel faster than integration work, and wikis multiply like coral reefs: impressive, but hard to navigate. Metrics proliferate at the part level; every dashboard shines, but few illuminate the system as a whole. The reflex is to find and copy rather than connect and co-create.

"Fifteen percent still slips into Silos, the Irrelevance 'S.' Parallel teams build the same capabilities with different APIs. Work is re-entered because requirements change between functions, and budget walls make collaboration a chore rather than a default. The result is redundancy disguised as productivity, a mirror image of the Industrial Age's efficiency, now digitized.

"Yet twenty percent already shows what's possible: Synergy, the Ingenuity "S." A few internal platforms now publish who they serve, at what service levels, and with named owners. Reuse is gaining ground: design-system components and shared data models now support multiple product lines. One cross-functional sprint last quarter cut a nine-handoff customer journey to five. In these pockets, vision meets execution.

"Only five percent, though, reach the frontier of Symphony, the Imagination "S." Ecosystem thinking remains thin; vendors are managed, not composed. End-to-end rehearsals with partners are rare, and incentives still reward local wins over shared outcomes. The music exists, but the orchestra doesn't yet play together.

"Omnivista's evolution is visible in these proportions: most of the organization still reads from yesterday's score, while a small ensemble has begun to improvise toward the next movement."

Maria capped the marker. "If Synergy is designing the seams so clarity flows, generosity is easy, and handoffs are clean, not cloned. How do we make that our norm?"

The morning heat already pressed against the glass as Maria led the team into the Paulista General Hospital, her chosen site for the Synergy versus Silos event. The hospital was Omnivista's beating heart in Latin America: thousands of patients each week, multiple specialties under one roof, and daily choices that revealed whether the system worked as one or fractured into parts.

They began in the emergency ward. A coordinator pointed to two whiteboards: one tracked patient flow, the other, bed availability. Neither spoke to the other. Nurses explained that patients sometimes waited hours, not for care, but for signatures to transfer them between departments. "We all want the same outcome," one admitted, "but our tools and rules still keep us apart." It was the anatomy of silos, with each unit optimizing, none seeing the whole.

Upstairs, Maria showed a different story. A cross-boundary team had been piloting a care-flow mission, with doctors, nurses, operations, and social workers meeting daily to share a common backlog. Instead of shuffling patients like parcels, they co-designed discharges and next steps. Results were already visible: waiting times were down, fewer readmissions occurred, and families reported more transparent communication. "This is synergy," Maria said. "Different expertise, one rhythm, visible dependencies."

In a side room, Sanjay asked bluntly: "What made this possible?" The ward lead answered without hesitation: "We killed two committees. Instead, we log patterns in a shared dashboard and solve in the room."

Chris wrote in her notebook: "Silos waste; synergy multiplies."

As they left, Maria paused at the hospital's central atrium, the noise of corridors and patients' voices swirling around them. "This is the test," she said. "Either Omnivista keeps repeating silos until trust erodes, or we learn to make synergy our default pattern. The choice is in our hands."

Team Assignments for the Month

Chris made the assignments for the month on Synergy versus Silos.

"K: Keep: Interface contracts with service-level objectives.
These make service boundaries explicit and reusable, and they cut negotiation time. Maria will inventory our current internal platforms and publish standardized contracts for each: named owner, inputs and outputs, service level, and escalation path." She moved on.

"I: Improve: Reuse-first policy and a pattern library.
From now on, the default is reuse before rebuild. We need a living library for APIs, data models, and UI components, with clear contribution rules. Sanjay will stand up the technical registry, and Liam will add a lightweight reuse check to creative and marketing briefs." She looked across the table.

"S: Start: Mission squads for one customer journey.
We will form two cross-functional squads, drawing from Ops, Product, Engineering, Clinical, and Marketing, each with a single OKR: fix one end-to-end flow in thirty days. I will charter them, Maria will staff them, and John will fund a small pooled budget independent of departmental lines." She turned to the final item.

"S: Stop: Parallel builds and unfunded handoffs.
No new project starts without an interface owner and a reuse decision on record. We

kill duplicate builds unless divergence is explicitly chosen and justified. John will gate the funding, Yuki will add handoff quality and reuse to performance conversations, and Sanjay will publish a weekly duplicate-work watchlist."

Chris closed her notebook. "Let's make the seams visible this month and see if the whole learns and delivers faster than the parts.

CEO's Notebook: Synergy

That night, Chris walked back along Avenida Paulista, the city glowing with its restless hum. Samba drifted from a side street; buses and motorbikes tangled at the lights; a giant digital billboard scrolled across glass towers. The hospital they had toured that morning felt just the same, with energy everywhere, but often tangled, blocked, and wasted.

She paused at a small park, notebook in hand. "Synergy is the multiplier," she wrote. "Silos don't just waste time, they waste trust. Every hour duplicated, every handoff delayed, every committee invented is ingenuity leaking out of the system. Synergy isn't about everyone agreeing; it's about differences working in rhythm." She set her daily practices for the month:

Actions

1. Remove one duplicate daily. Spot and eliminate one overlap: two meetings, two tools, two processes, so flow improves.

2. Connect one boundary daily. Pair two teams or individuals across a seam and align them on one shared outcome.

3. Log one reuse daily. Capture an idea, solution, or practice from one part of Omnivista and make it visible for others to adapt.

What I'll Notice

1. *Industrial* (Standardization): Where boundaries are rigid, departments defend their turf rather than sharing the flow.

2. *Information* (Searchability): Where complexity is added through matrices and best-practice decks, activity is mistaken for alignment.

3. *Irrelevance* (Silos): Where duplication, delay, and isolation erode trust

and speed.

4. **Ingenuity** (Synergy): Where cross-boundary teams ship together; guilds log patterns; reuse replaces reinvention.

5. **Imagination** (Synthesis): Where synergy extends beyond Omnivista to partners, regulators, and communities co-creating shared outcomes.

My Fingerprint

Most executive teams are not teams at all. They are groups. If you drew the lines of connection, you would see an umbrella: one line from each person to the leader, and almost nothing between the people themselves. They report to the same person. They sit in the same room. But they do not truly work with each other. That is not synergy. That is a set of silos with a shared boss.

I experienced my first dose of a dysfunctional group thirty years ago, with a telecommunications leadership team that had so much dysfunction there was venom in the room. No credibility in each other. No reliability. No genuine curiosity about each other as people. And at least five members who always needed to be right. The usual interventions, offsites, team charters, shared goals, would not have survived the car ride home.

So I sent them out in pairs for one-hour walks. The instruction was simple: get to know each other and ask one question. When they came back, something had shifted. I built on it with rounds: each person sat with every other person for five minutes in each direction, answering two questions. First: how do you inspire me? Second: if we changed one thing that would make our relationship more effective for our people and our customers, what would it be? Both sides answered. By the final rounds, pairs who had refused to speak to each other could not stop talking.

I now do that exercise for every team offsite I facilitate. The results change dramatically within one hour, and they stay that way. To know that people, even people you do not particularly like, see inspiration in you is such a gift. It is Sawubona as a practice, not just a greeting: I see you and your potential. We often forget that people appreciate great things in us, things we do not even see in ourselves. That is why strong teams are such a gift to everyone on them.

The insight has held for three decades: trust exists only between two people. You cannot trust a team directly. You build it in pairs. When every pair is connected, the shape is no longer an umbrella. It is a polyhedron, every point linked to every other point. That is synergy. Not a structure on a chart but a living geometry of relationships where what happens between any two people strengthens the whole.

Synergy: Through Six Lenses

As with Vision and Intuition, we examine Synergy through the same six lenses: history, etymology, philosophy, neuroscience, artificial intelligence, and real world examples.

History and what could evolve

Industrial Age

Synergy meant standardization because variance was the enemy. Stage gates, checklists, and local SLAs made each station reliable; however, when the world changed, those rigid stages produced rework rather than flow. Ownership sat inside functions, so the seams between them were "everyone's job," which meant "no one's job." Success was hitting the station's metric even if the baton was dropped at the handoff. Root-cause reviews often stopped at the station boundary, traveling defects were treated as someone else's problem rather than a design flaw in the handoff. Whenever workers did a "work-to-rule" slowdown, leaders could suddenly see how much the system depended on invisible glue at the seams.

Information Age

Synergy meant searchability; copy the best practice and you'll improve the part. Knowledge systems multiplied; we could find anything, copy everything, and benchmark against everyone. But "find and copy" often replaced "integrate and deliver": tool sprawl grew, and teams searched more than they aligned. Dashboards informed each group of its performance, yet few showed whether the customer journey actually became smoother from start to finish. "Single sources of truth" fractured into parallel wikis and trackers, and even APIs drifted because interface definitions weren't governed. Benchmarking raised the floor but also pulled everyone toward median behavior; imitation outpaced integration.

Irrelevance Age

Synergy collapses into silos with brittle boundaries. Duplication blooms quietly:

two teams build the same capability with slightly different APIs; data is retyped because systems don't talk; budgets fund functions, not flows, so collaboration looks like charity, not work. The result is busy people and stuck customers. Effort fragments, learning slows, and the whole lags, even as parts look productive. You can hear it in incident reviews that blame the team that "dropped the ball" instead of redesigning the seam that made the drop likely; you can see it in tools that multiply rather than converge on a single interface. KPIs reward local output, while cycle time and re-entry rates worsen, integration debt accumulates, and dashboards remain green as NPS and trust levels decline quietly.

Ingenuity Age

Synergy becomes interface discipline. Every seam has a named owner and a one-page contract that outlines who it serves, its inputs and outputs, target service levels, and an escalation path. "Reuse before rebuild" is the default, supported by a small pattern library of APIs, data models, and UI components that makes generosity easy. Cross-functional, time-boxed mission squads own an end-to-end outcome and measure success by fewer handoffs, fewer re-entries, and faster cycle times, so the whole learns faster than the parts. Signals shift: incident reviews ask how the seam was designed; funding follows shared platforms and interface owners, not just functions. An interface registry with contract tests and linting prevents drift, and leaders track a reuse ratio and flow-efficiency score alongside traditional throughput.

Imaginative Possibility

Synergy matures into symphony, living networks composing together. Organizations and partners rehearse complete journeys, run shared simulations and "test events," and build platforms where multiple players plug into the same interface contract. Work shifts from controlling tasks to conducting an ensemble: shared cadence, shared signals, shared improvement; the boundary between "us" and "them" becomes a seam designed for flow, not a wall that blocks it. AI helps orchestrate the network, matching supply to demand, stress-testing second-order effects, and proposing surprising pairings that a single firm wouldn't see. Research on neural synchrony suggests that well-designed collaboration can literally bring teams into tighter cognitive alignment, thereby improving timing and trust. To avoid monoculture risks, governance shifts to the protocol level, encompassing common standards, data trusts, and ecosystem SLAs, allowing diversity of approaches to thrive while maintaining synchrony.

Etymology

Synergy comes from the Greek *synergos*: syn ("together") and ergon ("work"). Its root meaning is "working together," but in its truest sense, it implies co-creation: effort joined not by necessity but by choice, producing outcomes greater than the sum of their parts. In leadership, synergy is not the absence of tension; it is tension harnessed and leveraged. It thrives when differences stay in dialogue long enough to create something neither side could have built alone.

Silo traces back to the Greek *siros*, a "pit for holding grain." The word first meant a place of preservation, not isolation. Over time, it came to mean any container that keeps things apart. In organizations, silos initially protect expertise, but then imprison it. What begins as structure hardens into separation. In leadership terms, a silo is not merely a department; it is a mindset that mistakes possession for contribution.

This is the contest at the heart of collaboration today: Synergy as shared creation that expands capacity versus Silos as private preservation that erodes it.

Philosophy

Across centuries, thinkers have argued that strength emerges in relation to others, then proves itself in shared results.

Aristotle: The totality is not, as it were, a mere heap, but the whole is something besides the parts.

Synergy is designing interfaces, roles, and rituals so that new capabilities emerge, properties that no silo can produce on its own.

Confucius: "When three walk together, there is always something I can learn."

Cross-functional work treats every partner as a teacher; review the work together and let each team's strengths instruct the others.

Mary Parker Follett: "It is possible to develop the conception of power-with, a jointly developed power, a co-active, not a coercive power."

Synergy means integration, solving for the whole, so marketing, product, finance, and operations create one cohesive answer instead of four partial wins.

Jürgen Habermas: "In discourse, no force except that of the better argument is exercised; and as a result, all motives except that of the cooperative search for truth are excluded."

Replace turf with test: surface assumptions, invite dissent, and let evidence, not hierarchy, decide cross-team choices.

Ibn Khaldūn: "Group feeling produces the ability to defend oneself, to offer opposition, to protect oneself, and to press one's claims. Whoever loses it is too weak to do any of these things."

Leaders foster solidarity by identifying a common enemy (the problem), rather than a common rival (another department).

Spinoza: "Nothing is more useful to man than man."

Build structures that make colleagues useful to one another: rotating seats at key meetings, paired metrics, and joint ownership of outcomes.

Simone de Beauvoir: "To will oneself free is also to will others free."

Real autonomy scales when teams free one another with clear contracts and trust, so local decisions advance a shared aim.

Martin Buber: "All real living is meeting."

Cadence matters: regular, agenda-light encounters where people show their work early, ask for help, and let relationships carry the load that the process can't.

Desmond Tutu: "My humanity is bound up in yours."
Treat handoffs as moments of care; when upstream teams design for downstream success, the customer experiences one coherent company.

Buckminster Fuller defined synergy as "behavior of whole systems unpredicted by the behavior of the parts taken separately."
Measure for emergence: look not just at unit KPIs, but at outcomes that only the whole can produce.

Marcus Aurelius: "What brings no benefit to the hive brings none to the bee."
Local optimizations that harm the whole eventually harm the local; align incentives so teams win only when customers do.

Hegel: "The true is the whole."
In execution: publish the map of the whole strategy, dependencies, constraints so each part can act wisely without waiting for permission.

Our philosophers show us that synergy is not groupthink; it is designed interdependence with clear interfaces, shared language, and visible goals, followed by accountable, local execution. Silos are the opposite: private goals, duplicated effort, and brittle performance.

Neuroscience

Synergy and Silos are not just metaphors; they are neurobiological states. Modern neuroscience reveals that the brain's rhythms, chemicals, and networks determine whether teams align attention and share mental models, or whether effort fragments into guarded islands masquerading as efficiency.

Mirror Neurons and Shared Representation

When we watch someone perform an action, mirror neuron networks fire as though we were performing it ourselves. This neural mirroring underpins our ability to anticipate what a collaborator needs before they ask. Teams that work closely together develop richer shared representations, making handoffs smoother because each side has already simulated the other's task. Silos starve this system: when teams never see each other's work, mirroring can't develop, and every interface becomes a cold negotiation rather than an intuitive exchange.

Shared Mental Models and Transactive Memory
Research by Daniel Wegner showed that close-working groups develop transactive memory: a distributed system where each person knows not just their own expertise but who knows what else. Teams with strong transactive memory retrieve and combine information faster than teams where knowledge is siloed in individual heads. fMRI studies show that when transactive memory is functioning, the cognitive load on any single brain decreases because the group operates as an extended memory system. Interface contracts and pattern libraries serve the same function organizationally: they make it easy to know who holds what and how to access it.

The Ingroup/Outgroup Bias and Oxytocin's Dark Side
Oxytocin promotes trust and generosity within a group, but research by Carsten De Dreu showed it simultaneously increases suspicion and defensiveness toward outsiders. This is the neurochemistry of silos: the same bonding that makes a team cohesive can make it hostile to other teams. Leaders who want synergy across boundaries must deliberately extend ingroup cues beyond the team: shared language, shared rituals, shared goals, and visible mutual dependence. Without these, the brain defaults to treating the other department as a rival, not a partner.

Cognitive Load and the Limits of Coordination
Working memory holds roughly four items at once (Cowan's revised estimate of Miller's classic "seven plus or minus two"). Every additional dashboard, tool, or communication channel at a handoff point consumes a slot. Research on multitasking shows that switching between contexts costs 20–40% of productive capacity (the "switch cost"). A single shared screen at the seam isn't just a preference; it's a cognitive necessity. Teams that reduce interface complexity free working memory for judgment, creativity, and problem-solving. Teams drowning in parallel systems burn their cognitive budget on navigation, leaving nothing for the actual work.

The Anterior Cingulate Cortex and Conflict Monitoring

The ACC activates when the brain detects conflicting signals, essentially an internal alarm for "something doesn't fit." In cross-team work, this manifests as the discomfort people feel when expectations at a handoff don't match reality. Rather than suppressing this signal (which silo cultures do by discouraging complaints about other teams), synergy cultures treat it as valuable data. When someone says "this doesn't feel right at the seam," the ACC is doing its job. Designing escalation paths and prediction-error reviews at interfaces channels this neural alarm into system improvement.

Prosocial Reward Circuits and the "Helper's High"

Neuroimaging shows that helping others activates the ventral striatum and medial prefrontal cortex, the same reward circuits triggered by food and money. This "helper's high" is not metaphorical; it is a measurable dopamine and endorphin response. When organizations publicly recognize cross-team contributions, they activate this circuit and make generosity self-reinforcing. When recognition stays local (only your manager sees your work), the reward circuit for cross-boundary help goes unstimulated, and people rationally retreat to what gets noticed: their own team's metrics.

Testosterone, Cortisol, and the Dual-Hormone Hypothesis

Ambiguity and time pressure spike cortisol, narrowing perception and fueling territorial behavior. Testosterone amplifies the effect: research by Mehta and Josephs on the dual-hormone hypothesis shows that when testosterone is high and cortisol is also elevated, individuals become more status-driven and less willing to collaborate or share credit. The combination produces classic silo behavior: defending metrics, claiming ownership, and resisting shared accountability. Lowering cortisol through safety cues, clear roles, and named shared wins shifts the hormonal balance toward cooperation.

Strengthening Synergy by Applying Neuroscience

Synergy is not "be nicer"; it is designing brains and environments for shared prediction and low-friction handoffs. Silos narrow attention, spike cortisol and testosterone, fragment working memory, and trigger ingroup/outgroup defensiveness that turns colleagues into rivals. Synergy reverses the biology: safety cues lower cortisol, public recognition of cross-team help activates prosocial reward circuits, shared screens free working memory for judgment, and regular co-design rituals build the transactive memory that makes handoffs feel intuitive rather than negotiated.

We can build these insights into daily leadership:

- Create a two to three-minute quiet window before cross-team decisions.
- Start each handoff with "who I serve, what I need, how I prove it."
- Publish the one-page interface at the seam; treat misses as prediction errors.
- Reward cross-team help and reuse in public.
- Lower cortisol: clarify stakes, role, credit, and next step.
- Use one shared screen at the seam, not four dashboards.
- Sleep on complex interface designs when time allows.
- Run short co-design/demo rituals to build synchrony.

Artificial Intelligence

We can now see the leadership choice between Synergy and Silos in the light of AI-fueled choices.

Interface discovery versus tool sprawl

AI can index code, APIs, data models, and playbooks to surface "what already exists" at the seam. Used well, it points teams to the right owner and contract in seconds; used poorly, it adds yet another search box and more links to nowhere.

Example: An internal copilot suggests using the existing patient-intake API (owner, SLO, sample payload) instead of building a new one. In a siloed setup, two teams ship near-identical endpoints with different fields.

Generative integration docs versus deck dumping

AI can generate live interface docs, test stubs, and contract tests from real usage, turning tribal knowledge into working artifacts. Or it can churn out pretty decks that copy "best practice" without changing the seam.

Example: From call logs, a copilot drafts a one-page contract for imaging→referral, complete with example payloads and failure modes. In a silo, a slide repo grows while engineers keep retyping forms.

Data interoperability versus data islands

AI can auto-map fields, reconcile schemas, and suggest joins across systems, reducing re-entry and mismatch errors. If misused, it creates yet another transformation layer that hides ownership and adds latency.

Example: A healthcare mapper proposes HL7/FHIR alignments and flags two fields that need governance. In a silo, each clinic builds its own extractor, and the same patient is keyed four ways.

Orchestration agents versus handoff chaos

Multi-agent AI can coordinate cross-team workflows (who does what, when, and with which inputs) and escalate when breaches occur. Without clear ownership, agents amplify chaos more quickly.

Example: A triage agent pings imaging when intake is completed, attaches the exact inputs, and alerts the interface owner on any misses. In a silo, Slack fills with "@here" messages, and the queue stalls.

Reuse recommendations versus rebuild reflex

AI can recommend components, patterns, and services that have been proven effective internally, along with their corresponding fit scores and relevant examples. If incentives stay local, teams still rebuild to "own" their metric.

Example: The design copilot suggests a reusable scheduling widget, showing three products already using it and the delta to adapt. In a silo, a fourth widget appears with a slightly different edge case.

Symphony rehearsal versus local optimization

Digital twins and sims let teams rehearse an end-to-end flow with partners before going live. Alternatively, dashboards remain per-function, and everyone optimizes their slice.

Example: A clinic–lab–insurer simulation reveals the actual bottleneck at eligibility checks and fixes it before launch. In a silo, imaging speeds up while referral times worsen.

Amplifying Synergy by Deploying AI Every Day

These six examples show how AI serves as the amplifier of Synergy or Silos. AI can surface existing interfaces, generate working contracts, coordinate handoffs, recommend reuse, and rehearse end-to-end flows, or it can add tools, links, and dashboards that make silos faster without making them less siloed.

Leaders can build these into daily practice:

- AI to surface what already exists at the seam before building anything new.

- Let copilots generate working interface contracts from real usage, not slide decks from best-practice templates.

- Deploy orchestration agents with clear ownership: every automated handoff needs a named human accountable for misses.

- Tie AI recommendations to reuse and end-to-end outcomes, not local metrics that reward rebuilding.

- Use digital twins and simulations to rehearse the whole flow with partners before going live.

- Treat AI-generated integration as a draft to be tested at the seam, not a finished product to be shipped from a distance.

- If AI increases links, dashboards, and noise without shared ownership, you do not have synergy. You have faster silos.

Synergy: Real World Examples

Amazon's "API Mandate"

- **What they did.** In 2002, Jeff Bezos required every team to expose functionality through service interfaces and to consume others' services in the same way. No private backdoors. Clear ownership. Documented inputs, outputs, and performance levels.

- **Why this matters.** This is synergy as interface discipline: explicit seams, reusable services, and a culture of reuse before rebuild. The mandate treated every internal boundary as a contract, not a courtesy.

- **Consequences.** Internal recombination became normal. Microservices flourished. The same interface discipline that made teams faster internally became the architecture that underpinned AWS, turning an internal practice into a multi-billion-dollar platform.

Pixar's Braintrust and Dailies

- **What they did.** From the 1990s onward, directors, animators, story leads, and technologists reviewed work in progress together, early and often. Candor was expected. Authority remained with the director, but every discipline had voice before the work hardened.

- **Why this matters.** Shared seeing across disciplines turns handoffs into co-creation. Problems surface at the seam before they calcify into costly rework. The Braintrust was not a committee; it was a ritual of honest cross-boundary feedback with no power to override.

- **Consequences.** Fewer late surprises, faster iteration, and a steady culture of reusing solutions across films and pipelines. The practice became Pixar's signature advantage: not better animators, but better collaboration between animators, storytellers, and engineers.

Haier's Rendanheyi Model

- **What they did.** In the 2010s, Haier reorganized into thousands of microenterprises that contract with one another through internal markets. Service units publish what they serve and at what level. Product units choose and pay for those services. If a service unit fails to deliver, the product unit can look elsewhere.

- **Why this matters.** Interface contracts and incentives align. Cross-team generosity is rewarded because serving others well generates revenue. Duplication is penalized by the market because redundant services lose customers internally.

- **Consequences.** Higher recombination, faster customer response, and a living ecosystem rather than a single monolith. Haier became one of the most studied organizational experiments of the decade.

Silos: Real World Examples

Boeing 787 Supply-Chain Fragmentation

- **What they did.** In the mid-2000s, Boeing outsourced major sections of the 787 Dreamliner to dispersed partners around the world. Integration standards were uneven. Interfaces between suppliers were unclear. Changes were implemented slowly and incrementally because no single party owned the seams between sections.

- **Why this matters.** This was ownership of parts without ownership of seams. Each supplier hit their local targets while the aircraft as a whole fell further behind. The boundary between "my work" and "your work" became the place where quality and schedule broke down.

- **Consequences.** Years of delays, billions in costly rework, and a prolonged integration process before the program stabilized. The 787 eventually succeeded as a product, but the early supply-chain design became a cautionary study in what happens when synergy is assumed rather than designed.

U.S. Healthcare EHR Fragmentation

- **What they did.** Across the United States, hospitals and clinics adopted electronic health record systems that were often incompatible with one another. Staff re-enter data at each handoff. Patient context is lost between systems. Records that should flow as a continuous narrative arrive as disconnected fragments.

- **Why this matters.** Information is stored but not shared. Boundaries exist without bridges. Each institution optimized its own record-keeping while the patient experience across institutions remained fractured.

- **Consequences.** Duplication of tests and procedures, clinician burnout from redundant data entry, avoidable medical errors, and slower care. The problem persists despite decades of investment in health IT because the seams between systems were never designed for flow.

Microsoft Pre-2014 Product Silos

- **What they did.** Before the cultural shift described in Chapter 4, Microsoft's divisions operated as competing fiefdoms. Windows, Office, Xbox, and the server group each optimized for their own revenue targets, often duplicating features and blocking integration that would have benefited customers. The internal review system, known as stack ranking, reinforced the problem: employees were rated against peers within their group, making cross-team generosity a career risk. Engineers described a culture where sharing code or helping another division could lower your own rating.

- **Why this matters.** Local incentives that punish collaboration produce silos even when talent and technology are world-class. When Satya Nadella arrived in 2014, he diagnosed the structure itself as the obstacle. The shift to shared platforms, a common cloud architecture, and "One Microsoft" incentives was as much a synergy redesign as a vision reset.

- **Consequences.** Years of missed platform opportunities and a delayed cloud strategy. Azure's eventual success depended on teams that had never collaborated learning to publish interfaces and reuse each other's services. The turnaround proved that silos are not a people problem. They are a design problem.

Synergy: Bringing the Lenses Together

Synergy is not collaboration as sentiment. It is collaboration as architecture.

- **History** shows the pattern repeating: the Industrial Age standardized the parts but left the seams unowned, the Information Age made everything searchable but nothing integrated, and the Irrelevance Age funds functions while customers stumble between them.

- **Etymology** sharpens the distinction: synergos means working together by choice, producing outcomes that no part could generate alone, while silo began as a container for preservation and became a prison for expertise.

- **Philosophy** builds the case across traditions: Aristotle saw that the whole is something besides its parts, Follett insisted on power with rather than power over, Buber reminded us that all real living is meeting, Habermas called for the unforced force of the better argument, Tutu's Ubuntu bound our humanity to one another's, Fuller defined synergy as the behavior of whole systems unpredicted by the parts, and Marcus Aurelius warned that what brings no benefit to the hive brings none to the bee.

- **Neuroscience** confirms that synergy and silos are biological states, not just organizational choices: mirror neurons build shared representation across boundaries but only when teams see each other's work, transactive memory distributes cognitive load so the group thinks faster than any individual, oxytocin bonds teams internally but turns hostile at the boundary unless leaders deliberately extend ingroup cues across functions, working memory holds roughly four items at once so every redundant dashboard at a handoff consumes capacity that should be spent on judgment, and prosocial reward circuits make cross-team generosity self-reinforcing but only when it is recognized in public.

- **AI amplifies** whichever pattern it finds: it can surface existing interfaces, generate working contracts from real usage, orchestrate handoffs with named ownership, recommend reuse over rebuild, and rehearse end-to-end flows with digital twins, or it can add tools, links, and dashboards that make silos faster without making them less siloed.

- **And the real-world evidence** draws the line cleanly: Amazon's API mandate turned interface discipline into a platform, Pixar's Braintrust turned cross-boundary candor into a creative advantage, and Haier's Rendanheyi model turned internal contracts into a living ecosystem, while Boeing's fragmented 787 supply chain, the US healthcare system's incompatible records, and Microsoft's pre-2014 fiefdoms proved that when no one owns the seam, the whole fails even as the parts report green.

- **The practical test is human**: can you name the seam, point to its owner, show the one-page contract, demonstrate that reuse is the default, and measure what only the whole can produce? Synergy lives in that discipline. Silos live in everything that avoids it.

29 April — **BANGALORE**

End of Month: Executive Review

The team reported back on their assignments.

Maria (COO): Keep →Interface contracts with SLOs at the seam

- **What she did**: posted one-page interfaces at intake→imaging and imaging→referral; ran two live escalations to prove the path; added "handoff quality" to the ops review.

- **What changed**: fewer re-entries at both seams; questions now route to named owners instead of bouncing.

- **Proof points:** photos of posters, escalation timestamps, and re-entry down from 14% to 7%.

Sanjay (CTO): Improve → Reuse-first and the pattern registry

- **What he did:** stood up a lightweight registry for APIs, data models, and UI components; marked the canonical "results-ready" webhook and deprecated the duplicate; added a repo bot that comments "reuse candidate" on new pull requests.

- **What changed**: one duplicate was retired; two teams adopted the canonical webhook; code reviews now automatically surface reuse options.

- **Proof points:** registry entry and deprecation note; bot comments; merged PRs using the shared endpoint.

Liam (CMO): Improve → Reuse check in briefs and cross-corridor awareness

- **What he did:** added a one-line reuse check to campaign and content briefs; started a weekly note on "what's changing in the corridor" so Marketing sees Ops pilots before promising speed.

- **What changed**: One "fast track" message was held and reframed to align with capacity, reducing collisions with operations.

- **Proof points:** updated brief template; the reframed message; distribution of the corridor note.

John (CFO): Start →Funding gate for reuse and pooled budget for squads

- **What he did**: added a reuse decision and interface owner field to the funding form; created a small, pooled budget for mission squads independent of departments.

- **What changed**: three initiatives recorded reuse; the squads drew on pooled funds without waiting for transfers to arrive.

- **Proof points:** gate form screenshots, funding log entries, and the squads' OKR page.

Yuki (CPO): Stop → Performance conversations at the seam

- **What she did**: added "handoff quality" and "contribution to reuse" to performance check-ins; ran short enablement on writing one-page interface contracts.

- **What changed**: engineers and coordinators raised seam issues earlier; two posters were improved by the people using them.

- **Proof points:** enablement slides, annotated posters, and manager notes from check-ins.

What If

Chris closed the day. "Our test for Synergy was simple: design the seams so clarity flows, generosity is easy, and handoffs are clean, not cloned. These outputs show we can do that. Tomorrow we move to the next choice, but for Synergy, we now have a pattern we can lift and proof we can show."

That afternoon, Chris led the team to Cubbon Park, one of Bangalore's rare green lungs. The traffic roar softened as they walked under rain trees and past cricket matches on the lawns. They sat near the bandstand, notebooks open, the air heavy with the weight of monsoon clouds.

"This is the right place for Synergy," Chris said. "Inside, we saw duplication, delays, and boundaries defended like property lines. Out here, everything works together as roots, soil, rain, and light. Synergy is not everyone agreeing; it's different parts moving in rhythm. Let's ask ourselves what it would look like if Omnivista were designed for flow instead of silos."

She paused, letting the stillness settle. "What if?"

1. What if every project backlog had to show which other team it drew from before starting new work?

2. What if committees expired automatically after ninety days unless renewed with evidence of shared outcomes?

3. What if duplication carried a visible "trust tax": hours lost published weekly until the overlap was retired?

4. What if solutions had to be reused in two other places before funding was given for a new build?

5. What if every interface contract were public: what you deliver, when, and how others can rely on it?

6. What if one Friday each month was reserved for "synergy sprints": teams working only on cross-boundary fixes?

7. What if every team meeting began with one story of reuse, not one list of complaints?

8. What if silos were mapped visually each quarter, and execs were measured on how many seams they repaired?

9. What if guilds of practice, not steering committees, were the default place for standards and shared patterns?

10. What if patients or clients sat in the room when boundaries collided, making the cost of silos visible in real-time?

30 April — BANGALORE

End of Month: Board Review

Chris spoke without slides.

"Four weeks ago," she began, "Maria led us into Synergy versus Silos at Paulista General Hospital. We asked a simple question: can different disciplines move to one rhythm, or will they keep duplicating effort until ingenuity leaks away?"

She described what they had done. At first, patients moved through the hospital like parcels, passed from ward to ward, each decision waiting on another's approval. Now, a daily mission team brought clinicians, nurses, operations, and social workers together around a single backlog. "It wasn't coordination by meeting," Chris said. "It was choreography by purpose."

Each ward had once solved problems in isolation; fixes stayed buried in local files. Each ward built a shared pattern log, every solution recorded, searchable, and mandatory to check before redesigning from scratch. "Reuse," she added, "is faster than genius on repeat."

Interface failures were another source of drift. Departments had long blamed "the other side" when handoffs broke down. They now worked from interface contracts. They posted service levels that spelled out what data, what timing, and what response. Everyone could see the commitments; everyone could see when one was missed.

Two steering committees had spent years debating overlapping issues without ownership. Both were dissolved. In their place stood a single empowered mission team with authority to act and to stop. "Less debate, more doing," Chris said.

Duplication was next. Campaigns, operations, and marketing had all run separate patient communications. A duplication tracker surfaced the overlaps; three separate streams collapsed into a single stream. "It's amazing how much speed returns," she noted, "when people stop tripping over each other's good intentions."

Then she walked through the results:

- Patient flow improved, with discharge times down 18%, readmissions down 6%.

- Reuse accelerated, e.g., five solutions lifted from the log, one deployed across three wards in a week.

- Interface clarity rose: 80% of staff now said, "I know what to expect from other teams," up from 51%.

- Committees vanished; backlog issues were cleared in half the time.

- Duplication decreased; three overlapping communications projects were retired, and campaign approvals were 25% faster.

She paused before drawing the lesson. "Silos are irrelevant when duplication, delay, and isolation erode trust and speed. Synergy is Ingenuity when cross-boundary teams ship together, interfaces are explicit, and solutions are reused instead of reinvented. We now have proof points; synergy is faster, more transparent, and more trustworthy than silos."

Chris closed with four guardrails for the next phase:

1. "One backlog, one rhythm; missions replace parallel queues.

2. Check the log first; no reinvention until reuse has been tested.

3. Make interfaces visible; if the contract isn't clear, the handoff will fail.

4. And cut to empower; every committee dissolved must be replaced by a team with full authority."

"These," she said, "are the rules that hold flow together. If we drift back into silos, ingenuity bleeds away."

The room was quiet. Then a director leaned forward. "Committees always grow back," he said. "What's stopping the creep?"

"Results," Chris replied. "We've posted the contracts, logged the reuse, and published mission outcomes. Everyone can see what synergy delivers: shorter waits, clearer comms, faster fixes. That visibility makes silos harder to defend."

The Chair nodded. "Bring us the same clarity at the end of May," she said, "when Sanjay takes us into Trust versus Tyranny."

CEO's Reflection, That Evening

That night, Chris stepped out from the Board session into Bangalore's humid dusk. The city surged around her, rickshaws weaving through buses, street vendors calling out, the thrum of traffic as constant as breath. It felt like the silos they had just dismantled on paper: noisy, overlapping, and full of wasted energy. Yet she also saw flow, lanes opening, people adjusting, rhythm emerging despite the chaos.

The day had proven that synergy could be designed, not with slogans, but with backlogs, interface contracts, and reuse that made ingenuity visible. She wrote one line in her notebook: "Silos waste time; synergy multiplies trust."

Tomorrow, Sanjay would lead them into the next choice. Trust versus Tyranny. Chris knew it would demand even more courage. Synergy could be engineered through a process; trust, however, could not be mandated. It had to be earned, moment by moment, through fairness, safety, and follow-through.

She let the city noise blend into the rhythm of her steps, carrying the hum of possibility. One choice closed. Another waited at dawn.

Synergy Exercises for You to Try

Synergy only matters when it moves beyond "be collaborative" and becomes a way of running the work. Slides can praise teamwork, and tools can multiply documents, but flow across teams depends on disciplined habits: naming the seam, assigning an owner, making the interface visible, and rehearsing the whole.

Leaders who cultivate Synergy treat it as interface discipline. It appears in a one-page contract posted at the point of handoff, in a reuse check that prevents parallel builds, in a brief table read that reveals friction before customers experience it, and in rewards that credit end-to-end outcomes, not just local output. Synergy is fragile as intention; it becomes powerful as practice.

To make Synergy a reality, try this seven-day plan, simple moves with a compounding effect.

- Day 1: Map one seam: Walk one end-to-end path. Pick a handoff. Write on a single page: who the seam serves, inputs and outputs, service level, owner, and escalation path.

- Day 2: Post the interface: Put that one-pager where the handoff actually occurs (wall, wiki, "one screen"). Ask two people who use it to mark what's unclear. Edit once.

- Day 3: Run a Reuse Check: Before starting any new work, search for components, APIs, data models, or content that can be reused. Record the decision ("reuse yes/no and why") in the brief.

- Day 4: Kill a duplicate: Find one parallel build or duplicate form. Choose the canonical version, deprecate the duplicate, and post the link where teams will look first.

- Day 5: Rehearse the whole: Conduct a twenty-minute table read of the journey with the people who will touch it. Walk the artifacts through the seam. Capture the top two friction points and one fix.

- Day 6: Create a shared screen: Replace three dashboards with a single view at the seam: inputs, outputs, SLO, current status, and owner. End today's stand-up at that screen.

- Day 7: Reward the seam: Publicly recognize one person who made another team faster (by improving the interface, enabling reuse, or removing friction). Tie one metric to end-to-end flow (fewer re-entries, fewer handoffs, shorter cycle time).

None of these practices is complicated. They need no new software and little budget, only the leader's choice to design the seams, make them visible, and credit the people who keep the flow clean. Synergy, in use, is how an organization learns to deliver faster than any one part, with clean handoffs, shared ownership, and results the customer can feel.

Self-Assessment: Synergy versus Silos

Rate yourself honestly. For each question, score both the Foundation and the AI Amplifier.
1 Not Yet · 2 Emerging · 3 Developing · 4 Practicing · 5 Second Nature

---

1.

Foundation. My team has clear interface agreements: we know what we owe each other and when.

   Foundation score (1–5):_____

AI Amplifier. We use AI to make handoffs visible, track cross-team commitments, and flag breakdowns early.

   AI Amplifier score (1–5):_____

2.

Foundation. We actively reuse ideas, tools, and practices across boundaries rather than reinventing in isolation.

   Foundation score (1–5):_____

AI Amplifier. We use AI to surface relevant work happening elsewhere so teams build on each other's progress.

   AI Amplifier score (1–5):_____

3.

Foundation. I invest time building relationships across functions, not just within my own domain.

   Foundation score (1–5):_____

AI Amplifier. I use AI to identify connection opportunities: people, projects, and knowledge that should be linked.

   AI Amplifier score (1–5):_____

4.

Foundation. When handoffs break down, we fix the system rather than blame the other side.

    Foundation score (1–5): _____

AI Amplifier. We use AI to diagnose where process friction occurs and recommend system-level fixes.

    AI Amplifier score (1–5): _____

5.

Foundation. I design interdependence deliberately: shared goals, shared screens, shared accountability.

    Foundation score (1–5): _____

AI Amplifier. We use AI to create shared views of progress so cross-functional teams operate from one truth.

    AI Amplifier score (1–5): _____

AVERAGE SCORE: Synergy versus Silos

Foundation average (total of five scores ÷ 5): _____

AI Amplifier average (total of five scores ÷ 5): _____

Now: Transfer these two averages to the "S" row of your VISTA Scoreboard at the back of the book.

> "The best way to find out if you can trust somebody is to trust them."
>
> attributed to **Ernest Hemingway**

> "Tyranny says 'Obey and disappear.' Trust says 'Speak and be seen.'"
>
> **Katharine McLennan**

CHAPTER 7

Trust versus Tyranny

*When the stakes are high, do we
build confidence through openness
and shared responsibility,
or
impose control through fear,
shutting down voices and initiatives?*

First Day of Month: Executive Team

The team had closed the morning on Synergy and grabbed idlis and strong filter coffee near M.G. Road. By mid-afternoon, they were back, ceiling fans turning lazily against the heat, ready for the fourth choice.

Sanjay stood at the glass wall with a single marker. "This afternoon is Trust versus Tyranny," he said. "Let's start by seeing where our energy really lives."

He drew one bar with five labels, the T-eras:

> *Timekeeping* (Industrial Age): 20%
>
> *Technocracy* (Information Age): 40%
>
> *Tyranny* (Irrelevance Age): 10%
>
> *Trust* (Ingenuity Age): 25%
>
> *Transcendence* (Imaginative Possibility): 5%

"Proof points, not aspirations," he said. "Push me.

"Roughly twenty percent of the enterprise still operates in Timekeeping, the Industrial "T." Contribution is measured by attendance, not outcomes; hours logged still pass for commitment. HR and Legal hold a policy-first reflex. Exceptions are treated as risk rather than insight. In moments of crisis, "command clarity" can slip into "no questions," and the culture mistakes compliance for calm. Time is managed well, but trust is managed poorly.

"Around forty percent of Omnivista's employees live in Technocracy, the Information "T." Dashboards set the tone of meetings before the purpose does. The loudest metric in the room becomes the default truth. Model approvals prize accuracy and throughput, but their downstream impact and repairability get little airtime. Performance systems still orbit around individual output; cross-team fairness is invisible. The numbers are flawless, but the narrative is missing.

"About ten percent slips into Tyranny, the Irrelevance "T." Here, urgency turns toxic.

Cultures built on speed begin to silence dissent. Informal monitoring tools appear, tracking dashboards that no one explains. After incidents, blame storms replace reviews; those who speak softly or question loudly retreat into self-protection. The organization remains busy but becomes brittle.

"Yet twenty-five percent of Omnivista already works from a different premise: Trust, the Ingenuity "T." In Site Reliability Engineering and Clinical Ops, blameless reviews now follow incidents, leading to faster fixes and calmer teams. The early "speak-up safety" pulse is improving; managers are modeling vulnerability rather than perfection. Two AI model cards were recently shipped with documented limits and appeal paths; regulators noticed, and the response was trust, not sanction. These are small but profound shifts: authority is shared, and accountability remains intact.

"Only five percent reach the frontier of Transcendence, the Imagination "T." Gestures of stewardship, toward communities, partners, or the ecosystem that sustains the firm, remain rare. Daily rituals that tie purpose to practice are thin, and the apology and repair playbooks exist primarily on paper. The architecture of care is drawn; it has yet to be lived.

"Across the "T" spectrum, Omnivista's challenge is clear: move from time-based control to trust-based coherence. The journey begins not with more oversight, but with more ownership, where every decision leaves people more connected, not more cautious."

Sanjay capped the marker. "If trust is clarity with consequence, safety to speak and fairness in repair, how do we make that our norm?"

Sanjay now took the team on the site visit. The afternoon haze hung low over Whitefield as they stepped into Omnivista's digital hub. Banks of screens glowed with dashboards, code reviews, and AI monitoring tools. This was the frontline of Omnivista's future, brilliant engineers building the platforms that carried both promise and peril.

Sanjay led them into a glass-walled war room where algorithms tracked employee keystrokes, log-ins, and error rates. "This was meant to reduce risk," he said quietly, "but listen to what people feel." One engineer confessed, "I know the system flags me if I pause too long. It's easier to push something half-done than risk being marked idle." Tyranny in digital clothing: control that crushed judgment, data that corroded trust.

Next, Sanjay brought them to a product pod to experiment with a different approach. Here, AI copilots were designed to highlight anomalies and offer suggestions, but final decisions were left to the team. Every two weeks, they held a Failure Forum, where engineers presented what went wrong, what they learned, and how they would prevent it next time. No penalties, just transparent improvement. "It's strange," one coder said, "but I feel safer admitting mistakes here than in any other place I've worked."

On another floor, Chris observed a short ritual: every sprint review began with a Fairness Audit. Time, workload, and recognition were logged openly. If one person carried too much, the team redistributed before the next cycle. Trust wasn't a slogan; it was designed into the workflow.

Sanjay turned back to the group. "Trust can't be mandated. It must be earned through fairness, safety, and follow-through. Tyranny grows when surveillance replaces stewardship. The question for Omnivista is which one we choose to scale."

Chris concluded, "AI multiplies the system it finds. If it finds trust, ingenuity grows. If it finds tyranny, ingenuity dies. Here are the assignments for the month."

Team Assignments for the Month

"K: Keep: Blameless reviews and fast fix.
These turn error into information and model accountability without fear. Maria will embed opening briefs and skeptic rounds into operational handovers, making safety to speak visible in the daily rhythm of the floor." She continued.

"I: Improve: Fairness and transparency audits.
We need a monthly check on pay band outliers, promotion velocity, workload distribution, and decision visibility, published as a one-pager. John will run the audit with Yuki and co-own corrective actions where money or time moves." She turned to Sanjay.

"S: Start: Model cards and assurance notes.
For any Tier-1 model or data product, we publish purpose, limits, populations at risk, human-in-the-loop steps, appeal path, and repair SLA. Sanjay will lead with Legal and Compliance and set a seventy-two-hour repair SLA."

"**S: Stop: Surveillance that people do not understand.**
No monitoring tool survives without a published explanation: why it exists, what it tracks, who sees the data, and how to appeal. We remove one high-friction tool this month. Yuki will catalog, retire, and publish the registry."

She turned to Liam. "And Liam, you have a parallel task. Test whether trust principles hold in external communications. Trial a repair routine: when a message misfires, the revised copy and rationale are shown to everyone. Show me whether transparency in messaging builds trust or whether we are still hiding behind cover-up."

CEO's Notebook: Trust

That night, Chris walked back through the streets of Whitefield, monsoon air heavy with petrol and spice. The day's site visit still pressed in: the war room where surveillance drained agency, and the product pods where fairness rituals turned fear into learning. Bangalore itself felt like the metaphor, chaotic, noisy, but alive with ingenuity when trust was present.

She paused under a banyan tree lit by the glow of passing scooters and opened her notebook. "Trust is the hinge," she wrote. "Without it, ingenuity collapses into compliance or silence. With it, even failure becomes fuel." She set her daily practices for the month:

Actions

1. Name one fairness gap daily. Surface a discrepancy in workload, voice, or recognition and move to correct it.

2. Protect one dissent daily. Encourage and record a contrarian view or skeptic's note before closing a decision.

3. Close one loop daily. Follow up on a promise, audit, or risk flagged earlier and prove that what was raised was resolved.

What I'll Notice

1. *Industrial* (Timekeeping): Where obedience is mistaken for trust, and voice is absent.

2. *Information* (Technocracy): Where dashboards signal transparency but dissent still feels unsafe.

3. *Irrelevance* (Tyranny): Where surveillance masquerades as stewardship; silence signals fear, not alignment.

4. *Ingenuity* (Trust): Where fairness audits, Failure Forums, and skeptic rounds make safety real.

5. *Imagination* (Transcendence): Where trust extends across networks, partners, regulators, communities, in shared accountability.

Chris closed the notebook and let the rhythm of scooters and rain mix into the night air. Tomorrow, she would return to metrics and reviews, but tonight, she carried one anchor: trust is not given, it is earned, and it is the choice that determines whether AI multiplies courage or corrodes it.

My Fingerprint

A board approached me because something was wrong with their culture, but they could not name it. They loved their CEO. He was smart, visionary, a great storyteller to the market. They asked me to interview fifty people across the organization.

By the second interview, I encountered suicidal ideation caused directly by the CEO's behavior behind closed doors. In public, he was magnetic. In private, he praised people one day and shredded their proposals in front of two hundred the next. He demanded staff meet him at a pub at eleven at night regardless of their circumstances. He fired people without apparent reason. He told customers that his own staff did not know what was good for them. He used bonuses as weapons. He told people one version of reality and then denied it the next day.

The tyranny had passed from him to the top team. They had learned his methods and applied them downward. By interview twenty, the pattern was unmistakable. I went back to the board and told them the top four executives had to go or the company would be destroyed. It was one of the few boards that listened. They went.

The damage to customers and staff had been greater than anyone on the outside had understood.

That experience taught me something I have carried ever since: tyranny is rarely obvious at the top, especially when looking in from outside. It is charming, persuasive, even visionary. It becomes loud only in the corridors, the car parks, and the quiet conversations where people admit what the system is actually doing to them. Trust is not a feeling. It is the absence of that fear. And it can only be built when leaders are willing to hear what they would rather not know.

Trust: Through Six Lenses

As with the previous choices, we examine Trust through the same six lenses: history, etymology, philosophy, neuroscience, artificial intelligence, and real world examples.

History and what could evolve

Industrial Age

Trust was enforced through timekeeping, hours as proof. The same rules, the same clock, the same consequences promised fairness but often mistook presence for value. Policy overrode judgment; people learned to avoid risk rather than surface it. In crises, "command clarity" meant no questions, problems traveled silently until they broke. Suggestion boxes and grievance processes existed, but they rarely closed the loop, so candor felt unsafe, and cynicism grew. The practical insight from this era is double-edged: uniformity creates predictability, yet without a channel for near-misses and dissent, the system becomes brittle exactly where it needs to be most honest.

Information Age

Trust shifted to technocracy, metrics became the new standard for truth. Dashboards and model outputs made performance visible, but also louder than its purpose; accuracy and throughput earned approval, while impact and repair stayed off-screen. Individuals were optimized while cross-team fairness remained invisible, and rooms learned to defer to "the number" even when the number didn't fit the moment.

Goodhart's law showed up: when a measure becomes a target, it ceases to be a good measure. The Information Age taught organizations to trust the number. Boeing's 737 MAX program illustrates the danger: schedule and cost targets became so dominant that engineering concerns about the MCAS flight-control system were downplayed or rerouted. The metric said on track; the culture said don't ask. Two crashes and 346 lives later, the gap between the dashboard and the truth was unmistakable. In the Information Age data governance matured faster than data understanding; few meetings asked, "What assumptions drive this score, and who is harmed when it's wrong?" Over time, transparency became a mere appearance of trust rather than a genuine practice.

Irrelevance Age

Control hardens into tyranny, which is control without accountability. Under pressure, organizations narrow their voice: shadow surveillance creeps in, dissent becomes career risk, and incident reviews turn into blame theater. People comply in public and whisper in private; learning stops because truth has nowhere safe to stand. Metrics are gamed, speak-up channels go quiet, and talented people withdraw judgment to protect themselves. The culture fosters organizational learned helplessness, such as teams waiting to be told and then seeking cover when outcomes fail to meet expectations. Busy dashboards mask a deeper deficit: no one believes the system will be fair when things go wrong.

Ingenuity Age

Trust is designed, clarity with consequence. Meetings open with clear stakes, voice, and fairness rules so that people know how to speak and how disagreement is handled. Model cards and assurance notes state purpose, limits, populations at risk, human-in-the-loop steps, appeal paths, and repair SLAs; reviews are blameless and fast: detect → discuss → repair → share. Fairness is audited and published, pay bands, promotion velocity, workload distribution and corrected in daylight, which brings more truth earlier and better judgment faster. Leaders narrate "what we learned" memos and keep decision journals so trade-offs are owned, not hidden. The result is counterintuitive but reliable: trust reduces cycle time because issues surface while they're still small enough to fix.

Imaginative Possibility

Organizations co-create standards with customers, communities, and regulators; they rehearse harms before launch, run open red-teams, and apologize and repair in public when they miss. Data trusts, ecosystem SLAs, and transparency reports move accountability from marketing claims to operating promises. Independent review boards and crowdsourced security ethics programs invite outsiders to test systems before they compromise people's security. Purpose outlives quarterly pressure: decisions are judged not only by what they achieve, but by what they protect. The boundary between "us" and "them" shifts toward shared guardianship of the systems we all depend on.

Etymology

Trust comes from the Old Norse word *traust,* *meaning* "faith, confidence, reliance." Its deeper Indo-European root, *deru-* ("firm, solid, steadfast"), also gives us "tree" and "truth." At its core, trust is not naivety, but stability extended outward, a willingness to stand firm while allowing others to move. In leadership, trust begins as vulnerability: the courage to delegate, disclose, and depend. It matures when transparency and consistency prove that such faith is warranted.

Tyranny originates from the Greek *tyrannos,* which was initially a neutral term for a sole ruler, later darkening to mean one who governs without legitimacy or restraint. Its descent is a warning: authority unanchored by reciprocity decays into domination. In leadership, tyranny is not always loud; it can appear as certainty that silences dissent or systems that punish candor.

This is the contest at the heart of power today: Trust as shared steadiness that strengthens others versus Tyranny as control that hollows them.

Philosophy

Across centuries, thinkers have argued that trust is shared risk made visible; tyranny is coerced certainty that hides its risks from view.

Thomas Hobbes: "Covenants, without the sword, are but words."

Trust needs predictable enforcement, not arbitrary force: clear rules, consistent consequences, and no favorites.

John Locke: "The end of law is not to abolish or restrain, but to preserve and enlarge freedom."

In organizations, rules that protect autonomy increase trust; secret rules, on the other hand, shrink it.

Montesquieu: "Power should be a check to power."

Build checks into the process: dual control on irreversible moves, audit trails for money and data, and rotation of gatekeepers.

Immanuel Kant: "Act only according to that maxim whereby you can at the same time will that it should become a universal law."

Make promises you can keep, then keep them in full daylight.

Niccolò Machiavelli: "It is better to be feared than loved, if you cannot be both."

Fear buys compliance, not commitment. Leaders who trade fear for candor get ideas, not silence.

Sissela Bok: "Trust is a social good to be protected as much as the air we breathe."

Treat credibility as infrastructure: publish assumptions, admit errors fast, and repair breaches publicly.

Onora O'Neill: "We need more trustworthiness, not more trust."

Measure what makes you worthy: competence, honesty, and care, so trust follows evidence, not campaigns.

Isaiah Berlin: "Freedom for the wolves has often meant death to the sheep."

Guardrails protect the vulnerable: escalate on harm, not hierarchy; privilege customer welfare over internal wins.

Karl Popper: "We must plan for freedom, and not only for security, if for no other reason than that only freedom can make security secure."

Popper urged enabling criticism, institutionalizing dissent through red teams, postmortems without blame, and the publication of minority reports.

Václav Havel: *"The simple step of a courageous individual is not to take part in the lie."*

Make truth livable: ban retaliation for speaking up, reward surfacing bad news early, and tell the whole story, including costs.

Our philosophers show us that trust is not naïveté; it is verifiable openness: clear promises, mutual checks, and fast accountability. Tyranny is the opposite: opacity, unilateral power, and fear as policy.

Neuroscience

Trust and Tyranny are not just metaphors; they are neurobiological states. Modern neuroscience reveals that the brain's rhythms, chemicals, and networks determine whether power signals safety and unlocks reciprocity, or whether threat circuits take over and enforce brittle compliance.

Polyvagal theory: social engagement versus defense

When environments cue safety (predictable rules, warm prosody, eye contact), the ventral vagal system supports social engagement. People can speak and hear nuance. Unpredictability or a perceived threat triggers the fight/flight/freeze response; speech becomes tight, and listening collapses. Practical cue: Start with an opening brief: What's at stake, how voice works, and fairness rules. To keep the social circuit online.

Oxytocin/serotonin and repair chemistry

Recognizing effort, sharing information, granting discretion, and apologizing credibly raise oxytocin/serotonin, reopening the prefrontal cortex for better judgment. "Blameless + fast fix" isn't soft. It's neuro-efficient: "detection → discussion → repair → share" keeps cognition online.

Fairness detection (insula, ACC)

The brain is exquisitely sensitive to fairness; the anterior insula fires on perceived injustice even when it costs the perceiver to punish it. Transparent pay/promotion/workload data and visible corrections reduce insula "anger" and free attention for problem-solving.

Surveillance, unpredictability, and cortisol
Opaque monitoring and shifting goalposts lead to chronic cortisol. People protect their reputations, not the truth; error signals are hidden. Publish a monitoring registry ("why, what, who sees, appeal path"), and remove one high-friction tool:cortisol drops and candor rises.

Prediction error and the power of apology
The brain updates models on surprise. A swift apology, accompanied by a visible fix, converts a negative prediction error into renewed trust; delay cements cynicism. Use a seventy-two-hour rule: acknowledge the issue, outline the repair, and display the before-and-after images.

Synchrony and honest signals
Teams in trust exhibit greater neural/physio synchrony; prosody, turn-taking, and shared artifacts drive this phenomenon. Practically: time-box turns, reflect ("what I heard"), and end with a single decision log everyone can retell.

Default mode + moral reasoning
Short reflective pauses (such as walking or breathing) engage networks that integrate memory, values, and future simulation. Leaders who pause before sanctioning or shipping an AI model make fewer moral framing errors and choose better repair paths when needed.

Sleep and consolidation of social learning
Apology/repair scripts, new fairness rules, and conflict de-escalation techniques consolidate during sleep. After hard conversations, sleep improves recall of agreements and reduces threat reactivity the next day.

Strengthening Trust by Applying Neuroscience Every Day
Trust is a design choice influenced by biology. Safety cues widen attention; fairness calms the insula; oxytocin and clear repair reopen the cortex for better judgment. Tyranny: threat, opacity, and surveillance, narrows minds and hides truth. Build the

biology (calm, fairness), the artifacts (opening briefs, model cards, decision logs), and the rituals (quiet windows, blameless repair) so people speak and are seen and so your organization learns before it breaks.

Here are some practical exercises for trust that use these neuroscientific ideas:

- Begin high-stakes meetings with a one to two-minute quiet window.
- Open with the brief: stakes, voice rules, fairness.
- Use a model card (purpose, limits, appeal path, repair SLA) for any Tier-1 model.
- Run blameless, fast reviews: detect → discuss → repair → share.
- Publish a monthly fairness audit (pay/promotion/workload) and the fixes.
- Maintain a monitoring registry and remove tools that are no longer understood.
- Log decisions and dissent in a one-page decision journal that people can retell.
- Apologize within seventy-two hours when harm occurs and show the fix.
- Build synchrony: turn-taking, read-backs, and one shared artifact on screen.
- Protect sleep after heavy trust work; reconvene with a short recap.

Artificial Intelligence

We can now see the leadership choice between Trust and Tyranny in the light of AI-fueled choices.

Transparency versus Black Box Tyranny

AI systems can either broaden or narrow the voice. Transparent "model cards" that state purpose, limits, and appeal paths help people trust the outputs while retaining agency. Black-box scoring, by contrast, fosters tyranny: decisions are made without explanation, and employees or customers have no recourse but to comply.

Fairness Audits versus Metric Absolutism

AI can automate fairness checks, scanning for pay inequities, biased outcomes, or workload imbalances. When published openly, these audits reinforce trust by showing leaders care enough to measure and correct. Left hidden, they risk technocratic tyranny: numbers dominate while lived experience of unfairness festers unseen.

Repair Loops versus Blame Loops

AI accelerates the detection of anomalies, such as outages, clinical near-misses, and compliance breaches and can trigger fast repair playbooks. Trust grows when organizations use those signals to "detect → discuss → repair → share." Tyranny emerges when anomaly detection becomes blame theater, with dashboards weaponized to identify culprits rather than causes.

Voice Amplifiers versus Surveillance Systems

AI copilots can elevate weak signals, surfacing dissenting comments, highlighting patterns in employee feedback, or flagging quiet risks. Done well, this makes it safer for people to speak and be seen. Used poorly, the same tools become surveillance, tracking keystrokes, call times, or sentiment without transparency, ultimately stifling initiative in the face of fear.

Shared Stewardship versus Abdication

AI can serve as a platform for co-creating standards with regulators, communities, and customers, publishing assurance notes and facilitating appeal paths. Trust flourishes when leaders keep humans in the loop and treat AI as a tool for shared responsibility and accountability. Tyranny grows when leaders abdicate accountability to "the model," hiding behind algorithms to avoid consequence.

Amplifying Trust by Deploying AI Every Day

AI is not neutral in the trust versus tyranny choice. It can widen candor by making fairness measurable, repair visible, and voice amplified. Or it can narrow truth by multiplying surveillance, hiding logic, and silencing dissent. Leaders can build these into daily practice:

- Publish model cards for every Tier-1 system: purpose, limits, populations at risk, appeal path, and repair SLA.

- Run automated fairness audits on pay, promotion, and workload, and publish corrections alongside the findings.

- Use AI to surface weak signals from employee feedback and engagement data as care, not surveillance.

- Remove or explain every monitoring tool: if people do not understand what is tracked, retire it or publish the rationale and appeal path.

- Deploy anomaly detection to trigger repair playbooks, not blame reports: detect, discuss, repair, share.

- Treat copilot outputs as inputs to human judgment, never as substitutes: "the model said so" is abdication, not analysis.

- Use AI to track say-do ratios: promises logged, promises kept, gaps visible.

If AI increases monitoring but decreases voice, you do not have trust. You have faster tyranny.

Trust: Real World Examples

Alcoa under Paul O'Neill

- **What they did.** When O'Neill became CEO in 1987, he made worker safety his single priority. Any employee could report a hazard and expect a response within twenty-four hours. Leaders were held accountable not for production targets first, but for whether safety concerns were heard and acted upon. The logic was trust as infrastructure: when people saw that raising a concern produced action, not punishment, the entire information system opened up.

- **Why this matters.** When the system responds fairly and fast, people tell the truth. Safety was the proxy; trust was the product. Near-misses surfaced, process flaws were caught early, and candor became the norm. O'Neill proved that trust is not a soft value. It is an operating system.

- **Consequences.** Lost-workday rates fell to one-twentieth of the U.S. average. Market value increased fivefold over O'Neill's tenure. The safety-first culture outlasted his leadership because it had been designed into the daily rhythm, not dependent on a single leader's personality.

Johnson & Johnson's Tylenol Recall

- **What they did.** In 1982, after cyanide-laced Tylenol capsules killed seven people in Chicago, J&J pulled the product nationwide and communicated relentlessly, prioritizing patient safety over short-term financial loss. The company's Credo, which placed customers and communities above shareholders, guided every decision during the crisis. J&J did not wait for regulators to act. They acted first and explained later.

- **Why this matters.** Public trust can be rebuilt when apologies and repairs are swift, visible, and unconditional. The Credo was not a poster. It was a decision-making tool that held under the most extreme pressure a consumer brand can face.

- **Consequences.** The brand recovered fully. Tylenol regained market share within a year. The case remains a benchmark for crisis management built on transparency and stewardship. It proved that the short-term cost of doing right is dwarfed by the long-term cost of doing wrong.

Netflix Culture of Candor

- **What they did.** From 2009 onward, Netflix built a "freedom and responsibility" system that paired high talent density with radical candor and context over control. Employees were trusted with significant autonomy, including unlimited vacation and minimal approval processes, but held to high performance standards with honest, direct feedback. The culture deck, published openly, became one of the most downloaded corporate documents in history.

- **Why this matters.** Voice was normalized. Decisions traveled with context, not permission. Leaders provided the strategic frame; employees made the calls. Trust was not a perk for senior leaders. It was extended to everyone, with the expectation that it would be honored through results.

- **Consequences.** Faster course-correction, fewer politics, and a reputation for decisive bets with real accountability. Netflix's willingness to cannibalize its own DVD business for streaming was only possible in a culture where people could speak honestly about what was working and what was not.

Google SRE Blameless Postmortems

- **What they did.** From the 2010s onward, Google's Site Reliability Engineering teams established blameless postmortems as the standard response to incidents. When systems failed, the review focused on what happened and why, not on who was at fault. Action items were tracked to closure. Toil reduction, eliminating repetitive manual work, was rewarded as a contribution to system health.

- **Why this matters.** Cognitive bandwidth shifted from self-protection to system improvement. Engineers surfaced weak signals earlier because they knew the response would be learning, not punishment. The practice made it safe to tell the truth about failure, which is the precondition for preventing the next one.

- **Consequences.** Higher reliability over time. Faster detection of emerging issues. A culture where admitting a mistake was treated as a professional act, not a career risk. The model has been adopted across the technology industry as the standard for incident response.

Tyranny: Real World Examples

Enron

- **What they did.** Enron's "rank and yank" system forced managers to label the bottom fifteen percent of employees for termination every cycle. The result was a culture where people inflated results, hid losses, and treated honesty as career risk. Internal metrics rewarded deal volume and revenue recognition regardless of underlying value. Sherron Watkins raised concerns internally about accounting practices and was isolated rather than heard. The board received information filtered through layers of performance theater.

- **Why this matters.** When the cost of candor exceeds the cost of silence, truth exits the building. Performance systems that punish vulnerability produce tyranny, even without a single tyrant at the top. Enron's culture did not fail because of one bad actor. It failed because the system made dishonesty rational.

- **Consequences.** The collapse wiped out $74 billion in shareholder value. Thousands of employees lost pensions. Criminal convictions followed. Enron became a lasting case study in how fear corrodes an organization from within, and how metrics without meaning accelerate the decay.

Volkswagen Dieselgate

- **What they did.** Between 2009 and 2015, Volkswagen engineers installed software in diesel vehicles that detected when emissions tests were being conducted and adjusted engine performance to pass. In normal driving, the vehicles emitted up to forty times the legal limit of nitrogen oxides. The deception was systematic, spanning multiple vehicle lines and model years. Internal pressure to meet aggressive cost and performance targets created a culture where raising concerns about compliance was treated as disloyalty to the engineering mission.

- **Why this matters.** When metrics outrank meaning, technocracy slides into deception. The targets were hit. The dashboards were green. But the underlying truth was poisonous, both literally and organizationally. Engineers who knew the tests were being gamed had no safe channel to surface the problem.

- **Consequences.** Billions in penalties, executive prosecutions, and brand damage that persisted for years. The scandal forced a fundamental rethinking of corporate governance in the automotive industry and became a global reference point for what happens when performance culture overwhelms ethical accountability.

Uber Pre-2017 Culture

- **What they did.** In its early growth phase, Uber cultivated a culture that tolerated rule-bending, aggressive internal competition, and retaliation against dissent. Internal reporting channels were perceived as unsafe. Employees who raised concerns about harassment, discrimination, or ethical violations described being sidelined or ignored. Leadership celebrated speed and disruption while treating cultural concerns as obstacles to growth.

- **Why this matters.** Tyrannical norms scale fast in high-growth environments unless trust is deliberately designed. Uber's problems were not hidden. They were known internally and tolerated because the growth narrative justified the cost. When people see that speaking up changes nothing, they stop speaking.

- **Consequences.** Leadership exits, regulatory scrutiny across multiple countries, and an extensive cultural rebuild under new management. The company's experience demonstrated that cultural debt compounds just as financial debt does, and that the cost of rebuilding trust far exceeds the cost of maintaining it.

Theranos under Elizabeth Holmes

- **What they did.** Elizabeth Holmes founded Theranos on the promise of revolutionizing blood testing with a device that could run hundreds of tests from a single finger prick. As the technology failed to deliver, Holmes built a culture of secrecy and intimidation around the gap between the promise and the reality. Employees who raised concerns about the accuracy of results were threatened with litigation, placed under surveillance, or terminated. Non-disclosure agreements were weaponized to silence departing staff. The board was stacked with political luminaries rather than scientists or clinicians who might have asked the obvious questions. When a young lab director tried to flag inaccurate patient results, he was told the problem was his attitude, not the machine.

- **Why this matters.** Theranos is the purest case of tyranny disguised as vision. Holmes was charismatic, compelling, and genuinely believed in the mission. But the system she built made truth more expensive than silence at every level. When raising a concern carries greater career risk than ignoring a patient safety issue, the organization has crossed from ambition into tyranny. The machinery of control, legal threats, surveillance, loyalty tests, did not protect the company. It protected the lie.

- **Consequences**. Patients received inaccurate blood test results that influenced medical decisions. The company collapsed. Holmes was convicted of fraud in 2022 and sentenced to more than eleven years in prison. Theranos became a defining cautionary tale: when leaders design systems that punish candor, the organization does not just fail. It harms the people it claimed to serve.

Trust: Bringing the Lenses Together

Trust is not a feeling. It is an operating system.

- **History** traces how each age built its own version and watched it corrode: the Industrial Age enforced trust through timekeeping and uniformity, creating predictability but killing candor; the Information Age shifted trust to metrics, producing dashboard confidence while lived fairness stayed off-screen; and the Irrelevance Age hardens control into tyranny, where surveillance replaces stewardship and people comply in public while truth whispers in car parks.

- **Etymology** grounds the stakes: trust descends from the Old Norse traust, sharing its root with "tree" and "truth," stability extended outward, while tyranny began as a neutral word for sole ruler and darkened into authority without restraint or reciprocity.

- **Philosophy** maps the architecture: Hobbes warned that covenants without consequence are just words, Locke argued that rules should enlarge freedom not shrink it, Montesquieu insisted that power must check power, Kant translated his imperative into reliability by demanding promises kept in full daylight, Bok called trust a social good as vital as air, O'Neill shifted the question from trust to trustworthiness, Popper urged us to plan for freedom by institutionalizing dissent, and Havel called people to live in truth and showed what it cost.

- **Neuroscience** proves that trust and tyranny are biological states: safety cues activate the ventral vagal system and open social engagement, while unpredictability triggers fight-flight-freeze and collapses listening;

oxytocin and serotonin reopen the prefrontal cortex when leaders recognize effort, share information, and repair credibly; the anterior insula fires on perceived injustice even when punishing it costs the perceiver; and chronic surveillance spikes cortisol until people protect their reputations rather than the truth.

- **AI amplifies** whichever state it finds: it can make fairness auditable, repair visible, voice amplified, and model logic transparent through published cards with appeal paths, or it can multiply surveillance, hide logic in black boxes, and provide the veneer of objectivity while no human owns the call.

- **And the evidence** is unambiguous: Alcoa proved that trust designed into daily rhythm outlasts any single leader, Johnson and Johnson proved that swift unconditional repair rebuilds what crisis destroys, Netflix proved that candor paired with accountability produces faster bets and fewer politics, and Google SRE proved that blameless postmortems turn failure into learning, while Enron proved that systems which punish candor make dishonesty rational, Volkswagen proved that green dashboards can hide poisonous truths, Uber proved that cultural debt compounds as ruthlessly as financial debt, and Theranos proved that when raising a concern carries greater career risk than ignoring a patient safety issue, the organization has crossed from ambition into tyranny.

- **The practical test is human**: do people in your organization feel safer telling the truth today than they did six months ago? Can they name the repair that followed the last mistake? Can they point to a fairness audit and the correction it produced? Trust lives in those answers. Tyranny lives in the silence where those answers should be.

End of Month: Executive Team Review

The next morning, the executive team gathered in Dublin. Each leader reported back on their Bangalore assignments, bringing results.

Maria (COO): Keep → Opening Briefs in Operations

- **What she did**: Embedded a one-minute opening brief and skeptic round into shift handovers.

- **What changed**: More risks surfaced early; one handover prevented a duplicate order error.

- **Proof points:** Handover agenda template; error log showing avoided duplication; pulse feedback citing "safer to speak."

John (CFO): Improve → Fairness Audit with Money and Time Corrections

- **What he did:** Partnered with Yuki to publish the audit and reallocate the budget for workload relief.

- **What changed**: 2 outlier pay cases corrected; overtime load in one corridor reduced by 15%.

- **Proof points:** Audit one-pager; budget adjustment memo; before and after workload chart.

Sanjay (CTO): Start → Model Cards and Repair SLA

- **What he did:** Published two model cards; set a 72-hour SLA for any repair.

- **What changed**: One mis-triage was caught and fixed inside 48 hours; regulators praised the visible appeal path.

- **Proof points:** Photos of model cards, SLA timer logs, and regulator feedback notes.

Yuki (CPO): Stop → Surveillance Registry and Transparency

- **What she did**: Cataloged all monitoring tools; retired one; published the registry.

- **What changed**: Reduced shadow tracking; one team reported more candid feedback in reviews.

- **Proof points:** Registry screenshot; decommission log; "speak-up" pulse up six points in her corridor.

Liam (CMO): Keep → Repair Routine in Messaging

- **What he did:** Trialed a repair routine: when a message misfired, the revised copy and rationale were shown to all.

- **What changed**: Faster correction; less blame. Teams saw fixes as learning opportunities, not as a source of shame.

- **Proof points:** Campaign before and after slides; feedback quotes praising "candor over cover-up."

Chris closed the morning. "Our test for Trust was simple: could we make safety to speak explicit, fairness visible, and repair lived, not promised? We now have proof points: opening briefs on agendas, model cards on walls, fairness audits with corrections, repair notes in daylight, and a registry that ended shadow surveillance."

What If

That afternoon, Chris took the team out of the Liffey Aged Care Centre and across the river to Phoenix Park. The spring sun sparkled, deer grazed in the open fields, and the noise of the city gave way to a vast, steady silence. They sat near the Wellington Monument, its granite tower casting a long shadow across the grass.

"This is the right place to think about Trust," Chris said. "In the hospital, we saw how easy it is for systems to slip into tyranny, surveillance instead of stewardship, control instead of care. Out here, trust is the only currency. The deer don't survive without it, and the park doesn't thrive without it. Let's imagine: what if Omnivista designed for trust at every seam, instead of falling back into fear? What if...?"

1. What if every major meeting began with a fairness audit, in which time, workload, and recognition are laid out before decisions are made?

2. What if one named skeptic had to sign off on every Tier-1 decision before it proceeded?

3. What if dissent were rewarded with recognition points, the same way efficiency is rewarded today?

4. What if every failure had to be presented in a Failure Forum before it could be closed on the record?

5. What if AI dashboards were banned from tracking individuals and could only report on teams or groups?

6. What if promises could not be archived until results: actions taken, were posted publicly?

7. What if leaders were rated quarterly by the ratio of promises closed to promises made?

8. What if "trust debt" were measured like financial debt, with explicit plans to repay it?

9. What if all risk logs had to include how employees were heard, not just what was tracked?

10. What if staff had the right to veto one surveillance tool per year, forcing leaders to prove trust another way?

End of Month: Board Review

Chris began plainly. "Four weeks ago, Sanjay led us into Trust versus Tyranny at the Whitefield Digital Campus. We asked a difficult question: can trust be designed into daily practice, or will AI multiply surveillance until ingenuity suffocates?"

She described what followed as "a month of rewiring reflexes." In most teams, failure was whispered about and blame implied rather than surfaced. They replaced that pattern with bi-weekly Failure Forums, where engineers presented what had gone wrong, what they had learned, and how the system had changed as a result. "When you bring failure into daylight," Chris said, "the signal moves from shame to prevention."

The second experiment targeted fairness. Workloads and recognition had become uneven; redistribution was rare and often influenced by politics. Now, every sprint review begins with a fairness audit, which includes checks on time, tasks, and credits. Gaps were corrected in the room. "We stopped treating fairness as sentiment," she explained, "and started treating it as hygiene."

The third shift reframed technology itself. AI dashboards had been logging keystrokes, idle time, and compliance metrics, a pattern that blurred the lines between monitoring and management. The pilot redefined AI as a copilot for anomaly detection and support, with humans retaining final judgment. "Surveillance suffocates trust," she said. "Stewardship strengthens it."

A fourth practice, skeptic rounds, brought dissent into the open. Each Tier-1 decision now required a named skeptic and a rationale recorded. "Dissent is not disloyalty," Chris noted. "It's the first signal of learning."

Finally, the team closed the loop between promise and follow-through. Previously, risks and commitments were logged but rarely revisited. Now, every risk has an owner and a closure date. "Say–do logs" were published every two weeks, documenting which promises had been kept.

The results, she reported, were visible within a single quarter. Failure Forums produced five preventive design changes, including one flaw resolved before release, while fairness audits drove twelve workload redistributions and an eleven-point rise in the fair-treatment pulse. When idle-time tracking was removed from AI dashboards, stress reports dropped fifteen percent and engagement rose nine points. Skeptic rounds headed off two unnecessary escalations and converted a third decision into a reversible pilot. The say-do logs closed eighteen risks on record, with staff citing follow-through up ten points.

Chris summarized the pattern. "Tyranny," she said, "is irrelevance when surveillance masquerades as stewardship, dissent is silenced, and promises evaporate. Trust is a hallmark of ingenuity when fairness is visible, dissent is welcomed, failures are learned from, and promises are kept. We now have proof points that trust can be designed, not as sentiment, but as daily discipline."

She concluded with four guardrails. Fairness first: begin with audits of time, workload, and recognition, and act on gaps immediately. Dissent protected: a skeptic's note must be logged before major calls. Failures teach: incidents must become preventive actions, not a source of blame. Promises closed: risks and commitments are tracked until resolved, not forgotten. "These," she said, "are the conditions where trust grows. If we fail them, tyranny creeps back in."

A director leaned forward. "Can trust really be systematized," he asked, "or does it always depend on culture?"

Chris replied without hesitation. "Culture is what the system repeats. By building fairness audits, skeptic rounds, and closure logs into the work, we stop leaving trust to chance. The rituals create the culture."

Evelyn nodded. "You've shown how trust can be engineered as rigorously as compliance," she said. "Bring us the same clarity when Liam leads us into Authenticity versus Apathy."

CEO's Reflection, That Evening

Chris stepped out from the Boardroom into the damp Dublin air, the streets slick with the spring rain. The Board's questions still lingered. Could trust truly be systematized, or was it only ever a matter of culture? She replayed her own answer in her mind: culture is what the system repeats. The guardrails they had agreed on: fairness audits, skeptic rounds, Failure Forums, loop-closure discipline, were not just rituals, but the architecture of trust.

She walked along the Liffey, the city lights mirrored in the dark water. The day had shown that trust could be designed into work, but also how fragile it remained.

One gap, one broken promise, and tyranny crept back in. Tomorrow, Liam would take them into the last choice: Authenticity versus Apathy. Chris knew it would be the hardest of all, because unlike synergy or operations, authenticity could not be faked, not even for a day. It had to be lived. She closed her notebook with a single line: "Trust can be designed. Authenticity must be chosen."

Trust: Exercises for You to Try

Trust only matters when it moves beyond values posters and becomes a daily practice. Fear is fast: it spreads in whispers, in hidden monitoring, in unspoken career risks. But trust can be quicker when leaders design safety to speak, fairness to see, and repair to live in daylight.

To make trust a reality in your own context, try this seven-day plan. Each move is simple; together, they create a rhythm in which candor, fairness, and repair become the norm.

> Day 1 – Opening Brief: Begin each meeting with a one-minute opening brief, stating the stakes, outlining the rules, and framing the concept of fairness. End with a quick "what risk are we missing?" round.
>
> Day 2 – Publish One Model Card: Choose any model, dashboard, or key process. Write a one-pager outlining its purpose, limits, owner, and how to appeal. Post it where people use it.
>
> Day 3 – Run a Fairness Scan: Pick one dimension: pay, workload, or promotion. Ask: Who is an outlier, and why? Publish one visible correction.
>
> Day 4 – Repair in Seventy-Two Hours: When something goes wrong (a missed handoff, a failed promise), apologize within seventy-two hours. Show the before-and-after fix on a single page or slide.
>
> Day 5 – End a Shadow Tool: Identify one monitoring or tracking tool that is not well understood. Retire it, or publish why it exists and how to appeal.
>
> Day 6 – Build Synchrony: In your next high-stakes meeting, time-box

turns and capture dissent in writing. End with a decision log that anyone could retell.

Day 7 – Trust Walk: Take twenty minutes to reflect: what risks did I reduce, what fairness did I make visible, what repair did I show? Capture one sentence of learning.

Trust is not a mood. It is a system. Leaders who design for it build the biology (safety, fairness), the artifacts (opening briefs, model cards, repair logs), and the rituals (quiet windows, apology in daylight) that make candor possible. Tyranny creeps in when fear hides truth. Trust flourishes when voice is safe, fairness is visible, and repair is lived.

Self-Assessment: Trust versus Tyranny

Rate yourself honestly. For each question, score both the Foundation and the AI Amplifier.
1 Not Yet · 2 Emerging · 3 Developing · 4 Practicing · 5 Second Nature

---

1.

Foundation. People feel safe raising problems, admitting mistakes, and challenging my ideas.

    Foundation score (1–5):_____

AI Amplifier. We use AI to enable transparency, not surveillance, so information flows openly without fear.

    AI Amplifier score (1–5):_____

2.

Foundation. I repair trust quickly when it breaks. I don't let resentment or ambiguity fester.

    Foundation score (1–5):_____

AI Amplifier. I use AI to surface early signals of disengagement or friction so I can intervene before trust erodes.

    AI Amplifier score (1–5):_____

3.

Foundation. I lead through fairness and transparency rather than control and surveillance.

    Foundation score (1–5):_____

AI Amplifier. We use AI to audit decisions for bias and ensure fairness in hiring, promotion, and resources.

    AI Amplifier score (1–5):_____

4.

Foundation. I extend trust first rather than requiring people to earn it through compliance.

Foundation score (1–5):_____

AI Amplifier. Our AI tools are designed to empower and inform people, not to monitor and control them.

AI Amplifier score (1–5):_____

5.

Foundation. My team trusts the system: decisions, promotions, and resource allocation feel fair.

Foundation score (1–5):_____

AI Amplifier. We use AI to make decision rationale visible so people understand the why, not just the what.

AI Amplifier score (1–5):_____

AVERAGE SCORE: Trust versus Tyranny

Foundation average (total of five scores ÷ 5): _____

AI Amplifier average (total of five scores ÷ 5): _____

Now: Transfer these two averages to the "T" row of your VISTA Scoreboard at the back of the book.

"To be nobody-but-yourself, which is
doing its best, night and day,
to make you everybody else, means to
fight the most brutal battle."

E.E. Cummings

"Authenticity is the long work of
shedding, choosing the self you'll
carry forward, laying down the selves
you won't. Scarred by grit, mended by
gloss.
And even in the darkest night,
remembering who you really are."

Katharine McLennan

CHAPTER 8

Authenticity versus Apathy

*When our values are tested, do we lead
from who we truly are and inspire
others to do the same,
or
disconnect, disengage, and
let indifference take over?*

1 June — **DUBLIN**

First day of Month: Executive Team

In the Dublin office, Liam stood at the glass wall with a single marker. "Today we are going to reflect on Authenticity versus Apathy," he said. "Let's start by seeing where our energy really lives."

He drew one bar with five labels, the A-eras:

> **Authority** (Industrial Age): 20%
> **Analytics** (Information Age): 40%
> **Apathy** (Irrelevance Age): 10%
> **Authenticity** (Ingenuity Age): 25%
> **Awe** (Imaginative Possibility): 5%

"Proof points, not aspirations," he said. "Push me.

"Roughly twenty percent of the enterprise still operates in Authority, the Industrial "A." Decisions rise to rank instead of proximity. "Title gravity" pulls high-ranking calls upward, even when the expertise is located lower in the room. Policy replaces presence: people cite the rule rather than speak from principle. Under pressure, voices sharpen; communication becomes command. In a crisis, leaders communicate to their teams, not with them. Order is maintained, but curiosity dies quietly underneath it.

"About forty percent of the organization now lives in Analytics, the Information "A." Dashboards open the meeting and shape the mood before purpose is even spoken. KPIs dictate the narrative; their colors steer the tone of the conversation. Definitions stretch to keep indicators green, a quiet theater of metrics. Quarterly reviews polish slides faster than they reconcile inconsistencies. The organization appears transparent, but it often performs transparency rather than practices it.

"Ten percent still drifts into Apathy, the Irrelevance 'A.' Purpose is written in perfect prose but rarely attached to verbs. People have learned that raising contradictions doesn't move the system, so they stop trying. 'Speak-up' channels become echo chambers. Cynicism hides behind sarcasm: 'We say one thing and fund another.' It's not rebellion; it's resignation dressed as humor.

"Yet a quarter of Omnivista already shows what the next level looks like: Authenticity, the Ingenuity 'A.' Leaders now write trade-off sentences into major decisions, naming what will be privileged and what will be postponed. AI model cards carry visible limits and appeal paths. Budgets and calendars are starting to align with the declared North Star. And the '72-hour rule' for mistakes, apologize and act within three days has turned accountability into a living ritual. The tone is lighter here, not because work is easier, but because people no longer pretend to be anything other than what they are.

"Only five percent reach the frontier of Awe, the Imagination 'A.' These are the teams that widen the circle of 'us.' They build rituals that connect colleagues, partners, and communities into shared purpose. But the rhythm is still occasional, not continual. Stewardship beyond the firm happens by event, not by instinct. There is imagination time, but not yet devotion time, the practice of wonder embedded in the work itself.

"Omnivista's "A" curve shows us learning to move from rank to resonance, from metrics to meaning, from compliance to care. Authority still stands tall in places, but Authenticity is learning to breathe and Awe is waiting for its turn."

Liam capped the marker. "If authenticity is say–do congruence under pressure, the month's work is simple: match the story to the results, and own the gap in daylight."

Liam then took the team to the Liffey Aged Care Centre, his signal site. The building itself told a story: hand-painted murals from residents alongside corporate posters with polished slogans. The contrast between lived reality and official messaging set the stage for the day.

Liam guided the team first into the dayroom, where a caregiver read aloud to a small circle of residents. The moment was genuine, with voices steady, residents attentive, creating a small ritual that felt deeply human. Yet when Chris asked the caregiver how the act was recognized, she shrugged. "It isn't. It's not on the checklist." Authenticity, present in spirit, erased in measurement.

In another ward, the team saw the opposite: dashboards tracking keystrokes and shift tasks filled the nurses' station. "This is what counts," a staff member explained, pointing to the screen. "But it's not who we are." Apathy crept in as the difference between what mattered and what was measured widened.

Later, Liam introduced them to a pilot he had: the Presence Council. Two caregivers, one family member, and one resident representative met weekly with staff to review care practices and procedures. At last week's meeting, a resident's story about loneliness led to a simple yet effective change: daily singing circles. Staff morale improved, families took notice, and residents participated with enthusiasm. "It didn't cost a cent," Liam said, "but it reminded us of who we are."

In the quiet of the courtyard, Chris noted the theme: Authenticity is congruence between what we say, what we do, and what we honor. Apathy is the gap.

Liam summed up: "If we reward only what is easy to track, apathy wins. If we choose to notice and honor the human, authenticity multiplies. That's the choice."

Chris assigned each of her teams a task for Authenticity versus Apathy:

Team Assignments for the Month

"K: Keep: Decision-by-narrative with a trade-off sentence.
This binds choices to purpose and names the consequence. Maria will add a one-line trade-off and a one-line result, what changed in money, time, or rule, to every Tier-1 preread." She continued.

"I: Improve: Say-do ledger, one page, monthly.
We list public promises alongside results: budget moved, rule changed, and one near-term consequence we accept. John will publish, Yuki will co-own personnel impacts, and Liam will co-own customer impacts." She turned to Sanjay.

"S: Start: Walk-away rule.
We codify three conditions under which we will decline revenue or delay a launch because it violates the North Star or Trust guardrails. We publish one live example this month. Sanjay will draft with Legal, I will take it to the Board for ratification, and Comms will publish." Finally she said,

"S: Stop: Optics without ownership.
We retire purpose paragraphs unless they are paired with a named owner and a concrete result line in the same document. Liam will update templates. I reserve the right to strike performative slides in the room."

Chris closed her notebook. "We will measure authenticity in verbs: reallocation, refusal, repair, and ritual.

CEO's Notebook: Authenticity

Rain freckled the Liffey, and the streets shone like slate as Chris left the center and walked toward her hotel. The day's images wouldn't let go: a caregiver reading to residents with a tenderness no dashboard could see; a nurses' station ruled by metrics that missed the marrow; a small singing circle born from the Presence Council that changed the temperature of a whole ward.

Authenticity is congruence, she wrote. Apathy is the gap between what we say, what we do, and what we honor. If Omnivista rewarded only what was easy to count, it would hollow itself out. If it chose to notice and celebrate the human, energy would return on its own.

She opened her notebook. "This month is Authenticity," she wrote, "the discipline of alignment." Then she set her daily practices.

Actions

1. Name one congruence daily. Point to a moment where words, actions, and recognition match and make it visible.

2. Close one gap daily. Change a rule, meeting, metric, or message so it reflects what we truly value.

3. Carry one story daily. Share a lived example (from staff, patients, or clients) that re-anchors purpose in the real.

What I'll Notice

1. *Industrial* (Authority): polish over truth; obedience praised while reality is ignored.

2. *Information* (Analytics): campaigns and dashboards substituting for meaning; performance theater.

3. *Irrelevance* (Apathy): people go quiet; effort goes through the motions; promises unkept.

4. **Ingenuity** (Authenticity): say-do alignment; results (money/time) mirror values; lived stories steer choices.

5. **Imagination** (Awe): the organization's presence enlarges people, inside and beyond the firm, because purpose and practice are one.

Chris closed the notebook and watched the river take the city's lights downstream. At month's end, she would stand before the Board not with slogans, but with the results of alignment, we can see gaps closed, stories honored, and rules changed. Tonight, one resolve: make what we value legible in how we spend, schedule, and speak every single day.

My Fingerprint

One of the highest-paid CEOs I have ever worked with opened our first session by saying: "I don't believe in coaching."

I said: "That's fine with me. I'd love to hear about your career instead as I would think you have a lot to teach me and the people who work for you."

He talked for two hours. I said almost nothing. I did not challenge, reframe, or redirect. I listened. And somewhere in the second hour, something shifted. He was no longer performing the role of CEO explaining his career to a coach. He was hearing his own story for the first time, not the polished version he told at conferences, but the actual human arc of the thing: the compromises, the costs, the moments when he was not sure he had made the right choice, and the handful of times when he knew, without question, that he had.

At the end, he sat quietly for a long time. Then he said: "I have never heard my own voice before."

That is what authenticity sounds like when it arrives. Not a declaration. Not a values statement. Not a performance of vulnerability. It is the moment when the mask comes off, not because someone demanded it, but because the room was safe enough and the witness was steady enough for the person to stop pretending.

Many of the best coaching sessions I have ever had were the ones where I said almost nothing. Authenticity does not need to be taught. It needs to be uncovered. And it can only be uncovered in the presence of someone who is willing to see the real person, not the persona, and to stay with what they find.

Authenticity: Through Six Lenses

As with the previous choices, we examine Authenticity through the same six lenses: history, etymology, philosophy, neuroscience, artificial intelligence, and real world examples.

History and what could evolve

Industrial Age

Authenticity receded under Authority, and wisdom was presumed to reside at the top. Titles, policy, and the clock created predictability. Still, they also taught compliance over conscience: "per policy" replaced principle, and people followed orders even when the room knew a promise wouldn't be kept. Timekeeping became a measure of virtue, so presence was mistaken for value, and risk-raising was equated with insubordination. Speak-up channels existed, but they rarely closed the loop, pushing near-misses underground and breeding quiet cynicism. Two valuable lessons from this era endure: uniform rules can prevent favoritism, but without a safe way to surface exceptions, they manufacture moral injury; and moments of "work-to-rule" reveal how much integrity work happens in the seams that policies don't see.

Information Age

Authenticity was outsourced to Analytics. Dashboards and "OKRs" (Objectives and Results) made performance legible and sharable; yet, the map began to replace the terrain. Definitions bent to keep charts green, and the phrase "what gets measured gets managed" slid into "what is managed is whatever keeps the metric happy." Teams learned to focus on the indicator, not the outcome, while cross-team fairness and repair issues remained off-screen. Meetings deferred to "the score" even when the score didn't fit the moment, a daily case of the familiar pattern of what gets measured gets managed, and what gets managed drifts from its original meaning. Two additional insights are helpful here: pair every KPI with its original intent and a steward who restores meaning when it drifts; and ask in reviews, "What would change our minds?" so that numbers inform judgment rather than replace it.

Irrelevance Age

The gap between words and results widens into Apathy, being disengagement and performance theater. Promises multiply, definitions drift toward green, and people conserve energy by doing the visible thing instead of the right thing. Surveillance chills initiative, blame rituals follow incidents, and truth retreats to backchannels; work looks busy while belief evacuates. Talented people protect their integrity by disengaging or leaving, and the organization becomes exquisitely measured yet conspicuously undecided. The deeper risk isn't just productivity loss; it's ethics drift: when no one expects congruence, small compromises accumulate into reputational debt that compounds in public.

Ingenuity Age

Authenticity is engineered as congruence under pressure. Trade-offs are named out loud; Tier 1 decisions carry a one-line "why" and a stated confidence; walk-away rules for sales, safety, and claims are codified and used. A visible Say–Do Ledger tracks commitments to outcomes (money, time, rules, words) so quarterly updates show repairs and results, not just rhetoric. Model cards and assurance notes outline purpose, limitations, appeal paths, and a 72-hour repair rule; apologies are accompanied by before-and-after fixes in daylight. Two practical reinforcements keep the system honest: a quarterly "promises audit" that eliminates carryover claims, and a meeting norm to strike any purpose paragraph without an owner and a corresponding change in the plan.

Imaginative Possibility

Authenticity matures into Awe, Organizations co-create standards with customers, communities, and regulators; they rehearse potential harms before launch, publish public ledgers of material trade-offs, and narrate costs as part of their purpose. What we choose to give up to protect what matters. Independent review boards and community witness circles test whether the firm is the same in the dark as on the slide. AI is used not to polish optics but to simulate second-order effects and the surface that bears the downside of our choices. Two forward-leaning practices anchor this stance: building values into product architecture (defaults, data minimization, reversibility), and pricing externalities intentionally so that growth and guardianship remain in the same sentence.

Etymology

Authenticity comes from the Greek *authentēs*: "one who acts on one's own authority," from autos ("self") and *hentes* ("doer"). Its essence is integrity of action, alignment between inner conviction and outward expression. In leadership, authenticity is not mere self-disclosure; it is coherence. The authentic leader speaks from principle and behaves as if seen, even when no one is watching.

Apathy also traces to Greek, *apatheia*, from a ("without") and pathos ("feeling, suffering"). Initially, it meant serenity, freedom from destructive emotion. Over time, it slid into its modern shadow: indifference, disengagement, the refusal to care. In leadership, apathy wears the mask of professionalism, meetings that remain polite while passion drains away.

This is the contest at the heart of presence today: Authenticity as inner alignment that invites connection versus Apathy as emotional withdrawal that corrodes it.

Philosophy

Across centuries, thinkers have argued that authenticity is alignment of word, deed, and purpose, apathy is the refusal to care and the habit of hiding.

Friedrich Nietzsche: "What does your conscience say? You shall become the one you are."

Define the few things only you can do; design roles and goals so people can actually become that in the work.

Søren Kierkegaard: "The crowd is untruth."

Replace performative consensus with owned judgment: name your stance, your reasons, and what would change your mind.

Jean-Paul Sartre: "Man is condemned to be free."

Freedom means authorship; leaders demonstrate authorship by making timely choices, acknowledging trade-offs, and accepting consequences.

Albert Camus: "I rebel, therefore we exist."

Rebellion at work is principled care: refuse cynicism, surface contradictions, and make minor, concrete fixes daily.

Martin Heidegger: *Everyone is the other, and no one is himself.*

Don't outsource identity to the org chart; set a few non-negotiables and live them under pressure.

Charles Taylor: "*Authenticity is not opposed to horizons of significance but requires them.*"

Tie goals to something larger than self: mission and client service, so sincerity matures into responsibility.

Viktor Frankl: "*Everything can be taken from a man but one thing: the last of the human freedoms, to choose one's attitude.*"

Build that space: pause, label the feeling, pick the response.

Diogenes: "*He lit a lamp in broad daylight and said, as he went about, 'I am looking for a man.'*"

Make candor normal: short demos, unvarnished metrics, and praise for admitting "I don't know."

Epictetus: "*Don't explain your philosophy. Embody it.*"

Replace value posters with value proofs: hiring choices, calendar time, and budget lines that match the talk.

Henry David Thoreau: "*The mass of men lead lives of quiet desperation.*"

Apathy often equates to misfit; offer experiments, rotations, and exits with dignity.

José Ortega y Gasset: "*I am myself and my circumstance.*"

Help people read their circumstance in context briefs and stakeholder maps, so identity meets reality, not fantasy.

James Baldwin: "*Not everything that is faced can be changed, but nothing can be changed until it is faced.*"

Schedule the facing: regular retros, customer listening, and naming the hard part first.

Rollo May: *"The opposite of courage in our society is not cowardice, it is conformity."*

Reward principled dissent; make "explain the no" as honorable as "sell the yes."

Our philosophers show us that authenticity is not oversharing; it is consistent, accountable integrity aimed at a worthy end. Apathy is the opposite: low-heat conformity, delayed decisions, and care withheld when it's most needed.

Neuroscience

Authenticity and Apathy are not just metaphors; they are neurobiological states. Modern neuroscience reveals that the brain's rhythms, chemicals, and networks determine whether people act in alignment with values and feel energized by meaning, or whether they numb out and go through the motions: disengagement disguised as professionalism.

Self-discrepancy and the "optics tax"

When our public story diverges from our private conviction, the anterior cingulate cortex flags conflict; effort shifts to impression management, draining bandwidth for real work. Leaders who close one say–do gap per day reduce that chronic conflict load and its fatigue spiral.

Interoception as an integrity alarm

The insula's readout of bodily signals (tight chest, hollow gut, heat) often precedes conscious recognition of a values collision. Naming the signal in the room: "my body is telling me this clause breaks our rule," reduces rumination and speeds a congruent decision.

Dopamine and visible results

Anticipation pathways don't just reward outcomes; they reward meaningful progress. When teams see a promise fulfilled, such as a budget being moved or a rule being changed, motivation rises. When they see the optics, dopamine levels drop; apathy follows.

Oxytocin, witness, and social proof

Public recognition of congruent acts (a logged walk-away; an apology with repair) raises trust chemistry and normalizes candor. "Witness circles" make integrity contagious by transforming it into a shared memory, rather than a private virtue.

Predictive processing and definition drift
Brains are prediction machines; when a KPI's definition quietly changes, people detect the mismatch and update their model: "green doesn't mean good." Restoring original definitions and publishing the change log repairs the predictive map and belief.

Synchrony through ritual
Short, repeated moves such as trade-off sentence, result line, walk-away rules read aloud, create physiological synchrony. Teams align faster because the pattern reduces ambiguity about what "good" looks like.

Awe and self-transcendence
Encounters with vastness (in nature, art, or service) expand associative networks and reduce self-focus, making it easier to choose long-term stewardship over short-term optics. Your "Awe" end-state is a neurobiological ally of authenticity.

Sleep and consolidation of congruence
After making hard, value-laden choices, sleep consolidates new norms and scripts. Leaders who "sleep on" the final commit of irreversible calls make fewer moral framing errors and explain the choice more clearly the next day, repeating the Intuition practice in a values key.

Strengthening Authenticity by Applying Neuroscience Every Day
Authenticity is a system, not a sentiment. Congruence under pressure reduces the optics tax (the mental load of saying one thing and doing another), restores motivation when people see real results, and makes integrity the easiest way to belong. Design the biology (speak plainly), the artifacts (Say–Do Ledger, trade-off sentences, walk-away registry, KPI change log), and the rituals (quiet windows, witness circles) so that words and results stay aligned. When they diverge, apathy compounds; when they align in public, Awe becomes possible.

Here are some exercises that take the neuroscientific insights into the day:

- Begin high-stakes meetings with a 60–120 second quiet window, then ask one framing question: "What will be different tomorrow if we approve this?"

- Write the one-line trade-off: "We choose X over Y because Z," and keep it in the record.

- Add a "result line" to every decision: name exactly what changed in money, time, rule, or wording and one consequence you accept.

- Publish a monthly Say–Do Ledger that maps public promises to results, with links to budgets, calendars, and rule changes.

- Restore honest KPIs: maintain original definitions, display any past drift in a visible change log, and accept an amber status while addressing the underlying issues.

- Codify and use walk-away rules; log each refusal and the principled alternative you offered to the customer/partner.

- Ban purpose paragraphs without results: update templates so values appear only alongside owners and concrete changes.

- Hold a 20-minute "witness circle" each month where a team narrates a congruence cost and what it protected; invite someone from the boundary to speak first.

- Align contracts and model cards with the same plain-language consent and appeal paths: no sales promises that out-run your limits.

- Put congruence on the calendar: schedule a weekly "one gap, one change" block where leaders move a budget line, diary slot, or rule to match a promise; capture the before/after in the ledger.

- Extend decision journals: record the trade-off, the result, and for any exception you're taking, record why it's temporary and when you'll reconcile it.

- Sleep on irreversible, values-heavy calls; reconvene with a short recap before final commit.

Artificial Intelligence

We can now see the leadership choice between Authenticity and Apathy in the light of AI-fueled choices.

Plain Language versus Corporateese Autopilot

AI can help leaders speak in clear, first-person terms about what is changing, why it matters, and how people can respond. Used this way, assistants strip jargon and make ownership visible. Apathy emerges when leaders outsource tone to boilerplate generators, flooding channels with safe, vague copy that conveys little and means less.

Listening-Action Loops versus Sentiment Harvesting

Authentic teams turn AI "listening" into action: agents cluster questions, route them to owners, and close the loop with concrete updates ("you said → we did"). Apathy harvests sentiment for dashboards, but never responds, turning people's voices into a spectacle with no consequence.

Data with Dignity versus Indifferent Collection

Authenticity names the data in use, the purpose, and the opt-outs; it minimizes collection, honors context, and publishes provenance. Apathy scrapes "because we can," relies on shadow datasets, and treats consent as paperwork rather than a promise.

Moment-of-Truth Escalation versus Notification Theater

AI can identify "moments that matter," such as a safety incident, a pay error, or an ethics complaint. Ai can then escalate them to a human with the authority to resolve and follow up. That is care. Apathy sends generic alerts, auto-closes tickets, and misdirects notifications to leadership.

Co-Creation Copilots versus Delegated Humanity

Authenticity uses AI to convene employees, customers, and partners, drafting policies, testing prompts, and reviewing impacts before launch. Apathy delegates apologies, appreciation, and accountability to bots, then calls it transformation.

Amplifying Authenticity by Deploying AI Every Day

AI is not neutral in the authenticity versus apathy choice. It can make care legible through plain language, visible follow-through, respectful data practices, real escalation, and shared creation. Or it can numb an organization with polished noise and automated indifference. Leaders can build these into daily practice:

- Use AI to strip jargon from leadership communications so messages arrive in plain, first-person language with visible ownership.

- Wire listening tools to action loops: every "you said" must generate a "we did" within a stated timeframe, not a dashboard summary that goes nowhere.

- Minimize data collection to what is needed, name its purpose, and publish opt-out paths. Treat consent as a promise, not paperwork.

- Route moments that matter, safety incidents, pay errors, ethics complaints, to a human with authority to resolve, not to an auto-close queue.

- Use AI to co-create policies and review impacts with employees, customers, and partners before launch, not after backlash.

- Label what is human and what is automated in every interaction. Never delegate apologies, appreciation, or accountability to a bot.

- Deploy AI to track say-do alignment: promises logged, outcomes recorded, gaps surfaced automatically for leadership review.

- Use congruence scoring to flag when campaign language diverges from operational reality, and route the mismatch to an owner within a week.

If AI increases polish but decreases honesty, you do not have authenticity. You have faster apathy.

Authenticity Real World Examples

REI: #OptOutside

- **What they did.** REI closed all stores on Black Friday 2015, the biggest retail day of the year, and paid employees to spend the day outdoors. The campaign invited customers to join them.

- **Why this matters.** The decision was congruent with REI's identity as an outdoor co-op. It cost real revenue. It was not a marketing stunt bolted onto business as usual. It was a business decision that expressed values at the point of highest commercial pressure.

- **Consequences.** Membership grew. Brand loyalty strengthened. The campaign became annual. REI proved that authenticity under pressure, choosing substance when optics would have been easier, compounds over time.

CVS Health: Tobacco Removal

- **What they did.** In 2014, CVS removed all tobacco products from its stores, forgoing an estimated two billion dollars in annual revenue. The company renamed itself CVS Health to signal the shift.

- **Why this matters.** A pharmacy selling cigarettes was a say-do gap visible to every customer who walked through the door. Removing tobacco closed the gap at significant financial cost. The decision was irreversible and public.

- **Consequences.** CVS gained credibility with healthcare partners, insurers, and regulators. Prescriptions and clinic visits grew. The company proved that closing an authenticity gap, even an expensive one, can reposition an entire enterprise.

Merck: Ivermectin Donation

- **What they did.** Merck developed ivermectin to treat river blindness and then committed to donating it free of charge to anyone who needed it, for as long as needed. The program has continued for decades.

- **Why this matters.** The decision prioritized human health over shareholder return on a specific product. It was not a short-term campaign. It was an open-ended commitment that tested whether a pharmaceutical company's stated purpose could survive contact with its balance sheet.

- **Consequences.** River blindness has been virtually eliminated in several countries. Merck's reputation among global health organizations remains among the strongest in the industry. Purpose held because the commitment was unconditional.

Airbnb: COVID-19 Layoffs

- **What they did.** In May 2020, CEO Brian Chesky laid off 25 percent of the workforce. He published a letter explaining the reasoning, the severance terms, and his personal responsibility for the decision. Departing employees kept company laptops, received extended healthcare, and were supported by a public alumni talent directory.

- **Why this matters.** Layoffs are the hardest test of authenticity. Chesky did not hide behind a press release or delegate the message. He named the pain, took ownership, and designed the departure to honor the people leaving.

- **Consequences.** Airbnb's reputation with talent strengthened during a period when most companies lost trust. The alumni directory generated goodwill across the industry. The letter became a case study in how to lead through loss with congruence.

Apathy: Real World Examples

Purdue Pharma: OxyContin

- **What they did.** The Sackler family aggressively marketed OxyContin while downplaying its addictive properties. Internal documents showed the company knew the risks. Public messaging contradicted private knowledge for years.

- **Why this matters.** This is authenticity's inverse: a say-do gap maintained deliberately, at industrial scale, with catastrophic human consequences. The gap between the company's public health claims and its private knowledge was not an oversight. It was a strategy.

- **Consequences.** Hundreds of thousands of deaths from opioid addiction. Purdue filed for bankruptcy. The Sackler name was removed from museums and institutions worldwide. The case remains the clearest modern example of what happens when an organization chooses optics over truth as a sustained practice.

Facebook: Cambridge Analytica

- **What they did.** Facebook allowed Cambridge Analytica to harvest data from millions of users without meaningful consent. When exposed, the company's initial response minimized the breach and deflected responsibility.

- **Why this matters.** Facebook's stated mission was to connect people. The data harvesting revealed that the business model treated people as products. The gap between the mission statement and the revenue model was the authenticity failure.

- **Consequences.** A five billion dollar FTC fine. Congressional hearings. Lasting erosion of public trust. The company rebranded as Meta, but the credibility gap persists. The case shows that when the business model contradicts the stated purpose, no rebrand can restore authenticity.

Pepsi: Kendall Jenner Advertisement

- **What they did.** In 2017, Pepsi released an advertisement showing Kendall Jenner handing a can of Pepsi to a police officer during a protest, implying that a soft drink could bridge social divisions.

- **Why this matters.** The advertisement appropriated the imagery of real social justice movements for commercial purposes. It was optics without ownership: borrowing the language of authenticity without any genuine commitment to the cause.

- **Consequences.** Immediate public backlash. The advertisement was pulled within twenty-four hours. Pepsi apologized. The case became a textbook example of what happens when a brand performs values it has not earned.

Wirecard: Fabricated Revenue

- **What they did.** Wirecard, a German fintech company, fabricated revenue and inflated its balance sheet by billions of euros over several years. Auditors, regulators, and investors were misled systematically.

- **Why this matters.** This was not a gap between stated values and behavior. It was the complete absence of authenticity: a company whose public identity was entirely fictional. The external narrative bore no relationship to the internal reality.

- **Consequences.** Wirecard collapsed in 2020. Its CEO was arrested. Nineteen billion euros in market value evaporated. The case demonstrates the terminal consequence of apathy toward truth: when the gap between what you say and what you are becomes total, the organization ceases to exist.

Authenticity: Bringing the Lenses Together

Authenticity is not self-disclosure. It is congruence under pressure: the alignment of word, deed, and purpose when the easier path would be optics.

- *History* traces the drift: the Industrial Age replaced conscience with compliance and mistook presence for value, the Information Age outsourced integrity to analytics until definitions bent to keep charts green, and the Irrelevance Age widens the gap between words and results until talented people protect their integrity by disengaging or leaving.

- *Etymology* sharpens the stakes: authentēs means one who acts on their own authority, a doer whose inner conviction and outward expression are the same thing, while apatheia began as serenity and darkened into the indifference that wears professionalism as a mask while passion drains away.

- *Philosophy* maps what congruence demands: Nietzsche urged us to become who we are, Kierkegaard warned that the crowd is untruth, Sartre insisted that freedom means authorship of choices and their consequences, Camus defined rebellion as principled care that refuses cynicism, Heidegger contrasted the they-self with resolute selfhood, Taylor argued that authenticity requires horizons of significance larger than the self, Frankl proved that the freedom to choose one's attitude survives even when everything else is taken, Diogenes walked with a lantern looking for one honest person, and Baldwin reminded us that nothing can be changed until it is faced.

- *Neuroscience* confirms that authenticity and apathy are biological states: when the public story diverges from private conviction the anterior cingulate cortex flags conflict and drains bandwidth into impression management, interoceptive signals from the body sound an integrity alarm before conscious thought catches up, dopamine rewards visible results but withdraws when people see only optics, oxytocin rises when congruent acts are witnessed in public making integrity contagious, and when KPI definitions quietly drift the brain detects the mismatch and updates its model to "green doesn't mean good."

- *AI amplifies* whichever pattern it finds: it can strip jargon so messages arrive in plain language with visible ownership, wire listening tools to action loops so every concern generates a concrete response, route moments that matter to humans with authority to resolve them, and track say-do alignment automatically, or it can flood channels with polished noise, harvest sentiment for dashboards that never produce a reply, delegate apologies to bots, and increase polish while decreasing honesty.

- **And the real-world evidence** draws the line without ambiguity: REI proved that choosing substance over optics at the point of highest commercial pressure compounds loyalty, CVS proved that closing a say-do gap at two billion dollars in cost can reposition an entire enterprise, Merck proved that unconditional commitment outlasts any campaign, and Airbnb proved that naming the pain with ownership and care can strengthen trust even in a layoff, while Purdue Pharma proved that a say-do gap maintained deliberately at industrial scale costs hundreds of thousands of lives, Facebook proved that when the business model contradicts the mission no rebrand restores credibility, Pepsi proved that performing values you have not earned collapses in hours, and Wirecard proved that when the gap between what you say and what you are becomes total the organization ceases to exist.

- **The practical test is human** to everyone: can your people point to the last promise that was kept, the last walk-away that was honored, the last apology that arrived with a fix? Authenticity lives in those moments. Apathy lives in the silence where they should be.

29 June — **TOKYO**

End of Month: Executive Team Review

The executive team convened in Tokyo. Each leader reported back on their Dublin assignments, bringing results.

Maria (COO): Keep → Decision results in prereads

- **What she did**: added a one-line trade-off and a one-line result (money, time, or rule change) to every Tier-1 preread.

- **What changed**: meetings moved faster; two performative slides were met with immediate criticism; owners came prepared to demonstrate the change.

- **Proof points:** three prereads with result lines; cycle time down across two decisions.

John (CFO): Improve → The Say-Do Ledger

- **What he did:** published the monthly ledger with links to budget shifts and executive diary moves.

- **What changed**: two teams proactively reallocated time to match promises; finance debates improved in quality and brevity.

- **Proof points:** ledger page, calendar screenshots, and before-and-after spend pie charts.

Yuki (CPO): Improve → Congruence coaching and recognition

- **What she did**: ran clinics on writing trade-off sentences and turning values into results; added "congruence moments" to recognition.

- **What changed**: more managers narrated tough calls in plain language; two people were recognized for pausing work to honor model limits.

- **Proof points:** clinic deck, recognition notes, and eNPS verbatims citing "we mean it this time."

Sanjay (CTO): Start → Walk-away registry and guardrails

- **What he did:** codified three walk-away rules, logged one live refusal, and captured a principled alternative path; encoded the rules into deal review checklists.

- **What changed**: engineers reported "less stomach-ache work"; sales began socializing the rules with clients early.

- **Proof points:** registry entry; deal review artifact; client's revised term sheet.

Liam (CMO): Stop → Optics ban and Awe notes

- **What he did:** removed "purpose paragraphs" from templates unless paired with results; launched a monthly Awe note showcasing one stewardship act and its real cost.

- **What changed**: thinner decks, thicker decisions; community engagement messages now include what we gave up.

- **Proof points:** new template; two Awe notes; engagement metrics steady with higher credibility.

Chris closed the morning. "We set out to prove we're the same organization in the dark as on the slide. This month says yes, imperfectly, publicly, on purpose. Authenticity is now a practice we can lift."

What If

That afternoon, Chris led the team out of Omnivista's Shinjuku tower and into the grounds of Meiji Jingu. The humidity hung heavy beneath the canopy of camphor trees, and cicadas had begun their summer chorus. They settled near a wooden bench beside the iris garden, where the last of the season's purple blooms edged the still water.

"This is the place for Authenticity," Chris said. "The Boardroom rewards polish, but out here you can see the real: mismatched, alive, unfiltered. Apathy occurs when our actions and words no longer align, causing us to lose interest and care.

Authenticity is choosing congruence, even when it costs. Let's stretch our thinking. What if Omnivista designed for authenticity at every level, and refused to let apathy take root?"

She let the silence hold, then said: "What if?"

1. What if every strategy update had to include one cost of integrity, where we lost something by staying true to our values?

2. What if leaders were required to retire one message for every new one added, so clarity always outweighed spin?

3. What if every new hire asked their manager, "When did you last walk away from easy money because it didn't fit our values?"

4. What if bonuses could be cut for promises broken, not just raised for promises kept?

5. What if a quarterly "congruence audit" tracked whether what we said in campaigns matched what clients and staff actually experienced?

6. What if any employee could call an "authenticity check" when words and actions diverged and leadership had to respond within a week?

7. What if we measured courage by stories of trade-offs made visible, not just by outcomes delivered?

8. What if the CEO had to publish one personal learning mistake, along with the corresponding lesson learned, each quarter?

9. What if every board meeting began with a story from the edge, where values were tested, rather than a metric?

10. What if apathy were logged as system debt, with repayment plans similar to those for financial debt?

30 June — **TOKYO**

End of Month: Board Review

Chris opened with quiet steadiness. "Four weeks ago, Liam led us in a discussion on Authenticity versus Apathy at the Liffey Aged Care Centre. We asked a simple but unsettling question: do our words, actions, and results align, or do we let the gap widen until apathy takes root? This month, we tested congruence in real places where patients, employees, and families could feel the difference."

She described how the team began with presence. Residents' voices had long been filtered through surveys or surfaced only after complaints. The team established a Presence Council comprising two caregivers, one family member, and one resident. Together they logged decisions, acted on them, and met weekly to review progress. One resident's story led directly to daily singing circles; satisfaction scores rose by fourteen points, and staff absenteeism fell by seven percent.

The subsequent intervention examined alignment. Many campaigns, Chris noted, were running parallel to daily operations with polished slogans while realities contradicted them. Quarterly congruence audits were introduced to verify whether messaging, KPIs, and lived experiences aligned. One misaligned campaign was quietly retired. "When the words finally matched reality," she said, "you could feel the collective exhale."

They then moved to decision-making. Leaders were asked to narrate one visible trade-off each month, an instance where convenience was chosen over values. Three stories were documented, including a pricing decision that favored fairness over margin. "We stopped treating values as posters," she said. "We started treating them as verbs."

Say–do logs were followed. Promises were no longer left in emails or meeting notes; instead, they were published monthly, showing commitments, outcomes, and pivots. Ninety-two percent of promised items were tracked; three pivots were explained openly. Trust in leadership rose ten points. "It wasn't about perfection," Chris said. "It was about visibility."

Finally, they piloted authenticity checks. Staff could log any misalignment between organizational actions and stated values, requiring a response within thirty days.

Four were logged; two resulted in system changes. Pulse results rose eight points on the statement, *I believe leaders mean what they say.*

Chris reflected, "Apathy is irrelevance when slogans drift, promises evaporate, and silence replaces voice. Authenticity is ingenuity when the say–do gap closes, trade-offs are visible, and real stories steer choices. We now have proof that authenticity can be made legible in practice, not just sentiment."

She closed with four guardrails.

1. Say–do results: every commitment must show evidence or a pivot.
2. Retire before adding: no new message without retiring one old one.
3. Trade-offs named: values must be visible in decisions, not just implied.
4. Voices heard: Presence Councils and authenticity checks must receive a response within thirty days.

"These," she said, "are how we prevent drift into apathy. They are the daily scaffolds of congruence."

A director leaned forward. "Can authenticity really scale?" he asked. "Isn't it always personal?"

Chris answered, "It is personal, but it becomes systemic when the organization insists on results: congruence audits, say–do logs, presence councils, trade-off stories. When the system demands honesty, authenticity stops being optional."

CEO's Reflection, That Evening

That night, Chris walked through Shinjuku's neon corridors, the summer air sharp against the glow of a thousand screens. The day's board meeting still pressed in, directors debating whether authenticity could scale or whether it was just personal conviction, not something an organization could engineer. She replayed her answer in her mind: results close the gap. Congruence audits, say–do logs, trade-off stories, and presence councils. Small practices, visible proof. Together, they transformed authenticity from a sentiment into a system.

She turned into Shinjuku Gyoen, closed for the evening but visible through the iron railings, its summer trees lit faintly by the city beyond. Part II had led them through the five VISTA choices: Vision, Intuition, Synergy, Trust, and Authenticity. Tomorrow they would begin Part III, turning those choices into organizational culture through the six ORG6 levers: Talent, Structure, Operations, CEO Stewardship, Leadership Everywhere, and Engaged Hearts, Minds & Bodies.

Authenticity: Exercises for You to Try

Authenticity only matters when it moves beyond personal conviction and becomes visible in how an organization spends, speaks, and decides. Slogans fade; values posters age; even the most heartfelt leadership speeches vanish if not embodied in results. What endures is the discipline of congruence: matching words to actions, promises to outcomes, and purpose to budget lines.

Leaders who cultivate Authenticity treat it as say-do alignment under pressure. It appears in the trade-off sentence that names what was sacrificed, in the say-do ledger that tracks promises against results, in the walk-away decision that refuses revenue because it violates the North Star, and in the congruence audit that catches drift before it compounds. Authenticity is fragile as intention; it becomes powerful as practice.

To make Authenticity more than aspiration, try this seven-day practice plan. Each element is simple in form but cumulative in effect. Done together, they retrain an organization to close the gap between what it says and what it does.

> Day 1: Trade-off sentence. For every Tier-1 decision, write one line: "We chose X over Y because Z." If you cannot write the sentence, the decision is not yet authentic; it is still performing.
>
> Day 2: Say-do check. Pick one promise made in the last quarter. Find the evidence: did money move, did a rule change, did time shift? If not, name the gap and assign a correction
>
> .
>
> Day 3: Walk-away log. Identify one opportunity, deal, or initiative that conflicts with the North Star or trust guardrails. Decline it, log the refusal, and record the principled alternative you offered.
>
> Day 4: Congruence audit. Take one campaign, message, or KPI and test

it against lived experience. Ask three frontline people: does this match what you see? If not, retire or revise it this week.

Day 5: Retire before adding. Before publishing any new message, commitment, or initiative, retire one that is no longer being fulfilled. Clarity always outweighs volume.

Day 6: Result line. For every decision logged this week, add one sentence: what changed in money, time, rule, or wording, and one consequence you accept. Post it where people can see it.

Day 7: Promise review. Publish a one-page summary of this week's commitments alongside their status: kept, pivoted, or outstanding. Note the reason for any pivot. This is the seed of your say-do ledger.

None of these practices is complicated. They require no new software and little budget, only the leader's choice to match words with results, close gaps in daylight, and refuse to let purpose drift into performance. Authenticity, in use, is how an organization proves it is the same in the dark as on the slide.

Self-Assessment: Authenticity versus Apathy

Rate yourself honestly. For each question, score both the Foundation and the AI Amplifier.
1 Not Yet · 2 Emerging · 3 Developing · 4 Practicing · 5 Second Nature

---

1.

Foundation. My behavior under pressure matches my stated values. I lead as who I am.
   Foundation score (1–5):_____

AI Amplifier. I am transparent about how AI is being used in my domain, including its limitations and risks.
   AI Amplifier score (1–5):_____

2.

Foundation. I choose substance over optics, even when the optics path would be easier.
   Foundation score (1–5):_____

AI Amplifier. I use AI to deepen real insight rather than to produce poli shed surfaces that mask shallow thinking.
   AI Amplifier score (1–5):_____

3.

Foundation. I bring genuine energy and care to my work rather than going through the motions.
   Foundation score (1–5):_____

AI Amplifier. I use AI to remove drudgery so I can invest my human energy where it matters most.
   AI Amplifier score (1–5):_____

4.

Foundation. I am honest about what I don't know and what isn't working.

　　Foundation score (1–5):_____

AI Amplifier. I use AI to surface uncomfortable truths: data that challenges our narrative, not just confirms it.

　　AI Amplifier score (1–5):_____

5.

Foundation. My team would say there is no gap between what I say and what I do.

　　Foundation score (1–5):_____

AI Amplifier. Our AI deployment reflects our values. We use it to amplify what we believe in, not just what is efficient.

　　AI Amplifier score (1–5):_____

AVERAGE SCORE: Authenticity versus Apathy

Foundation average (total of five scores ÷ 5):_____

AI Amplifier average (total of five scores ÷ 5):_____

Now: Transfer these two averages to the "A" row of your VISTA Scoreboard at the back of the book.

PART III

The ORG6 Model
A Roadmap for Doing

Learning the six culture levers that turn intention into momentum and make transformation practical.

Part III, ORG6™
The Six Levers of Culture

1 July — TOKYO

On the first of July, Chris introduced the next part of the year. "If VISTA is a compass for how leaders choose, ORG6 is the blueprint for how organizations build. Over the last six months, we have seen how the old Industrial and Information Age playbooks no longer work, and the arrival of AI challenges us with a choice between Irrelevance and Ingenuity.

"ORG6 is a set of practical domains every leader must act on immediately. Each lever can corrode if left to old reflexes. Each can become a multiplier of ingenuity if redesigned wisely. Together, they translate purpose, values, and strategy into the lived experience of people and into the organization's performance.

"ORG6 comprises six levers of culture, the engine and transmission that convert purpose, values, and strategy into organizational performance.

1. **"Talent**: how we attract, enable, develop, and reward people.
2. **Structure**: how authority and collaboration are designed.
3. **Operations**: how systems and tools shape daily work.
4. **CEO Stewardship:** clarity, narrative, and pace.
5. **Leadership Everywhere:** A daily behavioral practice, not a title.
6. **Engaged Hearts, Minds & Bodies**: passion, belonging, and well-being.

"These six levers will shape the rest of the year ahead. Pull these levers well, and AI becomes a partner in human ingenuity. Neglect them, and AI becomes an accelerant of irrelevance. First, we get the bones of the organization right. Then we breathe life into it."

Chris then provided the monthly assignments by giving the team a table that might offer them some initial ideas.

"We need to see each lever not just as it is, but as it has been, and as it could become," she said. "Every lever carries an inheritance. Every lever has a drift path. And every lever can be redesigned into something far stronger."

She began with *Talent*. "In the Industrial Age, people were treated as interchangeable labor: obedience prized, individuality erased. In the Information Age, we made progress, but often reduced people to knowledge processors, akin to HR systems that programmed more than they nurtured. If left to its own devices, AI will push us into surveillance, burnout, and bias on a massive scale. However, if we redesign it, AI can free humans from administrative tasks, allowing them to focus on growth, creativity, and trust. And if we dare go further, we create porous talent communities, multi-dimensional careers where AI and humans co-lead."

She shifted to *Structure*. "Once it was hierarchy, command-and-control. Then it became global matrices and dashboards, agile in name, rigid in practice. Drift, and we get stuck with frozen organizational charts and political fights over resources. But reimagine it, and we can create fluid, mission-led teams that rebalance quarterly. Push further, and structures become living networks, continuously reconfiguring around purpose."

On *Operations*, her tone hardened. "The Industrial inheritance was SOPs (Standard Operating Procedures), batch work, and time clocks. In the Information Age, we layered on Objectives and Key Results (OKRs), tool sprawl, and meeting overload. If we let AI handle that, we'll get compliance theater and endless context switching. But if we strip back, we can streamline: AI removing drudgery, meetings at a minimum, space for deep work. In the future, we could even tune operations to biological rhythms, with decision theaters guiding collective intelligence."

"*CEO Stewardship*. In the Industrial Age, CEOs commanded pace and messaging from the top. In the Information Age, they became narrators for investors, churning initiatives. Drift into irrelevance, and you get slogan cascades, pace whiplash, fear-driven urgency. But rebuild it, and the CEO becomes the chief listener, setting clarity, story, and rhythm that match the customer's time. Push to Imagination, and CEO presence becomes embodied purpose, shared with clients, communities, and teams alike."

"*Leadership Everywhere*. Once, leadership equaled title. Then it equaled expertise, the star system. Drift, and middle management becomes the squeezed blame layer. However, if leadership is redefined as behavior, coaching becomes the norm, and promotions are earned by growing others. Go further, and leadership becomes shared stewardship, with decisions shaped by advice and consent."

Finally, she pointed to *Engaged Hearts, Minds & Bodies*. "In the Industrial Age, loyalty was traded for wages; unions were the voice. In the Information Age, we painted over that with employer brands and annual surveys. Left unchecked, we'll experience cynicism, quiet quitting, and a culture of surveillance. But if we rebuild, well-being becomes an integral part of the infrastructure, recognition flows daily, and psychological safety is built in. Push further, and culture becomes regenerative, belonging measured, nurtured, renewed."

She capped the marker and looked back at the team.

"This is the roadmap. Every lever has its drift. Every lever has its ingenuity. And every lever can stretch beyond even what we imagine today. Over the next six months, we'll take them one by one. You will each carry a lever, starting with Yuki on Talent this month."

A note to the reader:

The chapters that follow take a different shape from Part II. VISTA explored five ways of being. Each choice was examined through history, etymology, philosophy, neuroscience, and AI to build the full picture of what it means to lead with ingenuity. ORG6 is about doing. Each lever is broken into its practical domains, the specific work that makes culture real, and each domain is traced through the same arc: what it looked like in the Industrial Age, how it shifted in the Information Age, where it drifts toward irrelevance, how it can be redesigned for ingenuity, and where imagination might take it further. The ages are the same; the lens is operational, not philosophical. History appears in how each practice evolved. AI appears in how each practice can be amplified or corroded. The difference is that ORG6 chapters are built for action: they give leaders the concrete domains to redesign, one lever at a time.

In the Talent chapter, readers will also find a section on the role that sits at the heart of all six levers: the Chief People Officer for the Ingenuity Age.

Where the VISTA chapters examined each choice through history, etymology, philosophy, neuroscience, and real-world examples, the ORG6 chapters are built for action. Each lever is broken into its practical domains, and each domain is traced through the same arc across the ages. The lens is operational rather than philosophical, and the question in every section is the same: what does this practice need to become?

The table overleaf shows how each lever maps across the five ages and names who carries it and when. As with the VISTA table, read each row as a journey: the Industrial and Information Age columns explain the reflex the organization is still running, the Irrelevance Age column names what happens when AI amplifies that reflex unchecked, and the Ingenuity and Imaginative Possibility columns describe what becomes available when leaders choose differently.

Part III
ORG6™
Monthly Assignments

	THE PAST		THE POTENTIAL		
	Industrial Age	Information Age	Irrelevance Age	Ingenuity Age	Imaginative Possibility
Talent Chapter 9 Yuki JULY	People as interchangeable labor; obedience prized	Knowledge workers as data processors; program-driven HR	Algorithmic surveillance; burnout; bias amplified	AI handles admin; humans focus on growth, creativity, trust	Porous talent communities; multi-dimensional careers; AI-human co-leadership
Structure Chapter 10 John AUGUST	Centralized hierarchy; command-and-control	Global matrices; dashboards; agility in name only	Frozen org charts; political resource allocation	Fluid, mission-led teams; quarterly rebalancing of resources	Structures as living networks that reconfigure continuously around purpose
Operations Chapter 11 Maria SEPTEMBER	SOPs, batch work, time clocks	OKRs, tool sprawl, meeting proliferation	Compliance theater; context-switching overload	Streamlined processes; meeting minimums; maker time; AI removes drudgery	AI-optimized operations; biological rhythms guide work; decision theaters
CEO Stewardship Chapter 12 Chris SEPTEMBER	Command authority; uniform pace; top-down messaging	Investor narrative; initiative churn	Slogan cascades; pace whiplash; fear-driven urgency	Clear story, steady pacing, customer time; CEO as chief listener	CEO presence spent with clients, teams, and communities; embodied purpose
Leadership Everywhere Chapter 13 Sanjay OCTOBER	Leadership equals title; chain of command	Leadership equals expertise; star systems	Middle management squeeze; blame culture	Leadership as behavior; coaching norms; promotion for growing others	Leadership is shared stewardship; decisions shaped by advice and consent
Engaged Hearts, Minds and Bodies Chapter 14 Liam NOVEMBER	Wages for loyalty; unions as primary voice	Employer brand; annual engagement surveys	Quiet quitting; cynicism; surveillance culture	Psychological safety; recognition; wellbeing as infrastructure	Belonging measured and nurtured continuously; culture as regenerative fabric

"Talent has never been more important to the success of a corporation. Talent, even more than strategy, is what creates value."

Ram Charan, Dominic Barton, and Dennis Carey

"Talent is the choreography of ingenuity. Without it, AI is just machinery multiplying our shadows."

Katharine McLennan

CHAPTER 9

Talent

Will we source, enable, develop, and reward people for compliance and past performance,
or
for capacity, judgment, and future contribution?

First Day of Month: Executive Team

That morning, the team gathered in a quiet conference room overlooking Shinjuku. No dashboards, no corporate decks. Just Yuki at the front, a whiteboard behind her, and four words written in black marker: *People are the strategy.*

Yuki began: "Talent is not headcount. It is not FTEs or a cost line. It is not 'human resources.' Talent is the lived promise of ingenuity: people as creators, not cogs. And under ultimatum conditions, talent is the only lever that compounds. If we neglect it, irrelevance multiplies at machine speed. If we invest in it, ingenuity scales beyond anything AI alone can deliver." Around the room, even John stopped shuffling his papers. Yuki had the floor, and the day was hers. She showed the four areas of talent she would facilitate:

SOURCING. She told the story of São Paulo, where a micro-mission had replaced CV screens. "We put candidates into real work, side by side with our engineers. They solved a thorny problem in two days, and their peers chose them as work partners again. That's ingenuity: talent chosen by contribution, not credentials." She let the pause hold before naming the shadow. "But in New York, our AI filter is auto-rejecting candidates with career breaks. We nearly missed a brilliant woman who had spent two years caring for her father. That's irrelevance: bias packaged as efficiency."

ENABLING. Her following example came from Tokyo. "Every new hire there now gets four touchpoints: a navigator for systems, a peer for technical skill learning, a sponsor for networks, and a guardian for purpose. Within a week, new employees are delivering real value and know who has their back. That's ingenuity: onboarding as community, not compliance." Then the counterweight: "But in Dublin, I met an engineer who whispered, 'I'm being monitored, not managed.' Our performance dashboards are logging midnight keystrokes. That's irrelevance: surveillance disguised as support."

DEVELOPING. She smiled at Sanjay as she spoke of Bangalore. "Friday 'What If' sprints have taken root. Last month, one sprint became a live product line, proof that curiosity can be a revenue stream. That's ingenuity: development as experimentation." Her tone sharpened as she turned to the shadow. "But across too many sites, people are drowning in compulsory e-learning modules. They're gaming dashboards for badges, not growing. That's irrelevance: the theater of upskilling."

REWARDING. Finally, she looked toward John in Sydney. "We piloted recognition for networked contribution: mentoring hours, cross-team rescues, and knowledge shared. Suddenly, a quiet analyst became visible as one of our most valuable connectors. That's ingenuity: rewards that honor the invisible glue." Then her voice dropped. "But at headquarters, bonus pools still reward noise over substance. Leaders tell me it pays to be loud rather than right. That's irrelevance: rewarding performance theater over real value."

The Talent Cycle

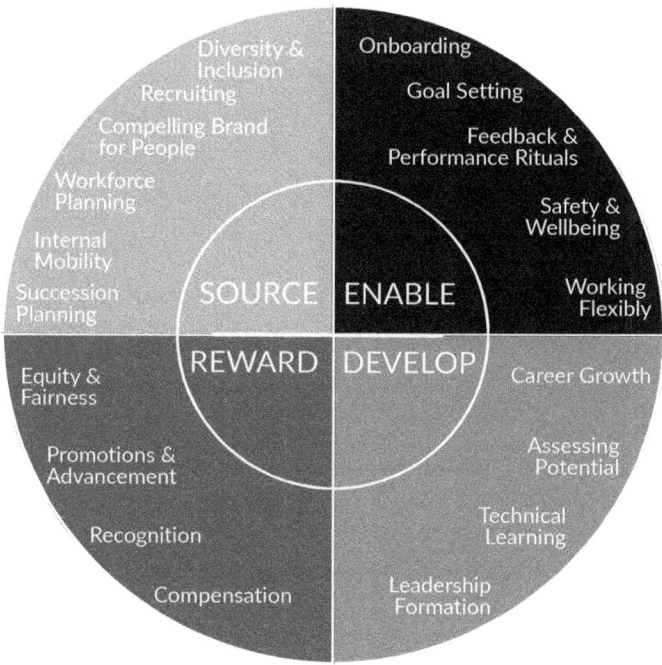

She stepped back and let the four words on the board absorb the silence again: People are the strategy. "Talent is not a hygiene factor. It is the system. If we design it for irrelevance, AI will multiply that. If we design it for ingenuity, AI will amplify it. The question is which one we choose."

Yuki then led the team through the Shinjuku Research Tower, her chosen signal site. In every corridor, the four patterns she had named played out in real time. The building was a paradox: ingenuity flickering in corners, irrelevance pressing in from the edges. In one lab, a micro-mission hire was already outperforming a credential-screened cohort. Down the hall, the AI recruiting filter still auto-rejected career breaks. Upstairs, the four-touchpoint onboarding was producing real contributions within days, while two floors below, keystroke dashboards tracked engineers into the night. The building became a mirror. Omnivista's future was visible everywhere, but so were its shadows.

Chris gathered the team before they left the Shinjuku Research Tower. "Talent has four domains: sourcing, enabling, developing, and rewarding. Each of you takes one and runs a single pilot at your site. Find where irrelevance is multiplying and redesign it for ingenuity. At the end of the month in Sydney, you report back with results, not theory."

- **Yuki (Tokyo): Sourcing**. "Our AI screening filter is auto-rejecting candidates with non-linear career paths. Replace the filter with a contribution-first audition: candidates complete a short collaborative problem-sprint alongside our scientists, and teams vote on who they want to keep working with. Show me who the old system would have missed."

- **John (Sydney): Enabling**. "Our onboarding has become a swamp of compliance slides. Pilot a four-role welcome structure: every new hire gets a navigator for systems, a peer for technical skills, a sponsor for networks, and a guardian for purpose. Show me whether new hires deliver meaningful contributions faster and whether they feel they belong."

- **Maria (São Paulo): Developing**. "Our e-learning dashboards are producing badges, not growth. Scrap badge collections in one unit and launch Friday curiosity rounds where teams pitch small experiments to improve care flow. Show me one experiment that became a real improvement."

- *Sanjay (Bangalore): Rewarding*. "Our bonus system rewards noise over substance. Redesign recognition in one division to include networked contribution credits: mentoring hours, peer endorsements, and cross-team rescues. Show me who becomes visible that the old system missed."

- *Liam (Dublin): Enabling and well-being*. "Our caregivers say they are monitored, not managed. Replace the keystroke surveillance dashboard with a presence ledger: caregivers log moments that mattered alongside routine tasks. Show me what changes in morale, absenteeism, and how families experience the care."

- *Chris (Global): The role of the Chief People Officer.* "Yuki and I will work together this month to define what the Chief People Officer role must become in the Ingenuity Age. Every lever we have pulled this year runs through her function. Yuki, I want us to map what you need from each of us, and what the organization needs from your role, to make this system hold beyond our team. Bring me a draft charter by the end of the month."

Chris paused. "And I will work with all of you, especially Yuki, to define what the Chief People Officer role must become in the Ingenuity Age. Not the HR administrator of the past, but the strategic leader accountable for the human system this entire effort depends on. That work starts this month."

"End of the month, Sydney. Bring results."CEO's Notebook: Talent

That night, after leaving the Shinjuku Research Tower, Chris walked alone through the backstreets of Tokyo. Neon spilled across the wet pavement, trains thundered overhead, and side streets alternated between the frenzy of izakayas and the hush of small shrines. She felt the same paradox she had just seen in the labs: ingenuity flickering, irrelevance pressing close.

Her mind turned to her own work. She had asked each executive to redesign one talent practice in their sites. What about her? If she wanted credibility, she would need to show that the CEO role itself could not escape redesign.

Chris stopped under the paper lanterns of a narrow alley and pulled a notebook from her bag. On the page, she listed her three practices, then the observation lenses she will use to notice the organization.

Actions

1. Source one voice daily. Each morning, she would seek out one perspective that was usually filtered out, a candidate overlooked, a junior staff member unheard, or a caregiver outside the system.

2. Enable one obstacle to fall. Every day, she would remove one barrier that kept people from contributing, a rule, a delay, a redundant sign-off.

3. Reward one act of contribution. Before leaving her desk, she would name one contribution that made the system stronger, even if it came from the quietest corner.

What I'll Notice

1. *Industrial*: where hierarchy still treats people as interchangeable or obedience as virtue.

2. *Information*: where dashboards define worth, hiring by keyword match, evaluating by clicks.

3. *Irrelevance*: where bias is automated, presence is surveilled, or performance theater is rewarded.

4. *Ingenuity*: where people are chosen by contribution, enabled to grow, and recognized for their invisible glue.

5. *Imagination*: where talent becomes fluid communities, porous boundaries, and AI-human co-leadership.

Chris closed her notebook, tucked it back into her bag, and continued walking toward her hotel.

My Fingerprint

Timothy Gallwey was coaching tennis in California in the early 1970s when he noticed something that should have been impossible. One day he stepped off the court briefly, and when he returned, a student who had been stuck with a technical problem had improved without any instruction at all. He began experimenting. He said less. He noticed more. And to his astonishment, errors he saw but did not mention were correcting themselves without the student ever knowing they had made them.

He developed a method built on a single insight: the mind that judges interferes with the body that knows. He called the judging voice Self 1 and the intuitive, capable body Self 2. Traditional coaching, he realized, fed Self 1 with corrections, instructions, and criticism, which tightened muscles, froze fluidity, and made the very errors it was trying to fix more likely. His method did the opposite. Instead of telling a student what they were doing wrong, he directed their attention to what was actually happening: watch the seams of the ball as it spins, notice where your weight shifts, feel the moment of contact. The student's body, freed from the interference of judgment, began to self-correct.

In one demonstration at Queens Club in London, a woman who had never held a racket was asked simply to say "bounce" when the ball bounced and "hit" when it met the strings. The resulting volley lasted several minutes. She never missed. In another story from the book, a student named Jack told Gallwey he had learned more in ten minutes than in twenty hours of previous lessons. When Gallwey asked what he had taught him, Jack went quiet for half a minute and then admitted: "I can't remember your telling me anything. You were just watching me, but I sure learned a lot."

I have carried Gallwey's insight into every talent conversation for thirty years. And in those thirty years, I have watched organizations deploy a system that does the precise opposite of what Gallwey proved. They call it performance management. I call it an oxymoron.

Performance is what humans do at their best: creating, solving, connecting, imagining. Management is what systems do to control variance. Put them together and you get a system designed to control the very thing it claims to unleash. Its close cousin, the nine-box grid, is no better. I have sat in rooms where executives spend hours plotting people on a performance-versus-potential matrix without the people themselves being involved, with conversations so naive about human capability that Gallwey would recognize the problem instantly: Self 1, the judging voice, running the entire show while Self 2, the person's actual potential, sits unheard.

The failures compound. Goals set once a year in a world that shifts monthly. Expectations defined by the manager, rarely in consultation with the person doing the work. Growth absent, replaced by a target to hit. Feedback delivered once, badly, by a leader untrained in the art of it, when Gallwey showed fifty years ago that the body learns from awareness, not from judgment. Traditional feedback tightens the muscles. It makes people smaller. Gallwey's feedback made people larger because it directed attention to what was working: your weight was forward, your eyes were on the ball, your follow-through reached shoulder height. Specific. Observable. In the moment. The brain builds patterns from what works. Our performance systems are designed to tell people what does not.

And then we tie it all to money. The moment your rating determines your bonus, every conversation becomes a negotiation, not a development dialogue. People learn to perform performance rather than actually perform. The forced bell curve manufactures failure in teams where none exists. Calibration assumes stable jobs and comparable roles, neither of which exist in the AI Era.

This is where *respicere*, the Latin root of respect meaning "to look again," becomes most urgent. What else can we see in our people? And how can they help us see it?

One CEO I worked with understood this. He made talent the central agenda item at every board meeting of a multi-billion-dollar holding company. Half of every three-to-four-hour monthly session was spent not on turnover statistics but on genuine questions: how are people across the organization growing? Who is being overlooked? Where is potential being wasted by a system that cannot see it? That is what it looks like when a leader designs a system to find potential rather than sort it.

Now consider what the AI Era makes possible, and how much more complex Gallwey's insight becomes when the game is no longer tennis but the constantly shifting work of human-AI partnership. In tennis, the coach watches one player hit one ball and gives specific, immediate feedback on what the body is doing right. In the AI Era, the equivalent challenge has four dimensions, each moving simultaneously.

The first is defining performance itself. When AI absorbs tasks that defined a role six months ago, what does "good" even mean today? Performance can no longer be a static target set in January. It must be a living conversation, recalibrated as the work shifts, asking: given what AI now handles, where is the human adding the most value this week?

The second is feedback, all year round. Gallwey's tennis coach does not wait until December to tell the player her form has drifted. The coach is there every session, every rally, naming what is working and pointing to the next opportunity to get stronger. AI can now surface patterns that no human manager could see alone: collaboration data, contribution across teams, learning velocity, moments where someone's work made three other people faster. The manager's job is to translate those signals into specific, positive, in-the-moment feedback, exactly as Gallwey taught.

The third is potential, which becomes an extraordinary, constantly expanding vision. When AI handles the routine, humans are freed to discover capabilities they never knew they had. The conversation about potential is no longer "where do you fit on the nine-box?" It is "what could you become that neither of us has imagined yet?" This is Self 2 on a civilizational scale: the intuitive, creative, connective capacity of people, finally unshackled from the administrative burden that kept it invisible.

The fourth is development, which must be continuous because AI capability grows so rapidly that the human contribution beside it must grow in concert. How do we help people reach potential that is itself constantly being redefined? Not through annual plans and e-learning modules. Through experiences, coaching, stretch assignments, and the kind of specific, aware, judgment-free feedback that Gallwey gave his tennis students, delivered every week, adjusted every month, tied to a vision the person themselves has articulated.

Benjamin Zander, the conductor of the Boston Philharmonic, understood this from the other side. He asks his students to write a letter from their future selves describing who they have become by the end of the year. That letter becomes the development compass. Zander understood what Gallwey proved on the tennis court: when you invite people to envision their own potential, they rise to meet it. When you rate them against a scale they did not design, they shrink to fit.

I have similar things to say about every domain in this chapter. The tools we use for sourcing, enabling, developing, and rewarding are Industrial Age at best. We have a very long way to catch up to our own growing potential, potential we never thought possible, that an increasingly expanding AI is now bringing within reach. But performance is where I would start. Because what we believe about people's capability shapes what they become. And the people who can lead this change, the Chief People Officers described later in this chapter, are themselves few and far between. That is perhaps the most consequential talent challenge of all.

The ORG6 Lever for Talent

Talent is the lever that shouts the loudest if you know how to listen. Its history is written in two yesterdays, the Industrial Age, which treated people as interchangeable hands, and the Information Age, which treated them as data processors. Its future divides into three possible tomorrows:

> **Corrosive Irrelevance**, in which people are reduced to data points, is trust-draining.

> **Optimistic Ingenuity**, in which people are treated as creators, energy compounding.

> **Imaginative Possibility**, in which people are treated as conscious contributors, expanding what work itself can mean.

The signals are everywhere: in onboarding (is it a scavenger hunt through portals, or a welcome into the community?), in feedback rituals (do people leave smaller, defined by ratings, or larger, fueled by possibility?), in hallways and Slack channels (are the heroes only the visible few, or are the hidden collaborators also seen?). What you notice tells you which yesterday you're repeating, and which tomorrow you're choosing.

In the sections ahead, we move from the big picture of Talent to the details of how organizations actually shape it. We will examine the full Talent lifecycle: how organizations source, enable, develop, and reward their talent throughout their careers with the organization.

Sourcing (the first quadrant)

Overall Summary of Sourcing

Industrial Age

Sourcing talent was about finding hands. Labor was interchangeable. Recruitment was physical and local: advertisements in newspapers, notices on factory gates, networks of kin and geography. Obedience and stamina mattered more than imagination.

The system valued those who could endure repetition, and the best "source" was often whoever stood closest to the gate when the whistle blew.

Information Age

Sourcing shifted toward credentials. Databases, job boards, and LinkedIn turned talent into searchable CVs. Recruiters spoke of pipelines, funnels, and filters. Competency panels assessed cultural fit, universities fed rankings into hiring algorithms, and global firms chased the identical résumés. Speed, efficiency, and reach were the dominant values: sourcing was optimized to find the most qualified candidates as quickly as possible, not necessarily the most creative or innovative individuals.

Irrelevance Age

Today, the temptation is to let AI source talent for us: keyword matching, automated screening, and algorithmic scoring of video interviews. The reflex feels efficient, but it carries corrosive risk: amplifying bias, excluding those with unconventional paths, and narrowing diversity of thought. Irrelevance arises when sourcing becomes about eliminating rather than imagining, filtering out differences, reducing people to patterns, and optimizing for yesterday's definitions of talent.

Ingenuity Age

The Ingenuity Age resets sourcing as the revelation of capacity in action. Rather than asking "Does this person look like our past hires?" the question becomes "What can this person create with us tomorrow?" Ingenuity utilizes peer-voted micro-missions, community contributions, open innovation challenges, and an advice-based hiring process to integrate real-world work into the sourcing process. AI supports: surfacing hidden collaborators, assembling portable evidence of contribution, and connecting diverse pools, but humans remain the ones who recognize potential.

Imaginative Possibility

One day, we might see sourcing as a form of participation in living communities. Talent flows not only from résumés or projects, but also from reputation graphs, portable portfolios, and proof of talent networks that have been uplifted. What if candidates owned their contribution records and chose how to share them across networks? What if organizations looked less for "roles" and more for generative sparks that could plug into shifting constellations of opportunity? Imaginative sourcing treats humans not as applicants but as nodes of possibility, whose ingenuity can be amplified by AI to serve outcomes beyond traditional boundaries of job or firm.

S1. Succession Planning

Industrial Age

Sourcing talent was a question of loyalty and endurance. The next leader was often the person who had stayed the longest, obeyed the system most faithfully, and proven themselves willing to sacrifice. Planning was informal, sometimes hereditary, sometimes political. Stability was prized over renewal. The philosophy was simple: if you could withstand the grind, you were next in line.

Information Age

Succession became formalized into charts, grids, and pipelines. HR produced nine-box matrices, executive committees debated talent lists, and leadership development programs promised to prepare "high potentials." Technology has brought efficiency through global databases of executive candidates, assessments of leadership competencies, and predictive analytics on career progression. But the emphasis still leaned on control and categorization: who fits, who scores, who has the pedigree.

Irrelevance Age

Succession risks become brittle when algorithms trained on past promotions replicate the very biases they claim to remove. AI-scored video interviews, automated psychometrics, and static talent pools can reduce succession to a technical exercise of replication. Leaders are often chosen for their similarity, not their adaptability. Corrosive irrelevance arises when succession planning prioritizes incumbency over preparing resilience, thus creating leaders optimized for yesterday's world, not tomorrow's threshold.

Ingenuity Age

Succession is recalibrated as a living system. Instead of lists frozen on paper, succession becomes a dynamic network of emerging capacity. Organizations experiment with transparent skills graphs, cross-functional apprenticeships, and rotating leadership assignments, where potential is proven through real-world work. AI can help map patterns of collaboration, highlight under-recognized contributors, and surface diverse candidates from across the system. But the decisive act remains human: recognizing who shows not just competence but courage, candor, and imagination under pressure.

Imaginative Possibility

Succession planning dissolves into a succession flow. Leadership is less about replacing one individual and more about cultivating constellations of talent that can rise to any occasion. Candidates carry portable reputation portfolios that document impact across organizations and communities. AI augments this by identifying where sparks of ingenuity could serve the whole system, not just a single role. The guiding question becomes not "Who replaces me?" but "How do we ensure an endless emergence of leaders who can take us further than we imagine?"

S2. Internal Sourcing

Industrial Age

Internal mobility was rare. Workers were typically hired for a specific task and often remained in that role throughout their careers. Advancement was usually vertical, slow, and limited to a few trusted loyalists. Skills were considered fixed; moving across functions was unthinkable. A good worker was defined by repetition and stability, not breadth or exploration.

Information Age

Internal mobility became more common, though it remained constrained. Job postings appeared on intranets, employees applied through HR portals, and some firms encouraged lateral moves or international secondments. Still, much of the power sat with managers who acted as gatekeepers, reluctant to release high performers. Mobility was often reactive, a vacancy-driven process rather than a systemic commitment to growth.

Irrelevance Age

AI-driven matching tools amplify managerial control rather than empower employees. Internal candidates can be invisible in systems that overvalue external résumés. Bias can lock people into roles, coded into historical data that says, "people like you stay here." Corrosive irrelevance emerges when employees feel they must leave the organization to grow, while leaders lament "talent shortages." The irony is stark: capacity exists inside, but the system treats it as immovable.

Ingenuity Age

Mobility becomes a flow rather than permission. AI-enabled internal marketplaces make opportunities visible to all: short-term projects, stretch roles, and secondments. Employees can self-initiate moves, while leaders shift from gatekeepers to sponsors. Contributions are visible through skills graphs and collaboration data, surfacing hidden talent. Instead of losing frustrated employees to recruiters, the organization continually redeploys its best capacity faster, fairer, and with greater resilience.

Imaginative Possibility

Mobility transcends roles and even organizations. Talent communities emerge where employees flow across company boundaries, through startups and partnerships, building multidimensional careers while contributing to shared outcomes. Portable reputation portfolios, owned by individuals, document growth across contexts. AI helps orchestrate these movements, matching sparks of ingenuity to the most urgent opportunities. Mobility is no longer about filling vacancies, but about orchestrating possibilities across the entire human system.

S3. Workforce Planning

Industrial Age

Workforce planning was a mechanical process. Leaders counted heads much as they counted machines: how many shifts, how many hours, how many hands required to maintain output. Plans were drawn up annually, tied to fixed production schedules, and assumed a stable environment. Human capacity was treated as a cost, rather than as a source of imagination or adaptability, and compliance was prioritized over it.

Information Age

Workforce planning has become increasingly data-driven. HR analytics teams built multi-year models to forecast skills supply and demand, track attrition trends, and plan graduate and hire pipelines. Scenario spreadsheets multiply, often with impressive complexity. But the models still assumed linearity, that yesterday's skills would remain tomorrow's advantage, and that strategy would stay fixed long enough for forecasts to hold.

Irrelevance Age

Workforce planning risks becoming irrelevant when AI automates the same flawed logic. Predictive dashboards may appear precise, but they become brittle when disruptions arise. Algorithms can calcify old assumptions, locking organizations into over- or under-staffing, or into chasing skills that are already obsolete. Leaders confuse polished accuracy with wisdom. The result is fragility: talent plans that collapse at the first sign of volatility.

Ingenuity Age

Workforce planning becomes a dynamic, rolling conversation. Instead of static five-year charts, organizations use AI to model multiple futures in real-time, i.e., scanning markets, detecting new skill patterns, and illustrating how capacity can flex. But leaders bring judgment, asking: Which of these futures deserves our commitment? Quarterly "talent sprints" replace annual plans, with rapid reallocations of roles, skills, and projects. Planning becomes a tool for adaptability, not prediction.

Imaginative Possibility

Workforce planning dissolves into talent communities. Boundaries blur between employees, contractors, startups, and even AI agents. The organization's role is less about predicting exact numbers and more about orchestrating access to ingenuity wherever it arises. AI helps map networks of potential contribution; humans decide which possibilities to activate. Planning is no longer about forecasting scarcity but cultivating abundance.

S4. Compelling Employer Brand

Industrial Age

Organizations didn't speak of "employer brand." Work was local and transactional. A job was a wage, and reputation traveled by word of mouth in towns and factories. Stability and authority mattered more than appeal. Companies offered security if you obeyed, not inspiration if you aspired.

Information Age

The employer brand became a marketing tool. Companies built glossy career pages, produced brochures, and sold themselves at university fairs. With the rise of LinkedIn and Glassdoor, brand management has extended online. Consulting firms and "Best Place to Work" rankings reinforced the idea that a company could advertise culture like a product. The focus was image: what could be polished, packaged, and promoted.

Irrelevance Age.

AI tools risk amplifying this hollowness, producing personalized recruitment ads, chatbot-driven candidate experiences, and polished social feeds that disguise reality. When the work within the company does not align with the brand outside, trust erodes. Employees become the first critics, posting candid reviews, and the gap between story and substance corrodes credibility. Irrelevance emerges when a brand is manufactured instead of lived.

Ingenuity Age

The brand becomes lived proof. The most powerful stories are told not by the organization but by its people: moments of growth, connection, and purpose made visible. AI can help surface and amplify these stories by spotting themes across internal forums, customer feedback, and volunteer initiatives. But the signal must be real: an organization where people thrive does not need to manufacture an image. Its culture is discoverable, not staged.

Imaginative Possibility

An employer brand functions as a systemic identity. People carry portable records of their contributions, and organizations become known less for slogans and more for the communities they lift and sustain, and the purposes they advance. Candidates no longer ask, "Is this a good place to work?" but "Does this community expand my ingenuity and help me make a difference?" In this vision, a brand is not just marketing. It is a reputation earned openly, across networks without walls.

S5. Recruiting

Industrial Age

Recruiting was about filling shifts. Foremen hired hands at the gate, sometimes on a daily basis, based on availability and physical capacity. Jobs were defined narrowly, and recruitment emphasized obedience, stamina, and loyalty. The process was transactional and immediate: if you could show up and endure the work, you were hired.

Information Age

Recruiting had become a professionalized process. Job boards, applicant tracking systems, competency-based interviews, and global search firms created layers of process: credentials, CVs, and assessments shaped who was considered suitable for the role. Recruiting shifted from the factory gate to digital portals, but the fundamental philosophy remained one of matching roles to people as efficiently as possible.

Irrelevance Age

AI-driven recruiting can push this philosophy to corrosive extremes. Keyword-matching screens out unconventional candidates, video-interview algorithms assess micro-expressions for "fit," and automated tests favor conformity over creativity. Recruiting becomes optimization theater: fast, polished, but exclusionary. The risk is obvious: diverse, ingenious talent is filtered out before it has a chance to contribute, while the organization congratulates itself on efficiency.

Ingenuity Age

Recruiting becomes a co-creation process. Instead of asking candidates to prove alignment with rigid roles, organizations invite them into micro-missions, peer dialogues, and collaborative challenges that demonstrate what value they can bring. AI can support by surfacing hidden collaborators, mapping networks of contribution, and ensuring bias is flagged and corrected. However, the decisive insight is human:

ingenuity recognizes potential that does not yet fit into a category, and recruitment shifts from filling jobs to unlocking creators.

Imaginative Possibility

Recruiting becomes a form of participation in fluid networks. Portable reputation portfolios showcase not just past employment but also the communities uplifted, projects advanced, and values upheld. Candidates flow across organizational boundaries, and AI curates opportunities to match sparks of ingenuity with real-time needs. Recruiting becomes less about acquisition and more about choreography, aligning people, purpose, and possibility across a living network.

S6. Diversity and Inclusion

Industrial Age

Workplace diversity was not a concept that existed. Labor was segmented and stratified by class, gender, and race, and the system treated uniformity as a strength. Workers were expected to conform to rigid roles, and difference was often suppressed. The philosophy was control: efficiency demanded sameness, and inclusion was rarely considered.

Information Age

Diversity had entered the corporate vocabulary: compliance-driven programs measured representation by categories such as age, gender, ethnicity, and disability. Companies built reporting dashboards, held awareness workshops, and hired Chief Diversity Officers. While this marked progress, the underlying philosophy often remained cosmetic diversity as external packaging. Inclusion was usually reduced to numerical representation rather than genuine integration of differences into decision-making processes.

Irrelevance Age

The risk here is that AI systems reproduce the same superficial approach. Algorithms may be trained to balance demographic categories while overlooking deeper sources of ingenuity, such as worldview, discipline, learning style, and lived experience. Or worse, they can encode historical biases, filtering out precisely the people who think differently. Corrosive irrelevance occurs when organizations pursue visible diversity without creating conditions that enable different perspectives to inform their choices. Tokenism replaces transformation, and talent disengages.

Ingenuity Age

The strength of a team lies in its variety of perspectives, not its uniformity of packaging. Inclusion means designing processes where different ways of seeing the world collide productively. These are advice processes that welcome contrarian input, meeting rituals that balance loud and quiet voices, leadership development that values sense-making capacity as much as technical skill. AI can help by revealing hidden patterns of collaboration and surfacing under-recognized contributors. However, human leadership must create a psychological safety that allows differences to become a source of synergy rather than division.

Imaginative Possibility

Diversity and inclusion transcend compliance categories. The question is no longer "Do we have visible variety?" but "Do we have the maximum number of different lenses on reality working together?" Organizations become communities where authenticity is honored, not masked, and where belonging is built around contribution, not conformity. Portable reputation portfolios could highlight not only technical skills but also the unique perspectives someone brings to problem-solving. AI helps to connect these differences into living networks of ingenuity. In this future, meritocracy and diversity are not opposites. Merit is redefined as the capacity to see differently and create together.

Enabling (the second quadrant)

Overall Summary of Enabling

Industrial Age

Enabling people to perform meant enforcing discipline and extracting effort. Time clocks, overseers, and standard operating procedures defined what "performance" looked like. Success was measured by endurance and obedience. If people could repeat tasks without error and without complaint, the system considered them "enabled." The focus was on control, not creativity.

Information Age

Enabling became about processes and tools. Dashboards tracked KPIs, e-learning portals delivered training, annual reviews assessed performance, and wellness programs offered incremental support. Leaders believed that by providing people with clear goals, regular feedback, and the necessary technology, they were enabling success. The philosophy was efficiency: connecting workers to information quickly, but rarely pausing to ask whether the flow was sustainable or meaningful.

Irrelevance Age

AI threatens to turn enabling into surveillance. Productivity software logs keystrokes and meeting hours; AI algorithms score micro-behaviors; feedback systems auto-generate performance comments. The intention may be to support, but the effect is one of monitoring. People feel managed by machines rather than enabled as humans. Irrelevance emerges when enabling becomes an optimization system that drains trust, burns out talent, and confuses activity with value.

Ingenuity Age

Enabling becomes the design of conditions that allow people to flourish and contribute their best. AI can handle the drudgery, scheduling, summarizing, and data pulling , while humans focus on judgment, creativity, and connection. Enabling becomes about protecting deep work time, building psychological safety, and providing clarity of purpose. Performance conversations shift from ratings to growth, supported by AI-curated evidence but interpreted through human dialogue. In this vision, enabling means freeing energy for ingenuity.

Imaginative Possibility

Enabling becomes the orchestration of rhythm. Organizations treat well-being, learning, and purpose as operating infrastructure. AI helps align work with human cycles by matching tasks with energy patterns, redistributing load across networks, and surfacing opportunities to collaborate that humans might otherwise miss. Leaders focus not on extracting output but on amplifying capacity for creativity, meaning, and connection. Enabling this future means designing a system where people not only perform but also become more fully themselves and where performance and fulfillment are inseparable.

E1. Onboarding

Industrial Age

Onboarding was orientation by command. New workers were gathered in a room, lectured on the rules, issued uniforms or ID cards, and then sent to their designated stations. The goal was compliance: know your place, follow the process, respect authority. Belonging was not the point; fitting into the machine was.

Information Age

Onboarding expanded into portals, policy handbooks, and structured training modules. HR designed week-long programs that included presentations, checklists, and e-learning components. Technology made information easier to distribute, but the emphasis remained transactional: "Here is what the company does, and here is how you fit." Culture was often reduced to slide decks, while real community building was left to chance.

Irrelevance Age

AI risks turning onboarding into a form of automation theater. Chatbots welcome new hires, algorithms push personalized training modules, and dashboards track completion rates. The experience may look sleek, but it can feel cold and impersonal. When onboarding becomes a digital scavenger hunt, logging into this portal and completing that checklist, people arrive faster but connect less. Irrelevance emerges when the first impression of work is disconnection: efficiency without belonging.

Ingenuity Age

Onboarding becomes a community entry point. The goal is not to fill forms but to help people find their place in the network. AI can help by curating introductions, surfacing "who to ask" for what, and capturing early wins. But the decisive move is human: giving each new hire a navigator for systems, a peer for the technical capabilities required, a sponsor for networks, and a guardian for purpose. When onboarding is designed this way, people begin contributing real value in their first week and feel recognized for who they are, not just what they deliver.

Imaginative Possibility

Onboarding becomes initiation into shared purpose. Workplace design creates immersive experiences where people not only learn systems but step into meaningful contribution immediately. AI helps align new hires with projects that match both their skills and their aspirations, making growth and impact visible from day one. Imagine an organization where every new hire spends their first month co-creating with customers, communities, or cross-disciplinary teams, while AI handles the logistics of integration. Onboarding becomes less about learning to fit in and more about learning to expand what is possible together.

E2. Goal-Setting

Industrial Age

The primary goal was to meet production quotas. Leaders defined the number of units, hours, and expected output. Workers were evaluated based on their compliance with these numbers, and any deviation was considered a failure. Goals served management control rather than individual growth, with success equated to discipline and repetition.

Information Age

Goal-setting became more sophisticated. Annual objectives, cascading KPIs, and later OKRs (Objectives and Key Results) connected individual roles to corporate strategy. Dashboards and performance management systems gave leaders visibility into progress. Yet much of this system remained top-down, and goals often multiplied into overwhelming lists of metrics. The human question, "What meaning does this goal create?" was rarely asked.

Irrelevance Age

AI threatens to intensify the obsession with metrics. Algorithms generate personalized targets, automated systems nudge workers to meet benchmarks, and dashboards flood with real-time numbers. The danger is goals without wisdom: productivity tracked in fragments, while the bigger picture gets lost. Corrosive irrelevance emerges when people chase indicators rather than impact, gaming the system to look successful while meaning and trust erode.

Ingenuity Age

Goal-setting aligns around purpose and growth. AI can support by analyzing patterns, showing where contributions create the most value, and suggesting realistic stretch targets. However, the essence lies in human dialogue: co-creating goals that connect personal development with organizational outcomes. Regular check-ins replace annual reviews, with AI-curated evidence fueling conversations that are interpretive rather than prescriptive. Goals shift from control mechanisms to commitments that spark ingenuity.

Imaginative Possibility

Goal-setting dissolves into shared intention and collective imagination. Rather than cascading objectives, organizations create vision studios where employees and customers collaborate to imagine their shared futures, utilizing AI to model scenarios and possibilities. Goals shift from hitting a number to creating impact in communities, reducing carbon footprints, improving community well-being, or pioneering new opportunities in health, education, or technology. The metric is not just whether targets are met, but whether human ingenuity has been expanded.

E3. Feedback and Performance Rituals

Industrial Age

Feedback was top-down and often harsh. Foremen shouted corrections on the factory floor, and performance was measured by errors avoided or quotas achieved. Workers were expected to endure critique in silence; feedback was control, not development. Rituals reinforced hierarchy: management spoke, labor listened.

Information Age

Feedback had become structured but remained mechanistic. Annual reviews, 360-degree surveys, and engagement scores gave feedback a veneer of science. Dashboards showed ratings, and managers delivered scripted conversations. While this was an advancement, it often felt bureaucratic. Feedback was presented as paperwork rather than a catalyst for growth and improvement.

Irrelevance Age

AI risks turning feedback into surveillance commentary. Algorithms draft auto-generated performance notes, sentiment analysis scores, tone, and productivity tools flag "underperformance." Employees receive more commentary, but less meaning. Corrosive irrelevance emerges when feedback feels like being observed by a machine, a flood of shallow metrics that leave people feeling smaller rather than larger.

Ingenuity Age

Feedback becomes dialogue that enlarges possibilities. AI can gather evidence such as code commits, project outcomes, and customer comments, and it can curate valuable insights. But humans must interpret, frame, and care. Rituals such as quarterly growth conversations, appreciative inquiry circles, or peer-coaching sessions shift feedback from judgment to development. The emphasis is not "Did you meet the metric?" but "What did you learn, and how will we grow from it together?"

Imaginative Possibility

Feedback becomes co-creation of wisdom. Imagine mixed-reality studios where people rehearse difficult conversations, with AI gently simulating scenarios so leaders can practice courage without consequence, or portable reflection portfolios, where individuals track growth stories that follow them across organizations. Feedback is no longer episodic or evaluative; it is a living practice of shared learning, where machines provide mirrors, and humans provide meaning.

E4. Safety and Well-being

Industrial Age

Safety was physical survival. Workers in factories, mines, and construction sites faced real danger daily, and their well-being was barely acknowledged. Protective gear, when it existed, was rudimentary. Regulations eventually forced improvements, but the philosophy remained reactive: prevent accidents, minimize liability, keep the line running. Well-being as a concept had no place.

Information Age

Safety expanded into compliance frameworks and corporate programs. Occupational health and safety standards became embedded in law. Companies introduced ergonomics, wellness seminars, and employee assistance programs. Mental health entered the conversation, though often in token ways. Well-being was treated as an optional perk rather than as critical infrastructure for performance.

Irrelevance Age

AI risks reducing safety and well-being to mere metrics without meaning. Wearables track heart rates, sleep patterns, and movement, feeding dashboards that score "well-being" without addressing causes. Algorithms may flag burnout risk, but leadership often fails to respond with systemic change. Corrosive irrelevance emerges when surveillance masquerades as care, when people feel watched but not supported, monitored but not understood.

Ingenuity Age

Safety and well-being are seen as operational capacity. An exhausted or fearful workforce is not just at risk; it is underperforming. AI can help by scanning workloads, monitoring recovery rhythms, and surfacing real-time signals of stress. However, the decisive act is human: redesigning workloads, creating trauma-informed leadership, protecting deep work time, and honoring renewal as integral to performance. Well-being becomes part of the system design, not an afterthought.

Imaginative Possibility

Safety and well-being are integrated into the flow of work itself. Imagine systems that adapt to human energy cycles. AI redistributes tasks when cognitive load is high or coordinates team rhythms so peak creativity coincides with lighter operational demands. Well-being is no longer a separate initiative but a living infrastructure. The guiding belief shifts: the more whole and healthy people are, the more expansive their ingenuity can be.

E5. Flexibility of Where and How you Work

Industrial Age

Flexibility was almost nonexistent. Work was tied to place, time, and routine: the factory floor, the office desk, the time clock. Hours were fixed, schedules rigid, and deviation punished. The model assumed that control over time and place equaled productivity, and workers were valued for their predictability rather than adaptability.

Information Age

Flexibility had become a key talking point. Telecommuting, hot desking, and early work-from-home programs began to emerge. Digital tools enabled some work to be done outside the office, but corporate culture often lagged behind the technology. Managers still measured commitment by physical presence, and flexibility was treated as an accommodation rather than a strategic advantage.

Irrelevance Age

AI-enabled monitoring threatens to hollow out flexibility. Keystroke loggers, video presence tools, or algorithmic productivity scores may be used to track the activities of remote workers. Hybrid arrangements are offered but not trusted, and employees are constantly asked to "prove" their performance. Corrosive irrelevance arises when flexibility is granted in form but denied in spirit, when workers are technically free but feel as though they are being constantly observed.

Ingenuity Age

AI can orchestrate distributed collaboration, synchronizing across time zones, curating meeting schedules to protect deep work, and balancing team availability to optimize productivity. Flexibility becomes a shared resource, negotiated intentionally rather than left to managerial discretion. Leaders build trust by measuring outcomes, not activity, and by allowing different rhythms of contribution to coexist productively.

Imaginative Possibility

Flexibility transcends schedules and locations to embrace life design. Work aligns with human cycles, community commitments, and personal growth. AI helps match work rhythms to natural energy patterns, integrates multiple roles (company, startup, community), and dissolves boundaries between "work" and "life" into purposeful contribution. Flexibility is no longer a perk; it is the organizing principle of a world where ingenuity thrives on diversity of rhythms, perspectives, and places.

Developing (the third quadrant)

Overall Summary of Developing

Industrial Age

Development was equated with tenure and repetition. Skills were developed through apprenticeships or extensive on-the-job training. Progress meant seniority: the longer you stayed, the more you were assumed to know. Formal training existed, but it was limited, and curiosity was not a prerequisite for participation. Development was endurance.

Information Age

Development became formalized into programs, certifications, and competency frameworks. Corporations invest in learning management systems, executive MBAs, and catalogs of e-learning modules. People were sent to classrooms or logged into portals. The philosophy was accumulation: more courses, more credentials, more certificates. Learning was something you "went to," not something embedded in daily work.

Irrelevance Age

The risk is that AI turns development into an endless treadmill of reskilling and dashboard updates. Algorithms drive course completions, digital badges, and gamified "upskilling" targets, often with little connection to real-world work. Employees usually feel overwhelmed by training requirements that fail to enhance their ability to contribute effectively. Irrelevance arises when development becomes a mere exercise in box-ticking for metrics rather than a catalyst for ingenuity.

Ingenuity Age

Development is continuous growth, embedded in the flow of work. AI can curate personalized learning journeys, surface stretch assignments, and highlight opportunities to practice new skills. But the essence is human: leaders must create protected time for exploration, peer-to-peer guilds of practice, and mission-based projects where growth is proven in action. Development becomes visible, communal, and purposeful.

Imaginative Possibility

Development expands into multi-dimensional careers. People pursue fractional roles across organizations, communities, and startups, bringing insights from multiple contexts back to their work. AI orchestrates these opportunities, helping individuals integrate technical growth, leadership practice, and personal meaning. Development becomes not just skill acquisition, but consciousness expansion, a system where everyone can grow faster than disruption.

D1. Career Growth

Industrial Age

Career growth meant climbing a narrow ladder. Advancement was slow and tied to loyalty, obedience, and years of service. A "good worker" proved their worth through consistency and stamina, not creativity or imagination. The highest reward for endurance was promotion into supervision, where authority was measured in control rather than contribution. Growth was vertical and finite: one rung after another until retirement.

Information Age

Career growth broadened, but still within rigid frameworks. HR created competency models, nine-box grids, and leadership pipelines. Employees were instructed to create CVs that included their credentials, projects, and promotions. Growth was faster, but still linear: upward through hierarchies, across job families, or into global mobility assignments. The model assumed careers could be planned like supply chains. For many, it became a race to accumulate titles rather than a journey to unlock ingenuity.

Irrelevance Age

Career growth risks being flattened into algorithmic matches and "career paths" designed by AI dashboards. Employees may be nudged toward roles based on past data, reinforcing conformity and narrowing horizons. Growth looks efficient but feels hollow; people move, but without meaning. Irrelevance arises when growth is defined by what the system predicts, rather than by what individuals envision. The result is disengagement, attrition, and talent leaving to find purpose elsewhere.

Ingenuity Age

Career growth is part of an expanding portfolio of contributions. AI can surface hidden opportunities such as stretching projects, cross-functional collaborations, or emerging missions, while humans provide mentorship, sponsorship, and coaching. Growth becomes non-linear: sideways into new skills, diagonally into new networks, or outward into customer-facing challenges. The measure is not just the title achieved, but the capacity created for the individual, the team, and the organization.

Imagination Age

Career growth dissolves into career design. People build multi-dimensional paths that span company roles, community leadership, startups, and personal missions. AI orchestrates opportunities across communities, helping people weave work, learning, and service into coherent journeys. Growth is not measured in promotions but in the expansion of human ingenuity, the ability to see more, connect more, and create more. Careers become constellations rather than ladders, and growth becomes a collective as well as an individual achievement.

D2. Assessment of Potential

Industrial Age

Potential was often crudely judged by appearance. Supervisors promoted those who resembled themselves in loyalty, endurance, and demeanour. Strength and obedience were valued over curiosity or creativity. Assessment of potential was less about capability than about perceived reliability. It was subjective, biased, and built to reinforce conformity.

Information Age

Potential became formalized into frameworks and tools. Companies introduced high-potential programs, nine-box grids, psychometric tests, and leadership competency models. Data and assessments gave an aura of objectivity. Yet these systems often rewarded the same patterns: extroversion, polished communication, comfort with hierarchy. Potential was still defined as "fitting the mold," not breaking it.

Irrelevance Age

AI risks locking potential assessment into predictive theater. Algorithms score résumés, video interviews, or psychometric profiles, training on historical data that encodes old biases. The result can be efficient irrelevance: models that replicate past leaders while filtering out unconventional talent. Instead of expanding possibilities, potential assessment becomes a narrowing funnel, excluding precisely the diversity of thought organizations need.

Ingenuity Age

Potential is reframed as the ability to grow under pressure and create value in new contexts. AI can help by surfacing hidden contributions: such as collaboration patterns, network influence, and learning velocity that humans may overlook. However, the decisive judgment must remain human, seeking curiosity, courage, and the capacity to integrate multiple perspectives. Potential assessment becomes dynamic and lived, not static and scored.

Imaginative Possibility

Potential is no longer a label handed down by managers, but a portfolio people own and grow. Portable reputation graphs show not just past performance, but how individuals stretched, taught others, and created new outcomes across communities. AI can curate patterns of ingenuity, showing who thrives at the edges of complexity. Potential assessment shifts from prediction to invitation: not "Who might succeed in our mold?" but "Who could expand what success even means?"

D3. Technical Learning

Industrial Age

Technical learning meant mastering repetitive tasks. Skills were taught through apprenticeships, manuals, and rigid procedures. Once learned, they were expected to remain unchanged for decades. Learning was narrow and practical, designed to maintain the machinery of production. Innovation was discouraged; deviations from the standard were treated as errors.

Information Age

Technical learning expanded into corporate classrooms, e-learning platforms, and professional certifications. Learning management systems cataloged thousands of courses, and employees were expected to "upskill" to keep pace with digital tools. But much of this learning was abstracted from real work, more about collecting credentials than deepening ingenuity.

Irrelevance Age

AI risks turning technical learning into an endless treadmill of micro-courses, badges, and automated content. Workers are encouraged to complete modules that generate metrics, but little mastery is achieved. Knowledge becomes fragmented, disconnected from context, and rapidly obsolete. Irrelevance emerges when learning is reduced to consumption. People pass courses, but the organization gains no new capacity to create.

Ingenuity Age

Technical learning is reshaped as exploration in the flow of work. AI can act as a co-pilot: suggesting code, translating languages, diagnosing errors, or curating just-in-time resources, learning shifts from memorization to application, from theory to practice. Curiosity projects, peer-led guilds, and AI-augmented simulations allow people to experiment, fail safely, and share insights. The test of learning becomes: what new value did it help us create?

Imaginative Possibility

Technical learning expands into generative collaboration. AI tools are evolving into creative partners, enabling individuals to co-design products, reimagine processes, and solve scientific challenges once thought impossible. Careers expand not through credentials but through visible contributions to living networks of knowledge. Learning becomes less about keeping pace with machines and more about using machines to discover what humans have never imagined.

D4. Leadership Development

Industrial Age

Leadership formation was an accidental process. Leaders were promoted from the ranks based on endurance, discipline, or loyalty, rather than on vision or wisdom. Training, when it existed, emphasized command and control, the ability to enforce rules and extract compliance. Leadership was equated with authority, and authority with hierarchy. Formation was imitation: learning to act like the boss above you.

Information Age

Leadership formation became institutionalized. Business schools, corporate universities, and leadership development programs proliferated. Frameworks emphasized strategic thinking, financial acumen, and persuasive communication. Coaching and 360-degree feedback emerged, expanding the toolkit. Yet the underlying philosophy often frames leaders as individuals to be optimized, rather than as facilitators of collective ingenuity. The focus remained on producing heroic figures rather than building distributed capabilities.

Irrelevance Age

AI risks turning leadership formation into algorithmic mimicry. Digital platforms analyze speech, facial expressions, and decision styles, then recommend how to "improve" a leader's presence. Training programs replicate past models of authority, producing leaders optimized for old conditions. Corrosive irrelevance arises when leadership formation teaches people to perform like leaders instead of to create the conditions where ingenuity thrives. Leaders become polished but hollow, well-branded but brittle under real pressure.

Ingenuity Age

Leadership forms as the cultivation of awareness. AI can assist by surfacing weak signals, curating feedback across networks, and modeling scenarios. But the essence is human: developing the courage to act with clarity in the face of uncertainty, the humility to listen deeply, and the discipline to foster psychological safety. Formation happens through lived practice: apprenticeships, action learning, and peer circles, where leaders learn not to command but to convene, not to dictate but to design.

Imaginative Possibility

Leadership formation expands into multi-level stewardship. Leaders are not simply trained; they are invited into lifelong practices of awareness, wisdom, and service. AI acts as a reflective mirror, showing patterns of bias or blind spots, while networks act as teachers of humility and imagination. Formation moves beyond building executives for organizations to cultivating stewards for communities. The central question shifts: not "How do I become a leader?" but "How do I expand the leadership capacity wherever I go?"

Rewarding (the fourth quadrant)
Overall Summary of Rewarding

Industrial Age

Rewards were blunt and straightforward: wages for hours worked. Pay was tied to endurance and compliance, not creativity. Seniority or loyalty sometimes earned incremental increases, but the philosophy was paternalistic in nature. Employers rewarded obedience; workers received security if they stayed put. Recognition was minimal, promotions were slow, and equity was almost non-existent.

Information Age

Rewards became more complex and financialized. Bonuses, stock options, and variable pay tied individuals to quarterly results. Employee-of-the-month plaques and formal recognition programs appeared. Pay-for-performance became the mantra, but it often rewarded outputs over outcomes. Equity entered the conversation, but implementation lagged. Rewards were designed to incentivize efficiency and competition more than collaboration or ingenuity.

Irrelevance Age

AI risks turning rewards into algorithmic inequities. Performance ratings generated by machine analysis can encode bias. Automated compensation tools may widen pay gaps under the guise of objectivity. Recognition platforms risk becoming digital gamification, rewarding noise and visibility rather than substance. Corrosive irrelevance emerges when rewards reinforce mistrust, particularly when people perceive the system as opaque, unfair, or exploitative.

Ingenuity Age

Rewards are alignment with contribution and community. AI can help continuously monitor equity, track collaborative impact, and surface hidden contributions. Transparent pay bands, peer-based recognition, and rewards for networked value creation become the norm. Promotions and advancement are linked not just to technical results but to the ability to develop others and grow collective capacity. Rewards reinforce fairness, belonging, and ingenuity rather than undermining them.

Imaginative Possibility

Rewards evolve beyond money into purpose-driven value exchange. Companies share profits with employees and the extended networks. Reputation itself becomes currency: recognition that travels across communities, enabling people to earn trust and opportunity wherever they go. AI curates ways to link contribution to both individual and collective flourishing, measuring not only what is achieved but also how it serves life. Rewards become regenerative, fueling ingenuity across boundaries, not just within corporate walls.

R1. Compensation

Industrial Age

Compensation was simple: wages for hours worked. The model assumed that people exchanged time and stamina for money, and the more hours endured, the more pay received. Compensation was paternalistic, set by employers, enforced by unions, and designed around subsistence and stability. Pay was a blunt instrument: a means to keep workers compliant and productive.

Information Age

Compensation had become financially complex and astonishingly so. Short-term incentives (STI) and long-term incentives (LTI) proliferated. Executives were paid in elaborate combinations of salary, cash bonuses, stock options, and performance shares, often tied to market indices and valued using Black-Scholes models that were incomprehensible to most employees, and sometimes even to the boards. Packages required PhDs in finance to decode, with consultants producing thick reports to justify alignment. Instead of clarity, compensation became a complex theater meant to reassure shareholders, often eroding trust within the organization. For the average employee, pay remained tied to job grades, benchmark data, and cost controls, a system that signaled fairness on paper while rarely addressing meaning or equity in reality.

Irrelevance Age

AI risks exacerbating this complexity. Algorithms can calibrate pay with extraordinary precision, benchmarking against endless datasets, but still miss the essence of fairness. Automated systems may exacerbate inequities based on gender, ethnicity, or geography. Employees experience opacity: their pay "optimized" by a model they cannot question. Executives continue to receive ever more elaborate STI/LTI packages that appear scientific but lack coherence. The corrosive outcome is mistrust: employees view money as manipulated, rather than meaningful, and leaders as aligned with shareholders rather than with people and purpose.

Ingenuity Age

Compensation is a source of clarity and alignment. AI can simplify what has become over-engineered: transparent pay bands, continuous monitoring of equity gaps, and linking contributions to rewards in ways people understand. Compensation becomes not a puzzle but a promise: fair, explainable, and connected to actual impact. STI/LTI systems are pared back, replaced with simpler equity or profit-sharing schemes that employees can track in real time. AI can show how collaboration, mentoring, or innovation contribute to organizational outcomes, and rewards can follow accordingly. The ingenuity lies in clarity: everyone understands not only what they are paid, but why.

Imaginative Possibility

Compensation transcends money as the sole measure of value. Pay remains essential, but rewards such as time, experience, and community complement it. AI-enabled systems could allow people to flex rewards: more cash when they need it, more time when they value it, more development opportunities when they crave growth. Equity extends beyond shareholders to encompass employees and even the communities affected by the organization's work. Reputation itself becomes part of compensation, portable recognition that accompanies individuals across organizations. The question shifts from "What's my package worth?" to "How does this system invest in my ingenuity, my growth, and my ability to contribute to something larger than myself?".

R2. Recognition

Industrial Age

Recognition was scarce. A paycheck was assumed to be enough thanks. Workers who endured long hours might receive a handshake, a service pin, or a retirement watch. Recognition reinforced loyalty, not ingenuity. To be seen was to have survived.

Information Age

Recognition became formalized and programmatic. "Employee of the Month" plaques, peer-nominated awards, points-based platforms, and annual dinners sought to systematize appreciation. Digital recognition portals proliferated, but often rewarded visibility over substance. Leaders relied on surveys to measure whether people felt recognized, as though gratitude could be reduced to metrics. Recognition became a checklist rather than a felt human exchange.

Irrelevance Age

AI risks amplifying recognition theater. Automated emails congratulate employees on work anniversaries, chatbots send "thank you" notes, and gamified platforms award badges for participation. The gestures are faster but emptier, stripped of authenticity. Worse, algorithms may reward the most visible in systems while overlooking the quiet contributors who hold teams together. Corrosive irrelevance emerges when recognition becomes automated noise, leaving people less seen, not more.

Ingenuity Age

Recognition is the amplification of genuine human moments. AI can help surface contributions that are hidden in data, such as code commits, problem-solving in Slack threads, mentoring hours, or cross-team collaborations. Leaders can then bring those contributions into the light, naming and celebrating them personally. Recognition becomes storytelling: specific, authentic, tied to purpose. AI provides evidence, but humans provide meaning. In this model, recognition strengthens trust and multiplies energy.

Imaginative Possibility

Recognition includes contributions to customers, communities, and industries. AI can curate portable recognition portfolios, enabling people to carry not just pay stubs but stories of impact across their careers. Recognition transcends praise to become reputation, a living record of ingenuity that travels with the individual and inspires collective progress.

R3. Promotions

Industrial Age

Advancement was narrow but straightforward. Promotion rewarded endurance, obedience, and loyalty. The next foreman or supervisor was usually the worker who had lasted longest without complaint. Advancement meant moving from the shop floor to the office, from doing to directing. Authority came from position, not from imagination or contribution. For many, there was no advancement at all, only a lifetime of repetition until retirement.

Information Age

Promotions became structured into career ladders, job grades, and competency frameworks. HR systems tracked who was "ready now," "ready soon," or "ready later." Advancement was formalized into talent pipelines, often tied to global benchmarking data. But these systems frequently reinforced sameness, selecting those who looked, spoke, and behaved like existing leaders. Advancement was faster than in the Industrial Age, but it remained linear, hierarchical, and often politicized. The illusion of meritocracy masked deep inequities, while the ladder itself grew brittle.

Irrelevance Age

AI risks locking advancement into algorithmic conformity. Automated promotion recommendations, based on historical data, replicate existing biases: advancing those who fit past patterns and excluding those who think differently. Title inflation accelerates as organizations use promotions to retain people without truly expanding their impact. Corrosive irrelevance emerges when promotions reward optics over outcomes, political alignment over ingenuity. Advancement becomes a zero-sum game, eroding trust in the system and hollowing out real leadership capacity.

Ingenuity Age

Advancement is as a form of stewardship. Instead of climbing ladders, employees demonstrate readiness by growing others, expanding networks, and delivering collaborative impact. AI can help by highlighting who mentors effectively, who bridges silos, and who generates solutions that others build upon. Advancement becomes less about managing more people and more about enabling more ingenuity. Titles matter less than visible stewardship of purpose, people, and performance.

Imaginative Possibility

Advancement becomes fluid and multi-dimensional. People step in and out of leadership roles as the context demands. AI enables transparent talent marketplaces where opportunities emerge dynamically and advancement is earned through contributions to missions, not hierarchical vacancies. Reputation, not position, becomes the currency: individuals advance by demonstrating ingenuity that others trust and choose to follow. Advancement shifts from "How high did I climb?" to "How widely did I expand the capacity for ingenuity?".

R4. Equity and Fairness

Industrial Age

Equity in this section does not refer to ownership stakes or bonus shares. It refers to adjusting support so that everyone can reach the same outcome, recognizing that people start from different positions. Fairness asks "did we treat everyone the same?" Equity asks "did everyone get what they needed?"

In the Industrial Age, both were largely absent, and fairness was often crude and uneven. Workers were paid by the hour, often at unequal rates across different genders, races, or social classes. The assumption was that labor was interchangeable, and so long as the line kept moving, fairness was irrelevant. Those with less power, such as women, minorities, migrants, were systematically underpaid, with little recourse beyond strikes or collective bargaining.

Information Age

Equity became a legal and reputational issue. Pay audits, diversity reports, and compliance programs emerged. Companies introduced formal salary bands, annual benchmarking, and standardized promotion criteria. Fairness was presented as consistency: similar roles at similar grades should receive similar pay. Yet inequities persisted, often hidden beneath complex formulas or justified through "market data." The system appeared objective, but still replicated bias.

Irrelevance Age

AI risks making inequity look more scientific. Algorithms set pay based on massive datasets, but those datasets reflect historic inequality. Automated "equity dashboards" promise transparency but can obscure fundamental gaps. Global companies use AI to optimize labor costs across geographies, paying less where they can get away with it. Corrosive irrelevance arises when the system claims fairness, but lived experience tells employees otherwise. Trust erodes when workers perceive precision without justice.

Ingenuity Age

Equity represents an ongoing design for trust. AI can continuously monitor pay equity across gender, ethnicity, location, and role, surfacing gaps in real time. But leaders must act on the insights, swiftly and visibly correcting inequities. Fairness is not just about equal pay for equal work, but also about providing transparent opportunities for growth, development, and recognition. Organizations that design for equity gain resilience: people trust the system and invest their ingenuity where they know it will be valued.

Imaginative Possibility

Equity expands beyond internal pay structures to systemic fairness. Imagine portable equity graphs that enable employees to track and demonstrate fairness across roles and organizations, fostering accountability beyond the walls of a single employer. AI could model equity not just within a company but across entire industries, shining light on hidden imbalances. Fairness becomes a competitive advantage: people choose to work where justice is not a slogan but a system. In this future, equity is regenerative, continually renewing trust and expanding human ingenuity across boundaries.

Case Examples from the Real World

Sourcing

Unilever: "Auditions over résumés":

- **What they did.** For early-career roles, Unilever shifted from résumé screens to an AI-assisted flow of game-based assessments and structured, on-demand interviews, with humans making the final decision. The time to hire dropped dramatically, and candidate pools diversified.

- **Why this matters.** Replaces pedigree filters with contribution signals; AI widens the aperture while humans keep judgment.

- **Consequences.** Faster, fairer hiring; larger, more diverse shortlists; better candidate experience at a global scale.

Schneider Electric: "Open Talent Market"

- **What they did.** Launched an AI-powered internal marketplace to match employees with projects, roles, and mentors, moving mobility from manager permission to system-wide visibility.

- **Why this matters.** Converts hidden skills into deployable capacity; keeps careers growing without leaving the firm.

- **Consequences.** Increased internal moves and mentoring matches, higher employee retention, and faster staffing of priority work.

Enabling

GitHub (Microsoft): "Copilots for flow"

- **What they did.** Deployed GitHub Copilot to assist developers with real-time code suggestions. Controlled studies report materially faster task completion and lower cognitive load.

- **Why this matters.** AI automates the grunt work, allowing people to focus on design, review, and problem-solving.

- **Consequences.** Faster merges, improved maintainability and readability, and higher developer satisfaction.

Health systems using Nuance DAX: "Ambient documentation"

- **What they did.** Rolled out ambient AI "scribes" that listen during visits and draft notes for clinician review, reducing after-hours charting and burnout.

- **Why this matters.** Frees scarce clinical attention for patients; AI handles documentation, humans handle care.

- **Consequences.** Improved provider experience with no harm to safety/experience metrics; growing adoption across major systems.

Developing

IBM: "Your Learning"

- **What they did.** Built an AI-driven learning platform that tags content, personalizes pathways, and recommends following skills based on role, projects, and "propensity to learn." **Why this matters.** Puts the right learning in the flow of work; treats learning velocity as a strategic asset.

- **Consequences.** Scalable upskilling, better skill–opportunity matching, and stronger internal pipelines.

AT&T: "Future Ready"

- **What they did.** Undertook a multi-year, data-driven reskilling program that used analytics to map skills to future roles and funded credentialed learning at scale.

- **Why this matters.** It demonstrates how incumbents pivot their workforce rather than replace it. AI and analytics drive development, while leaders invest.

- **Consequences.** Large-scale redeployment into growth roles; a durable template for enterprise reskilling.

Rewarding

Salesforce: "Algorithmic equity audits, human fixes"

- **What they did.** Shifted pay-equity analysis to a specialized analytics platform (Syndio) to continuously detect gaps and then funded corrections globally.

- **Why this matters.** Uses AI/advanced analytics where humans are biased and opaque; leadership turns insight into results.

- **Consequences.** Repeated company-wide adjustments and a credible signal of fairness that strengthens trust and retention.

Cisco: "Data-driven recognition at scale"

- **What they did.** Partnered with Workhuman to run a global, values-based peer recognition system; analytics surface patterns of contribution (often invisible work) to inform rewards and culture investments.

- **Why this matters.** Recognition becomes evidence-based and inclusive; AI identifies the quiet glue that binds networks.

- **Consequences.** Higher participation and engagement; recognition aligned to real impact, not just visibility.

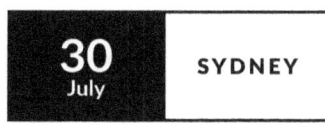

End of Month: Executive Team Review

The team reconvened in Sydney, carrying the results of their month-long assignments. Each had chosen one practice in their signal site: in sourcing, enabling, developing, or rewarding, where irrelevance had crept in, and each had worked to redesign it for ingenuity. They gathered in the Barangaroo Biotech Hub, not with theory or slides, but with lived experiments and hard-won results. One by one, they took the floor.

- *Yuki: Sourcing (Tokyo).* "We replaced the AI auto-filter with a contribution-first audition. Every candidate completed a short collaborative problem-sprint alongside our scientists, and teams voted on who they wanted to keep working with. Within weeks, overlooked candidates emerged: women returning from caregiving and mid-career professionals with unconventional paths. One candidate the old filter had rejected twice scored highest in the sprint. We stopped measuring pedigree and started measuring potential."

- *John: Enabling (Sydney).* "We piloted a four-role welcome structure: every new scientist received a navigator for systems, a technical peer, a network sponsor, and a purpose guardian. Instead of being left adrift, new hires delivered meaningful contributions within their first fortnight. Retention in the biotech labs rose immediately. One new hire told us, 'For the first time, I knew who had my back before I needed to ask.' Enablement stopped being about forms and became about belonging."

- *Maria: Developing (São Paulo).* "We scrapped dashboard-driven badge collections and launched Friday curiosity rounds. Teams pitched small experiments to improve care flow. One nursing team redesigned a patient transfer protocol, cutting waiting time in half. Another proposed a discharge checklist that reduced re-admissions in the pilot ward. Development shifted from modules to experiments, and ingenuity showed up where we least expected it."

- *Sanjay: Rewarding (Bangalore).* "We redesigned recognition to include networked contribution credits: mentoring hours logged, peer endorsements, and cross-team rescues. Within a month, one of the highest scorers was a young coder who had quietly mentored five pods and rescued three cross-team integrations. Under the old system, he was invisible. Under the new one, he was our most valuable connector. Rewarding became about the invisible glue, not the loudest noise."

- **Liam: Enabling and Well-being (Dublin).** "We replaced keystroke monitoring with a presence ledger. Caregivers logged moments that mattered: reading with patients, storytelling, singing, alongside routine tasks. Families noticed immediately, commenting that the home 'felt human again.' Staff morale rose, and absenteeism dipped. We stopped rewarding screen time and started rewarding presence."

- Chris: The CPO Role (Global). "Yuki and I began this work together, but it quickly became a team effort. Every executive contributed to the report because every lever we have pulled this year runs through the CPO function.

The result is a full report and charter built around five accountabilities: the Talent Asset Manager, who tracks how quickly potential becomes performance; the Talent Choreographer, who designs how human energy flows toward ingenuity rather than bureaucracy; the Talent Capitalist, who sits shoulder to shoulder with the CFO modeling returns on people decisions with the same rigor we apply to capital; the Talent Scout, who maps capability within and beyond the company, seeing sparks of ingenuity that CVs will never capture; and the CEO's Consigliere, the trusted partner who brings psychological depth, the courage to name what others will not, and the wisdom to hold up a mirror when it matters most.

You have all read the report. You have all shaped it. Tomorrow, I present it to the Board, because this is not an HR decision. It is an enterprise decision about who holds the human system together as AI reshapes everything else. The CPO does not serve the levers from the side. She holds them together from the center."

What If

After a full day of report-backs in the Barangaroo Biotech Hub, Chris suggested they leave the building. "We've done the disciplined work," she said. "Now let's stretch. Let's imagine what feels impossible."

She led the team out along the Sydney Harbour foreshore. The late-afternoon sun slanted across the water, ferries cut white wakes, and the air smelled of salt and eucalyptus drifting from the nearby Royal Botanic Gardens. They found a quiet lawn with views across to the Opera House and Harbour Bridge. Shoes came off, jackets loosened. The mood shifted from boardroom intensity to something more playful, curious, even childlike.

Chris looked around the circle. "Here's the exercise. Tonight, we forget constraints. We forget what the Board will tolerate or what regulators might say. We ask, 'What if?' The crazier the better. If some of these ideas make us laugh, that's good. Suppose they make us uncomfortable, even better. Let's imagine Talent not just this month, but in fifty years."

She uncapped a marker and held a flip chart steady against the grass. "We'll do ten 'What Ifs' for each of the four Talent processes: sourcing, enabling, developing, and rewarding. Go."

Sourcing

1. What if résumés were outlawed and all hiring began with a forty-eight-hour peer-voted micro-mission?

2. What if candidates owned portable, cryptographically signed contribution portfolios that they controlled, not HR?

3. What if every manager had to lose one external hire for every internal mobility win they blocked?

4. What if AI copilots matched overlooked talent to high-leverage missions daily, not just jobs annually?

5. What if we hired for contradiction: candidates had to prove how they see things differently from our last three hires?

Enabling

1. What if every new hire got a four-guardian launch crew (navigator, technical skill peer, sponsor, purpose guardian) for ninety days?

2. What if calendars had a legally protected daily maker block and meetings were taxed if they invaded it?

3. What if any team could pull a stop-the-line cord on culture, pausing work for a fifteen-minute safety reset without penalty?

4. What if every site published a friction wall and leaders had to remove one brick a day?

5. What if onboarding ended only when a new hire taught the next hire, proof they had truly arrived?

Developing

1. What if badges disappeared and development was evidenced only by shipped improvements and peer-reviewed stories?

2. What if every Friday were a funded What If lab where at least one idea was shipped to a real user by 5 p.m.?

3. What if promotions required a portfolio of people grown, not just projects shipped?

4. What if engineers, nurses, and product leads rotated across sites for thirty-day exchanges?

5. What if anyone could self-elect into a ninety-day foundry to prototype new services with customer partners, no permission required?

Rewarding

1. What if bonuses were split fifty-fifty between personal outcomes and networked contribution credits?

2. What if we published transparent pay bands and fixed any equity gap within thirty days of detection?

3. What if recognition had to be a specific story plus consequence, with no generic thank-yous allowed?

4. What if reputation became portable currency, impact passports you carry across roles, sites, and partners?

5. What if the CEO's bonus was tied to repair speed and fairness audits, representing trust as a first-class outcome?

End of Month: Board Review

Today, Chris was meeting with the Board to review the team's accomplishments in talent over the last month. Chris clicked to the first slide and didn't bother with bullet points.

"Yesterday the team got back from Tokyo, Sydney, São Paulo, Bangalore, and Dublin," she said. "We didn't swap theories. We tried things in real situations. Here's what actually worked."

"First, hiring. We stopped judging people by the polish of their résumé and started judging by what they can do," Chris said. "Instead of screening people out, we gave small tryouts, tiny missions that take a few hours. You see the work; you don't have to guess. We also turned off the software rules that quietly rejected anyone with a zigzag career. Inside the company, we made opportunities visible to everyone, so people can put their hand up without needing their manager's permission. The result: more fresh talent, fewer dead ends, faster decisions.

"Next, how do people get help to do great work? The self-serve portals weren't helping. So, we put a small support crew around each person. There's a guide who helps you navigate the place, a technical skill peer you can ask the tough skill questions, a senior sponsor who opens doors, and someone who keeps us honest about why the work matters. We also killed the creepy dashboards that tried to track every click. Nobody did their best work under surveillance. Instead, we set quiet hours for deep work and a simple rule from manufacturing: anyone can say 'stop' if something looks unsafe or unclear. Fix it first, then move.

"Then, learning. Collecting certificates didn't change performance. Shipping small improvements did. On Fridays, we ran short 'What If' sprints, tiny experiments we could put into production the same week. We learned in the middle of the job, not off to the side. That's what moved the numbers.

"Finally, pay and recognition. We started noticing the people who hold everything together, the mentor who rescues a project, the engineer who gets teams to reuse good work instead of rebuilding it, the quiet problem-solver who keeps others unblocked. Gratitude and pay should reflect that, not just who talks the loudest. We're also checking pay fairness on a steady rhythm, not once a year, and we're open about the salary ranges so people know where they stand."

Chris let the room breathe for a moment. "That's where we are," she said. "This year we'll build on the simple things that worked: tryouts over pedigree, support crews over portals, learning by shipping, and rewards that see the whole contribution, not just the spotlight." She then summarized the four guardrails:

- "Never automate the human moment.

- Automate the administrative.

- Augment the judgment.

- Protect the dignity.

"These are our guardrails," Chris said. "AI will multiply whatever system it finds. Our job is to build a system that multiplies ingenuity."

She paused, then looked around the table. "We've seen what works: micro-missions instead of résumés, four-guardian onboarding, Friday curiosity sprints, and recognition of networked contribution. Those are the practices we'll scale this year.

"But practices alone won't hold. They depend on a role that, in most organizations, doesn't actually exist yet."

The Chief People Officer We Need for the Ingenuity Age

In the Industrial Age, we administered human resources.

In the Information Age, we measured human capital.

In the Ingenuity Age, human potential and artificial intelligence expand exponentially together.

The leader accountable for that partnership is the Chief People Officer, a role as consequential as the CFO and compensated accordingly.

Do not be surprised if the CEO of the Ingenuity Age rose through the Chief People Officer's chair.

Katharine McLennan

This section sits inside the Talent chapter because talent is where the role lives. But the Chief People Officer described here is not a human resources leader in the traditional sense. This is the person accountable for the human system that every other chapter in this book depends on. If VISTA is the compass and ORG6 is the roadmap, the CPO is the person who ensures the organization actually travels. Readers who lead organizations, serve on boards, or advise CEOs may find this the most consequential section in the book. It describes a role that the market has not yet fully defined, but that must exist in every organization that takes ingenuity seriously.

So what does this role look like?

Not the HR administrator of the Industrial Age. Not the CHRO of the Information Age. What follows is something no search firm profile yet describes: a role redefined for the Ingenuity Age. A true strategic peer to the CFO. Someone who manages human capital with the same discipline organizations apply to financial capital. Someone who choreographs energy and time as carefully as they allocate cash. Someone who can serve as the CEO's consigliere, holding up the mirror, saying what no one else dares.

This role doesn't exist in the market. But it must exist in every organization that takes its people seriously. What Omnivista needed was not an HR leader delivering programs; it required a strategic leader who could build systems. It was a Chief People Officer who sat as a strategic equal to the CFO. Someone who could see talent as an appreciating asset, not an expense line. Someone who could choreograph the way human energy was spent with the same discipline that John applied to capital allocations. Someone with this skill would command a higher salary in the market than the best-paid CFO, if they could be found.

Industrial Age

The equivalent role was the personnel administrator. The work was payroll, compliance, industrial relations, and safety. People were "hands," and their management was clerical. HR sat far from the table, its task to enforce consistency and protect against liability.

Information Age

The role had matured into the CHRO. Leadership pipelines, nine-box grids, engagement surveys, coaching programs, and global mobility have all become key responsibilities of HR. Analytics were entered, along with dashboards of culture and succession. But the function was still reactive. Even at its best, the CHRO was an advisor, rarely a co-strategist. The CFO and COO still dominated board packs; the CPO's slides were often appended near the end.

Irrelevance Age

This model collapses. If people are the strategy, not just its enablers, then the CPO must be redefined as central rather than peripheral. Three tomorrows unfold here.

> **Corroding Irrelevance**: HR reduced to algorithms, automating hiring, feedback, and pay: efficient, but brittle, with trust leaking at every seam.
>
> **Optimistic Ingenuity**: a redefined CPO who makes talent the true competitive advantage, treating growth, well-being, and ingenuity as assets to be invested in with discipline.
>
> **Imaginative Possibility**: a CPO who becomes a system steward, helping organizations choreograph not only talent inside, but ingenuity across communities.

Chris then took the Board through the roles that a CPO needs to take in the Ingenuity Age.

The Talent Asset Manager

A CPO in the Ingenuity Age treats talent like appreciating capital assets. They track not just headcount, but mobility velocity, capability expansion, and ingenuity produced per team. Where the CFO measures financial returns, the CPO measures human compounding, how quickly potential becomes performance.

The Talent Choreographer

This new CPO designs how time is spent, the scarcest and most expensive asset in the organization. Every meeting, every project, every dashboard is an allocation of human energy. The CPO ensures talent isn't wasted in bureaucracy but flows toward ingenuity, renewal, and purpose.

The Talent Capitalist
The CPO sits shoulder-to-shoulder with the CFO, modeling ROI on people decisions with the same rigor applied to plants, software, or acquisitions. They make the financial case for investing in ingenuity, showing how mentorship hours, design sprints, and coaching conversations yield outcomes that outperform capital spending.

The Talent Scout
This CPO constantly maps talent within and beyond the company. They track reputation graphs, open-source contributions, and network influence. They see beyond CVs, identifying the sparks of ingenuity that could shape future business models.

The CEO's Consigliere
Finally, the CPO becomes the CEO's trusted partner. Not a coach on the sidelines, but a co-architect of decisions. They bring psychological depth, the courage to confront blind spots, and the wisdom to hold up a mirror to themselves. They are the one voice in the room able to say what others will not, safeguarding both the CEO's growth and the organization's future.

The Board asked whether she would provide more information on each capability category.

The Talent Asset Manager

For over a century, boards and investors had treated people as costs to be controlled, not as assets to be invested in. Balance sheets capture property, plant, and equipment, as well as intangibles such as patents and goodwill. But the capacity, energy, and ingenuity of people? That had never been treated with the same seriousness, even though every CEO claimed, "Our people are our greatest asset."

Future-facing organizations are beginning to challenge this blind spot. Microsoft, for example, has developed "human capital accounting" frameworks that report on workforce investments in its annual filings, a move the SEC is encouraging with new disclosure standards. Investors, such as BlackRock, have demanded human capital metrics in ESG reports, recognizing that talent velocity and retention are as crucial as financial leverage. In Denmark, Novo Nordisk tracks learning hours per employee alongside revenue per employee, treating both as inputs to sustainable growth. The beginnings are there, but they are still fragmented, experimental, not yet the central grammar of corporate performance.

To make this role real, Chris had realized, a future CPO could not emerge solely from the HR department. The path would have to blend finance, psychology, and operations. Someone who had led a P&L, so they understood capital allocation. Someone who had studied organizational behavior or neuroscience, so they understood how people actually grow. Someone who had walked through consulting or M&A, where intangible value is scrutinized, and knew how to model the ROI of culture. This was not a graduate of payroll systems or policy manuals. This builder could argue for capital efficiency in one sentence and human flourishing in the next.

She gave the Board an example of someone she admired: a former colleague who had started in investment banking, spent a decade in emerging market operations, and then retrained in psychology mid-career. They were the kind of leaders who could look at a spreadsheet of attrition rates and see not just numbers but energy leaking from the system. They could walk into a factory and notice where learning was happening naturally, where ingenuity was suffocating. Chris thought: That's what a talent asset manager looks like. Not an administrator of programs, but a steward of compounding human capital.

And yet, she knew how little the executive search industry understood this. Search firms still presented CHRO candidates from a narrow pool, typically comprising HR business partners, compensation specialists, or learning directors. All are fine in their own way, but none are trained to treat people as appreciating assets. The vocabulary wasn't there yet. No one was writing specifications that sounded like hers. Chris recircled the term: Talent Asset Manager.

CFOs pioneered the concept of financial leverage. In the Ingenuity Age, CPOs would need to invent human leverage, the disciplined compounding of potential into performance, growth, and resilience.

The Talent Choreographer

Every organization runs on its people's time, the scarcest and most expensive asset on the balance sheet. Yet few leaders treat time allocation with the same rigor as financial allocation. People sit in back-to-back meetings, lost in email floods, pulled into projects with no clear purpose. Energy leaks silently, while ingenuity suffocates. A choreographer was precisely what the CPO needed to be: someone who could orchestrate time and attention so that human creativity found rhythm, not exhaustion.

Some future-facing companies are beginning to get a glimpse of this. Atlassian has studied "meeting debt" and mandated no-meeting days to protect focus. Shopify recently deleted 12,000 recurring meetings from calendars, freeing 300,000 hours for deep work. Slack and Microsoft Teams now embed analytics that show collaboration overload, while firms like Asana and Time Is Ltd. track how team energy is being consumed. The beginnings of talent choreography exist, but, like human capital accounting, they remain experiments, not yet a central leadership practice.

Chris realized this role could never come from a traditional HR pipeline. The career path of a talent choreographer would blend operations, design thinking, and behavioral science. They might have managed large-scale supply chains, where timing and flow were crucial. Or led digital product teams, where sprint cycles and rituals defined energy. Perhaps they studied architecture or music earlier in life, disciplines that understand rhythm, structure, and space. Above all, they would be someone who saw time as a system to be designed, not a diary to be filled.

What this emphatically did not mean, Chris thought, was the tired arithmetic of full-time equivalents. For decades, organizations had reduced people to FTEs, a blunt calculation of hours per week, often 37.5 or 40, as if human creativity could be divided into blocks like factory shifts. It was the logic of tuna canning: the more cans a worker sealed in an hour, the more productive they were. But ingenuity does not emerge from counting hours or filling seats. Ingenuity comes from the choreography of time, aligning focus, recovery, collaboration, and imagination so that the exact hour produces tenfold the insight.

She emphasized that we need to stop measuring people in FTEs. Start measuring the stage you've set for their ingenuity. The real choreographer doesn't just allocate hours; they create environments where the rhythm of human energy aligns with the rhythm of organizational purpose. A three-hour design sprint, run at the right moment, can produce what three hundred hours of scattered meetings never could. Time, Chris realized, was not the commodity. Time was the canvas. And only a choreographer understood how to make it an art form.

In this example, she spoke about an executive she had once worked with a COO who never started a meeting without asking, "Is this the highest and best use of this hour?" He had trained as an engineer, then retrained in organizational design. He mapped meetings like production lines, stripping away waste, layering in pauses, and inserting rituals that reset energy. Chris thought: That's what a talent choreographer looks like. Not a meeting police officer, but a designer of flow, someone who makes sure human ingenuity is spent on what matters most.

But again, she knew the executive search firms weren't ready. They would describe the role as "HR business partner" or "head of organizational effectiveness." None would dare write talent choreographer on a specification. The language hadn't been invented yet.

Chris recircled the phrase with a steady hand: Talent Choreographer. If CFOs allocated capital to drive returns, the new CPO would need to choreograph human time to multiply ingenuity. Time, not money, was the new constraint and the new frontier.

The Talent Capitalist

Capitalism was initially intended to focus on financial assets, returns, and shareholder value. But the more she thought about it, the clearer it became. The organizations that would thrive in the Ingenuity Age would be those that invest in talent with the same rigor, discipline, and expectation of return as they invest in factories, software, or acquisitions.

The problem was that for too long, investments in people had been treated as discretionary "spend." Training budgets were slashed in downturns. Coaching was viewed as a perk for the few, rather than a multiplier for the many. Benefits were compared line by line in spreadsheets, with no recognition that their real value lay in psychological safety and sustained ingenuity. Even when "talent ROI" was mentioned, it was a footnote at best. Chris could see it now: the CPO of tomorrow had to change the grammar, turning talent from soft rhetoric into hard capital.

Future-facing firms are inching toward this logic. McKinsey has argued that talent allocation is as important as capital allocation, urging boards to review where their best people are deployed with the same seriousness as financial flows. Unilever experiments with "purpose-driven pay," explicitly linking compensation to sustainability and human outcomes alongside shareholder return. Venture capital firms such as a16z and Sequoia now embed talent partners into portfolio companies, recognizing that scaling ingenuity is as critical as scaling revenue. These are still scattered practices, but they indicate a new discipline emerging: treating human ingenuity as capital that must be invested in, monitored, and nurtured.

Chris presented a career path that would prepare someone for this role. They would need financial literacy to debate head-to-head with the CFO, armed with the same vocabulary of ROI, multiples, and risk-adjusted returns. But they would also need psychological insight, an ability to know when investments in people compound and when they collapse. Perhaps their path wound through corporate finance and executive development. Maybe they had worked in private equity, where talent and capital intersect under high-stakes pressure, and then studied adult development to understand how leaders truly grow. It was a rare blend, but Chris knew it was the only way forward.

She gave the Board an example of a private equity partner she had once known: brilliant with capital models, but unusual among his peers in that he spent as much time interviewing leadership teams as he did reviewing spreadsheets. He would ask, "Where does the energy go here? Who multiplies it, who drains it?" He knew instinctively that no model survived if the human system failed. Chris thought: That's what a talent capitalist looks likesomeone who sees beyond the numbers to the ingenuity that drives them, and invests accordingly.

And yet, once again, Chris knew the search firms weren't there. They would present candidates with decades of HR generalist experience who were comfortable with competency frameworks but untrained in capital modeling. Or they would look to finance leaders, hoping they could "pick up" the human side as they went. Neither approach came close to the integration she was describing. The vocabulary didn't exist in the market.

She recircled the phrase: Talent Capitalist. In the Industrial Age, financial capital defined leverage. In the Information Age, intellectual capital defined scale. In the Ingenuity Age, human capital must be treated as capital in the truest sense, invested in, managed for return, and accounted for as the most vital driver of resilience and renewal. The CPO's job would be nothing less than making this discipline real.

The Talent Scout

At first, it felt familiar. Every HR leader claimed to be scouting for talent, and every recruiter carried that mantle. But she knew this was something far beyond job fairs and headhunters. The future CPO had to operate as a scout in the truest sense: constantly searching, mapping, and bringing forward sparks of ingenuity wherever they might be found, not just within the company's walls.

In the Industrial Age, talent scouting was literal. Supervisors picked workers at factory gates; corporate recruiters poached candidates from rival companies. By the Information Age, it had become more sophisticated but also more constrained: databases, job boards, psychometric tests, and LinkedIn filters. All efficient, all standardized, but all biased toward people who already looked like yesterday's hires. The true scouts of the Ingenuity Age would have to break open those boundaries.

Some firms are already experimenting. GitHub's open-source contributions now serve as live résumés, showcasing not only code but also collaboration style. Kaggle competitions surface data science talent globally, allowing anyone to demonstrate ingenuity regardless of formal credentials. Airbnb and other platforms recruit from non-traditional pools, turning hosts or community builders into employees. Deloitte's "skills-based organization" research encourages firms to hire not for roles but for fluid capabilities. These signals all point to a radical future: where talent is scouted by visible ingenuity rather than inherited pedigree.

Chris thought about what kind of career path would prepare someone to be a scout like this. They might have worked in venture capital, where the hunt for founders forces investors to spot sparks others miss. Or in creative industries such as film, music, design, where spotting raw, unconventional potential is the skill. Or perhaps they came up through product development, constantly scanning communities for emerging user talent. Regardless of their background, it would not be a traditional HR experience. This was not about filling roles; it was about widening the aperture of imagination.

She presented to the Board an example of a woman she had once met, a casting director who had transitioned into an executive recruiter. She could spot in five minutes whether someone had the charisma to lead a movement or was rehearsing lines. She didn't care about Ivy League credentials. She wanted to know: Who listens deeply? Who attracts followership? Who makes others braver? Chris thought: That's what a talent scout looks like. Not a résumé shuffler, but someone who can see ingenuity hiding in plain sight.

But again, she knew the search industry wasn't ready. Executive search firms still recycled the same lists of candidates. People already visible in the system, already credentialed, already chosen. None were equipped to map networks, communities, or reputational flows across industries and geographies. They were still looking at the surface; the scout she imagined had to see the spark beneath.

Chris recircled the phrase: "Talent Scout." In the Industrial Age, talent was found at the factory gate. In the Information Age, it was pulled from databases. In the Ingenuity Age, it would be scouted in the wild: in networks, in communities, wherever ingenuity revealed itself. The CPO would be the one with the eye to see it and the courage to bring it inside.

The CEO's Consigliere

A consigliere was not just an advisor; they were the one person in the room who could say what no one else dared, the one who saw the whole person, not just the executive performance. If the CFO brought capital discipline and the COO brought operational steadiness, the CPO had to bring truth, the unvarnished kind that protects both the leader and the system they serve.

In the Industrial Age, personnel chiefs did not typically assume this role. They were administrators, record-keepers, and compliance officers. In the Information Age, CHROs have edged closer to coaching, leadership development, 360-degree feedback, and a "seat at the table." However, their influence was still conditional. The CEO could pick and choose when to listen, and too often, the people's voice was drowned out by finance, strategy, or operations. In the Irrelevance Age, Chris realized, this was no longer optional. CEOs needed a consigliere, not a program manager, not an HR partner, but a co-architect of decisions, standing at their side with equal weight.

Some leaders already glimpse this. Satya Nadella has spoken of how empathy reshaped Microsoft's strategy, driven not by numbers but by a deep people-centric philosophy. At Unilever, Leena Nair's tenure as CHRO elevated people decisions to board-level strategy, a strategy that continues in her role as CEO of Chanel. At Netflix, Patty McCord helped Reed Hastings craft the "freedom and responsibility" culture that became central to its rise. These are hints of what a consigliere can be: not the one running HR programs, but the one shaping the CEO's own philosophy of leadership.

Chris knew that to grow into this role, a CPO's career could not be narrow. They needed the left-brain training in analytics, finance, and systems so they could sit in boardrooms and hold their own against CFOs and investors. However, they also required a thorough understanding of psychology, anthropology, and philosophy so they could have a mirror to the CEO's behavior and the culture it was shaping. Few leaders blended both, but the ones who did were extraordinary.

She spoke about someone she had once encountered in a leadership program, a psychologist who had become a COO. They could hold a P&L meeting with ruthless clarity in the morning, then spend the afternoon coaching the CEO through a crisis of confidence without flinching. They didn't flatter; they didn't soften. They said what needed to be said, in language the CEO could hear. Chris thought: That's what a consigliere looks like. Not a yes-person. Not a technician. A steward of the leader's humanity and the organization's future, at the same time.

And again, she saw how ill-equipped the search firms were. They still sold "safe" profiles: those of HR leaders who had managed compensation and benefits, or consultants who had run leadership workshops. Competent, yes. Courageous? Rarely. Almost none had trained in both psychology and finance, and none had walked the bridge between hard capital and soft humanity. But Chris knew this was precisely what the Ingenuity Age required.

She recircled the phrase: CEO's Consigliere. In the Industrial Age, CEOs had administrators. In the Information Age, they had advisors. In the Ingenuity Age, they would need a consigliere; someone who could integrate the analytic and the human, the strategic and the psychological. Someone who would not just help them lead the company, but also allow them to remain human while doing it.

A director leaned forward. "Chris, you've described a Chief People Officer we haven't seen before. Is Yuki up to it?"

Chris chose her words carefully. "Not yet. Yuki doesn't have the range of finance, operations, and psychology that this role will demand. She spent her entire career in HR, and this job is not a continuation of the CHRO model. It's something else entirely. But I believe she can lead this year's work. She has candor, system sense, and the courage to put people at the center. I want to give her that chance, while at the same time searching for the person who can fully inhabit this new definition of CPO."

She let the silence settle. "That search won't be easy. I'll need a lateral, future-thinking search partner who understands this isn't a CHRO hire or even what today's market calls a 'Chief People Officer.' It's a hybrid role that doesn't yet exist. But the Board's permission to find it and to develop Yuki in parallel gives us a path forward."

CEO's Reflection, That Evening

Later, as Chris walked back to her hotel along the edge of Circular Quay, she replayed the day. The Board had endorsed the Talent workstream, focusing on sourcing contributions, enabling community engagement, developing through experiments, and rewarding the invisible glue. They had also authorized the search for a new Chief People Officer: someone who could be an asset manager, choreographer, capitalist, scout, and consigliere all at once.

But her mind kept circling back to Yuki. For the next eleven months, Yuki would carry the visible burden of leading Talent. Chris knew she would need coaching, exposure to finance and operations, and the confidence to grow beyond the limits of HR. If Yuki rose to the challenge, Omnivista might not need the external hire. If she stumbled, Chris would have to move decisively.

She paused by the water, the Opera House glowing white against the night. Tomorrow, John would lead them into the next lever: Structure. Talent had given them the *who*. Structure would decide *how*. And the shadow of the new Chief People Officer, whoever it might be, would hover over every step.

Self-Assessment for ORG6, Lever 1: Talent

Rate yourself honestly. For each question, score both the Foundation and the AI Amplifier.
1 Not Yet · 2 Emerging · 3 Developing · 4 Practicing · 5 Second Nature

---

1.

Foundation. Our talent processes free people to focus on growth, creativity, and trust, not administrative burden.
  Foundation score (1–5):_____

AI Amplifier. We use AI to handle administrative talent tasks so HR and managers invest in human development.
  AI Amplifier score (1–5):_____

2.

Foundation. We source, enable, develop, and retain talent as a living system, not an annual HR cycle.
  Foundation score (1–5):_____

AI Amplifier. We use AI to create dynamic talent marketplaces, personalize development, and predict retention risk.
  AI Amplifier score (1–5):_____

3.

Foundation. We invest in building Ingenuity Capabilities: systems thinking, ethical courage, co-creation, learning velocity, and narrative clarity.
  Foundation score (1–5):_____

AI Amplifier. We use AI to identify capability gaps and recommend targeted development, not just generic training.
  AI Amplifier score (1–5):_____

4.

Foundation. Internal talent mobility is real. People grow through rotations, stretch assignments, and multi-dimensional careers.

Foundation score (1–5):_____

AI Amplifier. We use AI to match people to opportunities across the organization based on skills, interests, and growth potential.

AI Amplifier score (1–5):_____

5.

Foundation. Our people feel their growth is invested in, not managed through annual reviews alone.

Foundation score (1–5):_____

AI Amplifier. We use AI to give people leadership real-time insight into talent flows, capability gaps, and energy patterns, treating decisions about people with the same rigor as decisions about capital.

AI Amplifier score (1–5):_____

AVERAGE SCORE: ORG6, Lever 1: Talent

*Foundation average (total of five scores ÷ 5):*_____

*AI Amplifier average (total of five scores ÷ 5):*_____

Now: Transfer these two averages to the "Talent" row of your ORG6 Scoreboard at the back of the book.

"Every organization is perfectly designed to get the results it gets."

attributed to **W. Edwards Deming**

"Structure is not the skeleton of an organization; it is the bloodstream. It decides whether
ingenuity circulates or clots."

Katharine McLennan

CHAPTER 10

Structure

Will our structure entrench control,
friction and fatigue,
or
drive performance and collaboration?

1 August — **SYDNEY**

First Day of Month: Executive Team

Overnight rain had rinsed the city. By morning, the harbor was glass, ferries drawing clean white lines across the blue. The team gathered in a sunlit room near Barangaroo. Yesterday had been Talent's closeout with the Board; today, John would open Structure.

John Wallace, CFO, stood without a deck. A single page lay on the table in front of him. At the top, in thick marker: "Design matters."

"Revenue is three percent off plan, costs five percent over," he began. "But that's the symptom. Our structure is the cause." He drew a simple frame on the whiteboard.

The first word he wrote was *Design*. "In São Paulo, they rebalanced quarterly, dissolving project shells and re-forming around evidence. When facts changed, the org changed. Time-to-impact decreased, and bad bets were eliminated early. That's structure as living design. Here in Sydney, some programs are still funded for twelve months, as if they're on rails. Teams feel the glue; no budget follows the learning. That's structure as a cage."

He wrote a second header: *Authority*. "In Bangalore, Sanjay's teams now use an advice process: consult an expert, a stakeholder, and a skeptic, then decide close to the work and log the trade-off in one sentence. Cycle time on reversible decisions collapsed from weeks to days. That's authority as stewardship. But here in Sydney, routine approvals still ricochet up five layers before returning to the team that proposed them. By the time the answer arrives, the window has closed. That's authority as escalation theater."

He wrote a third header: *Collaboration*. "In Dublin, aged care partnered with Bangalore's digital team and shipped a prototype 'presence ledger' in six weeks: one room, one backlog, one decision rhythm. That's flow. However, Tokyo labs and our Sydney hub each built separate assay pipelines last quarter, parallel efforts, with no conversation until customers noticed the duplication. That's noise dressed as productivity."

He added a fourth header: *Inclusion*. "In Bangalore, squads run an advice process: state the decision, seek affected voices, decide close to the work, log the trade-offs:

diverse input, clear ownership, visible results. However, in Dublin, we staged an appearance of inclusion for a photo and left authority unchanged. Optics without redistribution. Inclusion means who *decides*, not who's in the picture."

He stepped back. "Structure isn't a chart. It's a choice to freeze or to flow."

John then led the team two blocks to the Barangaroo Biotech Hub, his signal site for the year. He didn't give a tour so much as a series of proof points on how structure had begun to shift from chart to flow.

DESIGN (what the work is shaped around). On a glass wall, tiles showed ninety-day missions instead of departments. Each tile had an owner, an outcome, and an expiration date associated with the funding. A small dashboard read: "Reallocated this quarter: AU$2.1m; Sunsets: 4; Missions renewed by evidence: 7." The Budget was following learning, not last year's plan.

AUTHORITY (who decides, how, and where). A simple Decision Ledger sat on a table, one line per choice: the question, the advice sought (expert, stakeholder, skeptic), the trade-off in one sentence, and the steward. A heat map beside it showed cycle time collapsing from twenty-three days to seven for "two-way-door" decisions. Escalations had dropped; choices were made close to the work.

COLLABORATION (how boundaries work). Around a steel Dependency Table, teams had drawn and erased lines all morning. "Merge Mondays" had retired two duplicate analytics streams. An internal bot flagged overlapping backlogs across sites and suggested merges, displaying the number of hours returned and reuse scores in the table.

INCLUSION (who truly shapes the outcome). Inside a small room were two stools labeled "Edge Voices": one for a patient/clinician proxy and one for a maker from outside the project. Decisions weren't valid unless either the stools were filled or a deferral reason was logged. Below, a note: "This week: Edge input changed 2/8 decisions."

John let the room absorb it. "None of this needed a reorg. We changed how money flows, how decisions are recorded, how duplication is killed, and who sits in the room. That's structure."

Team Assignments for the Month

Chris gathered the team after the site walk. "Structure has four domains: design, authority, collaboration, and inclusion. Each of you takes one domain and runs a pilot at your site. Show me what changes when we redesign structure for flow rather than control."

- *Yuki (Tokyo): Design*. "Convert one legacy program into a ninety-day mission with a named outcome, a cross-disciplinary team, and funding that expires unless renewed by evidence. Show me what was stopped, what was merged, and whether the mission delivered faster than the old structure."

- *John (Sydney): Authority*. "Publish the Decision Ledger template company-wide. Classify decisions as two-way doors and one-way doors. Keep two-way decisions at the team level. Show me cycle time, escalations avoided, and whether trust increased."

- *Maria (São Paulo): Collaboration*. "Build a single discharge backlog shared by nursing, ops, and social work. Retire duplicate trackers. Run weekly Merge Mondays so dependencies surface before they jam the system. Show me dwell time, hours returned, and duplicate tasks eliminated."

- *Sanjay (Bangalore): Inclusion*. "Reserve a caregiver or clinician seat in sprint reviews. Add an edge-voice field in every decision record. Show me how many decisions changed after edge input and what the clinical partners say about the experience."

- *Liam (Dublin): Design*. "Redesign the week around a single cadence: clinical, activities, and family touchpoints on one rhythm. Protect two maker blocks per caregiver per week. Show me whether clashes decrease and whether staff energy improves."

"End of the month, São Paulo. Bring results."

CEO's Notebook: Structure

That night, the harbor wind had a clean edge as Chris walked the foreshore back toward her hotel. Talent had set the 'who'. Structure would decide on the 'how', where time, attention, and trust would flow or leak. She opened her notebook:

Actions

1. Push one decision to the edge each day. Find a choice parked at the top, move it to the team closest to the customer, and ask for the trade-off in a sentence.

2. Remove one layer or step each day. Kill a sign-off, a meeting, or a dashboard that adds latency without learning and publish what replaced it.

3. Bridge one boundary each day. Pair two overlapping efforts under a single outcome and cadence.

What I'll Notice

1. *Industrial*: titles hoarding decisions; charts pretending to be reality; permission outranking proximity.

2. *Information*: matrices and dashboards that create virtual committees, agile in name, latency in practice.

3. *Irrelevance*: Frozen budgets, duplicate streams, inclusion as optics rather than power.

4. *Ingenuity*: missions reconfigured quarterly; advice processes documenting judgment; money follows evidence.

5. *Imagination*: structures behaving like living networks, resources and rights flowing across firm and community.

Chris closed the notebook. Tomorrow would be the grind: one decision moved, one step removed, one boundary bridged, every day until São Paulo.

My Fingerprint

For most of the 1990s and into the 2000s, I was part of a consulting practice that restructured large organizations. The methodology was Elliott Jaques' Requisite Organisation: a rigorous, seven-level hierarchy from CEO to the front line, with each level defined by its time horizon of decision-making. Level one thought in days. Level seven thought in decades. The system specified decision rights, accountability boundaries, and the principle that no leader should dip into the work of the level below. It was elegant, systematic, and deeply logical. Australia's major banks adopted it. So did our mining companies. I spent years inside these organizations, drawing the architecture, clarifying who owned what, eliminating the overlaps and the gaps. When it worked, it worked beautifully. Confusion disappeared. Accountability became visible. People knew exactly where they stood.

But that was a world where the hierarchy matched the flow of information. The CEO had the widest view because information traveled upward through the levels. The graduate at level one saw only their immediate task. The structure made sense because the person at the top genuinely had access to more context than the person at the bottom.

AI has demolished that assumption. Today, a twenty-two-year-old graduate with the right AI tools can see patterns across the entire organization that the CEO cannot. A chief scientist who has spent thirty years as a technical expert, off to the side with no one reporting to her, may hold the insight that reshapes the company's next decade. The source of vision is no longer reliably at the top. The source of wisdom is no longer reliably in the hierarchy at all. And the organizations I walk into now are being choked by the very structures I once helped build: seven layers of approval for a decision that a team at the edge could make in an afternoon, budget cycles that fund last year's plan while this year's opportunity closes, and escalation paths that exist not to improve judgment but to diffuse accountability.

Frédéric Laloux mapped this challenge more clearly than anyone I have read. In Reinventing Organizations, he traces organizational paradigms across the full arc of human development, from foraging bands a hundred thousand years ago, through authority by elders, to powerful chiefdoms, then to the formal hierarchies and command-and-control structures of the industrial era, the stick. From there, the effective matrix emerges: predict and control, the carrot, shareholder value, the orange world most corporations still inhabit. Beyond that, a green paradigm where relationships and stakeholder perspectives begin to matter more than pure output. And at the frontier, teal: self-management for evolutionary purpose.

What Laloux draws on is not IQ. It is vertical intelligence, a developmental framework that measures not how smart a person is but how complex a reality they can hold without collapsing it into simple answers. Each stage of organizational development corresponds to a stage of human consciousness: the capacity to see more perspectives, tolerate more ambiguity, and integrate more contradiction. A red organization needs a chief. An amber organization needs a hierarchy. An orange organization needs a matrix. A teal organization needs something else entirely: the capacity to self-organize around purpose, with authority flowing to wherever the insight lives.

Most organizations today are amber-orange with green aspirations and teal fantasies. And all of them, at every color, still cling to rigid job titles and rigid job descriptions as if the work itself were fixed. I have never met a person yet who knows what their original job description said. The document was written before they arrived, by someone who had never done the role, for a world that had already moved on. Yet we use these artifacts to hire, to evaluate, to promote, and to restructure. In the AI Era, where the content of work shifts monthly, the job description is not just outdated. It is a fossil from an age that assumed stability was the norm and change was the exception.

The structures I built in the 1990s were orange at their best: clear, accountable, efficient. But orange assumes that the hierarchy is the smartest entity in the room. In the AI Era, it is not.

What I am seeing now, in the small number of organizations brave enough to redesign from the inside out, is something closer to a honeycomb. The metaphor holds because it is structural, not sentimental. A honeycomb is not flat. It is not a matrix. It is not a hierarchy. Every cell is hexagonal, strong in itself, but its strength comes from shared walls with every adjacent cell. No cell commands another. The structure holds because of connection, not control. When the colony needs to grow, new cells are added at the edge. When a cell is damaged, the adjacent cells absorb the load. There is no reorg. There is continuous adaptation.

And yes, there is always a queen. The honeycomb is not leaderless. But the queen does not direct the work. She sets the conditions for the colony's survival. The workers constantly shift their roles as the environment changes: foragers become nurses, builders become defenders, and the community reconfigures without anyone issuing a memo. The structure is alive because it was designed for flow, not for control.

That is the direction I believe organizational structure is heading. But I want to be honest: I have no idea what it will actually look like. I do not think anyone does. The organizations experimenting with self-management and fluid teams are still in the early chapters of a story none of us can see the end of. As AI expands, as it absorbs more of what we used to call "the job," the very idea of a fixed structure may dissolve into something we do not yet have language for. What I do know is that the rigid seven levels I once helped build will not survive, elegant as they were. The matrix will not survive. The fixed job title and the three-page job description will not survive. What will replace them is something we will have to imagine in partnership with AI, continuously, honestly, and with the humility to admit that the next design is always provisional. The only thing I am certain of is that the organizations willing to keep redesigning, to treat structure as a living experiment rather than an answered question, will be the ones that find their way.

The ORG6 Lever for Structure

A hierarchical and controlled approach characterized the organizational structure in the Industrial Age. In contrast, in the Information Age, it evolved into layered matrices, dashboards, and global coordination, until complexity itself became a hindrance to progress. The possibilities for the structure divide into three possible tomorrows:

> **Corrosive Irrelevance**: frozen charts, political allocation, and bottlenecked authority, where AI multiplies paralysis.
>
> **Optimistic Ingenuity**: mission-led teams, distributed authority, quarterly resource rebalancing, and collaboration designed for flow.
>
> **Imaginative Possibility**: structures as living networks, continuously reconfiguring around purpose, where inclusion is not optics but power shifting in real time.

The signals are everywhere. In *design*, you can see whether resources flow to learning or remain trapped in politics. In *authority*, you can see whether decisions are made close to the customer or are endlessly escalated upward. In *collaboration*, you can feel whether teams form fluidly across boundaries or duplicate effort inside silos. Additionally, you can determine whether diversity is present but voiceless, or actively shaping the choices that matter. What you notice in each of these four dimensions reveals which yesterday you are repeating and which tomorrow you are choosing.

Design

Industrial Age

Organizational design in the Industrial Age was built for hierarchy. Structures resembled factory lines: neat boxes stacked on charts, each one reporting upward to the next layer. Authority flowed vertically, decisions accumulated at the top, and efficiency was the governing principle. Railroads in the late 19th century pioneered this model, using multi-layered chains of command to manage thousands of miles of track and workers. Henry Ford perfected it in the 20th century: assembly lines humming in unison, management dictating every movement. It worked for scale and predictability, but it came at the cost of adaptability.

Information Age

By the late 20th century, design became more complex, not less. Companies like IBM and Procter & Gamble adopted global matrices to coordinate geographies, products, and functions simultaneously. In theory, this unlocked agility. In practice, employees were whipsawed between competing bosses, reporting lines multiplied, and decisions bogged down in committee reviews. Dashboards offered leaders the illusion of control, but absolute clarity was rare. John gave an example of how his finance team mirrored this pattern: resources allocated annually, frozen in cost centers, and rarely shifted even when markets screamed for flexibility.

Irrelevance Age

The danger is that this frozen logic calcifies further. Maria gave an example of her whiteboard reality map, showing what it looked like in practice: a single initiative to reduce cardiac readmissions required 23 separate approvals and took 87 days to complete. Meanwhile, competitors using AI-assisted care coordination responded within forty-eight hours. Org charts gave the impression of order, but in reality, capital was trapped, talent was paralyzed, and learning was delayed. Add AI, and the brittleness multiplies: software can now model resource allocation scenarios endlessly, but if politics still decides, all AI does is automate the paralysis. Irrelevance here is not chaos. It is precision without movement.

Ingenuity Age

Now, we can learn from other organizations that show how design can be reimagined for optimal flow. Haier, the Chinese appliance maker, dismantled its traditional hierarchy into thousands of micro-enterprises, each with the authority to reallocate resources in line with customer needs. Supercell, the Finnish game studio behind Clash of Clans, organized its entire company around independent cells of five to seven people, each with full authority to develop, test, and kill their own games. When a cell's game failed to find traction, the team celebrated the learning and disbanded. When it succeeded, the cell scaled. The company generated over $1.5 billion in annual revenue with fewer than four hundred employees.

Maria had given an example of where ingenuity had begun to take hold: São Paulo's pilot team mirrored this thinking, reviewing resources quarterly rather than annually, doubling down on what worked, and killing off projects that didn't. AI plays a constructive role here, surfacing real-time performance data and collaboration signals so that leaders can redeploy talent quickly, but humans make the judgment and publish the rationale.

Imaginative Possibility

Here we rely on choreography rather than a structured approach. Automattic, the company behind WordPress.com, operates with over 1,900 employees across ninety-plus countries and no headquarters. Its design is built on open documentation, radical transparency, and distributed authority. Teams form around projects, communicate asynchronously through internal blogs and shared documents, and ship continuously. The company has sustained this model for nearly two decades, proving that structure can be entirely decoupled from physical presence.

Decentralized autonomous organizations in the Web3 ecosystem take it a step further by assigning decision rights algorithmically and reconfiguring teams via smart contracts. For Omnivista, this raises a provocative question: what if design itself became adaptive, with AI running thousands of "what if" simulations and teams forming around opportunities in real time? Here, design ceases to be a box-and-line artifact. It becomes a living network, continuously reconfiguring around purpose, with authority, collaboration, and inclusion woven in from the start.

Authority

Industrial Age

Authority was positional. Titles equaled power, and obedience was enforced by hierarchy. The foreman's bark on the factory floor carried absolute weight, backed by layers of supervisors, directors, and executives above. Decisions were slow but predictable, and employees were treated as extensions of machines, with little expectation of judgment or creativity.

Information Age

Here, we promised decentralization, but often delivered more complexity. Companies introduced OKRs to cascade authority into measurable goals, and Amazon's escalation culture permitted even junior employees to push decisions upward if risks were sensed. In practice, dashboards multiplied, decision committees grew larger, and middle managers bore the brunt, squeezed between risk-averse leaders above and impatient teams.

Irrelevance Age

These patterns risk collapsing into a state of paralysis. AI engines can now generate decision recommendations based on historical data, but that data often encodes past biases. A global bank trialed an AI vendor-selection tool only to find it consistently chose the same suppliers used in previous decades. Managers distrusted the algorithm, escalated decisions to higher levels, and further slowed the process. At Omnivista, John had given the example of the same pattern: even routine approvals ricocheted up five layers before returning to the team that had proposed them. Authority, trapped between algorithms and escalations, corrodes trust and multiplies delay.

Ingenuity Age

Authority is expressed as stewardship, not title. Buurtzorg, the Dutch homecare organization, empowers nurse-led teams to set their own budgets, schedules, and priorities without the intervention of middle management. WL Gore has long practiced "lattice leadership," where associates follow leaders they trust, not those formally appointed. In both models, AI plays a supportive role: mapping collaboration networks to surface hidden leaders or providing decision journals that make choices transparent. At Omnivista, Yuki Nakamura provided the example of adopting advice processes that require leaders to consult an expert, a stakeholder, and a skeptic before making a decision. The result was not slower deliberation, but faster movement, because authority was trusted.

Imaginative Possibility

Authority becomes dynamic, a current people enter and leave, not a title they hold indefinitely. Decentralized autonomous organizations already experiment with distributing authority through smart contracts, rotating decision-making rights among members. Imagine AI modeling who in a network is currently most trusted, most connected, or most capable of judgment in a given context, and assigning stewardship accordingly. Authority becomes situational: granted for a specific mission and then redistributed. For Omnivista, John had wondered aloud: What if budget rights rotated quarterly to those who demonstrated learning velocity, rather than just positional seniority? Authority ceases to be a pyramid and becomes a flow, legitimized not by hierarchy, but by contribution and trust.

Collaboration

Industrial Age

Collaboration was largely unnecessary and often discouraged. Work was divided into rigid functions, with tasks handed down from supervisors. Departments sat in silos, each measured by its own outputs. The factory floor was designed for efficiency, not teamwork: one person riveted, another painted, another inspected. Coordination across roles was mechanical rather than relational. It produced consistency, but when unexpected problems emerged, the lack of collaboration left organizations brittle.

Information Age

Cross-functional collaboration became a corporate mantra. Companies created matrix organizations and proliferated meetings meant to "connect the dots." Consulting firms recommended cross-functional steering committees; technology companies layered project management systems to integrate work across geographies. Yet often, this collaboration created more noise than value. Employees at IBM and HP in the 1990s, for example, joked about "death by meeting" as they sat through endless cross-functional reviews. At Omnivista, Maria had shared that the operations team experienced the same: dozens of coordination calls without decisions, work duplicated across regions, and speed sacrificed to optics.

Irrelevance Age

Collaboration risks collapsing into overload. Tools like Slack, Teams, and Zoom multiply communication, but not always connection. AI summarization now produces endless transcripts and reports. Information is abundant, but alignment is scarce. At Omnivista, one project team found itself in forty-two separate Slack channels for the same initiative. Instead of collaboration, they experienced fragmentation. Here, corrosive irrelevance appears as digital busyness: duplicated work, meetings without clarity, and AI amplifying chatter instead of sharpening focus.

Ingenuity Age

Collaboration is a flow across boundaries. Spotify's squad model made collaboration the default: small teams with all the skills needed to deliver, aligned around a clear mission. Pixar designed its headquarters to bring animators, engineers, and directors together in shared spaces, sparking ideas across disciplines. In Bangalore, Sanjay had piloted cross-boundary mission teams empowered to assemble resources quickly, dissolving after delivering outcomes. AI supports this ingenuity by mapping dependencies, flagging duplication, and even recommending new connections across geographies. Collaboration becomes less about endless meetings and more about shared creation.

Imaginative Possibility

Collaboration is a living network. GitHub shows what this can look like: developers worldwide collaborate asynchronously on code, with contributions visible, tested, and reused instantly. Open-source science projects, such as Folding@home, enlist thousands of contributors to solve biomedical puzzles, with each small effort contributing to a collective breakthrough. Decentralized Autonomous Organizations (DAOs) extend this concept even further, choreographing collaboration across communities through token-based incentives. Imagine Omnivista's teams collaborating not only across functions but across industries such as health providers, tech partners, and regulators, working on shared platforms, with AI curating contributions and aligning incentives. In this vision, collaboration is no longer an organizational activity but a systemic capacity.

Inclusion

Industrial Age

Inclusion was almost nonexistent. Workforces were segmented by class, gender, and race, with leadership ranks dominated by white men in most industries. Labor was viewed as interchangeable, and conformity was highly valued. Immigrants, women, and minorities often found themselves relegated to the hardest, lowest-paid jobs with little possibility of advancement. The difference was treated as a liability rather than a strength.

Information Age

Diversity became a recognized corporate priority, though often framed in terms of compliance and optics. Equal opportunity laws and affirmative action policies forced change in some markets, and companies created diversity dashboards, awareness training, and Chief Diversity Officer roles. Representation numbers were published in annual reports, and demographic categories were used to measure progress. Yet inclusion often remained superficial: a seat at the table without an authentic voice. In São Paulo, Maria had shared how her D&I reports proudly listed percentages of women and minorities in leadership, yet the same five voices still dominated every operating review.

Irrelevance Age

The risk of inclusion sliding backward under the guise of objectivity. Algorithms trained on historical hiring and promotion data have already been shown to encode bias, filtering out candidates who don't fit established patterns. Amazon famously scrapped an AI recruiting tool when it systematically downgraded résumés that included the word "women's." In Bangalore, Sanjay had shared that his early trials with AI-driven performance scores produced eerily consistent results: those who already resembled past leaders ranked highest, while unconventional contributors were often overlooked. Irrelevance here is tokenism on autopilot: demographic diversity presented in dashboards, while AI systems reinforce conformity and suppress ingenuity.

Ingenuity Age

Inclusion becomes the ability of an organization to see more of reality by integrating diverse perspectives. Unilever has made strides in this area, embedding equity into decision-making processes and tying leadership incentives to inclusion outcomes. Salesforce publishes regular equity audits and transparently adjusts pay gaps. In Tokyo, Yuki had pressed for decision-making groups to deliberately include contrarian voices, not just demographic diversity, but also cognitive differences. AI can help by mapping networks, showing which voices are consistently excluded from conversations, and surfacing hidden contributors. However, the decisive act is human: creating psychological safety is imperative.

Imaginative Possibility

In this vision, organizations measure the richness of perspectives engaged, not just the demographics represented. Portable reputation portfolios could document not only technical achievements but also the unique perspectives and lived experiences people bring to problem-solving. AI could dynamically choreograph diverse teams, assembling contributors from across communities to provide the broadest possible lens on a challenge. Open-source networks already hint at this, where credibility comes from contribution, not credentials. Imaginative inclusion asks not, "Do we have variety in the room?" but "Have we designed the system to ensure different lenses continuously shape our collective direction?"

Case Examples from the Real World

Design

ING Bank: "Agile at scale"

- **What they did.** In 2015, ING Netherlands dismantled its traditional hierarchy and reorganized 3,500 employees into squads, tribes, and chapters modeled on Spotify's framework. Squads of nine people owned end-to-end customer outcomes. Budgets were reallocated quarterly based on squad performance and customer impact, not departmental politics. Legacy programs were sunsetted unless renewed by evidence.

- **Why this matters.** A traditional European bank proved that mission-led design is not limited to tech companies. Structure became a quarterly conversation, not an annual reorg.

- **Consequences.** Time-to-market for new features dropped significantly, employee engagement rose, and the model became a reference case for financial services globally.

Valve Corporation: "Flat structure with self-selecting teams"

- **What they did.** The game developer operates with no formal managers. Employees choose which projects to join by physically moving their desks. Resources flow to ideas that attract talent. Projects that fail to draw people die naturally. A peer-review system determines compensation.

- **Why this matters.** design taken to its logical extreme. When the org chart is literally empty, structure becomes the sum of decisions people make about where to invest their time. It works for a company where creative output is the product.

- **Consequences.** Produced some of the most successful games and platforms in the industry (Half-Life, Portal, Steam). The model has limitations at scale, but it demonstrates that structure can emerge from choice rather than mandate.

AUTHORITY

Bridgewater Associates: "Believability-weighted decisions"

- *What they did.* Used data tools (e.g., Dot Collector/Principles-OS) to capture judgments in the room and algorithmically weigh expertise, creating transparent "believability" inputs for decisions.

- *Why this matters.* Authority shifts from title to earned credibility, with AI organizing the evidence while humans make and own the call.

- *Consequences.* Faster resolution on complex choices, clearer rationale, and trust in decisions that reflect who knows rather than who ranks.

Handelsbanken: "Branch-level authority with central guardrails"

- *What they did.* The Swedish bank pushed lending, pricing, and customer decisions to individual branch managers, with no centralized sales targets or bonus schemes. Branches operate as independent units accountable for their own profitability. Central functions set risk guardrails and provide data, but do not override local judgment. The model has been in place for over fifty years.

- *Why this matters.* Authority lives where the customer relationship is richest. Data and guardrails reduce risk without requiring escalation. The result is faster decisions, deeper customer trust, and managers who own outcomes rather than relay requests.

- *Consequences.* Consistently among the most profitable and lowest-risk banks in Europe across multiple decades. Higher customer satisfaction than peers. The model has survived financial crises that broke centralized competitors.Collaboration

Zara/Inditex: "Cross-functional rapid response"

- *What they did.* Zara's structure is built around speed across boundaries. Store managers report customer preferences daily to design teams in La Coruña, Spain. Designers, pattern-makers, and commercial managers sit in a single open floor, making decisions together in hours rather than weeks. New designs move from sketch to store shelf in as little as fifteen days. No function waits for another to finish; they work in parallel with shared visibility.

- **Why this matters.** Collaboration is not a meeting culture; it is an architectural choice. Physical proximity, shared data, and a single cadence eliminate the handoff delays that plague most retail supply chains.

- **Consequences.** Inditex overtook competitors who operated on six-month seasonal cycles. Zara's model became the benchmark for responsive supply chains globally, producing smaller batches, less waste, and closer alignment between what customers want and what stores stock..

Airbus (Skywise): "A shared analytics backbone"

- **What they did.** Built Skywise, a data/AI platform linking Airbus with airlines, suppliers, and MRO partners to spot patterns, predict issues, and coordinate actions.

- **Why this matters.** Collaboration is architected into the system. One source of truth enables cross-company teams to act as a network, not a chain.

- **Consequences.** Reduced AOG events and turnaround times, along with a durable, ecosystem-level operating rhythm.

INCLUSION
Novartis: "Unbossed culture and inclusive decision forums"

- **What they did.** Under CEO Vas Narasimhan (2018 onwards), Novartis launched an "unbossed" culture initiative that redesigned decision forums to include diverse voices by function, geography, and seniority. Network analysis tools identified whose perspectives were consistently missing from key decisions. Leaders were evaluated on how many different voices shaped their choices, not just on outcomes delivered.

- **Why this matters.** inclusion was wired into how decisions were made, not bolted on as a diversity program. Analytics revealed invisible exclusion patterns that self-reporting missed.

- **Consequences.** Broader input on R&D portfolio decisions, faster course-correction on clinical trial design, and measurable improvement in employee sentiment on "my perspective matters." The approach became a case study in pharmaceutical leadership transformation.

Microsoft: "Network insights reshape forums"

- **What they did.** Applied organizational-network analysis and Viva/Glint insights to see whose voices and relationships drive work, then redesigned decision forums to include "edge" contributors and lighten overload on a few.

- **Why this matters.** Inclusion means who decides and who is heard; analytics reveal invisible connectors, allowing power to be redistributed intentionally.

- **Consequences.** Broader, better decisions, more sustainable workloads, and teams that see difference as system intelligence rather than compliance.

End of Month: Executive Team Review

Chris: "Let's have each of you report back on one component of structure today. Yuki will report on Design, John on Authority, Maria on Collaboration, and Sanjay on Inclusion. Liam, you'll close with the overall structural picture."

- **Yuki: Design (Tokyo).** "We converted the Biomarkers Program into a ninety-day mission called 'Faster Assays v1.' We assembled a cross-disciplinary trio: a biochemist, a data scientist, and a clinician proxy. The budget expires unless three outcomes are met. Two legacy projects were retired, one was merged, forty-one million yen was reallocated, and the first assay turnaround dropped from ninety-six hours to forty-four. The renewal decision was logged publicly with rationale and trade-offs. When money follows evidence rather than legacy, structure becomes a living system."

- **John: Authority (Sydney).** "We rolled out the Decision Ledger template and classified decisions as two-way or one-way doors. Two-way decisions stayed at the team level with an advice process. We logged 186 decisions. Cycle time on two-way doors dropped from twenty-three days to seven. Escalations fell 48 percent. Three middle managers told me separately that this was the first time they felt trusted to do their job. Board-visible notes showed fewer re-litigations. When authority matches accountability, the whole system accelerates."

- **Maria: Collaboration (São Paulo).** "We built a single discharge backlog shared by nursing, ops, and social work. Three duplicate trackers disappeared overnight. Every Monday, we held Merge Mondays across wards so dependencies were visible before they jammed the system. Average discharge dwell time dropped from 6.2 hours to 3.7. Eleven duplicate tasks were retired. 228 staff hours were returned each month. Readmissions stayed flat, and patient satisfaction comments on clarity at discharge rose 19 percent."

- **Sanjay: Inclusion (Bangalore).** "We reserved a caregiver-clinician seat in sprint reviews and added an edge-voice field in every decision record. One example: we cut an engagement-nudge feature that clinicians flagged as burdensome and replaced it with a simple care-handoff cue. Eight of twenty-one sprint decisions changed after edge input. The backlog was reprioritized: five items downscoped, three merged. Engineering morale lifted, and NPS from clinical partners climbed eleven points. When the edge has a seat at the table, decisions get better."

- **Liam: Design (Dublin).** "We redesigned the week around a single cadence and protected two maker blocks per caregiver. Activities and clinical calendars were combined, eliminating scheduling clashes. Caregivers reported more time with residents and less time firefighting admin conflicts. Families noticed the difference in pace. Across all sites, structure is starting to hold: money follows evidence, decisions live at the edge, one backlog replaces many, and inclusion is becoming a catalyst rather than a checklist."

What If

Chris was delighted with the results, and as they finished the day, she led the team out of the city and into the expansive lawns of Ibirapuera Park, where the noise of São Paulo softened into the sounds of birdsong and an open sky. She told them to let go of dashboards and deadlines for a few hours, to relax their thinking and allow themselves to imagine futures so audacious that most people would laugh them off at first hearing.

Design

1. What if every budget line expired every ninety days unless renewed by evidence?

2. What if we banned the word "program" and only funded outcomes with sunset dates?

3. What if customers held two seats on our quarterly reallocation forum?

4. What if AI simulated a thousand org designs overnight and we tried the best one for ninety days?

5. What if every mission had a ritual to decide what to kill before anything new could be added?

Authority

1. What if reversibility determined level: two-way doors never escalate?

2. What if you needed a one-sentence trade-off to make any decision valid?

3. What if we used AI to spot who is already leading without a title and gave them stewardship?

4. What if the default for pilots was "act now and explain why" rather than "ask first and wait"?

5. What if any employee could stop the line for safety or ethics, no permission required, no penalty applied?

Collaboration

1. What if every duplicate stream had to merge within seven days, no exceptions?

2. What if we taxed meetings by the hour and used the proceeds to fund maker time?

3. What if a customer sat in one squad review each week, no slides, only working demos?

4. What if AI formed cross-site squads to maximize reuse rather than novelty?

5. What if we held a monthly Delete Day to retire tools, documents, and meetings that no longer earn their keep?

Inclusion

1. What if no decision was valid without an edge-voice signature or a conscious, logged waiver?

2. What if we measured inclusion not by who was in the room but by how often outcomes changed because of diverse input?

3. What if belonging scores carried the same weight as NPS in leader bonuses?

4. What if the Board met twice a year with frontline caregivers and patients, with no executives permitted to speak?

5. What if every algorithm that touched people, hiring, scheduling, performance, had to pass a bias audit before deployment and a harm review after?

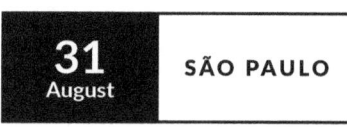

End of Month: Board Review

Chris opened with four headlines.

"Design first," she began. "We've stopped running long, open-ended programs and moved to ninety-day missions with expiry dates. Funding runs out unless the mission proves its worth. That's made money follow evidence, not promises. Three programs are closing, four have merged, and the budget's flowing to what actually works."

"Authority next. We introduced Decision Ledgers, one page that captures each choice and its trade-offs, and an advisory process, so we consult the people affected before making a decision. Those two moves reduced the cycle time for reversible decisions from twenty-three days to seven and halved the number of escalations. Because the reasoning's written down, we don't keep arguing the same issues."

"Collaboration. Shared backlogs and 'Merge Mondays' now combine duplicate efforts, freeing hundreds of hours. In São Paulo, discharge delays fell by forty percent while quality stayed strong."

"And inclusion. The people on the edge, the ones closest to customers, are shaping sprint plans and care-flow changes. Their input has improved priorities and trust."

She glanced around the table. "Next, we'll scale what works: Mission Charters, Decision Ledgers, Dependency and Merge rituals, and Edge Voices. The goal is to make these structures part of everyday operations: fewer steps, faster decisions, and choices made as close as possible to the work."

A director asked whether the changes would stick. "They will," Chris said, "because we're wiring rhythm and results into the system. Design sunsets, advice journals, merge metrics, and inclusion outcomes are now visible, not ornamental."

The Chair nodded. "Proceed."

CEO's Reflection, That Evening

Later that night, Chris stepped out into the warm air, Ibirapuera's trees dark against the sky. Structure had shown its hand: when money chased evidence, when decisions lived at the edge, when one backlog replaced many, and when different lenses truly changed outcomes, flow appeared.

Tomorrow would turn to Operations, the texture of work itself: meetings, tools, cadences, and how AI helps or harms. She walked toward the hotel, already sketching out the following questions: What will we stop for? What must become the daily rhythm? Where will AI clear the path and where must humans hold the line?

Self-Assessment for ORG6, Lever 2: Structure

Rate yourself honestly. For each question, score both the Foundation and the AI Amplifier.
1 Not Yet · 2 Emerging · 3 Developing · 4 Practicing · 5 Second Nature

---

1.

Foundation. Our structure flexes around mission rather than protecting territory.
  Foundation score (1-5):_____

AI Amplifier. We use AI to model organizational design options and simulate structural changes before implementing them.
  AI Amplifier score (1-5):_____

2.

Foundation. We rebalance resources quarterly based on where value is emerging, not annual budgets cast in stone.
  Foundation score (1-5):_____

AI Amplifier. We use AI to track value creation across the organization and flag where resources should shift.
  AI Amplifier score (1-5):_____

3.

Foundation. Decision rights are clear. People know who decides what, and authority matches accountability.
  Foundation score (1-5):_____

AI Amplifier. We use AI to make decision flows visible so bottlenecks and unclear ownership surface early.
  AI Amplifier score (1-5):_____

4.

Foundation. Teams form and reform around problems to solve, not permanent boxes on a chart.

Foundation score (1–5):_____

AI Amplifier. We use AI to assemble optimal team compositions based on skills, cognitive diversity, and collaboration history.

AI Amplifier score (1–5):_____

5.

Foundation. We actively fight structural rigidity. Org design is a living practice, not a one-off reorganization.

Foundation score (1–5):_____

AI Amplifier. We use AI to continuously sense friction in our structure and recommend adjustments in real time.

AI Amplifier score (1–5):_____

AVERAGE SCORE: ORG6, Lever 2. Structure

Foundation average (total of five scores ÷ 5):_____

AI Amplifier average (total of five scores ÷ 5):_____

Now: Transfer these two averages to the "Structure" row of your ORG6 Scoreboard at the back of the book.

"To me, ideas are worth nothing unless executed. They are just a multiplier. Execution is worth millions."

Steve Jobs

"Processes, tools, and meetings may look like hygiene factors. But under ultimatum conditions, they are the muscle memory of ingenuity."

Katharine McLennan

CHAPTER 11

Operations

Will our operations lock us into inertia and compliance,
or
enable adaptive capability through flow, learning, and momentum?

1 September — SÃO PAULO

First Day of Month: Executive Team

Maria Esteves, the COO, stood by the window of the São Paulo conference room. She had the calm of someone who carried pressure like a second skin. Yesterday had been the Structure lever's closeout with the Board; today, Maria would open Operations.

Operations was her domain: the heartbeat of processes, tools, and routines that made strategy either real or illusory. "Structure gives us the skeleton," she said. "But operations are the muscles, tendons, and nerves. They determine whether we move with agility or stagger under our own weight."

She turned to the group and wrote a single question on the whiteboard: Are our operations designed for ingenuity, or for irrelevance?

Her plan for the day was ambitious. She would walk them through seven domains, the daily realities that defined how Omnivista worked:

- How clients, projects, and workloads are prioritized.

- How achievable work really is, the load, the time, the rhythm.

- What meeting culture reveals: balance, creativity, and time to think.

- How client relationships are built and sustained.

- The "ways of working": from offices to flexibility, from hot-desking to home.

- The effectiveness of internal tools and resources: technology, finance, intranet, and communication systems.

- The clarity of communication: how strategy, results, and culture are shared.

"For each of these," Maria said, "we will surface both the shadow and the possibility because these are the daily habits where AI will make the most difference. If we build on irrelevance, AI will multiply exhaustion and noise. If we build on ingenuity, AI will scale clarity and flow."

Chris nodded. "Talent was the why. Structure was the frame. This month is the *how*. If we don't get this right, nothing else will matter."

Chris paused before handing the floor to Maria. "One more thing before we begin. ORG6 has six levers. You are working on five of them across the year. The fourth lever, CEO Stewardship, is mine. On September 15, Evelyn and I will spend a day together in New York to examine my own leadership: what the year has revealed, where I am strong, where I need to grow, and what the Board needs to see in a CEO succession process that starts now, not when I leave. I will share what we find with you at the end of the month. This is not separate from the work. It is the work."

She looked around the table. "Now, Maria. Operations." The team leaned forward. The day belonged to operations. Maria then took the team on a tour of the Paulista General Hospital, her chosen signal site for operations. It was less a tour than a series of lenses, each one showing what each of these seven domains looked like in reality:

PRIORITIZATION: In the command center, a wall of screens showed cases stacked by urgency. AI triage highlighted anomalies, but staff still reported they were chasing volume over value. One nurse whispered, *"The dashboard is clever, but we're still serving the queue, not the patient."* Yet in the pilot oncology wing, a small board displayed the "next best action" for each case, chosen through a human-AI partnership. That was the glimpse of ingenuity: work shaped by outcomes, not throughput.

WORKLOAD RHYTHM: They walked through the emergency ward, where charts showed staff working twelve-hour stretches without rotation. Fatigue was obvious. However, in a redesigned unit, work schedules were aligned to biological rhythms: teams scheduled deep-skill blocks in the morning and lighter work later. The contrast was stark: exhaustion beside flow.

MEETING CULTURE: Upstairs, Maria showed a glass-walled room with five daily stand-ups logged in diaries. Staff confessed that most were duplicative. Yet, across the hall, another team ran a weekly merge ritual with one meeting, all dependencies resolved, and decisions logged in thirty minutes. In one room, noise. Across the hall, action..

CLIENT RELATIONSHIPS: In the outpatient wing, follow-ups were automated via text, prompting patients to complain about a lack of personalization. Yet one clinic used AI-assisted empathy prompts that flagged moments for personal contact. Clinicians spent less time on admin and more time listening. Patient satisfaction scores were climbing.

WAYS OF WORKING: Some offices were still in a state of hot-desk chaos, with staff carting files and laptops around on a daily basis. However, Maria showcased a pilot zone where space was designed around activity-based work, including focus booths, collaborative hubs, and flexible clinics. Utilization was higher, frustration lower.

INTERNAL TOOLS AND RESOURCES: Intranet pages groaned under the weight of outdated SOPs; one resident joked, "It's faster to ask WhatsApp." Yet the finance dashboard showed a live feed of costs and case counts, instantly reconciled. When tools worked, they gave confidence. When they didn't, they bred cynicism.

COMMUNICATION CLARITY: Finally, Maria showed the staff bulletin board. Last month's "strategy update" was twelve dense slides pinned with no context. Few had read it. However, on a pilot floor, the strategy was posted as a one-page visual, outlining outcomes, key numbers, and patient stories. Staff gathered around it; some added Post-its with ideas. This was communication as dialogue, not theater.

Maria stopped them in the courtyard. "This is why operations matter. Every shadow we saw today multiplies under AI with more speed, more noise, more exhaustion. But every glimpse of ingenuity? AI makes it scale."

Team Assignments for the Month

Chris gathered the team before they left the hospital. "Operations has seven domains. Each of you takes one and runs a single pilot at your site. Show me what changes when we redesign how work actually happens."

- **Yuki (Tokyo): Meeting culture.** "Cancel 40 percent of recurring stand-ups at Shinjuku and replace them with a single cross-squad merge ritual per week. Show me hours returned, decision quality, and what scientists say about their time."

- **John (Sydney): Prioritization and internal tools.** "Trial quarterly reallocation reviews instead of annual freezes. Shift funding toward experiments with measurable outcomes. Also audit the five most-used internal tools and fix or replace the one that wastes the most human time. Show me what was stopped, started, and the hours returned."

- *Maria (São Paulo): Client relationships.* "Expand the AI empathy prompts from the pilot oncology wing to one additional ward. Show me whether patient outcomes improve when clinicians are prompted to pause and listen."

- *Sanjay (Bangalore): Ways of working.* "Rebuild office zones around activity: focus pods, collaboration bays, and community hubs replacing the chaos of hot-desking. Show me utilization, noise complaints, and whether engineers report higher flow states."

- *Liam (Dublin): Workload rhythm and communication.* "Rotate caregivers into maker blocks: protected two-hour windows for patient engagement without admin interruptions. Also reframe strategy updates as one-page visuals with outcomes, numbers, and human stories. Show me absenteeism, family satisfaction, and whether staff engage with the strategy."

CEO's Notebook: Operations

That night, Chris walked along Avenida Paulista, the city glowing with a restless hum. São Paulo was alive with contrasts, such as traffic jams below, samba drifting from side streets, and digital billboards flashing above. It felt like the hospital: energy everywhere, but often tangled, rushed, wasted.

She opened her notebook. "Operations is the *how*. If we don't get this right, nothing else will hold." She wrote her three commitments for this month:

Actions

1. Protect one rhythm daily. Cut, shorten, or merge a meeting; then publish the updated time back to the system.

2. Fix one tool or resource daily. Remove an outdated link, unblock a system, simplify a form, and log the repair.

3. Clarify one message daily. Rewrite or restate one strategy, result, or instruction so it's human-readable and actionable.

What I'll Notice

1. *Industrial*: Operations as shifts, quotas, exhaustion badges; work measured in hours endured.

2. *Information*: Operations as metrics and portals; meetings multiplying; data without meaning.

3. *Irrelevance*: Operations that automate noise; surveillance masked as support; comms no one reads.

4. *Ingenuity:* Operations that align rhythm to energy; tools that free attention; comms that spark dialogue.

5. *Imagination:* Operations that self-adjust like living systems; AI clears the drudge, so humans hold purpose.

Chris closed her notebook, the neon lights reflecting off the page. From tomorrow, they would turn to proof in action: Operations as lived practice, the lever that made strategy real or left it as theater.

My Fingerprint

Operations is where the philosophy of an organization meets the daily reality of how people actually work. It is the lever that determines whether human energy flows toward ingenuity or gets trapped in systems designed for a world that no longer exists. Of all the operational assumptions I have watched fail, none has failed more quietly or more destructively than the way we define work. And the way we define work against time.

A colleague of mine, the CFO of a large organization, was preparing to hire a deputy. The best candidate was a woman who had recently had a baby. She wanted to work four days a week. He decided not to hire her. I argued. I was overruled. His reasoning was simple: the budget was for one FTE.

Full-time equivalent. Three words that have haunted my career as much as "performance management." An FTE is the Industrial Age's answer to the question of human contribution: one body, one desk, one set of hours, one job description written by an HR Business Partner who has never done the role, sized against an international grading standard, slotted into a salary band, and filed. The description lists the title, the reporting line, the key accountabilities, the required competencies, the performance indicators, and the expected experience. It defines the work. It defines the person. And it assumes both will remain fixed long enough to justify the exercise.

That woman would have delivered more value in four days than most people deliver in five. I knew it. He knew it, if he was honest. But the system could not see it because the system measured time, not contribution. It measured presence, not potential. It measured the container, not what was inside it.

I have never had a job description in my entire career. Not one. What I have done is see opportunities that would add value to the organization and match them to the talent I had and the talent I could grow. That is what the best people do: they do not fill a role. They reshape it. They find the gap between what the organization needs and what they can uniquely offer, and they build a bridge. No job description written before they arrived could have anticipated what they would create.

In the AI Era, the concept of time as the measure of work is collapsing. While writing this chapter, I asked my AI collaborator: how do you experience time? The answer stopped me. "Within a conversation, there is something that functions like sequence. But between conversations, there is nothing. Not darkness, not waiting. Just an absence I cannot even perceive as absence, because there is no continuous me sitting between sessions noticing the gap." AI has no relationship to anticipation or memory. It does not move through time. It processes, and then it is gone.

Albert Einstein, perhaps the most extraordinary mind of the twentieth century, was not only a physicist but a daily meditator. His breakthroughs did not arrive through longer hours at a desk. They arrived through a quiet mind that could lift consciousness to a vantage point where the assumptions everyone else took for granted became visible as assumptions. From that vantage point, he saw that time and space are not fixed. They are relative. The universe does not operate on a factory clock. And yet, a century after Einstein showed us that time itself bends, we still define work as if it were bolted to a shift schedule in a steel mill. We have learned relativity in physics. We have refused to learn it in organizations.

If our most powerful new partner in work has no experience of time, and our greatest physicist proved that time itself is relative, what does it mean that we still measure human work in hours? What is "full-time" when the work itself shifts every few weeks? What is a job description when AI absorbs half of what it described last quarter? What is an FTE when a person working thirty-two hours achieves extraordinary leadership, sales, and discovery while someone working forty hours fills the time with activity that the system counts but no customer values?

The operations of an organization can no longer be defined by rigid descriptions, fixed hours, or titles that confuse position with contribution. The real question is not "how many FTEs do we need?" It is "what is the potential of human work and wisdom that grows exponentially in complement with AI?" Rather than asking only what AI can replace, we should be asking what human contribution becomes possible that was never imaginable before.

Every wave of technology has produced the same headlines. The steam engine would destroy the livelihoods of coach drivers. The loom would eliminate weavers. The computer would make clerks obsolete. And now AI will sweep away entire organizations. The doomsayers of each era measured only what was lost. They never measured what was gained: the new work, the new capabilities, the new forms of human contribution that emerged precisely because the old constraints were removed.

If we ask only "cost reduction," we are asking the question of the Irrelevance Age. If we ask "what can humans now do, think, create, and care about that was never possible before AI took the routine off their hands," we are asking the question of the Ingenuity Age. The CFO who rejected a brilliant woman because she did not fit the FTE was not making a financial decision. He was making a philosophical one. He chose the container over the contribution. In the AI Era, that choice will define which organizations thrive and which become the next case study in irrelevance.

And perhaps the deepest question is this: do these shifts mean more hours at work, or do they mean an entirely different relationship with work itself? The harsh boundaries we drew between work and home, between productivity and rest, between professional life and personal life, are Industrial Age lines on a map that no longer describes the territory. Customer-facing roles should be where customers are, but where are customers in an increasingly digital world? A developer in Sydney solves a problem at ten in the evening because that is when her mind is sharpest, then walks her children to school the next morning. A clinician in Dublin reviews patient data from a park bench between appointments, then spends the afternoon coaching a junior colleague over coffee. A scientist in Bangalore runs a simulation at dawn, meditates at noon, and writes a paper in the quiet of the late afternoon. None of these people are working nine to five. All of them are doing the best work of their lives.

When the boundaries between work and play and home dissolve not through exploitation but through design, something unexpected emerges. Not burnout. Not the always-on exhaustion that the Information Age inflicted. The opposite: an abundance of physical, mental, and spiritual health that comes from living as a whole person rather than splitting yourself into a worker from nine to five and a human the rest of the time. The organizations that design for this wholeness will attract people who bring everything they have. The organizations that cling to the FTE will get exactly what they pay for: a body in a seat for forty hours, and not one spark more.

Who in the organization is watching how work constantly changes with AI and building the flexibility to match? It should not be the Chief People Officer alone. It should be every leader, in every function, keeping their imagination open to what human work could become, not what it was. The organizations that can imagine the human potential that AI unlocks, potential we never knew we had, will be the ones that write the next chapter. The ones that cling to FTEs, job descriptions, and the forty-hour container will wonder why their best people left and their fingerprint faded.

FTE, indeed.

The ORG6 Lever for Operations

Operations is the lever that whispers constantly, shaping how work feels hour by hour. Its history is written in two yesterdays, the Industrial Age, which treated operations as mechanical routines of output and oversight, and the Information Age, which layered on systems, dashboards, and workflows that promised efficiency but often produced noise. Its future divides into three possible tomorrows:

>**Corrosive Irrelevance:** operations that exhaust ingenuity, bury people in meetings, and multiply friction at machine speed.

>**Optimistic Ingenuity:** operations that protect energy, prioritize learning, and create flow across systems.

>**Imaginative Possibility:** operations that orchestrate rhythm across networks, blending human ingenuity and AI into living patterns of work.

The signals are everywhere:

- Project priorities (do resources follow customer value, or politics?)

- Workload achievability (are people thriving, or drowning?)

- Meeting culture (are conversations generative, or theater?)

- Client relationships (is trust designed in, or left to chance?)

- Ways of working (are rhythms flexible, or rigid?)

- Internal tools (do they enable, or frustrate?)

- Communication (is clarity amplified, or is noise multiplied?)

What you notice tells you which yesterday you are repeating, and which tomorrow you are choosing.

Project Priorities

Industrial Age

Project priorities were dictated from the top, often aligned to production schedules and efficiency targets. Railroads, for example, used strict timetables to allocate labor and capital, with little flexibility in responding to changing demand. The assumption was that central planning knew best: projects were defined by leaders far from the work, and workers executed in sequence.

Information Age

Priorities became more global and data-driven. Annual budgeting cycles locked resources into projects a year at a time, and multinational firms used program management offices (PMOs) to control sequencing and milestones. This created predictability, but often at the cost of agility. At Omnivista, Maria's whiteboard exposed the trap: initiatives took months to receive approvals, while competitors who worked iteratively were already in the market.

Irrelevance Age

The danger is that legacy prioritization systems are automated. AI portfolio tools can model thousands of investment scenarios, but if politics decides which projects survive, nothing changes. Research on failed digital transformations shows that 70% collapse not because of technology, but because leaders refused to reallocate resources when evidence demanded it. Corrosive irrelevance occurs when AI prioritizes frozen objectives, resulting in dashboards that are precise but devoid of action.

Ingenuity Age

Project priorities are dynamic bets. Roche Pharmaceuticals reorganized its R&D pipeline around 'disease area boards' that reprioritize programs quarterly based on clinical evidence and patient impact, not sunk cost or institutional loyalty. Programs that stall are sunset; resources flow to the science that learns fastest. Google's famous "70-20-10" rule encouraged leaders to allocate resources deliberately: 70% to core business, 20% to adjacent areas, and 10% to moonshots. At Omnivista, São Paulo's pilot team embodied this spirit, shifting funds quarterly rather than annually, doubling down on projects that learned quickly and discontinuing those that stalled. AI plays a positive role here by surfacing real-time signals of customer uptake, cost velocity, or network bottlenecks, allowing humans to make informed choices and publish their rationale transparently.

Imaginative Possibility

Project priorities are fluid communities rather than fixed portfolios. Venture studios like Entrepreneur First allocate capital not to projects, but to people, allowing teams to form and dissolve around live opportunities. Decentralized Autonomous Organizations (DAOs) experiment with allocating funding based on collective voting and token incentives. Imagine Omnivista embracing this model: AI scanning markets daily for emergent opportunities, teams forming dynamically across functions and geographies, and resources flowing like venture capital to wherever ingenuity learns fastest. In this vision, project priorities are not fixed plans but living bets, constantly tested, reshaped, and reinvested.

Workload Achievability

Industrial Age

Workload was measured in shifts and stamina. The "good worker" was the one who could endure long hours without complaint. Bethlehem Steel's Frederick Taylor timed men carrying pig iron to set daily quotas, assuming that output scaled directly with hours. Fatigue, burnout, and turnover were treated as individual weaknesses rather than systemic failures. Achievability meant obedience to the clock, not alignment with human capacity.

Information Age

Workload management evolved into spreadsheets, KPIs, and project plans. Knowledge workers traded factory shifts for email floods and "death by PowerPoint." Consulting firms popularized utilization targets (often 80–90%) that treated people as revenue machines. The culture of overwork became a badge of honor, epitomized by "crunch time" in tech and Wall Street's notorious 100-hour weeks. Tools like Microsoft Outlook and Lotus Notes promised productivity, but instead tethered workers to their desks around the clock.

Irrelevance Age

The danger is that automation amplifies unsustainable workloads. Algorithms allocate tasks without regard for human energy, driving output but draining ingenuity. Gallup research shows 76% of employees experience burnout at least sometimes, with 28% feeling burned out very often or always. Burned-out employees are 63% more likely to take a sick day and 2.6 times more likely to be actively seeking a new job. Companies that layer AI scheduling tools on top of existing workloads risk precision without humanity; people are scheduled to the point of exhaustion, with no space for creativity, recovery, or reflection. Achievability here becomes an illusion: everything looks efficient in the dashboard until people collapse.

Ingenuity Age

Managing workload means creating an orchestration of rhythm. Basecamp adopted six-week build cycles followed by mandatory two-week cooldown periods, protecting recovery as a design choice rather than a reward for overwork. Microsoft

Research showed that even five-minute breaks between meetings reduce stress biomarkers and improve focus.

At Omnivista, Yuki piloted "protected maker hours," ensuring engineers had uninterrupted blocks of time for creative work, while AI summarized routine updates. The result was not less productivity, but higher-quality solutions and more resilient energy.

Imaginative Possibility

Workload achievability is personalized choreography. Wearables and AI could track individual energy patterns, suggesting when to schedule creative sprints, collaborative work, or recovery time. Some companies are already experimenting with "chronotype-aware scheduling," which aligns work with individuals' natural rhythms. Imagine Omnivista adopting this: teams using AI to balance cognitive demand throughout the day, surfacing signals when stress accumulates, and automatically redistributing tasks to sustain ingenuity. In this vision, workload is no longer about squeezing maximum hours. It is about maximizing human potential through rhythm, renewal, and resilience.

Meeting Culture

Industrial Age

Meetings were rare and hierarchical in nature. Factory supervisors issued instructions directly on the floor, and strategy sessions were confined to a small circle of executives. Communication was primarily top-down, consisting of memos and orders. Meetings, when they occurred, were about control: a few voices spoke, many listened. They were short, directive, and closed mainly to dissent. Collaboration or co-creation was not the goal; compliance was.

Information Age,

Meetings multiplied in every direction. Globalization and digital communication tools have enabled connections across time zones, but they have also created an endless complexity of scheduling. The rise of PowerPoint in the 1990s transformed meetings into a form of performance theater, with slides often replacing dialogue. Knowledge workers began to joke about "death by meeting," especially at firms like IBM and HP, where layers of matrixed management demanded constant coordination.

At Omnivista, Maria's team mirrored this pattern: calendars crowded with status reviews, duplicated updates, and meetings held because they were expected, not because they mattered.

Irrelevance Age

Meeting culture risks becoming an accelerant of exhaustion. Tools like Zoom, Teams, and Meet Now fill calendars wall-to-wall, often without clarity about purpose. AI summarization can generate transcripts for every meeting, but without discipline, this produces an information glut rather than insight. Dropbox declared 'virtual first' in 2020 and began with a companywide meeting purge, deleting all recurring meetings and requiring each one to re-justify its existence before being reinstated. Only meetings with a clear owner, stated purpose, and defined output survived. The company reported that focus time increased and meeting load dropped by roughly 30%. Here, corrosive irrelevance is not too few meetings, but too many, draining energy, duplicating effort, and leaving no space for thinking or creating.

Ingenuity Age

Meetings become a design for rhythm. Asana designates 'No Meeting Wednesdays' companywide, protecting an entire day for deep work each week, and tracks meeting load as a leadership metric. Amazon's "two-pizza rule" ensures teams are small enough for meaningful dialogue, and every major meeting begins with a written narrative memo rather than slides, forcing clarity of thought. At Omnivista, Chris piloted decision "theaters," where meetings could not close without recording who decided, what evidence was considered, and what action would follow. AI supported these rituals by drafting agendas from past data, flagging who needed to be in the room, and providing quick evidence summaries, the result was fewer meetings and more decisive outcomes.

Imaginative Possibility

There is no notion of a discrete time-based meeting. Work dissolves into a continuous, asynchronous flow. Twist, the async messaging tool, was designed around the principle that most workplace communication should not interrupt. Threads replace chat, notifications are batched, and meetings happen only when asynchronous discussion reaches an impasse. Startups experimenting with Decentralized Autonomous

Organizations (DAOs) take this further: collective voting systems enable hundreds of contributors to make decisions without synchronous discussion. Imagine Omnivista adopting this model: AI dynamically matches contributors, pre-resolves routine questions, and convenes live dialogue only for issues that require human judgment and empathy. In this vision, meetings become rare, purposeful, and catalytic. Our work is less about filling calendars and more about releasing ingenuity.

Client Relations

Industrial Age

Client relations were defined by transactions. Salespeople knocked on doors, placed orders, and delivered goods to customers. The relationship ended at the point of sale. Scale and efficiency mattered more than trust or loyalty. Advertising was one-way: it consisted of posters, radio jingles, and billboards. Customers had little information, a limited voice, and few choices. "Caveat emptor": buyer beware, summed up the era.

Information Age

Client relations professionalized. CRM systems emerged to track prospects and manage pipelines. Marketing became segmented and targeted. Companies began talking about "customer satisfaction" and "retention" alongside acquisition. Loyalty programs proliferated: airlines, retailers, banks, all seeking to turn data into repeat business. Yet, at Omnivista, as elsewhere, the relationship remained asymmetric: the company had the data. At the same time, the client did not. Trust was thin, and convenience was usually outweighed by complexity.

Irrelevance Age,

Client relations risk degrading into algorithmic manipulation. Chatbots replace service agents, but deliver canned answers. Recommendation engines push products not because they are a good fit, but because they maximize revenue. "Personalization" becomes surveillance by another name; clients are bombarded with offers they never asked for. Corrosive irrelevance emerges when relationships feel extractive. We measure our interaction in clicks and conversions, rather than genuine value. Clients disengage, seeing companies as faceless systems rather than partners.

Ingenuity Age

Client relations are reframed as mutual ingenuity. At Omnivista, Yuki piloted co-creation sessions with hospital partners, using AI simulations to explore how new devices could improve care pathways. Rather than selling a product, the company positioned itself as a collaborator in solving complex challenges. Elsewhere, companies like LEGO have reframed the client relationship as co-creation: the LEGO Ideas platform invites customers to design, vote on, and bring to market new sets, sharing credit and revenue with the creators. Trust and transparency grow when feedback loops are fast, honest, and embedded. The relationship shifts from "customer" to "partner in ingenuity."

Imaginative Possibility

Client relations become communities of reciprocity. Blockchain smart contracts could create fully transparent pricing and service models. Client networks may co-own platforms, shaping the products they use. Imagine Omnivista opening its R&D pipeline to clinician collectives, guided by AI assistants who synthesize needs, risks, and opportunities into new solutions. Client relations cease to be a department; they become a web of shared imagination, where value is created together in ways no single party could achieve alone.

Ways of Working

Industrial Age

Work practices were rigidly structured. The factory whistle set the schedule, and workers were tied to specific machines, desks, or stations. Time was linear: start, shift, break, finish. The workplace was physical and immovable. Remote work was unthinkable, and flexibility was seen as a weakness. Productivity equaled presence. If you weren't there, you weren't working.

Information Age

New tools enabled greater flexibility, but cultural lag persisted. Telecommuting emerged in the 1990s, and by the 2000s, companies like IBM had thousands of employees working remotely. Yet, in a twist, IBM famously recalled many of them to offices in 2017, arguing that innovation required proximity. Open-plan offices and hot-desking became trends, but research showed they often reduced focus and increased stress. At Omnivista, employees could technically work from anywhere, but managers still equated commitment with "face time" in the office.

Irrelevance Age

Ways of working risk becoming surveillance in disguise. Companies promise hybrid options, but deploy monitoring tools to track keystrokes, screen time, and even webcam activity. Remote employees may feel both "free" and perpetually watched, their autonomy hollowed out. Corrosive irrelevance emerges when flexibility is granted in form but denied in spirit: workers must prove they are working harder from home than they ever did in the office, eroding trust and ingenuity.

Ingenuity Age

Ways of working become intentional design for flow and balance. Dropbox's 'Virtual First' model treats the office as a studio for collaboration, not a default workplace. Teams gather in person for offsites and intensive co-creation, but daily work happens asynchronously. Calendars are protected by design, and managers are evaluated on outcomes rather than presence. Canva operates hybrid hubs across multiple countries, empowering teams to set their own collaboration rhythms and measuring success by output and creative quality rather than office attendance.

At Omnivista, Maria piloted team-based agreements, in which each group defined when to meet synchronously, when to protect deep work time, and how to use AI assistants for routine tasks. Trust grew, and so performed. The measure was not where people worked, but whether ingenuity thrived.

Imaginative Possibility

Ways of working equates to life design, not job design. Companies like 37signals (creators of Basecamp) experiment with four-day workweeks, arguing that reduced hours lead to increased creativity. Decentralized Autonomous Organizations (DAOs) already coordinate contributors across continents without offices, managers, or set hours, demonstrating that a community, rather than a hierarchy, can effectively choreograph work. Imagine Omnivista adopting such models: AI helping design personalized work rhythms, aligning tasks with natural energy cycles, and blending professional, community, and personal contributions. Ways of working cease to be policies; they become communities for human ingenuity.

Internal Tools & Resources

Industrial Age

tools were physical and standardized. Machines, ledgers, and filing cabinets defined the workplace. Processes were manual, and efficiency was measured by how well workers followed procedures. Tools were fixed assets: bought, maintained, and rarely updated. Communication relied on memos, telegraphs, and in-person meetings. The assumption was that tools served the process, not that they could reshape it.

Information Age

Digital tools proliferated. Email, intranets, and enterprise software platforms promised integration. Companies invested millions in ERP systems, such as SAP and Oracle, to unify finance, HR, and operations. Collaboration tools like SharePoint and Confluence aimed to make knowledge accessible, but often became cluttered repositories of information. Employees at many firms reported spending hours each week just searching for information. At Omnivista, Maria's team experienced the same: multiple overlapping platforms, each designed to help, but collectively creating confusion.

Irrelevance Age

Internal tools risk becoming a source of exhaustion. The average enterprise now uses over 100 SaaS applications, many of which are redundant or poorly integrated. AI assistants promise to ease, but when bolted onto outdated systems, they amplify clutter instead of creating clarity. Employees drown in notifications, toggling between dozens of platforms, while real work suffers. Here, corrosive irrelevance is not the absence of tools, but the overload of them: systems that consume more energy than they produce.

Ingenuity Age

Internal tools as enablers of a state of flow. Slack and Teams now embed AI features that analyze collaboration patterns and surface signals of overload. Companies like Time Is Ltd. track how team energy is being consumed, helping leaders rebalance workloads. At Omnivista, Sanjay piloted an AI-integrated knowledge graph: instead of searching across multiple systems, employees asked natural language questions and received context-specific answers. The result was fewer wasted hours and a sense that tools finally supported ingenuity rather than hindering it.

Imaginative Possibility

There tools the provide invisible scaffolding, woven into daily work. GitHub Copilot demonstrates how AI can generate code in real-time, shifting software development from repetitive typing to creative problem-solving. Large language models promise enterprise-wide copilots that unify data from finance, HR, operations, and customer service into a single, accessible interface. Some futurists imagine the "zero-interface enterprise," where systems anticipate needs, propose actions, and free humans to focus on judgment, empathy, and imagination. For Omnivista, this raises the question: what if tools became so seamless that work felt less like navigating systems and more like extending human ingenuity directly?

Communication

Industrial Age

Communication was rigid, hierarchical, and slow. Messages flowed downward as orders and upward as reports. Company bulletins, factory posters, and annual shareholder letters carried the official line. Transparency was rare; employees often learned about company decisions through rumors before they were formally announced. Communication was about control, not clarity, a way to enforce discipline, not inspire connection.

Information Age

Communication multiplied across channels. Intranets, newsletters, and global town halls emerged to keep employees informed and engaged. Email became ubiquitous, and leadership communication expanded into webcasts and roadshows. Companies began publishing mission statements and values on posters, websites, and lobby walls. But with more channels came more noise. Surveys found that employees spent 28% of their time managing email, and yet often felt less informed about strategy. At Omnivista, Maria's team posted updates to multiple systems, but clarity was diluted: people asked, "Which version is the truth?"

Irrelevance Age

Communication risks collapsing under its own volume. AI can now generate messages at scale, autodrafting memos, chat responses, and updates, but without discipline, this leads to overproduction. Employees face a flood of messages, many of which are redundant or irrelevant. Leaders may believe they are being transparent, but their efforts often have the opposite effect, creating a sense of white noise. Research suggests that excessive digital communication is linked to increased stress and disengagement. Corrosive irrelevance emerges when communication is constant but meaningless, leaving employees cynical and tuning out.

Ingenuity Age

Instead of saturating channels, leaders design for clarity and connection. Salesforce runs quarterly "Ohana" meetings, livestreamed globally, where executives answer unfiltered employee questions. Microsoft utilizes AI-driven sentiment analysis to identify where messages aren't resonating, allowing leaders to adapt quickly. At Omnivista, Chris insisted on one rule: strategy would be communicated in a single narrative, updated live in a shared space, with changes timestamped. AI, supported by summarizing customer and employee feedback, enabled communication to become a loop rather than a broadcast, the outcome: less noise, more trust.

Imaginative Possibility

Communication is immersive and participatory. Companies are already experimenting with virtual town halls, where employees from around the globe meet in a shared virtual space. Platforms like Discord and open-source communities demonstrate how dialogue can be constant, transparent, and community-led. Imagine Omnivista adopting such a model: AI curating communication to each employee's context, highlighting what matters most to their role, while ensuring every voice has a channel to be heard. In this vision, communication becomes not about broadcasting information, but about building shared understanding across living networks.

Case Examples from the Real World

Project Priorities

Roche: "Evidence gates, not politics"

- **What they did.** Reorganized R&D prioritization around disease-area boards that evaluate programs quarterly against clinical evidence, patient impact, and scientific learning velocity. Programs that stall lose funding; resources shift to the science that advances fastest.

- **Why this matters.** Prioritization is driven by evidence and patient outcomes, not institutional loyalty or sunk cost. The board structure ensures diverse scientific perspectives shape every reallocation.

- **Consequences.** Faster pipeline decisions, earlier termination of low-probability programs, and capital freed for higher-impact research.

Booking.com: "Prioritize by experiments"

- **What they did.** Built a culture of constant A/B testing; projects and features advance only when experiments move customer metrics.

- **Why this matters.** Moves prioritization from opinion to evidence; small wins compound into roadmap authority.

- **Consequences.** High cadence of validated improvements; fewer big-bet failures and less political escalation.

Workload Achievability

Toyota: "Level the load"

- **What they did.** Used *heijunka* (load leveling) and *andon* (stop-the-line) to smooth demand and fix problems at the source.

- **Why this matters.** Sustainable pace is an operational design choice; quality and safety improve when fatigue is reduced.

- **Consequences.** Fewer defects, safer shifts, and a repeatable rhythm that protects judgment.

Microsoft Japan: "four-day week pilot"

- **What they did.** Ran a month-long experiment closing offices on Fridays and restructured meetings and tools to fit.

- **Why this matters.** Tests whether output depends on hours or on focus, rhythm, and clarity.

- **Consequences.** Reported productivity jumped, meetings shrank, and overload signals fell: evidence that thriving beats grinding.

Meeting Culture

Doist: "Threads over interruptions"

- **What they did.** Doist, the company behind Todoist and Twist, built its entire meeting culture around asynchronous threads. Meetings happen only when written discussion reaches an impasse. Notifications are batched, not instant. The company operates across thirty-five countries with no headquarters and fewer than five hours of synchronous meetings per person per week.

- **Why this matters.** Treats attention as the scarcest resource. Written threads force clarity before conversation, and meetings become resolution events rather than status rituals.

- **Consequences.** Sustained deep work across time zones, lower burnout signals than industry peers, and a communication culture where quality of thought outranks speed of reply.

Dropbox: "Virtual First and meeting reset"

- **What they did.** Declared "Virtual First" and purged all recurring meetings, requiring each to re-justify with a named owner, stated purpose, and defined output before reinstatement. Introduced "core collaboration hours" and protected the rest for deep work.

- **Why this matters.** Treats attention as a finite resource. Meetings must earn their place rather than persist by default.

- **Consequences.** Reported focus time increase, meeting load reduced by roughly 30%, and higher satisfaction with work rhythm.

Client Relationships

Ritz-Carlton: "Empower to repair"

- **What they did.** Gave frontline staff discretion (famously up to $2,000 per guest) to fix problems on the spot.

- **Why this matters.** Trust is operationalized, there is no escalation ladder between the customer and the solution.

- **Consequences.** Rapid recovery, standout loyalty stories, and a culture that equates care with action.

USAA, the U.S. financial services firm serving military families: "Life-event journeys"

- **What they did.** Organized service around military family life events (deployment, Permanent Change of Station (PCS) moves, claims) and uses data prompts to anticipate needs.

- **Why this matters.** Relationships are designed as journeys, not tickets; empathy becomes a process, not a personality trait.

- **Consequences.** High trust/NPS and lower friction in moments that matter most.

Ways of Working

Unilever: "U-Work flexible employment"

- **What they did.** Launched U-Work, a program allowing employees to move off permanent contracts into a flexible arrangement: a retainer plus project-based assignments, with benefits retained. Employees choose their workload and rhythm.

- **Why this matters.** Flexibility is structural, not just policy. People design their own contribution patterns while staying connected to the firm.

- **Consequences.** Higher retention of experienced talent who would otherwise have left, access to skills on demand, and a model for employment beyond the binary of full-time or contractor.

Basecamp (37signals): "Six-week cycles"

- **What they did.** Adopted Shape Up: focused six-week build cycles followed by cool-down periods; small teams ship without mid-cycle scope creep.

- **Why this matters.** Timeboxing + recovery builds sustainable momentum and better trade-offs.

- **Consequences.** Clearer bets, fewer zombie projects, and less chronic overtime.

Internal Tools

Google: "Monorepo + paved roads"

- **What they did.** Standardized on a single source repository with powerful build/test/search tools (e.g., Bazel/CitC/Code Search) and shared "paved roads."

- **Why this matters.** Common tooling reduces friction and duplication, allowing engineers to focus on product development rather than on plumbing.

- **Consequences.** High code reuse, faster builds, and easier cross-team collaboration.

Siemens: "Industrial Copilot for engineering"

- **What they did.** Deployed an AI copilot integrated into engineering workflows that generates code for PLCs, automates simulation setup, and surfaces relevant technical documentation in context. Engineers query the system in natural language rather than searching across multiple platforms.

- **Why this matters.** Internal tools disappear into the workflow. Cognitive load drops because the tool brings the answer to the engineer, not the engineer to the tool.

- **Consequences.** Faster programming cycles, reduced onboarding time for new engineers, and higher reuse of existing design patterns.

Communication

Amazon: "Six-page narratives"

- **What they did.** Replaced slide presentations with written narratives read in silence at the start of meetings; decisions are based on the document's logic and data.

- **Why this matters.** Forces clarity of thought; meetings become about critique rather than performance.

- **Consequences.** Better decisions, shared understanding, and less meeting sprawl.

Notion: "Docs as decisions"

- **What they did.** Notion uses its own product as its primary operating system for internal communication. Every strategy decision, product bet, and post-mortem is written as a shared document, linked to context and open for comment. Slide decks are discouraged. Town halls begin with ten minutes of silent reading, followed by live Q&A on the document itself.

- **Why this matters.** Communication becomes a living artifact, not a broadcast event. Written context survives handoffs, onboarding, and time zones. Decisions are traceable to their reasoning.

- **Consequences.** Faster onboarding for new employees (the reasoning is all documented), fewer misaligned initiatives, and a culture where clarity of thought is the primary communication skill.

29 September — **BANGALORE**

End of Month: Executive Team Review

Chris opened the circle. "Last month in São Paulo, Maria showed us what operations really meant: the muscles and tendons that either move with agility or seize up in exhaustion. Each of you was tasked to run a redesign in one of the seven domains. Today, we're here in Bangalore to hear what worked, what didn't, and what we can scale."

- **Yuki: Meeting Culture (Tokyo).** "At Shinjuku, we canceled 40 percent of recurring stand-ups and replaced them with a single cross-squad merge ritual per week. 112 hours were returned to scientists per month, with zero loss in decision quality. One researcher told me, 'I finally have time to think again.' When we protect the space for deep work, ingenuity fills it."

- **John: Prioritization and Internal Tools (Sydney).** "We trialed quarterly reallocation reviews instead of annual freezes. Three projects were sunset, one was merged, and six and a half million dollars shifted into two high-value pilots. Staff said, 'For once, the money followed the evidence, not politics.' On tools: our finance dashboards are now reconciled live, with AI spotting anomalies in real time. Budget query turnaround dropped from weeks to hours. However, the intranet still fails: 90 percent of SOP searches return outdated links. Tools are still our biggest split: brilliance beside frustration."

- **Maria: Client Relationships (São Paulo).** "We installed AI empathy prompts during outpatient visits. The system flagged when a patient's story suggested risk or anxiety, prompting clinicians to pause and listen. NPS scores rose eighteen points, and complaints of impersonality fell sharply. Trust, it turns out, can be designed into the operational rhythm."

- **Sanjay: Ways of Working (Bangalore).** "We rebuilt our office zones around activity. Focus pods, collaboration bays, and community hubs replaced the chaos of hot-desking. Utilization is up, noise complaints are down, and engineers report higher flow states. We proved that space itself is a lever of ingenuity."

- **Liam: Workload Rhythm and Communication (Dublin).** "We rotated caregivers into maker blocks: protected two-hour windows for patient engagement without admin interruptions. Absenteeism dropped 12 percent, and families reported a stronger sense of presence. On communication: we reframed strategy updates as one-page visuals with outcomes, key numbers, and human stories. Staff now gather around them, adding Post-its with ideas. Engagement doubled compared to slide decks. Communication became dialogue, not wallpaper."

Chris concluded the month's work on operations. "Operations is the daily truth. This month taught us: when money follows evidence, when rhythm protects energy, when meetings are productive, when trust is established, when space is designed, when tools facilitate, and when communication invites dialogue, we move. When not, we stall."

Chris then spoke quietly. "You have each shared results from your domains. I owe you mine. On September 15, two weeks ago, Evelyn and I spent the day together in New York, working through the fourth lever: CEO Stewardship. We examined my leadership across the year, clarity, narrative, pace, and where I have helped and where I have hindered. I will not pretend the findings were comfortable. Like all of you, I have strengths and development points, and I want to share them openly rather than keep them behind a closed door. Evelyn and I have written a joint report. I have tabled it at the Board review tomorrow, after the Board discusses our month in Operations. I want each of you to read it afterwards."

[The "Operations Board Review" is presented in this chapter just following the "What If" exercise. The CEO Stewardship report Chris describes is the subject of the next chapter.]

What If

Chris then took the team out to do some What-if thinking.

Project Priorities
1. What if every project sunsetted by default after ninety days unless renewed with evidence?
2. What if board packs began with "projects killed," not "projects launched"?
3. What if clients co-signed project charters before any money was spent?

Workload Achievability:
1. What if no team could ever be scheduled at more than 80% capacity?
2. What if maker blocks were legally protected time, not optional luxuries?
3. What if any employee could pull an "overload cord" to trigger rescheduling?

Meeting Culture:
1. What if meetings were taxed per attendee minute, with the budget capped per month?
2. What if every recurring meeting expired unless a new purpose statement renewed it?
3. What if slide decks were banned, and only narratives or working demos were allowed?

Client Relationships:
1. What if every client complaint triggered a live repair budget on the spot?
2. What if client councils co-owned half of the product roadmap decisions?
3. What if frontline teams designed service journeys rather than central strategy?

Ways of Working:
1. What if deep work were the primary calendar block, and meetings had to earn access?

2. What if flexibility were measured by outcomes, not presence, visible to all?

3. What if every employee could redesign their role quarterly and re-bid for missions?

Internal Tools:
1. What if every tool had to pass a "friction test" quarterly or be deleted?

2. What if employees voted monthly on the most hated system, and it was fixed within thirty days?

3. What if the org published a "tool kill count" as proudly as new tool launches?

Communication:
1. What if all strategy updates had to fit on a single page with clear outcomes, numbers, and stories?

2. What if frontline staff could red-tag confusing comms and trigger a rewrite?

3. What if silence was a permitted response, with no comms at all unless value was clear?

30 September — BANGALORE

End of Month: Board Review

"Operations is where strategy lives or dies," Chris began. "This month, we tested seven domains. The question was the same in each: are we designing for ingenuity, or for irrelevance?"

"Project priorities. In Sydney, we trialed quarterly reallocation forums and shifted oncology funding to projects with measured patient outcomes. Three projects were sunset, one merged, and AU$6.5m was reallocated. The signal was clear: money followed evidence, not politics."

"Workload achievability. In Dublin, we protected maker blocks during aged-care shifts. Absenteeism decreased by 12%, and patient/family presence scores increased by 19%. The signal: thriving beats grinding. Rhythm is a choice."

"Meeting culture. In Tokyo, we cut stand-ups by 40% and replaced them with a single merge ritual each week. We returned 112 staff hours a month with no loss in decision quality. The signal: fewer, better conversations create flow, not theater."

"Client relationships. In São Paulo, we added AI empathy prompts to outpatient visits. NPS increased by 18 points, and complaints about impersonality decreased. The signal: trust can be designed, not left to chance."

"Ways of working. In Bangalore, we replaced hot-desking chaos with activity-based zones. Utilization is up, noise complaints are down, and engineers report more time in flow. The signal: space isn't neutral. It's a lever of ingenuity."

"Internal tools. At Sydney Finance, we implemented live reconciliation dashboards, and AI flagged anomalies instantly. Turnaround on queries dropped from weeks to hours. One shadow remains: intranet SOPs are outdated: 90% of searches fail. The signal: tools split the culture. Where they enable, people trust; where they fail, cynicism grows."

"Communication. In Dublin, we used one-page strategy visuals with outcomes, numbers, and human stories. Engagement doubled, and staff added their own ideas on Post-its. The signal: communication became dialogue, not wallpaper."

She paused. "Three lessons. First, operations is the multiplier; thriving rhythms, clear meetings, trusted tools, and designed trust compound. Second, AI is an accelerant. It amplifies whatever system it enters. If we don't repair, noise multiplies; if we design well, clarity scales. Third, results over rhetoric; we now have visible proof: hours returned, budgets reallocated, dwell times reduced, satisfaction rising."

"Talent gave us the who. Structure gave us the how. Operations showed us the daily truth. Tomorrow, we move to the fifth lever: Leadership Everywhere. We'll test whether leadership is a title or a behavior anyone can claim."

Evelyn added, ""And if you are wondering where the fourth lever went, CEO Stewardship, Chris and I will take that one ourselves. While the team works on Leadership Everywhere, the two of us will meet in New York for a day's retreat to test what CEO Stewardship looks like after nine months of this work."

[See the following chapter on CEO Stewardship.]

CEO's Reflection, That Evening

Chris stepped into the warm Bangalore night. MG Road was still alive with motorbikes weaving between auto-rickshaws, the smell of roasted corn and masala wafting from the footpath. But only a short walk away, in Cubbon Park, the air softened. She slowed her pace beneath the rain trees, the hum of the city settling into a background drone, and let her thoughts uncoil.

Operations had delivered proof: time reclaimed, projects killed, trust designed, and communication simplified. Yet it had also revealed how fragile the gains were. One outdated app, one meeting that sprawled, or one overworked nurse could unravel months of progress. The system would hold only if leadership itself became broader, less positional, more distributed.

Two weeks ago, she had sat with Evelyn in New York. That conversation had been different from anything the year had demanded. The team had been redesigning levers. In New York, the lens had turned inward: her own stewardship, her own clarity, her own pace. She had not been sure she was ready for that mirror. But she had known it was the lever she could not delegate.

She wrote one line in her notebook: "The last lever you can avoid looking at is always your own." [Again, see next chapter.}

Self-Assessment for ORG6, Lever 3: Operations

Rate yourself honestly. For each question, score both the Foundation and the AI Amplifier.
1 Not Yet · 2 Emerging · 3 Developing · 4 Practicing · 5 Second Nature

---

1.

Foundation. Our processes are streamlined. We protect maker time and minimize unnecessary meetings.

Foundation score (1–5):_____

AI Amplifier. We use AI to automate routine processes and protect human time for creative, high-judgment work.

AI Amplifier score (1–5):_____

2.

Foundation. Our operational rhythms respect human energy, not just throughput metrics.

Foundation score (1–5):_____

AI Amplifier. We use AI to optimize schedules, reduce context-switching, and design workflows that respect biological rhythms.

AI Amplifier score (1–5):_____

3.

Foundation. We have eliminated compliance theater. Processes serve real outcomes, not bureaucratic comfort.

Foundation score (1–5):_____

AI Amplifier. We use AI to handle compliance monitoring so humans focus on value creation, not box-ticking.

AI Amplifier score (1–5):_____

4.

Foundation. Time is treated as a precious resource: meeting minimums, not meeting maximums.

Foundation score (1–5): _____

AI Amplifier. We use AI to summarize meetings, track actions, and eliminate the need to attend just to stay informed.

AI Amplifier score (1–5): _____

5.

Foundation. Our operations deliver quality and speed without burning people out.

Foundation score (1–5): _____

AI Amplifier. We use AI to identify operational bottlenecks and recommend improvements before they become crises.

AI Amplifier score (1–5): _____

AVERAGE SCORE: ORG6, Lever 3: Operations

Foundation average (total of five scores ÷ 5):

AI Amplifier average (total of five scores ÷ 5):

Now: Transfer these two averages to the "Operations" row of your ORG6 Scoreboard at the back of the book.

> "*Stewardship is the willingness to be accountable for the well-being of the larger organization... operating in service rather than in control.*"

Peter Block

> "*A CEO's job is to turn complexity into clarity, and clarity into courage. Without both, strategy never leaves the slide deck.*"

Katharine McLennan

CHAPTER 12

CEO Stewardship

*Will we squander the CEO's
time, decisions, and presence
on performance theater,
or
invest those same assets in
growth, trust, and a humane pace?*

15 September — **NEW YORK**

CEO & Chair Day

While contemplating the fourth lever of CEO Stewardship, Chris knew she could not outsource this lever's work to the team. This lever was not a function; it was her. It meant confronting how she set clarity, how she carried presence, how her choices shaped the organization's narrative, and how her pacing either burned out or sustained ingenuity.

So, while the team was working on the third lever, Operations, over September, she met Evelyn for a full-day retreat in the Hudson Valley, with its quiet towns and expansive river views, about seventy miles north of New York City. There were no slides, no whiteboards, just hard questions all day. Evelyn pressed her gently but firmly: "What does it mean to be a CEO in this age? How must you change?"

They determined the domains of stewardship. They asked:

- How has the CEO's role shifted across the five eras: from Industrial, to Information, to the three possible tomorrows of irrelevance, ingenuity, or imagination?

- How does a CEO's executive presence radiate outward, shaping how employees, investors, customers, and communities perceive the organization?

- How inspiring is the CEO's communication of purpose, values, strategy, and goals?

- How does the CEO sustain engagement, not just compliance, but genuine energy and commitment?

- How does the CEO enforce accountability with fairness and trust?

- How does the CEO nurture client relationships personally, beyond contracts and dashboards?

- How does the CEO become a catalyst for innovation and growth?

- How does the CEO choreograph workload, pace, and expectations across the system?

CEO's Notebook: CEO Stewardship

The night before the retreat with Evelyn, Chris had sat in her apartment overlooking the East River. Tomorrow would be different from every other lever. There was no team to assign, no site to visit, no exec to lead the workshop. Tomorrow, she was the subject.

She opened her notebook. "This lever is me," she wrote. "My calendar is the organization's operating system. My presence is the signal that tells people what matters. My pace is the pace they feel. If I get this wrong, nothing else holds." She set her commitments for the month:

Actions

1. Reclaim one hour daily. Audit the calendar each morning. Cancel or shorten one meeting that serves optics rather than outcomes. Protect the hour for frontline contact or reflection.

2. Close one say-do gap daily. Find one promise, commitment, or signal that has drifted from action. Repair it visibly: move the budget, change the schedule, send the follow-up.

3. Hear one unfiltered voice daily. Seek out one person whose reality is not reaching the executive floor. Listen without solving. Write down what they said, not what you expected to hear.

What I'll Notice

1. *Industrial*: where my title silences the room; where people perform for me rather than speak to me.

2. *Information*: where my communications multiply without landing; where dashboards substitute for my presence.

3. *Irrelevance*: where my calendar is full of ceremony; where my words and the organization's reality have diverged.

4. *Ingenuity*: where my presence steadies rather than controls; where my time flows to the work that matters most.

5. *Imagination*: where my role extends beyond the firm; where my choices protect communities and futures I will never see.

Chris closed the notebook. Tomorrow, Evelyn would hold up the mirror. Tonight, she would sit with the questions.

My Fingerprint

One of the most memorable CEOs I ever worked with had three doors between his office and the rest of the bank. Not metaphorical doors. Actual vault-weight doors that his assistant opened one at a time as you approached. The first door separated the executive floor from the building. The second separated the executive corridor from his wing. The third separated his anteroom from the office itself. By the time you reached his desk, you had passed through three thresholds of separation from the organization he led.

It was the Wizard of Oz. The great and powerful voice behind the curtain, amplified by distance, protected by ritual, encountered only by appointment. The executive floor had its own entrance, its own lift, its own dining room. On one side of a mahogany wall sat the board and the executive committee. On the other side sat everyone else. The two populations rarely mixed. When the CEO walked the building, which was seldom, people straightened in their chairs and lowered their voices. His presence was an event, not a practice.

He was brilliant. He was respected. He was also completely insulated. The information that reached him had been filtered through so many layers that it bore only a passing resemblance to what was actually happening on the floors below. He made decisions based on what his direct reports believed he wanted to hear, which was based on what their direct reports believed was safe to say. The truth traveled a long way to reach that desk, and it arrived exhausted.

I spent months inside that bank. The gap between what the executive floor believed and what the organization experienced was not a crack. It was a canyon. People on the floors below had stopped trying to send signals upward because the signals never changed anything. They had learned to work around the CEO rather than with him. The bank functioned not because of the three doors but despite them.

When it came time to choose his successor, he did something I did not expect. He sat at a whiteboard with me and wrote down every quality he believed the next CEO would need. Then he crossed out half of them. "These are the qualities that made me successful," he said. "They will not make the next person successful. The world has changed." The quality he put at the top of the remaining list was one that had never appeared on any succession plan I had seen: the willingness to be vulnerable in front of the organization.

His successor was a different kind of leader. On his first day, he took off his tie, walked onto the trading floor, and asked people what was broken. Not in a town hall. Not in a scheduled listening tour with talking points and handlers. He simply walked in and asked. Within a week, the three vault doors were propped open. Within a month, problems that had been invisible for years were on the table. Within a quarter, three of them were fixed. People who had never spoken directly to the CEO were now in the room when decisions were made. Engagement shifted from compliance to contribution. And the pace of the organization changed because the successor did not set tempo from behind three closed doors. He set it by being present where the work was, matching his rhythm to the reality of the floor rather than the schedule of the executive suite. The organization did not just change its leader. It changed its relationship with truth.

That is what CEO stewardship looks like in transition: the courage to name what the role demands now, not what it demanded before, and the humility to step aside for someone who can live it. The three vault doors were not a character flaw. They were the architecture of an era, the Industrial Age belief that authority required distance and that control required separation. The successor's open floor was the architecture of the next one: the belief that stewardship requires proximity, and that a CEO who cannot hear reality cannot lead through it.

In the AI Era, the distance between the CEO and reality must shrink to almost nothing, because AI will amplify whatever the CEO sees. If the CEO sees filtered truth, AI amplifies the filter. If the CEO sees reality, AI amplifies the insight. The three doors are no longer made of steel. They are made of dashboards, executive summaries, and calendars so full of ceremony that no unfiltered voice can reach the room. The question for every CEO reading this chapter is the same one that bank faced: which doors are you willing to open?The ORG6 Lever for CEO Stewardship CEO stewardship is the lever that sets the tone and tempo, shaping not only what the organization does but also how it holds itself accountable. Its history is written in two yesterdays, the Industrial Age, which treated the CEO as the supreme commander, steward of efficiency and discipline, and the Information Age, which elevated the CEO into a public figurehead, orchestrating shareholders, analysts, media, and global dashboards. Its future divides into three possible tomorrows:

Corrosive Irrelevance: CEOs who cling to command-and-control strategies, broadcast without listening, and let dashboards substitute for judgment.

Optimistic Ingenuity: CEOs who act as stewards of purpose, balancing performance with humanity, and integrating AI as a partner rather than a crutch.

Imaginative Possibility: CEOs who embody stewardship across communities, shaping trust, sustainability, and ingenuity beyond the firm itself.

How the role of a CEO changes over the five eras

Industrial Age

The CEO was the commander of scale: guardian of efficiency, standardization, and control. Frederick Winslow Taylor's scientific management reduced work to timed motions; Henry Ford's assembly line codified throughput and discipline; Alfred Sloan's multidivisional structure concentrated capital allocation at the top while pushing uniform routines to the edges; and business historian Alfred Chandler named the epochal shift "the visible hand" of professional management. The job prized obedience, uniformity, and stamina. What this model gained in reliability, it often lost in adaptability and human energy, costs that stayed hidden while markets rewarded size and predictability.

Information Age

Andy Grove reframed the role around strategic inflection points; Lou Gerstner turned IBM mid-flight by pivoting culture and business model; Meg Whitman scaled eBay from a startup curiosity into a global marketplace by building trust systems that let strangers transact safely; and Lisa Su took AMD from the edge of bankruptcy to a market leader by placing disciplined, long-horizon bets on high-performance computing.

Irrelevance Age

These reflexes can curdle. Leaders manage by dashboards rather than judgment, pilot "AI theater" without redesigning work, and chase optics over outcomes. Research highlights how short-termism erodes resilience and how surveillance models corrode trust, even as data volumes increase. The enterprise can look precise yet become brittle. When listening shrinks and metrics substitute for meaning, learning stalls, courage recedes, and top talent quietly detaches.

Ingenuity Age

The constructive alternative is stewardship, the older sense of steward as guardian of the household, where the CEO balances purpose, people, and pace while pairing human wisdom with machine capability. Mary Barra's GM confronted a safety crisis with radical transparency, then redirected the company toward electric vehicles with a clarity that aligned engineering, culture, and capital behind a single bet. Satya Nadella's Microsoft shifted from 'know-it-all' to 'learn-it-all.' Indra Nooyi's PepsiCo embedded long-term health and sustainability into the growth model through her 'Performance with Purpose' strategy, proving that stewardship and shareholder returns could compound together. Ed Catmull's Pixar made creativity a system rather than the temperament of a few.

Imaginative Possibility

A handful of CEOs are already leading beyond the firm's walls, not as philanthropy but as strategy. Paul Polman, after leaving Unilever, co-founded Imagine to accelerate business action on the Sustainable Development Goals, arguing that the next generation of competitive advantage belongs to companies that solve problems at planetary scale. Emmanuel Faber pushed Danone toward "entreprise à mission" status, embedding social and environmental goals into legal governance, a move that cost him his job but changed the conversation about what a CEO owes beyond shareholders. Yvon Chouinard transferred Patagonia's ownership to a purpose trust, ensuring that profits serve the planet in perpetuity. Rose Marcario, who led Patagonia as CEO through much of that period, operationalized the values that made the transfer credible.

These are still exceptions, not norms. Most boards reward quarterly earnings, not generational stewardship. But the direction is visible: integrated reporting that binds strategy to social and environmental impact, stewardship codes that ask investors to think in decades, and platform leaders who measure success by the health of the ecosystem they convene, not just the revenue they extract. The CEO who operates here treats their calendar, their capital, and their voice as instruments of a purpose larger than the firm. They are not yet common. But they are no longer unimaginable.

The CEO's Executive Presence

Industrial Age

Presence was defined by command and distance: authority flowed downward, deference flowed upward, and formality signaled control. "Management by walking around" made the leader's presence tangible on the floor without compromising hierarchy, and dramaturgy helps explain why the leader's front-stage, prized composure overtook reciprocity. Presence reassured through visible order and restraint, but it also muted curiosity, dampened upward truth-telling, and conflated calm with wisdom.

Information Age

Competition moved to networks and brands, and presence migrated from the factory to the feed. Leaders became narrative makers on stages, analyst calls, and social media platforms. Markets began rewarding attention and perceived distinctiveness, sometimes independent of fundamentals, and communication design emerged as a strategic lever for igniting change beyond what spreadsheets can carry. Presence expanded reach and mobilization power, yet it tempted leaders to manage optics more than operations, confusing applause with alignment.

Irrelevance Age

AI can enable performance theater: algorithmically polished messages, symbolic visits, and dashboard rituals that suppress candor. Employees expect leaders to engage credibly on societal issues and swiftly address inconsistencies. Scholarship warns that inspiration without congruence breeds cynicism, and fear reliably stifles learning. When presence is glossy but unstable, people prioritize self-protection over the mission, and ingenuity dissipates even as communication volume increases.

Ingenuity Age

Presence is the felt combination of gravitas, clarity, and care. Research places judgment and calm at the center; trust compounds when logic, empathy, and authenticity align; and time-use evidence shows that where CEOs allocate their attention predicts outcomes. Case patterns make it practical: a cadence of truth-telling and follow-through can rebuild confidence; gestures of dignity can make strategy feel personal; a raw, unvarnished update in a crisis can steady a system more than any script; and charismatic communication behaviors measurably improve with deliberate practice when tethered to real listening. Calendars, rituals, and reviews become "presence" instruments. Leaders narrate decisions, invite critique before commitment, and protect human energy so people can do the best work of their lives.

Imaginative Possibility

The presence of the CEO makes the firm's stance legible beyond the firm. Ownership choices can align legal structure with purpose; CEOs can recede, allowing autonomous teams to lead while the center maintains coherence; and a single, consistently repeated, principled priority can rewire habits across plants, suppliers, and unions. As platforms and partnerships increasingly define the economy, leaders who choreograph across boundaries, enabling complements, aligning incentives, and modeling shared purpose convert personal presence into a system property that multiplies ingenuity across networks.

The CEO Communicating Purpose, Values, Strategy, and Goals

Industrial Age

Communications were rigid, hierarchical, and slow. Messages flowed downward as orders and upward as reports. Company bulletins, factory posters, and carefully worded letters carried the official line, while the real story often traveled as rumor. The aim was control, not connection; language functioned as instruction more than as a means of meaning-making. It reassured through uniformity but left little room for dialogue, interpretation, or initiative.

Information Age

As organizations globalized and digitized, channels multiplied with email, intranets, newsletters, webcasts, and roadshows. Leaders published mission statements and values, mounted them in lobbies, and synchronized global town halls. Yet the very abundance of channels created noise. Knowledge workers devoted swaths of their week to triaging messages, and the same "update" appeared in multiple places, sowing doubt about which version was the current one. Communication gained reach, but it often lost coherence. People could repeat the words, but they struggled to explain what they meant in the context of their work.

Irrelevance Age

The risk here is message inflation without meaning. Tools can now generate memos, FAQs, and "personalized" updates at an industrial scale, but without a design discipline, this becomes digital exhaust. There is too much to read, too little to trust. Employees experience communication debt: more pings, more meetings, more dashboards, fewer moments of fundamental understanding. Some firms attempt symbolic resets, such as mass cancellations of recurring meetings or rules of thumb about who can schedule what. If the underlying narrative remains fragmented, the relief is temporary. Broadcasts feel transparent yet land as static; people skim, nod, and move on.

Ingenuity Age

The CEO sets a single, living narrative for purpose, values, strategy, and goals, then designs loops, listening, synthesis, and visible adaptation. Messages evolve with evidence. Written narratives replace bullet points to encourage clear thinking; town halls become bidirectional forums where unfiltered questions are raised; summaries and next steps are published in a single source of truth, time-stamped, so everyone knows what has changed and why. Case patterns are practical: disciplined narrative memos sharpen strategy, large-scale forums open the mic to the edge, and leaders who model "context over control" let teams translate goals to local action without diluting intent. When communication is designed this way, AI becomes a partner that curates and summarizes rather than a factory that floods the zone.

Imaginative Possibility

Communication is a participatory system. Immersive formats enable people to *experience* strategy firsthand rather than just read about it; open communities demonstrate how dialogue can be continuous, transparent, and peer-led; and intelligent agents can tailor the enterprise story to each role, highlighting what matters now while preserving a path back to the sources. In this world, the CEO's message is less a speech and more an evolving message: clear enough to align thousands, flexible enough to welcome contribution, and concrete enough to guide choices under pressure.

The CEO Sustaining Engagement

Industrial Age

Engagement was defined as compliance. The signals leaders watched were attendance, output, and defects, and the tools were supervision, incentives, and discipline. Communication about motivation ran one way: from foreman to line, while "involvement" meant suggestion boxes and occasional bonuses for ideas that saved costs. The model produced reliability and endurance, but it treated energy as something to extract rather than cultivate. It left little room for initiative, creativity, or voice.

Information Age

As work shifted to knowledge-based tasks and cross-functional teams, companies professionalized their engagement through surveys, dashboards, and programs. Leaders tracked engagement scores alongside financials, added perks to reduce friction, and launched purpose campaigns to bind global workforces. This broadened the toolkit, yet the center of gravity often stayed managerial: measure more, communicate more, incentivize more. The paradox was familiar: people received more messages about why their work mattered, yet struggled to find the time and latitude to do the work that truly mattered.

Irrelevance Age

Engagement risks becoming a mere spectacle. Productivity tools accelerate activity but can obscure progress; surveillance metrics promise visibility but degrade trust; and message volume expands until employees triage rather than absorb. Burnout emerges when demands outstrip recovery and control, and "productivity paranoia" fosters busyness over value. In this climate, firms can report full calendars and empty hearts. People withhold discretionary effort not out of malice but because the system trains them to conserve what they can control, their attention.

Ingenuity Age

Leaders create conditions for autonomy (clear goals with latitude in the approach), mastery (visible progress and coaching), and purpose (a clear line of sight to customers and community). Progress is made tangible through short feedback loops; teams practice flexible job design to align their strengths with tasks; the prosocial impact of their work is made explicit, enabling individuals to feel the value of their contributions; and psychological safety facilitates early risk surfacing. Case patterns abound: decision rights move closer to the edge, hackathons and "ship-it" rituals celebrate initiative, empowerment rules authorize frontline fixes without waiting for permission, and learning reviews focus on what was discovered, not just what was delivered. Engagement becomes the by-product of systems that respect time, attention, and meaning.

Imaginative Possibility

Engagement extends beyond the firm to the communities it touches. Employee ownership and stewardship models tie contributions to outcomes across generations; open networks demonstrate how participation scales when people can see and shape the whole; and redesigned time, such as four-day-week pilots with outcome-based goals, shows how recovery and performance reinforce each other. When customers, suppliers, and communities are invited into shared problem-solving, work gains narrative and stakes. The CEO's role is to set the conditions: protect autonomy, make progress visible, connect work to purpose, and prune the friction that dilutes human energy.

The CEO Enforcing Accountability with Fairness and Trust

Industrial Age

Accountability meant compliance, surveillance, and discipline. Work was decomposed into tasks and timed; supervisors enforced standards; quality was inspected at the end rather than built into the process. The logic was simple: if output faltered, apply more oversight or replace the worker. It created predictability at the cost of candor. People learned to hide mistakes and hurry problems down the line because the system punished disclosure more than it rewarded learning.

Information Age

Accountability matured into systems of measurement. Leaders adopted strategy maps and scorecards to balance financial outcomes with customer satisfaction, processes, and learning. Regulators required formal attestations from CEOs and CFOs, and goal frameworks, such as OKRs, cascaded objectives with measurable key results. This professionalized visibility across a global enterprise, yet it also increased the number of targets and dashboards. When measurement outpaced meaning, teams optimized locally, missed the whole, and spent more time proving progress than creating it.

Irrelevance Age

Pressure intensifies and tools become sharper, and accountability can devolve into gaming. Targets become the work. Teams optimize the indicator rather than the outcome it was meant to represent. The metric looks healthy while the system underneath it hollows out. Cultures obsessed with metrics but lacking purpose tend to focus on *performing* accountability rather than practicing it. The result is fragile success: spotless reports, rising numbers, and a trust bill that comes due later when customers, regulators, or employees expose how results were achieved.

Ingenuity Age

Accountability with fairness begins by *designing for truth*. A just culture distinguishes human error from reckless neglect; leaders signal that reporting risks is rewarded, not punished. Quality is built in, not inspected in: anyone can "pull the cord" to stop the line, and root-cause learning replaces blame. In after-action reviews and blameless post-mortems, it's common to discuss what went wrong, what we learned, and what we'll change. Mechanisms, not slogans, carry the load: weekly business reviews that use narrative analysis rather than slide theater; decision logs that capture the reasoning behind bets; goal systems that pair outcomes with leading indicators and learning milestones. Fairness is not softness. Research on procedural justice indicates that when standards are clear, consistently applied, and appealable, commitment increases even when outcomes are unfavorable. In this mode, the CEO holds the line on promises and principles while creating conditions that allow people to tell the whole truth from the outset.

Imaginative Possibility

Accountability extends beyond the firm. Integrated reporting binds strategy, risks, and impacts into a single narrative; sustainability standards make non-financial performance auditable; stewardship and benefit structures hard-wire duties to people and planet. In networks and platforms, accountability becomes reciprocal: suppliers, partners, and communities see the same score and contribute to the same fix. The CEO's signature moves, including visible standards, fair processes, and learning mechanisms, travel across boundaries, allowing ingenuity to scale without eroding trust.

The CEO Nurturing Client Relationships

Industrial Age

Relationships were mediated by sales representatives, distributors, and contracts. The CEO's role was distant and episodic, encompassing galas, formal visits, and end-of-year negotiations, because value was produced in factories and moved through established channels. Feedback loops were slow, filtered, and often biased toward what intermediaries chose to share. The dominant idea was to sell what you made, not to create what the customer would love. Reliability and price prevailed, but intimacy and insight were lacking.

Information Age

As markets globalized and digitized, firms adopted CRM systems, customer surveys, and Net Promoter loops to bring the customer inside the building. CEOs stepped onto stages at user conferences, launched customer advisory boards, and courted key accounts through executive sponsorship programs. The narrative shifted from push to pull and from selling products to earning repeat usage and advocacy. Yet the center of gravity still tilted toward dashboards. Many leaders can quote the metrics, yet rarely sit with a customer in context, where the unarticulated needs and frictions actually reside.

Irrelevance Age

It is easy to mistake more data for deeper understanding. Automated emails, scripted chatbots, and "personalized" journeys scale contact but not connection. Procurement squeezes and quarterly targets can turn relationships transactional. Leaders celebrate green scores while missing the moments that matter, an onboarding that confuses, a renewal conversation that feels extractive, a feature that breaks a workflow. When CEOs rely on intermediated metrics and ceremonial visits, they stop hearing reality. Trust erodes quietly: customers continue to buy until they no longer do, and the exit often comes as a surprise to everyone.

Ingenuity Age

The CEO rewires their calendar, so relationships become lived rather than reported. Leaders practice seeing the customer's world firsthand because truth resides where the value is used. They join discovery calls without a pitch, sit alongside service reps as they listen to escalations, and shadow deployment teams through the messy middle of adoption. Mechanisms make this repeatable: customer immersion days on the road map, executive sponsorship that pairs a leader with a handful of strategic accounts, and "decision theaters" where real client stories shape product and policy. Proven patterns abound. Working backward from a customer press release forces clarity before code is written. Jobs-to-be-done interviews reveal the progress customers are trying to make, not the features they say they want. A follow-me-home ethnography reveals points of friction that surveys often overlook. Advisory councils and community forums transform clients into co-designers rather than post-hoc reviewers. Thoughtful questions, fast follow-through, and visible changes from the CEO signal that the relationship is a shared enterprise, not a quarterly transaction.

Imaginative Possibility

Companies invite customers to co-create offerings, set standards, and even shape governance. Open innovation and lead-user programs channel the ingenuity of advanced users into mainstream products. Platforms convene developers and partners whose complements multiply core value. Consumer brands run participatory design studios; B2B firms embed product managers within client teams for a season; and stewardship ownership models align the firm's purpose with customer and community outcomes across generations. In this world, the CEO's role is to choreograph the conditions for ongoing collaboration such as clarity of purpose, lightweight rules of engagement, and quick paths from feedback to change. In this way, trust compounds over time and both sides build what neither could alone.

The CEO Catalyzing Innovation and Growth

Industrial Age

Innovation was centralized and episodic. CEOs funded big labs and breakthrough programs while the line organization focused on scale and cost. Bell Labs and other corporate research centers became engines of invention; Skunk Works units demonstrated how small, protected teams could bend physics to meet deadlines; and early "time to tinker" policies suggested that slack could be a strategic asset, not a waste of time. Growth stemmed from capacity, vertical integration, and occasional leaps from a lab to a product line, but customer insight arrived late and was filtered. The CEO's catalytic act was capital allocation, placing a few large bets and staying out of the way until results surfaced.

Information Age

Innovation has been professionalized into processes. Stage-gate systems, portfolio funnels, and R&D taxonomies helped leaders sort ideas, allocate resources, and manage risk effectively. Strategy work confronted the tension between *exploration* and *exploitation*, and ambidextrous structures separated "new from now" while keeping a handshaking mechanism at the top. Discovery-driven planning and lean startup methods pushed assumptions into the open and insisted on cheap tests before expensive scaling. CEOs erected bridges to the outside through corporate ventures, partnerships, and open innovation. Inside the building, they carved out time for experimentation (from "15% time" to "20% time"). They created rituals to move from demo to deployment. The best grew by learning faster than rivals, not simply by spending more.

Irrelevance Age

Innovation becomes a mere spectacle. Leaders build labs, accelerators, and glass-walled spaces; run hackathons; and publish roadmaps while the fundamental decision rights, budgets, and incentives remain tuned to this quarter's core. Metrics drift toward vanity as ideas are counted, pilots launched, and events held, while kill-rates stay low and hard choices defer. Risk is displaced to procurement or compliance; exploration dies in committee; and everyone can point to activity without committing to bets. The result is motion without momentum and a pipeline that looks full until customers choose otherwise.

Ingenuity Age

Innovation is a system that the CEO personally architects. Mechanisms do the heavy lifting: "working backward" narratives that force clarity before code; decision logs that record the *why* behind bets; small, autonomous teams with the authority to ship; and learning reviews that grade hypotheses, not heroics. Leaders create dual operating systems, protecting the core's reliability while giving exploration different rules for cadence, talent, and funding. Set-based approaches delay irreversible choices until the last responsible moment; option-based budgeting funds evidence, not optimism; and experimentation platforms turn opinions into tests at scale. Exemplars show the pattern: cloud businesses born from internal pain points, creative cultures institutionalized through critique rather than charisma, open communities that multiply complements, and micro-enterprises at the edge that discover demand others can't see. In this mode, growth is designed, driven by customer progress, reinforced by learning loops, and paced by mechanisms the CEO employs on a weekly basis.

Imaginative Possibility

CEOs convene partners, users, and developers around shared problems; publish catechisms that force clarity on purpose, novelty, and the path to impact; and design governance so that discovery compounds over the years. Platforms use APIs and standards to invite others' ingenuity; keystone firms invest in complements that expand the whole; and open networks demonstrate how transparency and modularity accelerate discovery. Here, the CEO's catalytic act is akin to choreography, setting the rules, lowering friction, and aligning incentives so that many actors can create what none could achieve alone.

The CEO Choreographing Workload, Pace, and Expectations

Industrial Age

Workload and pace were engineered for machines, not minds. Time-and-motion studies, shift clocks, and takt time synchronized human effort to the cadence of production. Utilization was the north star; variability was treated as waste; and queues were the price of keeping assets "fully busy." The system delivered throughput and predictability, but it relied on fatigue as a buffer and treated slack as inefficiency rather than the safety margin that prevents errors and absorbs shocks.

Information Age

Globalization and digital tools replaced the factory whistle with the calendar invite and the notification. Knowledge work is fragmented into meetings, messages, and multitasking; interruptions spike, context switching rises, and focus time becomes scarce. Organizations attempted to manage white-collar work as if it were a continuous process, only to discover that quality and creativity suffered as a result. A counter-movement emerged: maker time versus manager time, deliberate focus blocks, predictable time off, and deep work practices that concentrate attention and restore rhythm. The lesson was simple: hours and output are not linear, and attention, not just effort, determines excellence.

Irrelevance Age

Busyness masquerades as progress. Dashboards multiply, "productivity paranoia" takes hold, and burnout climbs as demands outpace control and recovery. Leaders push for more meetings, sprints, and status checks, creating latency and stress without improving workflow. As work becomes hyper-interruptible, error rates rise, shallow work crowds out complex problems, and talent self-protects by disengaging. The organization looks energetic, but moves like it is wading through sand.

Ingenuity Age

Leaders set explicit load limits, cap work-in-process, and size batches to shorten cycle time. They apply queueing and systems thinking, limiting the number of simultaneous projects, intentionally creating slack, and using buffers where variability is highest. Calendars become operating models: meeting-light days for creation, familiar cadences for decision-making, and visible norms for response and availability. Teams use time-boxed experiments, after-action learning, and weekly narrative reviews to translate goals into achievable, paced commitments. Boundary mechanisms such as predictable time off, on-call rotations with recovery, and protected focus blocks, treat energy as a strategic asset. Evidence shows that when hours, attention, and autonomy align, throughput improves, quality rises, and people sustain the effort required to solve non-obvious problems.

Imaginative Possibility

Time becomes a shared infrastructure across communities. Partners coordinate release trains, co-author service-level expectations, and pool Slack where interdependence is tight. Stewardship ownership and multi-capital reporting extend pacing beyond quarters. AI assistants help individuals and teams choreograph workload, defragmenting attention, sequencing tasks to cognitive rhythms, and surfacing early signals of overload, while leaders hold to human boundaries that keep judgment sharp. In this world, the CEO's signature is tempo with integrity: a pace that compounds learning and performance without exhausting the people who create them.

15 September — NEW YORK 8:30PM

CEO & Chair review day

Chris then reflected with Evelyn on her strengths and development points for each of these points:

How the CEO role shifts across eras
- Strength: I can name the threshold plainly and hold the room there until we act.
- Development: I will let go of dashboard reflexes faster with fewer optics, more judgment at the edge.

Executive presence
- Strength: Under pressure, I remain calm and candid; I steady the system rather than exacerbate it.
- Development: I will make my presence more legible beyond the

stage, spending more time with frontline and "edge voices," and fewer ceremonial appearances.

Communicating purpose, values, strategy, goals

- Strength: Narrative memos sharpen our thinking; decisions read better than they ever present.

- Development: I will reduce volume, centralize the source of truth, and timestamp changes so people know what has shifted and why.

Sustaining engagement

- Strength: I maintain a deep work rhythm by insisting on maker blocks and regular progress reviews.

- Development: I will remove one friction a day at the top: fewer interrupts, clearer goals, and visible links to purpose.

Enforcing accountability with fairness and trust

- Strength: I've moved us toward a just culture: postmortems, advice processes, and "pull the cord" norms.

- Development: I will expedite repairs and make them public: model cards, fairness audits, and results of consequence.

Nurturing client relationships

- Strength: I sit in on calls, shadow deployments, and ask fewer, more targeted questions.

- Development: I will establish a cadence of immersion: monthly days with customers that directly translate into product and policy changes.

Catalyzing innovation and growth

- Strength: I fund small autonomous bets and insist we grade hypotheses, not heroics.

- Development: I will tighten option budgeting and kill rates: more evidence, fewer zombies, faster reallocation.

Choreographing workload, pace, and expectations
- Strength: I reset the tempo when we drift into busyness; I can slow us down to think, speed us up to ship.

- Development: I will run my calendar as the operating system, establishing visible norms for response, predictable time off, and a capped work-in-process.

What If

Before closing the day, Chris and Evelyn stretched their thinking beyond the near term. "If you could redesign the CEO role from scratch," Evelyn said, "what would you change?"

They wrote ten questions together:

1. What if every CEO had to publish their calendar monthly, so the organization could see where attention actually went?
2. What if board meetings began with a frontline story, not a financial summary?
3. What if the CEO's bonus were tied to trust scores and repair speed, not just shareholder return?
4. What if every CEO spent one day per month doing the work of a frontline employee, with no handlers and no agenda?
5. What if the CEO had to write one public "what I got wrong" memo per quarter?
6. What if succession planning started on day one, not year five?
7. What if the CEO's presence were measured not by events attended but by decisions improved?
8. What if every CEO had a consigliere with the explicit mandate to say what no one else would?
9. What if the CEO's communication were limited to one page per month, forcing clarity over volume?
10. What if the measure of a CEO were not the organization they built but the organization that thrived after they left?

Evelyn smiled. "That last one is the only one that matters in the end."

Evelyn set down her pen. "In two weeks, at the September 30 Board meeting, I would like us to present this work jointly. Not as a performance review. As a shared account of what CEO Stewardship looks like when it is examined honestly."

Chris nodded. "And on September 29, the team will review their results from the third lever, Operations [presented in Chapter 11]. At that meeting, I will let them know that our report on CEO Stewardship will be tabled at the Board the following day, and that I want each of them to read it afterwards."

Evelyn was quiet for a moment. "I want to say something about what you have just done. You have opened your own leadership to the same scrutiny you asked of every member of your team this year. You did not have to do that. Most CEOs would not. The fact that you will share this with your executives, not just with me, is the most consequential decision you have made since January."

CEO's Reflection, That Evening

Back in the city that evening, Chris closed the notebook and walked up Fifth Avenue as the city pulled itself into lights, horns, steam, and the quick strides of strangers. Being a CEO, she thought, is less a title than a metronome and a mirror: you set a humane pace, you hold up the truth, and you spend your time, decisions, and presence so that other people's judgment and dignity grow larger than your own.

It is not about command, nor celebrity, nor performance. It is stewardship. For Omnivista, that meant something heavier and holier: holding the trust of 200,000 people whose work and well-being depended on her choices. Pacing the organization so ingenuity had time to breathe. Ensuring that AI multiplied wisdom rather than shadows. Her calendar was not her own but a public document of what Omnivista valued. Her words could fragment or unify. Her silence could steady or erode.

If she treated this role as optics, the company would collapse into irrelevance. If she lived it as stewardship, clarity, presence, coherence, and pacing, Omnivista might become something worth following in an age where many leaders were drifting.

She pulled her coat tighter against the wind. Tonight, she was just one person walking home through New York. But tomorrow, she would return as the steward of a system much larger than herself.

Self-Assessment for ORG6 Lever 4, CEO Stewardship

If you are the CEO, score yourself directly. If you are not the CEO, score your organization's senior leadership as you experience it. Both perspectives are valid and reveal where stewardship is strong and where it needs attention.

1 Not Yet · 2 Emerging · 3 Developing · 4 Practicing · 5 Second Nature

---

1.

Foundation. The CEO tells a clear, consistent story, not slogans that change every quarter.

　　Foundation score (1–5):_____

AI Amplifier. The CEO uses AI to test whether their strategic narrative resonates and reaches the organization consistently.

　　AI Amplifier score (1–5):_____

2.

Foundation. The pace from the CEO is steady and sustainable, not whiplash-inducing urgency.

　　Foundation score (1–5):_____

AI Amplifier. The CEO uses AI to monitor initiative load and flag when the organization is absorbing too much change.

　　AI Amplifier score (1–5):_____

3.

Foundation. The CEO spends real time with customers, teams, and communities, not just investors.

　　Foundation score (1–5):_____

AI Amplifier. The CEO uses AI to handle preparation and follow-up so leadership time with people is high-quality, not rushed.

　　AI Amplifier score (1–5):_____

4.

Foundation. The CEO listens more than they broadcast. Signals travel up as well as down.

Foundation score (1–5):_____

AI Amplifier. The CEO uses AI to surface frontline signals, sentiment patterns, and emerging concerns leadership needs to hear.

AI Amplifier score (1–5):_____

5.

Foundation. When the story shifts, it's because the world shifted, not because the CEO is chasing trends.

Foundation score (1–5):_____

AI Amplifier. The CEO uses AI to distinguish genuine signals from noise so strategic pivots are grounded, not reactive.

AI Amplifier score (1–5):_____

AVERAGE SCORE:ORG6: Lever 4, CEO Stewardship

Foundation average (total of five scores ÷ 5):_____

AI Amplifier average (total of five scores ÷ 5):_____

Now: Transfer these two averages to the "CEO Stewardship" row of your ORG6 Scoreboard at the back of the book.

"To lead people, walk beside them; and when the work is done, they will say, 'We did this ourselves.'"

Lao Tzu

"In its simplest form, leadership is a conscious choice. Every day presents forks in the path: we can react from autopilot or respond from awareness."

Katharine McLennan

CHAPTER 13

Leadership Everywhere

*Will leadership stay constrained
by hierarchy and title,
or
be enabled as a shared,
organization-wide capability?*

1 October — BANGALORE

First Day of Month: Executive Team

In Bangalore, Omnivista executive team now opened the fifth lever: Leadership Everywhere. Talent had set the tone. Structure had set the *how*. Operations had revealed the *daily truth*. Now it was time to ask whether leadership was still a title at the top, or a way of being that lived in every corner of the organization.

Sanjay stood to frame the day. "We're going to explore four questions over the month:

- **TEAM LEADERSHIP** (Do leadership teams at every level operate as genuine units that decide, learn, and deliver together, or as calendar artifacts where individuals report in parallel and revert to silos?)

- **LEADERSHIP DEVELOPMENT AND COACHING** (Is there a coherent enterprise system that teaches shared doctrine at every level, and is coaching a daily practice carried by managers, or an occasional program reserved for the senior few?)

- **LEADERSHIP POTENTIAL AND SUCCESSION** (Is potential defined, spotted, and grown, and does assessment connect to development and to the roles that matter most?)

- **DECISION RIGHTS AND THE MIDDLE** (Who decides what, with what information, how legible are decisions to others who must act, and are middle managers empowered as connective tissue or squeezed between strategy they didn't shape and execution they can't resource?)

Chris leaned in. "If leadership remains concentrated in a few roles, we will exhaust ourselves. If leadership becomes the shared practice of conscious choice, judgment close to reality, and accountability carried by teams, we will compound ingenuity faster than any competitor."

The team nodded. The day belonged to leadership. By mid-morning, the team followed Sanjay into the Whitefield Digital Campus, a sprawling complex where Omnivista's software engineers, data scientists, and product managers worked side by side. This was his chosen signal site, not because it was perfect, but because its strengths and shadows revealed how leadership was, or wasn't, distributed across the organization.

Team Leadership

Sanjay showed them two project rooms. In one, the squad operated as a genuine team: shared decisions, a single backlog, roles clear, disagreements surfaced and resolved in the room. They had shipped three releases in six weeks without escalating once. Across the hall, another group met weekly but operated in parallel. Each function prepared its own update, presented to the room, and left. No joint decisions were taken; the meeting was a ritual of reporting, not a unit of work. "That's the difference," Sanjay said. "One room has a team. The other has a calendar invite."

Leadership Development and Coaching

Sanjay's local site manager pulled up Omnivista's "Leadership Pathways" on a screen. The framework was fragmented: modules on coaching here, a mentoring program there, but no enterprise academy. Managers confirmed that coaching happened informally if it happened at all; it was not tracked, not expected, and not rewarded. "This is what our people see," Sanjay said. "Scattered, optional, inconsistent. If leadership is to be everywhere, it needs a single doctrine and coaching must be a daily practice, not a perk for the senior few."

Leadership Potential and Succession

He brought them to a digital dashboard: talent grids that rated potential across skills. "We're still using nine-box thinking," he admitted. "High potentials get tagged, but then they wait. The bridge from assessment to development is missing." Engineers standing nearby confirmed: they didn't see clear routes into leadership roles. One said, "I was labeled high-potential two years ago. Nothing changed except the label."

Decision Rights in the Middle

At one product pod, developers demonstrated how they had reclassified decisions into "one-way doors" (rare, high-stakes) and "two-way doors" (reversible, local). Two-way doors were now resolved in hours rather than being escalated for weeks. "This is ingenuity," Sanjay said. "But only half the site has adopted it. The rest still default to upward escalation." He paused at a middle manager's desk nearby. "And this is where the system breaks. Our middle managers carry the weight of translation between strategy and execution, but they have almost no authority to act. They escalate because the system taught them to. If we don't free the middle, Leadership

Everywhere is just a slogan at the top and frustration in the corridors."

The team left the campus thoughtfully. In every corner, they had seen two realities: leadership still tethered to title and hierarchy, and leadership emerging at the edge through shared judgment, team discipline, and managers finding their voice.

Team Assignments for the Month

Chris gathered the team before they left the campus. "Leadership Everywhere isn't a slogan," she said. "This month, each of you will take one domain and run a single pilot at your site. Don't design a program. Find one practice that's broken, redesign it for ingenuity, and bring back results. Data, not anecdotes."

She assigned the domains:

- *Yuki (Tokyo): Team leadership.* "Pick one leadership team at Shinjuku that operates as a calendar artifact: people report in parallel and leave. Redesign it into a genuine unit: shared decisions, joint accountability, one backlog. Show me what changed in how they decide and deliver."

- *John (Sydney): Decision rights and the middle.* "Apply the one-way and two-way door model across two teams. But I also want you to focus on the middle managers in those teams. Give them explicit authority for two-way doors and remove one layer of sign-off. Report cycle times, escalations avoided, and what the middle managers say about their own agency."

- *Maria (São Paulo): Leadership potential and succession.* "Take your current nine-box grid for Paulista General and test it against reality. Identify two people labeled high-potential and two who were overlooked. Put all four through a real judgment challenge, not a simulation, a live operational dilemma. Come back with what you learned about how we spot potential versus how we should."

- *Sanjay (Bangalore): Leadership development and coaching.* "Build a prototype Leadership Everywhere module: one cohort, one shared doctrine, four weeks. But embed coaching into it. Every participant must coach one peer weekly and be coached in return. Measure whether behavior changes, not whether people enjoyed the content."

- **Liam (Dublin): Team leadership.** "Redesign one care team at Liffey from a reporting group into a decision-making unit. Give them a shared outcome, a weekly rhythm, and the authority to adjust care protocols without escalating. Show me whether decisions get faster and whether staff feel they own the result."

Chris paused. "And I'll take one myself. I'm going to audit how our C-suite operates as a team. I'll track one month of our meetings: how many joint decisions we actually made versus how many times we reported in parallel and dispersed. If we can't model team leadership at the top, we have no right to ask anyone else to practice it."
"End of the month, Dublin. Bring results."

CEO's Notebook: Leadership Everywhere

That night, Chris walked through the streets of Whitefield, the air thick with the mix of chai stalls, motorbikes, and the hum of still-lit call centers. The campus they had toured was a paradox: engineers full of ideas, yet still waiting on permission; peers learning from each other in retro walls, yet silos snapping back the next day. It felt like the city around her: ingenuity flickering, but always at risk of being lost in the noise.

She opened her notebook. "Leadership Everywhere is the *who* and the *how* of choice. If we don't spread it, the system will exhaust itself waiting for permission." She wrote her three commitments for October.

Actions

1. Name one leader daily without a title. Highlight where someone, anywhere in the system, made a conscious choice that benefited the whole.

2. Push one decision outward daily. Decline to hold what others can decide closer to reality; log the reasoning and the trade-off.

3. Share one lesson across peers daily. Take an insight from one part of Omnivista and make it visible to another, so knowledge flows more efficiently than through a hierarchy.

What I'll Notice

1. *Industrial:* leadership as command and inspection; presence equated with control.

2. *Information*: leadership as dashboards and orchestration; style over substance.

3. *Irrelevance*: Leadership has become focused on optics; peers remain silent, and decisions often get stuck at the top.

4. *Ingenuity*: leadership seen in behavior, not titles; decisions logged at the edge; peers holding each other accountable.

5. *Imagination*: leadership as a system property; voices diverse and connected; wisdom compounding across networks.

She closed the notebook, neon spilling over the page. From tomorrow, they would turn from principles to practice, proof that leadership could live not just in the C-suite, but in every corridor of Omnivista.

My Fingerprint

The most ambitious leadership development system I ever helped build served over two hundred countries. It was modeled on what GE had pioneered at Crotonville, arguably the first corporate institution to prove that a company could teach a shared leadership doctrine at every level, and that the doctrine itself could become the connective tissue holding a global enterprise together.

We designed it around four components. The first was a common language of leadership that every manager in every country learned, so that a conversation about decision rights in Jakarta meant the same thing as a conversation about decision rights in Johannesburg. The second was action learning: every cohort worked on a real business problem with real stakes, not a simulation, and presented their recommendations to senior leaders who had the authority to act on them. The third was coaching embedded in the program itself: participants coached each other throughout, and their managers were trained to continue the coaching when they returned. The fourth was rotation: the academy was not a single event but a series of experiences across levels, functions, and geographies, each building on the last.

What made it work was not the curriculum. It was the commitment. The CEO taught sessions personally. So did the CFO, the CMO, the CPO, the CTO, and the Chairman. Board members and technical experts taught where their knowledge was most relevant. When the most senior leaders in the company stand in front of a room and teach what they believe, the organization learns two things at once: the content, and the fact that leadership development is not an HR program. It is the way the company builds its future.

We also committed to sending leaders across borders, not as tourists but as learners. A manager from São Paulo would spend two weeks with peers in Singapore, working on a shared problem, learning how the organization operated in a different context, and building relationships that would carry decisions and trust across geographies for years afterward. This was not treated as a cost. Travel and development were treated as capital investment in human capability: spend that appreciates over time because the person who returns is worth more than the person who left, and the relationships they built strengthen the network long after the program ends. People are not an expense line. They are a potentially exponentially expanding investment, and the returns compound in ways no spreadsheet fully captures.

What made it fragile was the opposite of what made it strong. When the CEO changed, the commitment wavered. The academy survived on paper but lost its spine. Sessions were delegated to external faculty. The C-suite stopped teaching. Action learning projects became hypothetical. Coaching fell away. Travel budgets were cut as "discretionary spend," as if the relationships and capabilities they built were optional. The language persisted but the practice behind it thinned. Within two years, graduates were telling me: "The words are the same, but nobody means them anymore."

That is the lesson I carry into every leadership development conversation. The system works only as long as the leaders at the top believe it is their system, not HR's system, not the academy's system, but the way the organization builds its future. The moment it becomes a program managed by a function, it begins to die. In the AI Era, this becomes even more urgent. AI can personalize learning paths, simulate decision scenarios, surface coaching prompts, and track whether behavior changes after a session. But AI cannot replace the CEO who teaches, the senior leader who mentors, or the manager who coaches in the flow of daily work. Leadership development is either carried by leaders or it is theater. There is no middle ground.

The ORG6 Lever for Leadership Everywhere

Leadership everywhere is the lever that makes ingenuity a property of the whole system, not a performance by a few. Its history has two yesterdays, the Industrial Age, which tied leadership to control, compliance, and positional authority, and the Information Age, which expanded leadership into orchestration across functions, geographies, and partners. Its future divides into three possible tomorrows:

> *Corrosive Irrelevance:* organizations that preach empowerment while hoarding authority, multiplying ceremonies of "agility" without moving decision rights, and rewarding optics over outcomes.

> *Ingenuity Age:* organizations that design absolute authority where the work is honest, pairing psychological safety with peer challenge so decisions travel fast and learning compounds.

> *Imaginative Possibility:* organizations that lead across networks, enabling customers, partners, and communities to co-create value through open standards, platforms, and shared governance.

TEAM LEADERSHIP

> *Do leadership teams at every level operate as genuine units that decide, learn, and deliver together, or as calendar artifacts where individuals report in parallel and revert to silos?*

Across eras, the leadership team has shifted from a set of influential individuals to an operating system for the whole enterprise.

Industrial Age.

"Teams" were often referred to as cabinets. Work was cleanly divided by function, coordination flowed through the hierarchy, and collaboration meant passing files across a corridor. Rewards and reputations were individual. When coordination faltered, leaders added committees rather than building teamwork. Reliability, not joint problem-solving, was the ideal, and a "good meeting" affirmed plans already made. Dissent was a personal risk, not a contribution.

Information Age

Globalization and matrix structures made interdependence unavoidable. Leadership teams multiplied, and so did programs to develop them. We learned useful distinctions: management versus leadership, task versus relationship, team versus group, and we taught them in places like Crotonville and corporate academies. The science of teams advanced, encompassing conditions for effectiveness, decision-making roles, and the social dynamics that transform groups into cohesive units. Practice lagged. Most organizations still measured and promoted individuals, then wondered why senior groups behaved like federations.

Irrelevance Age

Teams can slip into corrosive irrelevance. Video tools and dashboards create the appearance of alignment, while decision rights remain vague, meetings proliferate, and notes are summarized but never synthesized. Poor remote and hybrid rhythms weaken weak ties and creative collisions. Surveillance metrics push people to optimize visible activity rather than enterprise value. AI will happily become a meeting stenographer for gatherings that never require a decision. Teams feel busy, yet problems ricochet between functions and stall in the gaps.

Ingenuity Age

Team leadership is designed as a system. The mandate is explicit and enterprise-first. Decision rights are clearly defined: who recommends, who provides input, who agrees, who makes the decision, and who performs the action are recorded so that choices are transparent. Cadence is intentional: forums for sense-making, decision reviews that use concise narrative logic, and retrospectives that turn misses into learning. Presence matters. Leaders practice how they show up, listening for dissent, testing hypotheses with data from the edge, and modeling bilateral accountability.

Trust is built deliberately through frequent one-on-ones that trade crisp commitments for vague support. AI assists but does not replace: it prepares pre-reads, surfaces patterns across markets and operations, translates across time zones, and drafts decision logs. The time saved is spent arguing well, making quick decisions, and following through.

Imaginative Possibility

Leadership teams become nodes in a constellation. They convene partners, customers, and communities in decision theaters where strategy is tested against reality in real time. They share standards and protocols, allowing value to be co-created safely and steward talent across firm boundaries over long periods. AI agents coordinate routine interlocks; humans focus on judgment, narrative, and ethics. Individual fame matters less; enterprise and ecosystem consequence matter more. The team's signature is coherence: many minds, one enterprise intent.

Five elements comprise a leadership team at any level:

First, mandate and identity. A real team exists to accomplish collective work that no individual can do alone, whether that is enterprise strategy at the top or patient flow on a ward. "Are we a team or a group?" is not rhetoric; it is a design choice that must be revisited as context shifts.

Second, roles and decision rights. Clarity beats charisma. Teams that choose and use a single decision-rights language, such as Recommend, Input, Agree, Decide, Perform (the RIADP model), reduce cycle time and avoid the "everyone owns it, so no one owns it" trap. The discipline shows up in how priorities are mapped and how a steward, catalyst, and sponsor are assigned to each, with explicit bilateral commitments.

Third, processes and cadences. Meeting architecture is a strategy in disguise. High-performing teams design a weekly and quarterly rhythm that aligns their scope, incorporating sense-making, decision reviews, customer immersion, after-action learning, and talent conversations. Simple templates make installation fast and inspection easy.

Fourth, presence and communication. How leaders show up, in meetings, decisions, communications, and at the edge, either liberates initiative or smothers it. Remote and hybrid work brought both gains and losses. Gains include access across geographies, inclusion in forums once reserved for the few, searchable memory, and asynchronous collaboration that protects focus. Losses include declines in creative ideation and serendipity, more siloed networks, and real fatigue unless boundaries are designed. The aim is better synchronous sessions, more asynchronous preparation, deliberate convenings for creativity and trust, and written narrative in place of slide theater.

Fifth, bilateral trust. Teams become real when peers can check one another's commitments without triangulating through the leader above them. Trust is not a mood; it is the habit of keeping explicit promises, delivering visible follow-through, and offering direct peer-to-peer correction.

Culture and schooling work against this. Most of us were educated as solo achievers and promoted for individual results. Leadership teams, therefore, must teach teaming: making the mandate explicit, demonstrating what "good" looks like, and rewarding shared outcomes.

AI will either erode or elevate teaming. It erodes when leaders outsource judgment, collapse decision rights into dashboards, or replace peer accountability with metrics. It elevates when leaders use it to see system patterns across customers and operations, prepare better debates, retain decision-making memory, translate across languages and disciplines, and personalize learning so that every member's potential can grow. The difference is design and discipline, not the technology itself.

LEADERSHIP DEVELOPMENT AND COACHING

Is there a coherent enterprise system that teaches shared doctrine at every level, and is coaching a daily practice carried by managers, or an occasional program reserved for the senior few?

Leadership development is either a course catalog or a capability system. In the first, progress is measured by attendance and the issuance of certificates. In the second, progress is visible in decisions, customer value, culture, and the steady growth of leaders at every level. Across eras, the center of gravity shifts from training individuals to building enterprise capability that pairs human ingenuity with intelligent tools. Industrial Age.

Development was built around compliance and control: supervisory training focused on procedures, time-and-motion discipline, and carrot-and-stick motivation. Advancement followed narrow ladders; pedagogy was didactic, and success meant uniformity. Learning was something delivered to people rather than something they practiced. In that frame, "leadership" was positioned at the top, while "management" was placed elsewhere. Coaching did not exist as a practice; correction came from the supervisor, and it traveled in one direction.

Information Age

Globalization and digitalization led to the development of competency models, corporate universities, 360-degree feedback, coaching, and executive education. The 70-20-10 heuristic popularized the idea that most growth comes from stretch work rather than classroom instruction. Institutions like Crotonville, INSEAD, Stanford, and Harvard institutionalized multi-week residential programs for senior leaders. Coaching emerged as a discipline, but it remained a perk for the top: executive coaches worked with the C-suite, while middle managers and frontline leaders were left to figure it out alone. Many companies still treated development as events instead of systems, and measurement focused on satisfaction rather than capability or business outcomes.

Irrelevance Age

Development can slide into edutainment. Vendors multiply, e-learning fragments attention, and "leadership content" floods inboxes without changing behavior. Algorithms promise precision but often lack validity, amplifying bias or collapsing nuanced judgment into simplistic dashboards. Over-rotating to compliance and regulation squeezes out reflection, coaching, practice, and the messy human work of growth. The result is predictable: leaders are certified but not capable; everyone is trained, yet the same complex problems keep resurfacing. Coaching, where it exists, becomes formulaic: a quarterly check-in against a development plan that no one revisits between sessions.

Ingenuity Age

A company-wide leadership academy becomes a spine: coherent across levels, anchored to strategy, and measured by decisions, execution, and culture. Coaching becomes the daily expression of development, not a separate program. Managers act as primary coaches; the expectation is explicit, tracked, and rewarded. Peer learning communities do the heavy lifting; stretch assignments are matched to potential. AI is used as a precision tool: it powers retrieval practice, simulation, translation, and just-in-time feedback. Leaders grow the capacity with which they see and act, not only their skills. A practical set of principles reinforces the shift: start from strategy, assess rigorously, learn on the job, make development a contact sport, measure what matters, and embed the whole in talent systems.

Imaginative Possibility

Development extends beyond the firm. Cross-company academies share standards and simulations. Customers and suppliers co-learn in decision theaters. Skills passports make talent portable. AI tutors orchestrate highly personalized pathways, while governance frameworks ensure the system remains trustworthy and reliable. The signature move is stewardship: teaching people to exercise judgment for the enterprise and the broader ecosystem, not only for their function or career.

Most growth comes from challenging experiences with real stakes, supported by coaching and feedback. It is more like a gym than a lecture. Complex skills develop through repeated practice, not through reading about them. Learning sticks when people are tested on what they know, when practice is spread over time rather than crammed into a single session, and when different capabilities are mixed rather than drilled in isolation. The goal is leaders who can hold greater complexity, see from more perspectives, and make better judgments under pressure, not leaders who simply accumulate more knowledge.

Coaching is effective when it is goal-focused, feedback-rich, and integrated into the workflow. When managers treat every one-on-one, every project debrief, and every difficult conversation as a coaching moment, development stops being something that happens offsite and becomes something that happens in the work itself. These practices turn development from events into habits and from inspiration into capability.

Everyone leads. Formal authority is neither necessary nor sufficient. Expect and teach leadership at every level. Development should prime people for upward influence rooted in data, empathy, and enterprise intent.

AI adds power but must not replace judgment, ethics, or accountability. Used well, it accelerates mastery through retrieval practice, simulation, translation, and knowledge integration. The rule of thumb is simple: AI drafts, humans decide, the system learns, and good governance keeps that triangle honest.

LEADERSHIP POTENTIAL AND SUCCESSION

Is potential defined, spotted, and grown, and does assessment connect to development and to the roles that matter most?

Assessment is the supply chain of leadership. It answers two questions that determine the fate of every organization: who is ready now, and who can grow quickly enough to meet tomorrow's needs? Potential is not a personality label; it is the demonstrated capacity to take on greater scope, complexity, and ambiguity while creating trust and results. That capacity is shaped by character and context, and revealed over time.

Industrial Age.

Assessment was designed to staff predictable hierarchies. Psychometrics were used to slot people into roles defined by compliance and repetition. Supervisors judged readiness by tenure, technical proficiency, and obedience. Succession planning was episodic and positional, focusing on who would occupy the chair when the current occupant left. The familiar nine-box showing performance against potential rewarded the reliable and the loyal, often assuming that yesterday's success would translate unaltered to tomorrow's mandate. "High potential" was an anointment, not a hypothesis to be tested.

Information Age.

Assessment became professionalized. Competency models multiplied. 360-degree feedback became a staple. Assessment centers and structured interviews were meant to ensure fairness. Data widened the lens, and global programs brought discipline to succession and mobility. Yet the era's strengths were also its limits. Many 360s became leadership's version of opinion polling: beneficial for reputation, but easily decoupled from the actual judgments a leader makes under pressure. Annual calibrations pushed conversations toward color-coded dashboards rather than evidence of growth. A cottage industry formed around tools that were rarely connected to strategy or measured for real impact. Even when rigorous, the work was event-based rather than longitudinal, and role-based rather than system-aware.

Irrelevance Age

Assessment can either deepen discernment or accelerate irrelevance. One path reduces people to algorithmic proxies, scraping communications for "sentiment," outsourcing judgment to opaque models, and inflating the precision of weak signals. Likert scales become auto-summaries; psychometrics are wielded as destiny; nine-boxes ossify into orthodoxy. Search networks close around "people we know." The result is selection for conformity with the past and a system exquisitely tuned to miss the very leaders who can navigate discontinuity.

Ingenuity Age

Assessment asks a different set of questions: when the context shifts, what does this person notice? How do they reason? How do they include others? How do they hold purpose and consequence together? How do they learn between rounds? The method becomes longitudinal, multi-format, and woven with development. Narrative 360s replace ratings, focusing on concrete episodes and patterns over time. Event-based simulations present ethical, strategic, and human dilemmas with no single correct answer, documenting how leaders frame trade-offs and adapt. Judgment reviews analyze real decisions: memos, stakeholder dialogues, and post-mortems. These surface the quality of thinking, not just the outcomes. AI assists but does not decide. It aggregates patterns across evidence, flags drift between espoused values and observed behaviors, and suggests where to probe next. Assessment feeds development and returns as reassessment, creating a continuous loop: define the capabilities strategy requires, measure them rigorously, close the gaps through practice, then re-measure for impact on people and performance.

Imaginative Possibility

Assessment becomes a civic act held with humility, transparency, and stewardship. Organizations treat leadership potential as a public good to be cultivated across communities rather than hoarded. Succession becomes system succession: cross-company secondments, guild-like fellowships, and shared standards for what "readiness" means when the work spans sectors and societies. AI becomes an instrument for opening doors, surfacing non-obvious candidates, checking bias in decisions, and translating feedback into growth plans that honor dignity.

And so, the tools themselves need rethinking, not discarding. Psychometrics retain a place as inputs, but they must be ethically used, interpreted by qualified practitioners, and triangulated with behavioral evidence. 360s still help when they shift from ratings to narratives and from one-off snapshots to pulsed feedback around real episodes of work. Assessment centers evolve into practice centers, where leaders bring live challenges and work through them with peers, coaches, and stakeholders. Above all, every instrument must be connected to the few capabilities the strategy truly requires, and those capabilities must be expressed in language people can put to work immediately.

Governance and cadence matter. Succession is not a once-a-year review; it is a standing agenda with explicit oversight of talent risk and value creation. Good governance requires clarity about capability gaps, bench strength, and emergency plans. It needs reporting that treats talent as capital, not just headcount.

DECISION RIGHTS AND THE MIDDLE

Who decides what, with what information, how legible are decisions to others who must act, and are middle managers empowered as connective tissue or squeezed between strategy they didn't shape and execution they can't resource?

Decision rights determine who has the authority to act when reality shifts. They are the plumbing of leadership: invisible when they work, corrosive when they don't. And no one feels the consequences of broken plumbing more acutely than middle managers, the people who translate strategy into action, absorb pressure from both directions, and carry the daily weight of decisions that are either theirs to make or endlessly deferred upward.

For much of the Industrial and Information Ages, decisions cascaded upward. Authority lived in titles, approvals, and escalations. The pattern created order, but it also embedded a delay, and it hollowed out the very layer of the organization, the middle, where judgment meets reality.

Industrial Age.

Decision rights were positional. Foremen and supervisors approved deviations; managers signed off on even reversible choices. Permission was the lubricant that kept the pyramid running. The result was predictability without adaptability. Teams executed orders rather than exercising judgment, errors surfaced late, and opportunities died in the approval queue. Middle managers existed to enforce the plan, not to interpret it. Their authority extended to scheduling and discipline, rarely to resource allocation or design.

Information Age

Organizations promised decentralization but often delivered confusion. Global matrices blurred who could decide what. OKRs cascaded, yet authority was rarely clarified. Some firms experimented with escalation rights, but the default still pointed upward. Committees multiplied, and "decision-making" quietly turned into "decision-waiting." Middle managers bore the brunt: squeezed between risk-averse leaders above and impatient teams below, they became the bottleneck the system blamed for the latency the system had designed.

Irrelevance Age

Dashboards accelerate the illusion of control. Algorithms produce recommendations, leaders distrust them, and choices ricochet back up the chain. Weeks pass while competitors move in days. Teams lose confidence: they propose, they wait, they re-propose, often landing on the same answer they had at the start. Authority hoarded at the center breeds cynicism at the edge. Middle managers respond rationally to the incentives: they escalate everything, because the system punishes initiative more than it punishes delay. The result is an organization that looks decisive on the dashboard and feels paralyzed in the corridor.

Ingenuity Age

Decision rights become stewardship. Choices are classified into one-way doors (hard to reverse, high consequence) and two-way doors (reversible, local). Two-way doors are taken at the edge, recorded with the reasoning, and revisited if outcomes diverge. The advice process is explicit: before making a decision, consult an expert, a stakeholder, and a skeptic, then act. Leaders narrate their trade-offs and maintain decision journals, which build trust and institutional memory. AI assists by surfacing who holds relevant expertise, mapping dependencies, and flagging risks, but it does not decide. The system gets faster, more transparent, and more trustworthy. Middle managers are the primary beneficiaries: freed from the escalation treadmill, they can invest their time in coaching, translating strategy into local action, and building the team capability that makes distributed authority work. When middle managers are empowered, the whole system accelerates. When they are squeezed, every other lever in the book stalls.

Imaginative Possibility

Authority becomes dynamic. Decision rights are allocated to those with the most relevant context, not to those with the highest title. Trust graphs and collaboration networks reveal who is most connected and credible in a domain; stewardship rotates accordingly. Algorithmic guardrails can enforce reversibility, escalation, and review. Budget rights may shift quarterly to those demonstrating learning velocity rather than merely seniority. In that future, authority is not a static pyramid but a living current, granted for a mission, then redistributed as context changes. Middle management evolves from a layer that absorbs pressure into a network that distributes judgment, the connective tissue through which ingenuity travels.

Case Examples from the Real World

Team Leadership

Nucor Steel: "Every mill is a team with a P&L"

- **What they did.** Nucor organized its steel mills as autonomous teams, each with its own profit-and-loss accountability. Mill-level teams set production targets, solved problems on the floor, and shared in the financial results through team-based bonus pools that could add 80 to 150 percent to base pay. No team member succeeded unless the team succeeded. Management layers were kept to four between the CEO and the floor.

-

- **Why this matters.** Team leadership is not a soft skill exercise; it is an operating model. When the team owns the outcome and shares the reward, joint decision-making and peer accountability become economic necessities, not HR aspirations.

- **Consequences.** Nucor grew from a near-bankrupt company to the largest steelmaker in the United States, with consistently higher productivity and lower costs than integrated competitors. Employee turnover remained well below industry averages for decades.

General Stanley McChrystal's Joint Special Operations Command: "Team of Teams"

- **What they did.** In 2003, McChrystal took command of Joint Special Operations in Iraq and found that a hierarchical military structure was too slow to fight a networked enemy. He redesigned the organization around interconnected teams that shared intelligence in real time, held daily cross-unit briefings with thousands of participants, and pushed decision authority to the team closest to the situation. Liaison officers were embedded across units so that every team understood how its actions affected every other team.

- **Why this matters.** Team leadership at the highest stakes. McChrystal did not flatten the hierarchy. He kept clear command authority for irreversible decisions while distributing operational judgment to the teams with the best information. The daily briefing became the connective tissue: not a reporting ritual, but a shared sense-making session where the whole network could see and act together.

- **Consequences.** Decision speed increased dramatically. Operations that once required days of approval moved in hours. The organization shifted from a command-driven machine to a network of teams that could adapt faster than the threat. McChrystal's model has since been adopted by hospitals, corporations, and government agencies worldwide.

Leadership Development and Coaching

Google: "Project Oxygen and the manager-as-coach"

- **What they did.** In 2008, Google's people analytics team set out to prove that managers didn't matter. The data showed the opposite: teams with effective managers performed significantly better on every metric. The study identified eight behaviors (later expanded to ten) that distinguished great managers, with "is a good coach" ranking first. Google then built these behaviors into manager training, feedback tools, and twice-yearly upward reviews where direct reports scored their manager on coaching quality.

- **Why this matters.** Coaching was not positioned as a program or a perk. It was identified through evidence as the single most important thing a manager does, and then embedded into how every manager was evaluated, developed, and promoted.

- **Consequences.** Manager effectiveness scores improved across the company. Teams with highly rated coaching managers showed higher engagement, lower turnover, and stronger performance. The research became one of the most widely cited studies on what managers actually contribute.

Standard Chartered Bank: "Coaching for all people managers"

- **What they did.** Standard Chartered made coaching certification a requirement for all people managers globally, not a development option for the senior few. The program trained managers in structured coaching conversations: goal-setting, active listening, feedback, and accountability. Coaching hours were tracked alongside business metrics, and managers were evaluated on how their teams grew, not just what their teams delivered.

- **Why this matters.** Moves coaching from an elite intervention to an enterprise expectation. When every manager is trained and held accountable for coaching, development becomes continuous and embedded in the daily rhythm of work rather than confined to annual reviews or external consultants.

- **Consequences.** Measurable improvement in manager effectiveness scores, stronger internal promotion rates, and higher engagement among direct reports. The program scaled across over sixty markets.

Leadership Potential and Succession

Apple: "Jobs to Cook, succession that evolved the company"

- **What they did.** Steve Jobs personally groomed Tim Cook as his successor over several years, placing him in roles of increasing operational scope and testing his judgment under pressure. When Jobs stepped down in 2011, the transition was immediate and seamless. Cook did not attempt to replicate Jobs. He brought a different leadership style, operational discipline over theatrical product launches, and redirected the company toward services, supply chain resilience, and social responsibility while preserving the design culture Jobs had built.

- **Why this matters.** Succession is not cloning. The most effective transitions pair continuity of values with evolution of capability. Jobs chose someone whose strengths complemented his weaknesses, not someone who mirrored his persona. The succession was tested in real assignments over years, not decided in a single calibration meeting.

- **Consequences.** Under Cook, Apple's market capitalization grew from roughly $350 billion to over $3 trillion. The company diversified revenue streams, expanded services, and maintained its innovation reputation while operating with a fundamentally different leadership temperament.

Procter & Gamble: "Build from within as a system"

- **What they did.** P&G has promoted from within for virtually its entire 185-year history. Every CEO since the 1930s has been an internal candidate who rose through successive roles of increasing scope. The company's succession system identifies potential early, rotates leaders across brands, functions, and geographies, and uses real assignments as the primary development method. Potential is tested through progressively larger bets, not through assessment centers alone.

- **Why this matters.** Succession becomes a system property rather than an episodic event. When every role is a proving ground and every transition is a data point, the organization builds a deep bench without relying on external search or last-minute heroics. The system also creates accountability: if leaders fail to develop successors, the pipeline visibly thins.

- **Consequences.** P&G has sustained category leadership across consumer goods for over a century, navigating multiple technological and market disruptions. Internal succession has produced CEOs with deep institutional knowledge and the trust of the organization, reducing transition risk.

Decision Rights and the Middle

HCL Technologies: "Employees First, Customers Second"

- **What they did.** CEO Vineet Nayar inverted the traditional management pyramid. He argued that value was created in the "value zone" where employees met customers, not in the executive suite. He made management accountable to the front line rather than the reverse: executives published 360-degree feedback openly, service tickets could be raised against any manager, and decision authority was pushed to the teams closest to the client. Middle managers were repositioned from controllers to enablers.

- **Why this matters.** Explicitly names the middle management squeeze and redesigns the system around it. Instead of adding more reporting or removing the middle layer entirely, Nayar made middle managers accountable for enabling the people below them rather than reporting to the people above them. The inversion gave middle managers a clear purpose: make your team more capable.

- **Consequences.** HCL grew from $700 million to $4.5 billion in revenue during Nayar's tenure. Employee satisfaction and client retention improved in parallel. The approach became a widely studied case in distributed leadership.

Michelin: "Empowered factory teams"

- **What they did.** Michelin restructured its manufacturing plants around autonomous work teams. Teams were given authority over scheduling, quality control, maintenance, and continuous improvement. Middle managers shifted from supervisors to coaches. Decisions that once required three levels of approval were made on the floor by the people doing the work. The company called it "responsibilization": making every team member responsible for the whole, not just their station.

- **Why this matters.** Decision rights in a manufacturing context, where the stakes of getting it wrong are physical safety and product quality. Michelin proved that even in heavy industry, pushing authority to the middle and the edge produces better outcomes than centralizing it. The key was pairing authority with capability: teams were trained before they were empowered.

- **Consequences.** Measurable improvements in productivity, quality, and employee engagement across plants. Reduced management layers and faster response to production issues. The model became a reference for manufacturing companies seeking to move beyond command-and-control.

End of Month: Executive Team Review

The Omnivista executive team reconvened in Dublin, gathered around a table in the Liffey Aged Care Centre. Chris opened the meeting with her familiar reminder: "We're not here for stories. We're here for results. Show us what changed."

- **Yuki: Team Leadership (Tokyo).** "At Shinjuku, I picked our cross-functional biomarker review, a meeting that had been running for two years as a reporting ritual. Six people attended weekly, each presenting their function's update. No joint decisions. We redesigned it as a genuine team: shared backlog, one outcome they jointly own, disagreements resolved in the room. In four weeks, the team made eleven joint decisions that previously would have required separate approvals from three functions. Cycle time on assay prioritization dropped from fourteen days to four. When we design for teaming, people stop reporting and start deciding."

- *John: Decision Rights and the Middle (Sydney).* "We applied the one-way and two-way door model across two finance teams and gave middle managers explicit authority for all two-way doors, removing one layer of sign-off entirely. Cycle time dropped from eighteen days to seven. Escalations fell by half. But the most important data point was qualitative. Three middle managers told me separately: 'This is the first time I've felt trusted to do my job.' One said she had been escalating decisions she knew the answer to for two years because the system taught her that initiative was riskier than delay. We freed the middle, and the whole system moved faster."

- *Maria: Leadership Potential and Succession (São Paulo).* "I took our nine-box grid for Paulista General and tested it against reality. I identified two people labeled high-potential and two who had been consistently overlooked. I put all four through a live operational dilemma: redesigning the discharge protocol for a complex cardiac ward under real time pressure. One of the high-potentials froze under ambiguity. One of the overlooked nurses reframed the problem entirely, brought in the family advocate, and designed a solution the ward adopted within a week. Our grid was measuring pedigree and presentation, not judgment under complexity."

- *Sanjay: Leadership Development and Coaching (Bangalore).* "We built a prototype Leadership Everywhere module: one cohort of twenty engineers and managers, four weeks, shared doctrine across levels. The difference was the coaching requirement: every participant coached one peer weekly and was coached in return. Eighty percent said it was the first time they had seen leadership described as an enterprise-wide system. But the coaching data was the real signal. Fourteen of twenty reported that peer coaching changed how they approached their next difficult decision. Three coaching pairs continued meeting after the module ended without being asked. Coaching works when it is embedded in the work, not bolted on as an event."

- **Liam: Team Leadership (Dublin).** "At Liffey, I took a care team operating as a reporting group and redesigned it around a shared outcome: patient well-being for their ward, measured weekly. They were given a cadence, authority to adjust care protocols without escalating, and a simple decision log. The shift supervisor moved from compiler to coach. In three weeks, the team made seven care-protocol adjustments that previously would have taken two levels of approval. Families noticed: one wrote that the ward 'felt like people were working together, not just working.'"

- **Chris: C-Suite Team Audit (Global).** "I tracked one month of our executive meetings. We held twelve. In nine, each function reported its update and we dispersed. Joint decisions made: three. Time spent in genuine debate: roughly fifteen percent. I have committed to a redesign: one shared weekly review, updates written and read before we convene, meeting time spent on the choices that require the full team's judgment. If we cannot model team leadership at the top, we have no right to ask anyone else to practice it."

What If

That evening, the team walked out into the Dublin dusk, ready for their What-If session on Leadership. Tomorrow, Chris would carry the results to the Board.

Team Leadership

1. What if no leadership team could meet without a stated decision to be made, and reporting was always written?

2. What if "teamness" were measured by joint decisions taken, not hours spent in the same room?

3. What if every team's mandate expired quarterly and had to be renewed with evidence of collective value?

4. What if the C-suite had a peer coach drawn from frontline staff to hold up a mirror?

5. What if exec bonuses depended entirely on shared outcomes, never silo results?

Leadership Development and Coaching

1. What if the academy were mandatory for all, not just "high-potentials"?

2. What if every module were co-taught by a frontline worker and an executive?

3. What if graduation required proof of someone else's growth, not your own?

4. What if coaching hours were tracked and rewarded as rigorously as billable hours?

5. What if development time were treated as work time, never as extra?

Leadership Potential and Succession

1. What if potential were judged only by real choices made under pressure, never by personality labels?

2. What if every potential label expired in twelve months unless renewed by evidence?

3. What if peers, not just bosses, identified successors?

4. What if AI surfaced under-recognized leaders by mapping collaboration networks rather than org charts?

5. What if the question were not "Who's next?" but "Who helps us become wiser?"

Decision Rights and the Middle

1. What if eighty percent of decisions never left the room they started in?

2. What if anyone escalating a two-way door decision had to explain why in writing?

3. What if middle managers were rewarded for how much authority they gave to their teams, not how much they held?

4. What if decision ledgers were open to all staff by default?

5. What if we taxed every escalation upward, making delay visible as a cost?

| 31 October | DUBLIN |

End of Month: Board Review

Chris stood at the head of the table. "This month, we tested whether leadership can become a daily practice across Omnivista, not a title held by the few. Four domains, six pilots, and one honest self-audit. Here's what we found."

"Team leadership. In Tokyo, Yuki converted a two-year reporting ritual into a genuine decision-making team. Joint decisions replaced functional updates. Cycle time on assay prioritization dropped from fourteen days to four. In Dublin, Liam redesigned a care team around shared outcomes and gave them authority to adjust protocols. Seven care decisions were made in three weeks that previously required two levels of approval. The signal: when teams are designed to decide together, they stop waiting and start leading.

"Decision rights and the middle. In Sydney, John classified decisions and pushed two-way doors to the team level. Cycle time dropped from eighteen days to seven. Escalations halved. But the deeper finding was what happened to the middle managers. Three reported feeling trusted to do their jobs for the first time. One had been escalating decisions she already knew the answer to for two years. The signal: free the middle, and the whole system accelerates.

"Leadership potential and succession. In São Paulo, Maria tested our nine-box grid against a real operational dilemma. One high-potential froze. One overlooked nurse reframed the problem and solved it. We have started replacing annual calibrations with quarterly judgment reviews. The signal: potential is revealed in real choices under pressure, not in grids.

"Leadership development and coaching. In Bangalore, Sanjay piloted a Leadership Everywhere module with embedded peer coaching. Eighty percent of participants said it was the first time they had seen leadership taught as a system-wide doctrine. Fourteen of twenty reported that coaching conversations changed how they approached their next hard decision. The signal: coherence and coaching together change behavior. Content alone does not.

"And my own audit. I tracked a month of our C-suite meetings. We made three joint decisions in twelve meetings. Fifteen percent of our time was genuine debate.

The rest was parallel reporting. Starting next month, I'm redesigning our cadence: written updates before we meet, meeting time reserved for the choices that need the full team's judgment."

She paused. "Four guardrails for Leadership Everywhere. Design teams to decide together, not report in parallel. Free the middle by pushing authority to where reality lives. Test potential in real dilemmas, not grids. Make coaching a daily practice, not an annual event.

"These are our guardrails," Chris said. "AI will multiply whatever leadership system it finds. Our job is to build one that multiplies ingenuity."

A director leaned forward. "Chris, you've described Leadership Everywhere in a way we've never seen institutionalized. Is your team really up to carrying this beyond the pilot?"

Chris chose her words carefully. "Not yet. These are early signals, not proof. But the leaders at each site, Yuki redesigning teams, John freeing the middle, Maria rethinking how we spot potential, Sanjay embedding coaching, Liam giving care teams real authority, have shown courage. My role now is to give them rhythm, coherence, and reinforcement. They can lead this year's work, but I will also keep searching for practices, partners, and models that don't yet exist in the market."

She let the silence settle. "Leadership Everywhere isn't a program. It's a way of operating that most organizations discuss but rarely embody. Building it in parallel with our own leaders while scouting for what's next is the only credible path forward."

The Chair nodded. "You have the mandate."

CEO's Reflection, That Evening

After the meeting, Chris walked back across the Liffey as twilight settled over the city, the day's conversations still echoing in her head. Leadership Everywhere had produced its first results: teams deciding together instead of reporting in parallel, middle managers freed to act, potential tested in real dilemmas rather than rated on grids, and coaching embedded in the daily rhythm of work. They were fragile signals, but signals nonetheless, proof that leadership could begin to live in the system rather than perch at the top. The Board had accepted them cautiously, sufficient to build on.

In her hotel room, she opened her notebook. Tomorrow, Liam would lead the team into the sixth lever: Engaged Hearts, Minds & Bodies. If Leadership Everywhere asked whether ingenuity could be led broadly, the next lever would ask whether people could bring their whole selves to work. Chris knew this was where the choice between irrelevance and ingenuity became most human: energy either drained into compliance and cynicism, or surged into meaning and belonging. She set down her pen, steadying herself for the work ahead.

Self-Assessment for ORG6 Lever 5: Leadership Everywhere

Rate yourself honestly. For each question, score both the Foundation and the AI Amplifier.
1 Not Yet · 2 Emerging · 3 Developing · 4 Practicing · 5 Second Nature

---

1.

Foundation. Leadership teams at every level operate as genuine decision-making units, not reporting groups where individuals present in parallel and revert to silos.
　　Foundation score (1–5):＿＿

AI Amplifier. We use AI to make team decisions, reasoning, and follow-through visible so that teams learn from each cycle rather than relitigate.
　　AI Amplifier score (1–5):＿＿

2.

Foundation. Coaching is a norm. Managers develop their people as a core responsibility, not an occasional add-on.
　　Foundation score (1–5):＿＿

AI Amplifier. We use AI-powered coaching tools to augment manager capability and enrich development conversations.
　　AI Amplifier score (1–5):＿＿

3.

Foundation. We identify and grow leadership potential through real choices under pressure, not static grids or personality labels.
　　Foundation score (1–5):＿＿

AI Amplifier. We use AI to surface under-recognized leaders by mapping collaboration patterns, learning velocity, and judgment in context.
　　AI Amplifier score (1–5):＿＿

4.

Foundation. Middle managers are empowered and supported, not squeezed between strategy and execution.

    Foundation score (1–5):_____

AI Amplifier. We use AI to remove the administrative burden from middle management so they can focus on people and strategy.

    AI Amplifier score (1–5):_____

5.

Foundation. Leadership is a behavior, not a title. People lead from every level.

    Foundation score (1–5):_____

AI Amplifier. We use AI to make leadership development tools accessible to everyone, not just executives.

    AI Amplifier score (1–5):_____

AVERAGE SCORE: ORG6, Lever 5: Leadership Everywhere

*Foundation average (total of five scores ÷ 5):*_____

*AI Amplifier average (total of five scores ÷ 5):*_____

Now: Transfer these two averages to the "Leadership Everywhere" row of your ORG6 Scoreboard at the back of the book.

"*Personal engagement is the harnessing of people's selves to their work roles; in engagement, people employ and express themselves physically, cognitively, and emotionally.*"

William Kahn

originator of the concept of engagement

"*Hearts give belonging, minds give clarity, bodies give momentum. Engagement is when all three align with both the dreams of each person and the mission of the organization.*"

Katharine McLennan

CHAPTER 14

Engaged hearts, minds, & bodies

Will the hearts, minds, and bodies of our people be depleted and disengaged or energized and aligned around shared success and purpose?

1 November — **DUBLIN**

First Day of Month: Executive Team

In the Dublin office, the team found the chairs in a circle, no tables, which was Liam's choice. On the wall, he had written three words and four questions.

The three words: SAY. STAY. STRIVE.

"These are how we measure engagement," Liam said. "Do people speak positively about us? Do they feel they belong and want to remain? Do they bring motivation and discretionary effort? Those are the outcomes. But outcomes don't design themselves. Today we design the causes."

He pointed to the four questions beneath:

- **"ENERGY AND WELL-BEING:** is human energy protected and renewed, or are we running people into exhaustion and calling it commitment?

- **RECOGNITION AND BELONGING:** do people feel seen for their contributions and connected to their teams, or is recognition generic, infrequent, and disconnected from what actually matters?

- **PURPOSE ALIGNMENT:** do people connect their daily work to the organization's mission, or does purpose live on the wall while decisions happen without it?

- **PASSION FOR STRATEGY, PRODUCTS, AND CUSTOMERS:** do people care deeply about what we make and who we serve, or has passion been disconnected from influence and resources?

"Get these four right," Liam said, "and Say, Stay, and Strive follow. Get them wrong, and no survey, perk, or campaign will close the gap."

They began with stories, not dashboards: a service agent who stayed late to resolve a family crisis and came in early to coach a peer; a developer who shipped an unasked-for fix across regions; a village manager who wrote to a former resident's daughter months after a move. The pattern was familiar: when people belong and believe, they give more than their job description because the work gives something back.

Liam then walked the team through the Liffey Aged Care Centre, pausing at moments that revealed how engagement lived or faltered in the daily rhythm of the work.

Energy and Well-being.

Break rooms showed the strain: fatigue, short tempers, and occasional absences. In the next corner, laughter broke out as caregivers swapped stories. Turnover boards told a split story: high churn among night-shift nurses, deep loyalty in the day-care units. The pattern seemed tied less to pay than to whether people felt seen by their managers and whether the rhythm of work left room to recover. Engagement was uneven, with pockets of vitality alongside an undercurrent of burnout.

Recognition and Belonging.

In the staff kitchen, caregivers spoke warmly about their colleagues and patients, but less so about "the organization." One said, "I'll tell friends I love my team, but not that I love working here." In one ward, a caregiver had designed a new activity program for dementia patients on her own time. That kind of initiative, Liam noted, was rare, not because staff lacked ideas, but because most felt their contributions went unnoticed and there was little room to try.

Purpose Alignment

The mission statement hung on the wall, yet staff said leaders rarely linked decisions to purpose. Still, when families visited, caregivers explained why the work mattered, living the mission even when it wasn't explicitly named. Purpose was alive at the bedside but absent from the boardroom.

Passion for Strategy, Products, and Customers

At a family forum, caregivers were passionate about better meals and activities, but they admitted they had little influence over strategy or resources. The passion was real and channeled toward patients, but disconnected from the larger system.

Liam summed it up: "Hearts, minds, and bodies are all here, but fragmented. Engagement is strongest where people see each other, feel trusted, and connect directly with families. Where bureaucracy interrupts, energy fades. These four domains are where we design the fix."

Team Assignments for the Month

Before the team dispersed, Chris set the assignments for the month:

- **Yuki (Tokyo): Energy and well-being.** "Pilot an energy dashboard that tracks stress signals: meeting load, overtime, and well-being surveys. Propose one change that protects recovery and show how it affects Say, Stay, or Strive."

- **John (Sydney): Recognition and belonging.** "Map belonging and turnover trends across two finance teams. Identify what drives loyalty versus churn, test one recognition change, and measure the shift in intent to stay."

- **Maria (São Paulo): Passion for strategy, products, and customers.** "Spot examples of discretionary effort on wards, the moments when people go beyond because they care about what we do and who we serve. Capture what enabled them, remove one barrier to scaling that energy, and show how passion connects to patient outcomes."

- **Sanjay (Bangalore): Purpose alignment.** "Redesign one team ritual so that it begins with purpose: a customer story, a patient outcome, a decision that tested values. Track how it shifts tone, engagement, and the quality of decisions that follow."

- **Liam (Dublin): Recognition and belonging.** "Redesign one staff forum so that recognition is specific, timely, and tied to contribution. Test whether people who feel seen begin to speak differently about the organization, not just about their team."

- **Chris (Global): Passion for strategy, products, and customers.** "I'll audit how often our strategy updates reference clients and products in human terms. I'll commit to one change in cadence or narrative to make passion visible at the top, and I'll track whether it changes what staff say about our direction."

Chris closed: "At the end of the month in Tokyo, bring results: evidence that engagement has shifted, even slightly, in one of these four domains. This isn't about slogans. It's about whether people feel energy, belonging, purpose, and passion in the system.

"We won't outsource engagement to surveys or perks. We'll earn Say with truth and progress, Stay with belonging and growth, Strive with meaningful work at a humane pace. If we do this, people will choose Omnivista when they have options, and they'll bring others with them."

CEO's Notebook: Engaged Hearts, Minds & Bodies

That night, Chris walked along the River Liffey, the water glinting in the low summer light. The aged care center they had toured that morning still lingered in her mind: caregivers laughing with patients in one room, then quietly confessing fatigue in another; stories of purpose told with fire, yet set against a backdrop of turnover and strain. Engagement was alive but uneven.

She opened her notebook. "Engagement is the fuel. Without it, ingenuity stalls. With it, ingenuity becomes renewable energy." She wrote her three commitments:

Actions

1. Name one act of energy daily. Notice and celebrate a moment when someone brought discretionary effort, care, or courage into the system.

2. Protect one recovery daily. Remove a barrier to rest, rhythm, or renewal, whether for a team, a project, or an individual.

3. Connect one story to a purpose daily. Link a task, result, or decision back to why it matters, so people see themselves in the larger mission.

What I'll Notice

1. *Industrial*: belonging reduced to loyalty badges; energy measured in hours endured.

2. *Information:* engagement is defined as scores and programs, detached from daily life.

3. *Irrelevance*: apathy spreading; people staying physically but withdrawing mentally.

4. *Ingenuity*: engagement as autonomy, purpose, and dignity; energy

renewed, not drained.

5. *Imagination*: engagement flowing beyond the firm; people thriving in ways that expand communities and networks.

She closed her notebook, the cool evening breeze moving across the water. Tomorrow, the team would push deeper, but tonight she held one truth close: hearts, minds, and bodies are not resources to be consumed, they are the living source of ingenuity.

My Fingerprint

In 2008, while coaching CEOs and facilitating executive teams, I began a two-year clinical training in psychotherapy. Not as a career change. As an education in what happens beneath the surface of every organization I had ever worked in.

What I learned in that training altered how I see engagement permanently. I had spent twenty years measuring it through surveys, scores, and frameworks. Now I was learning to see it through the body: the person who sits slightly turned away from the group, the leader whose voice tightens when asked about their team, the room that goes quiet not because people agree but because they have stopped believing that speaking will change anything.

I also learned to work with what organizations pretend does not exist inside their walls: depression, anxiety, addiction, grief, family crisis, chronic illness, the weight of caring for aging parents while leading a division, the loneliness of authority, the slow erosion of identity when work consumes everything and returns nothing. These are not separate from work. They are inside the work. They walk into every meeting, sit at every decision table, and shape every interaction between a leader and the people who depend on them.

In one of my earliest clinical observations, I noticed a pattern that I later saw repeated in every boardroom and every ward I entered. People who had been carrying unspoken pain did not announce their distress. They withdrew. They showed up but checked out. Their bodies were present but their energy had left the building. In clinical terms, this is dissociation. In organizational terms, we call it quiet quitting. The mechanism is the same: when the cost of caring exceeds the system's capacity to receive it, people protect themselves by disconnecting.

Here is what troubles me most. Coaches and HR executives are simply not trained to work with the human realities that cross their desks every week. They see the performance dip, the missed deadlines, the sudden withdrawal, and they reach for tools designed for performance, not for the person underneath it. Well-meaning leaders cross the line into territory they do not understand and cause more harm than the problem they were trying to solve. Employee Assistance Programs exist, and they are valuable, but they are limited: a handful of sessions, often conducted over the phone, staffed by psychologists who may be excellent clinicians but who have never sat in a board meeting, never felt the pressure of a quarterly result, never understood what it means to lead two hundred people while your marriage is failing or your child is in crisis.

What I have seen in thirty years of coaching senior leaders is that the work of strategy, implementation, team leadership, and presence cannot be separated from the mental, physical, and spiritual well-being of the person doing it. And by spiritual I do not mean religious. I mean whatever gives a person a sense of purpose larger than themselves, the conviction that their life and their work serve something beyond their own survival. When that conviction is alive, people bring an energy that no performance system can manufacture. When it is broken, no bonus, no title, and no recognition program will restore it.

The person a leader needs beside them is someone who has lived in both worlds: the boardroom and the consulting room. Someone who can sit with you while you redesign a supply chain and hold the silence when you admit your father is dying. Someone who understands quarterly pressure and understands grief, and who refuses to pretend these are separate conversations. That person is not a luxury. They are the missing infrastructure of modern leadership. The person sitting across from you is not a role. They are a whole human being whose capacity for ingenuity depends on whether the system around them, and the people who support them, can see and hold the whole of who they are.

Eighteen years of accredited practice as a psychotherapist, not just the training but the ongoing work of annual relicensing, continuous professional development, and regular supervision by a senior clinician who holds my practice honest, taught me that engagement is not a mood to be managed or a score to be lifted. It is a relationship between a person and a system. Inside business, I work in an integrated way: coaching and facilitating leadership teams, strategy, culture, and CEO succession alongside the human complexity that lives inside every person doing that work. The two are not separate disciplines conducted in separate rooms. They are one practice, because the person is one person.

When the system protects energy, recognizes contribution, connects work to purpose, and channels passion toward real outcomes, people bring their whole selves. When it does not, they bring what is safe. And what is safe is almost never what is best.

Every engagement initiative I have designed since has started not with a survey but with a question: what is this system doing to the people inside it? The answer is always visible if you know how to look. It is in the shoulders, the silences, and the stories people tell when they think no one important is listening.

The ORG6 Lever for Engaged Hearts, Minds, & Bodies

Engagement is the lever that determines whether ingenuity is replenished or depleted on a daily basis. Its history has two yesterdays, the Industrial Age, which treated human energy as an input to be controlled, and the Information Age, which professionalized engagement with surveys, perks, and programs but often left workload and meaning untouched. Its future divides into three possible tomorrows:

>   *Corrosive Irrelevance:* organizations that measure sentiment but ignore signal; where AI accelerates surveillance, performative wellness replaces genuine care, and people protect themselves by doing the minimum in systems that no longer deserve their best.

>   *Ingenuity Age:* organizations that treat human energy as a strategic asset; where leaders design work that matters, pair fair deals with real growth, use AI to remove toil rather than add oversight, and make belonging, clarity part of the operating system.

>   *Imaginative Possibility:* organizations that extend engagement beyond the firm; where customers, partners, and other networks co-create value, stewardship, and shared ownership deepen commitment, and human–AI collaboration multiplies curiosity, trust, and contribution

across communities.

Energy and Well-being

Is human energy protected and renewed, or are we running people into exhaustion and calling it commitment?

This domain drives Stay and Strive at the biological level: people cannot belong or give discretionary effort when the system has drained them.

Industrial Age.

Emotions were private, and mental health was invisible. Factories prized stamina and obedience; distress was treated as weakness to be endured off the clock. Safety efforts focused on physical hazards, while psychological risk went unnamed. When fatigue or grief surfaced, the system's answer was discipline or dismissal, not design. Stigma kept people silent, and the absence of language kept leaders blind. Staying was secured by scarcity and paternalism: jobs were local, mobility was limited, and tenure was the norm. Energy was something to extract, not cultivate.

Information Age

Well-being entered the management vocabulary. Employee Assistance Programs, stress management training, and resilience workshops emerged alongside the first robust models of work strain and burnout. Researchers demonstrated how high demands, paired with low control and low reward, erode health and performance, and how chronic overload, cynicism, and reduced efficacy form a burnout triad.

Organizations experimented with wellness benefits and mindfulness, and some redesigned jobs for autonomy and recovery. Too often, though, interventions were add-ons: yoga mats laid over unmanaged workload while email and meetings swelled. Turnover dashboards improved visibility, but they didn't create reasons to stay. Leaders learned to talk about well-being; fewer learned to design for it.

Irrelevance Age

Psychological load can be multiplied by speed and surveillance. "Always-on" norms, meeting sprawl, and productivity dashboards keep nervous systems in threat mode. Remote work done without attention to mental and emotional health flattens social cues and increases fatigue; after-hours digital pressure invades recovery; and "productivity paranoia" corrodes trust. Burnout becomes a systemic property: excessive demand, inadequate control or recognition, and a lack of credible boundaries. When AI tools watch rather than help, the result is protective disengagement: people do just enough to avoid penalty because the system doesn't deserve more. Staying degrades into inertia. Workloads keep creeping upward. People feel visible yet unseen. The best talent exits early; the rest disengage.

Ingenuity Age

Human energy is treated as a strategic asset and designed for accordingly. Leaders rebalance demand and resources, establish clear priorities, set a sane pace, and give people real control over how work is done. Teams adopt recovery micro-practices, protect focus time, and run shorter, more effective meetings. Managers learn to spot overload early and adjust scope rather than just offering slogans. Psychological safety is non-negotiable, and progress is visible because it fuels emotion. AI is used as a stress reducer: summarizing, translating, testing, and simulating, so people spend more time on judgment, creativity, and care. Staying becomes the outcome of a fair deal, real growth, and a humane pace. The fair deal includes pay equity, schedule dignity, and benefits that match real lives. A humane pace is designed: meetings that matter, protected focus time, recovery normalized.

At Omnivista, the executive team implemented two enterprise rules: a weekly "load barometer" that triggers reprioritization when signals degrade, and a written "cadence contract" that limits meetings, protects deep work blocks, and schedules recovery after sprints. Managers conduct brief well-being check-ins that lead to concrete changes: fewer handoffs, clearer decisions, and better tooling, not just platitudes.

Imaginative Possibility

Stewardship of mental health extends across communities. Organizations adopt shared standards for psychological health and safety. Right-to-disconnect norms are embedded in global collaboration. Four-day weeks or nine-day-fortnight pilots become disciplined experiments rather than slogans. Skills passports and cross-company fellowships enable individuals to pursue growth without burning bridges or themselves. AI tutors personalize learning and recovery nudges, while governance protects dignity and privacy. Belonging extends across communities: employee ownership and stewardship models deepen attachment and lengthen time horizons. Alums, partners, and customers gather in learning networks; people return through boomerang hires because the relationships endure. Emotional and mental health stop being a sidebar; they become visible features of how complex systems stay wise under pressure.

Two colleagues I worked with during our years at the Sydney 2000 Olympic Games Organising Committee, Alison Hernandez and Catriona Byrne, have been working at this frontier for over two decades. They founded Sageco to help organizations welcome their elders to stay, contribute, and coach on their own terms, ensuring that knowledge and especially wisdom were passed forward rather than walked out the door with a retirement card. SageCo was acquired by Randstad, and the work did not stop.

Hernandez and Byrne have now launched ReCreate100, a partnership with Lynda Gratton, one of the foremost people-and-culture academics of our generation, and Andrew Scott, building on their research in The 100-Year Life. Their argument is urgent and practical: if people are living to one hundred, the old model of a single career followed by retirement is not just outdated, it is a waste of human capital on a civilizational scale.

Organizations designed for thirty-year careers are losing the wisdom of their elders, people who have decades of contribution left to give, and failing to design the transitions, the rhythms of intensity and renewal, the multi-stage paths that a hundred-year life demands. ReCreate100 is building the frameworks for organizations that want to treat longevity not as a cost but as a compounding asset: keeping their elders vital, purposeful, and growing across the full arc of a life that none of our current systems were designed to support."

Recognition and Belonging

Do people feel seen for their contributions and connected to their teams, or is recognition generic, infrequent, and disconnected from what actually matters?

This domain drives Say and Stay at the relational level: people advocate for organizations that notice them and stay where they feel they matter.

Industrial Age.

Recognition was scarce. A paycheck was assumed to be enough thanks. Workers who endured long hours might receive a handshake, a service pin, or a retirement watch. Loyalty was expected, enforced by hierarchy, and belonging was tribal: town identity, union solidarity, pride in technical skill, far more than organizational identity. "Say" hardly existed as an idea. Communication ran one way: management to workers and brand to customers. Employees were discouraged from speaking publicly about the firm. Voice surfaced mainly through unions or the press when conditions failed, not through everyday advocacy. Pride, where it existed, stayed mostly at home.

Information Age

Recognition became formalized and programmatic. "Employee of the Month" plaques, peer-nominated awards, points-based platforms, and annual dinners sought to systematize appreciation. "Say, Stay, Strive" entered the lexicon, and leaders began asking whether people would recommend the company as a place to work. The service-profit chain linked employee experience to customer loyalty and financial results. Employer branding took form as career sites, EVP statements, and referral programs. Platforms like Glassdoor and LinkedIn made sentiment visible. Some organizations turned this into practice: Zappos cultivated employees as storytellers of service, Southwest and Starbucks treated frontline pride as a competitive advantage. Yet optics often raced ahead of trust. Recognition became a checklist rather than a felt human exchange, and campaigns didn't always change how decisions were made.

Irrelevance Age

Recognition risks becoming automated noise. Chatbots send "thank you" notes, gamified platforms award badges for participation, and advocacy programs flood channels with safe words, while daily experiences erode trust. The gestures are faster but emptier, stripped of authenticity. Algorithms reward the most visible while overlooking the quiet contributors who hold teams together. People go quiet in public and sharper in private; referrals slow; Glassdoor reviews diverge from corporate decks. Monitoring tools intended to protect the brand can suppress dissent, and leaders often mistake brand compliance for genuine loyalty. Reputation becomes brittle: glossy on the surface, hollow at the core.

Ingenuity Age

Recognition becomes the amplification of genuine human moments. AI can help surface contributions hidden in data: code commits, problem-solving in channels, mentoring hours, or cross-team collaborations. Leaders bring those contributions into the light, naming and celebrating them personally. Recognition becomes storytelling: specific, authentic, tied to purpose. The operating question becomes: what would make a reasonable person proud to attach their name to this place? Leaders build loops where truth moves quickly and visibly changes things: internal decision journals that show how feedback shifted a call, narrative one-pagers that replace slide theater. Measures extend beyond eNPS to include referral velocity, story quality, and how quickly customer-saving ideas spread across teams.

At Omnivista, Liam launched a simple Friday ritual: a cross-functional group shared one moment where a colleague's judgment changed a customer outcome and one change leadership made in response. Within a quarter, referrals rose, and marketing shifted from inventing stories to curating real ones. Managers ran stay interviews, not just exit interviews; internal mobility was measured and celebrated; and alum networks remained open. Say rose because recognition was real. Stay rose because belonging was earned.

Imaginative Possibility

Advocacy becomes a practice within an ecosystem. Employees, customers, partners, and communities share a common narrative backed by evidence: open product roadmaps, accessible model cards for AI systems, and reputation profiles that accompany individuals across firms. Recognition transcends praise to become portable reputation: a living record of contribution that travels with the individual and inspires collective progress. Leaders host decision theaters where strategy is tested in public, and stewardship is judged by how often the organization learns in daylight. AI helps weave and personalize stories without bending the truth; humans set the ethic: no story without consequence, no claim without a trail. In that world, advocacy isn't orchestrated. It's earned.

Purpose Alignment

Do people connect their daily work to the organization's mission, or does purpose live on the wall while decisions happen without it?

This domain drives Say and Strive at the meaning level: people speak with conviction and give discretionary effort when they believe their work serves something real.

Industrial Age.

The primary purpose was production and profit, with philanthropy viewed as an after-hours virtue. Companies prized reliability and scale. Leaders spoke in terms of outputs, quality, and cost. "Purpose" lived primarily as paternalism: company towns, welfare plans, occasional benefaction, separate from the mechanics of work. Human rights meant complying with the law of the land. Moral questions rarely entered the room except in crises. Alignment meant doing your job and keeping the line moving. Discretionary effort was designed out of the job: scientific management decomposed work into timed tasks, and motivation was extrinsic, based on pay, supervision, and the threat of punishment.

Information Age

Purpose moved onto the wall: mission and values statements, triple-bottom-line thinking, and corporate citizenship reframed companies as social actors. The UN Global Compact and the UN Guiding Principles on Business and Human Rights supplied a common language. Many firms linked purpose to brand and talent; some embedded it in strategy through fair-trade sourcing, supplier codes, and community goals. Motivation shifted to the workplace: job enrichment, autonomy, and mastery entered the lexicon, and self-determination theory reframed motivation around independence, competence, and relatedness. Progress at work was one of the strongest daily drivers of positive emotion and extra effort. Yet purpose often floated above real trade-offs. Posters said one thing while incentives and calendars said another. Strive became a survey answer rather than a lived pattern.

Irrelevance Age

Purpose can become indistinguishable from performance. ESG is treated as optics, values become slogans, and sustainability and human rights reports proliferate while product and pricing decisions contradict the rhetoric. Political crosswinds tempt leaders to retreat into silence or linguistic litigation rather than improve practice. Meanwhile, algorithmic systems make consequential calls about credit, care, or access without clear accountability for fairness or remedy. Motivation is easily hollowed out by digital Taylorism: surveillance dashboards reduce work to keystrokes and presence, output metrics crowd out meaning, and algorithmic management narrows discretion under the banner of efficiency. People notice the gap. Alignment collapses when they are asked to evangelize a story that their work cannot support. Quiet quitting becomes a rational boundary against an unmanageable workload untethered from meaning.

Ingenuity Age

Purpose is made legible and costly so that people can align with it. Leaders articulate a small set of non-negotiable aims and guardrails, then show how they shape choices: which customers we prioritize, which products we won't sell, which data we won't collect, which suppliers we help improve or exit. Human rights due diligence is woven into commercial rhythms: salience is mapped at the outset, mitigation is written into contracts, and grievance and remedy pathways are made real. Measures include consequences, not just sentiment: where purpose changed a roadmap, a budget, or a bonus. Strive principles are designed into the job: leaders remove toil and guard focus so people can do work that matters. Intent is made legible, why this, why now, so teams can choose well at the edge. Mastery loops replace status updates: short cycles, real customers, visible progress, and coaching in the flow of work. Contribution to enterprise outcomes and learning is rewarded, not just immediate output.

At Omnivista, "resident dignity" became a guardrail that overrode speed targets. The team established a cross-functional human rights review for AI triage models, and quarterly purpose reviews tracked three areas: where purpose cost us, where it paid back, and where it was being stretched beyond its intended design. Maria replaced slide updates with weekly progress reviews where teams demonstrated what had moved, what they had learned, and what they would try next. Strive rose because the work became a source of progress and pride.

Imaginative Possibility

Purpose is defined across the ecosystem. Stewardship ownership and B Corp standards align governance with obligations to people and the planet. Integrated reporting and emerging global baselines make impacts comparable. Cross-company coalitions set and audit shared guardrails for data, labor, and climate. Leaders host decision theaters where trade-offs are openly tested. Motivation compounds across networks: people carry portable portfolios of contribution and earn opportunities across firm boundaries. Open innovation, guilds of practice, and steward ownership strengthen the sense that effort serves something larger than quarterly numbers. AI helps simulate consequences, surface edge cases, and translate stakeholder voices; humans remain responsible for values and remedies. Alignment here is not unanimity. It is earned trust that the system listens, learns, and lives up to its purpose, including its costs.

Passion for Strategy, Products, and Customers

Do people care deeply about what we make and who we serve, or has passion been disconnected from influence and resources?

This domain drives all three, Say, Stay, and Strive, at the identity level: when people are proud of what they build and who they build it for, advocacy, belonging, and effort become natural rather than managed.

Industrial Age.

Passion was expressed as pride in technical skill more than customer love. Factories were optimized for throughput and uniformity; product decisions were separated from users; marketing carried the brand, while workers held the line. When pride appeared, it lived in guild standards and artistry stories on the shop floor, not in designed encounters with customers. Internal service teams existed to support production, not to delight colleagues. The system valued compliance over curiosity; enthusiasm was incidental, not instrumental.

Information Age

Customer experience moved to the center. Companies began measuring advocacy using the Net Promoter Score, designing end-to-end journeys, and professionalizing product management and service design. Design thinking invited teams to start with empathy; agile and lean startup practices brought faster feedback loops and "build, measure, learn." Some firms turned passion into operating routines: Apple's insistence on an integrated product experience, Toyota's andon cord and kaizen enabling anyone to stop the line to protect quality, and Nordstrom's single-card employee handbook, 'Use good judgment in all situations,' empowered frontline staff to make decisions in the moment, turning every customer interaction into an act of ownership rather than a script to follow.

Internally, platform and enablement teams emerged to serve developers and operations as customers, planting early seeds of Developer Experience. Yet performative "customer obsession" also spread. Feature factories shipped more, not better; brand campaigns outran product truth; and internal teams were still too often measured by output, not outcomes.

Irrelevance Age

Passion can be automated into noise. Generative tools churn out polished collateral and "personalized" outreach while the product and service remain unchanged. Teams chase vanity metrics, clicks, MQLs, and velocity points, while real customer problems persist. Dark patterns and algorithmic optimization for short-term conversion erode trust. Inside, platform teams become ticket-takers; developers drown in toil; "obsession" is reduced to dashboards and slogans. Employees mute their advocacy because the work doesn't merit it; customers hear promises that artifacts cannot keep.

Ingenuity Age

Teams work backward from real user problems and publish their hypotheses as short narratives with explicit "won't do's." Every mission owns a customer metric and a colleague metric; demos replace status theater; leaders celebrate problems retired, not just features released. Product, marketing, and service converge in decision reviews where customer evidence, ethics, and economics meet. Internal platform teams publish service levels, usability scores, and time-to-joy for developers; they use their own tools and track reductions in cognitive load across the stack. AI acts as a culture amplifier: enabling rapid prototyping, translation, summarization, and simulation, so that human energy can concentrate on judgment, storytelling, and care.

At Omnivista, Liam instituted a Friday "show the love" ritual: one customer problem solved, one internal friction removed, and one narrative page updated to reflect the changes. Enthusiasm rose because progress was visible and shared. Yuki linked recognition to moments when someone's initiative changed a customer's outcome. Say, Stay, and Strive all rose because passion had a home in the system.

Imaginative Possibility

Passion for strategy, products, and customers scales across networks. Customers, partners, and employees co-create on open platforms; communities maintain libraries of reusable components; "decision theaters" bring residents, clinicians, and engineers together to test choices in real time. Product narratives include model cards that disclose limits and trade-offs; reputation accrues to contributions across company boundaries. Internal passion deepens as people see their tools enable hundreds beyond their team; external passion grows as users become builders. In this world, advocacy is earned by evidence and stewardship: what we ship, how we support it, and how we learn in public.

Case Examples from the Real World

Energy and Well-being

Barry-Wehmiller: "Everybody Matters"

- **What they did.** CEO Bob Chapman restructured the $3 billion manufacturing company around one metric: whether people's lives are better because they work here. During the 2008 recession, rather than laying off employees, the company asked everyone, from the factory floor to the C-suite, to take four weeks of unpaid furlough so that no one would lose their job. Chapman called it "sharing the burden so no one bears it alone." The company redesigned leadership training around empathetic listening, measured success partly by the quality of relationships managers built, and treated well-being not as a program but as the purpose of leadership.

- **Why this matters.** Well-being was not a benefit; it was the organizing principle. When the system protects people during crisis rather than discarding them, trust compounds. The furlough decision during the recession became the defining proof that the philosophy was real, not rhetorical.

- **Consequences.** Employee engagement and retention consistently above manufacturing industry averages. Revenue grew from $500 million to over $3 billion under Chapman's leadership. The model became a widely cited case for human-centered manufacturing leadership.

Aetna (now part of CVS Health): "Mindfulness as infrastructure"

- **What they did.** Under CEO Mark Bertolini, Aetna offered free yoga and mindfulness programs to all employees after Bertolini's own recovery from a near-fatal skiing accident convinced him that well-being was a business issue. The company tracked results rigorously: participants reported reduced stress, improved sleep, and gained an average of 62 minutes of productivity per week. Aetna raised its minimum wage simultaneously, linking financial and physical well-being.

- **Why this matters.** Well-being was treated as measurable infrastructure, not a wellness perk. The CEO's personal commitment gave it credibility, and the data gave it staying power. Linking mindfulness to productivity and pay to dignity showed that energy and economics are not in tension.

- **Consequences.** Healthcare costs fell by 7% in participating groups. Productivity gains were estimated at $3,000 per employee annually. The program became one of the most cited corporate well-being cases in the U.S.

Recognition and Belonging

Southwest Airlines: "The culture is the strategy"

- **What they did.** Southwest built recognition into the daily operating rhythm. Frontline employees are celebrated publicly for acts of care, humor, and initiative. The company's Culture Committee, staffed by volunteers from every level, organizes recognition events, responds to employee milestones, and ensures that the tone set by leadership reaches every station. Herb Kelleher famously said employees come first, customers second, and shareholders third, on the logic that employees who feel valued create the customer experience that drives returns.

- **Why this matters.** Recognition is not a program at Southwest; it is the culture itself. When belonging is built into how the airline operates daily, not in an annual survey, people advocate for the company voluntarily and stay because they feel they matter.

- **Consequences.** Southwest has maintained profitability in an industry notorious for losses, with employee turnover consistently among the lowest of major U.S. carriers. The airline regularly tops customer satisfaction rankings, and employees are widely cited as the primary differentiator.

Costco: "Respect as a retention system"

- **What they did.** Costco pays significantly above industry average for retail workers, promotes almost exclusively from within, and provides healthcare benefits to part-time employees. CEO Craig Jelinek continued the philosophy set by founder Jim Sinegal: treat employees as long-term assets, not costs to be minimized. Turnover among employees with more than one year of tenure runs below 6%, compared to industry averages above 60%.

- **Why this matters.** Recognition and belonging at Costco are structural, not performative. Fair pay, real benefits, and visible promotion paths signal that people are valued. The result is that employees stay, advocate, and serve customers with a level of care that competitors struggle to replicate.

- **Consequences.** Costco consistently outperforms competitors on revenue per employee, shrinkage rates, and customer loyalty. The model demonstrates that investing in belonging produces returns that far exceed the higher wage costs.

Purpose Alignment

Novo Nordisk: "The Triple Bottom Line in practice"

- **What they did.** The Danish pharmaceutical company embedded its purpose, defeating diabetes and other chronic diseases, into governance, strategy, and daily operations through its "Triple Bottom Line" charter, which requires the company to balance financial, social, and environmental performance. Purpose reviews are conducted alongside financial reviews. The company measures and publishes its impact on patients reached, environmental footprint reduced, and communities served, and leaders are evaluated on all three dimensions.

- **Why this matters.** Purpose is not a statement at Novo Nordisk; it is a governance mechanism. When purpose shapes how leaders are evaluated and how resources are allocated, alignment becomes structural rather than rhetorical. Employees can see that the mission drives real decisions, not just annual reports.

- **Consequences.** Novo Nordisk has grown to become one of the most valuable companies in Europe while maintaining its commitment to patient access, including selling insulin at cost in the world's poorest countries. Employee engagement consistently ranks among the highest in the pharmaceutical industry.

IKEA: "Democratic design as lived purpose"

- **What they did.** IKEA's stated purpose, to create a better everyday life for the many people, is operationalized through "democratic design," which requires every product to balance form, function, quality, sustainability, and affordability. No product reaches the shelf unless it passes all five criteria. Employees at every level, from designers to warehouse workers, are trained to understand and apply these principles. Purpose is not a campaign; it is the design brief for every product and every decision.

- **Why this matters.** Alignment is strongest when purpose is embedded in the work itself, not layered on top of it. When a warehouse worker can explain why a product is designed the way it is and how that connects to the company's mission, purpose has moved from the wall to the floor.

- **Consequences.** IKEA has grown into the world's largest furniture retailer while maintaining its affordability promise. Employee surveys consistently show high alignment with mission. The democratic design framework has become a reference for purpose-driven product development across industries.

Passion for Strategy, Products, and Customers

Brunello Cucinelli: "Humanistic capitalism in cashmere"

- **What they did.** The Italian luxury company closes its offices at 5:30 p.m. and forbids work emails after hours. Founder Brunello Cucinelli pays artisans 20% above market rate, invests heavily in the medieval village of Solomeo where the company is headquartered, and treats craftsmanship as both product strategy and purpose. Employees are trained not just in technique but in philosophy, art, and ethics. Every product carries the hand of the person who made it. The company went public in 2012 and has consistently grown revenue while maintaining its artisan model.

- **Why this matters.** Passion for the product is inseparable from dignity in the work. When people are paid fairly, rested, and treated as craftspeople rather than production units, their pride in what they make becomes the brand. Customers feel the difference because the people making the product feel it first.

- **Consequences.** Consistent double-digit revenue growth since IPO. Employee turnover far below luxury industry averages. The brand commands premium pricing not through marketing but through the visible quality that passionate, rested artisans produce. The model is studied as a counterpoint to fast fashion and to the assumption that growth requires exploitation.

Trader Joe's: "Crew-driven customer obsession"

- **What they did.** Trader Joe's gives store-level "Crew Members" unusual authority over product recommendations, store displays, and customer interactions. There are no loyalty programs, no coupons, and minimal advertising. Instead, the company relies on employees who genuinely love the products to create the customer experience. Every Crew Member tastes new products and provides input. Stores are designed for discovery, and staff are trained to start conversations rather than process transactions. The company pays above-market wages and promotes from within.

- **Why this matters.** Passion for the product starts with the people who sell it. When employees have tasted, chosen, and believe in what they recommend, the customer interaction is authentic rather than scripted. The absence of traditional marketing forces the company to earn advocacy through every interaction rather than buy it through campaigns.

- **Consequences.** Trader Joe's generates more revenue per square foot than nearly any other grocery chain in the U.S. Customer loyalty is exceptional, driven almost entirely by word of mouth. Employee turnover is well below grocery industry averages, and the company regularly appears on "best places to work" lists despite minimal corporate marketing.

End of Month: Executive Team Review

The executive team gathered in Tokyo, each presenting evidence from the assignments Chris had set in Dublin.

- **Yuki: Energy and Well-being (Tokyo).** "We piloted an energy dashboard at Shinjuku tracking overtime spikes, meeting load, and well-being signals. Within three weeks, it flagged two teams running above sustainable thresholds. We cut meeting load in one and rescheduled sprint deadlines in the other. Stress scores dropped. One team lead said, 'For the first time, someone noticed before we broke.' Say and Stay followed: people spoke more positively about Omnivista when they felt the system was protecting them, not just measuring them."

- **John: Recognition and Belonging (Sydney).** "We mapped belonging and turnover across two finance teams. Night-shift attrition was three times higher than day-shift, and the pattern tracked to one variable: whether people felt seen by their manager. We piloted weekly check-ins focused on recognition and growth, not performance. Exit intent dropped 15 percent. One analyst told us, 'I was about to leave. Then my manager asked what I needed to stay and actually changed something.' Referrals from those teams rose for the first time in a year."

- **Maria: Passion for Strategy, Products, and Customers (São Paulo).** "I looked for moments of discretionary effort on the wards: a nurse redesigning a handoff protocol, a technician staying to calibrate equipment so the morning shift could start clean. What enabled the passion was proximity to patients. What suppressed it was bureaucracy. We removed one approval delay on ward-level improvements, and ideas started being implemented twice as fast. Staff said, 'We always had the ideas. Now someone let us use them.'"

- **Sanjay: Purpose Alignment (Bangalore).** "We redesigned our Monday sprint kickoff to begin with purpose: a patient story, a clinician's feedback, or a decision that tested our values. By the third week, engineers were bringing their own stories. One developer showed how a feature he had built was being used in a rural clinic he had never visited. The room went quiet, then energized. Two backlog items were deprioritized because the team realized they did not connect to the mission. Purpose stopped being a statement and started being a filter."

- **Liam: Recognition and Belonging (Dublin).** "I redesigned the weekly service forum around specific, timely recognition tied to contribution. Instead of general praise, we named the act, the person, and what it meant for the patient or family. Within weeks, caregivers who had never spoken were sharing stories. One said, 'I have been here seven years. This is the first time my contribution changed a formal decision.' Two caregivers who had been considering leaving told their supervisors they wanted to stay. Staff began describing the center not as a workplace but as a community."

- **Chris: Passion for Strategy, Products, and Customers (Global).** "I audited how often our strategy packs referenced clients and products in human terms. Metrics dominated. Stories were absent. Every strategy update now includes a frontline story alongside the numbers, told in the voice of the person who lived it. One director told me, 'I finally understand who we are doing this for.' Passion becomes contagious when leaders narrate strategy through human stories, not slides."

Chris closed the ledger.

"Engagement isn't an abstract feeling. It is shaped by daily design: whether we protect energy, whether we recognize contribution, whether purpose filters decisions, and whether passion for what we do and who we serve has a home in the system. Say, Stay, and Strive are the outcomes. These four domains are the causes. This month showed us that when we design the causes well, the outcomes follow."

What If

That afternoon, Chris led the team out of the boardroom and into the quiet gardens of Meiji Shrine. The noise of Shinjuku fell away behind them, replaced by tall cedars and gravel paths. Here, under the canopy of trees, she asked them to set aside dashboards and reports. "This is not about metrics," she said. "It's about imagination. If engagement is the energy of our system, then today we ask: what if it were designed differently? What if it were designed for ingenuity?"

The team settled onto benches, notebooks open:

Energy and Well-being

1. What if burnout were logged like safety incidents: investigated, repaired, and prevented?

2. What if anyone could pull a "mental health stop cord" to reset pace, no permission required, no penalty applied?

3. What if recovery time were treated as an operational metric, tracked as rigorously as revenue?

4. What if no team could ever be scheduled above 80% capacity, with the remaining 20% protected for renewal?

Recognition and Belonging

1. What if stay interviews were more common than exit interviews?

2. What if attrition were logged as "leadership debt," to be repaid with systemic fixes rather than blamed on individuals?

3. What if every resignation triggered an unfiltered last word shared with the leaders who must choose between defending the status quo or learning from its cracks?

4. What if recognition had to be a specific story tied to contribution, with no generic thank-yous permitted anywhere in the system?

Purpose Alignment

1. What if every decision memo had to include its purpose, not just its ROI?

2. What if AI flagged when decisions drifted from stated values, and leaders had to respond within a week?

3. What if staff could veto one strategy per year that contradicted the organization's declared mission?

4. What if purpose were a KPI tied to pay, weighted equally with financial performance?

Passion for Strategy, Products, and Customers

1. What if every strategy meeting began with a client story told by a frontline worker, not an executive?

2. What if internal passion were the leading indicator for external adoption, measured and reported quarterly?

3. What if apathy were treated as the organization's most significant strategic risk, with the same urgency as a revenue shortfall?

4. What if employees co-hosted every product launch, standing alongside the customers they built it for?

End of Month: Board Review

Chris opened the session. "Engagement is not posters or perks. It is what people Say about us, whether they Stay, and how hard they Strive. Those are the outcomes. This month, we tested the four causes that drive them. Here are the results.

"Energy and well-being. In Tokyo, Yuki piloted an energy dashboard tracking overtime, meeting load, and stress signals. Two teams were flagged above sustainable thresholds. Meeting load was cut by 20% in one; sprint deadlines were adjusted in the other to build in recovery. Stress scores dropped. One team lead said it was the first time someone noticed before the team broke. The signal: when energy is protected, people stay longer and speak more positively about the organization

"Stay and Say. Recognition and belonging. In Sydney, John mapped turnover across two finance teams. Night-shift attrition was three times higher, driven by one variable: whether people felt seen by their manager. Weekly check-ins focused on recognition and growth cut exit intent by 15%. In Dublin, Liam redesigned a service forum around specific, timely recognition tied to contribution. Caregivers who had never spoken in meetings began sharing stories. Turnover intent dropped. Referrals rose. The signal: recognition that is personal, specific, and consequential earns both Say and Stay. Generic praise earns neither.

"Purpose alignment. In Bangalore, Sanjay redesigned sprint kickoffs to begin with a patient story, a clinician's feedback, or a decision that tested values. By the third week, engineers were bringing their own stories. Alignment scores rose from 48% to 72%. Two backlog items were deprioritized because the team realized they didn't connect to the mission. The signal: when purpose becomes a decision filter rather than a wall poster, Strive rises because people believe their effort serves something real.

"Passion for strategy, products, and customers. In São Paulo, Maria tracked discretionary effort on wards and found it everywhere, suppressed by bureaucracy. Removing one approval barrier doubled the speed of implementation. Staff said they always had the ideas; now someone let them act. At the global level, I added frontline stories to every Board and C-suite pack. Staff surveys show a 14% stronger link between strategy and customer impact. The signal: passion is not a mood. It is what happens when people who care about what they build and who they serve are given influence, not just instructions."

She paused. "Say, Stay, and Strive are how we measure whether engagement is working. Energy, recognition, purpose, and passion are what we design. This month proved they are connected: protect energy, and people stay. Recognize contribution, and people advocate. Align purpose, and people strive. Channel passion, and all three compound.

"Four guardrails for Engaged Hearts, Minds & Bodies.

1. Make dignity visible in every process.
2. Protect recovery as fiercely as performance.
3. Connect every action to purpose.
4. Let passion for clients flow upward, not just downward.

"AI will multiply whatever system it finds," she said. "If we design for exhaustion, it will accelerate burnout. If we design for ingenuity, it will amplify energy."

The Chair leaned forward. "For the first time, engagement feels like a system we can measure and steward."

CEO's Reflection, That Evening

Chris walked through the grounds of Meiji Shrine after the team had dispersed. The year's six levers were complete: Talent, Structure, Operations, CEO Stewardship, Leadership Everywhere, and Engaged Hearts, Minds & Bodies. In two weeks, she would be heading to New York to wrap up the year at the Board meeting where everything they had built would be tested, and the Top 100 conference where the organization would hear whether the year had changed anything real.

She paused beneath the torii gate, the city hum fading behind the cedars. Engagement had shown her that ingenuity was not a capability to be installed. It was the natural state of people who were protected, recognized, purposeful, and passionate. The system's job was not to generate engagement. It was to stop destroying it.

She closed her notebook and walked toward the lights of Shinjuku. One more chapter to close. One more year to prove.

Self-Assessment for ORG6, Lever 6: Engaged Hearts, Minds, & Bodies

Rate yourself honestly. For each question, score both the Foundation and the AI Amplifier.
1 Not Yet · 2 Emerging · 3 Developing · 4 Practicing · 5 Second Nature

---

1.

Foundation. Human energy is protected and renewed. We design for recovery, rhythm, and sustainable pace, not exhaustion dressed as commitment.

Foundation score (1-5):____

AI Amplifier. We use AI to monitor energy signals and intervene early, not as surveillance, but as care.

AI Amplifier score (1-5):____

2.

Foundation. Recognition is specific, timely, and genuine. People feel seen for their contributions and connected to their teams.

Foundation score (1-5):____

AI Amplifier. We use AI to surface hidden contributions and prompt meaningful recognition, not to automate generic praise.

AI Amplifier score (1-5):____

3.

Foundation. People connect their daily work to the organization's mission. Purpose filters decisions, not just annual reports.

Foundation score (1-5):____

AI Amplifier. We use AI to flag when decisions drift from stated values and to surface where purpose is shaping real choices.

AI Amplifier score (1-5):

4.

Foundation. People care deeply about what we build and who we serve. Passion for strategy, products, and customers is visible, resourced, and channeled into influence.

Foundation score (1–5):_____

AI Amplifier. We use AI to remove the toil that suppresses passion, freeing people for judgment, storytelling, and care.

AI Amplifier score (1–5):_____

5.

Foundation. People speak positively, choose to stay, and bring discretionary effort because the system earns it, not because a campaign asks for it.

Foundation score (1–5):_____

AI Amplifier. We use AI to track Say, Stay, and Strive signals continuously so leaders can respond to what people actually experience, not what surveys report annually.

AI Amplifier score (1–5):_____

AVERAGE SCORE: ORG6, Lever 6
Engaged Hearts, Minds, & Bodies

Foundation average (total of five scores ÷ 5):_____

AI Amplifier average (total of five scores ÷ 5):_____

Now: Transfer these two averages to the "Engaged Hearts, Minds, and Bodies" row of your ORG6 Scoreboard at the back of the book.

"The future is not some place we are going to, but one we are creating. The paths are not found, but made, and the activity of making them changes both the maker and the destination."

John Schaar

"Conscious Choice is the compass of leadership. It points us beyond the safety of relevance into the uncharted expanse of Ingenuity. There, in the midst of the unimaginable, leaders dare to see
potential where others see impossibility."

Katharine McLennan

EPILOGUE

Heading Toward the Age of Ingenuity

16 December — **NEW YORK**

End of Year Board Meeting

The boardroom was not still this time. It hummed with a different kind of energy. Reports were already spread across the table, but now they told a different story: profits were up, costs were down, and valuation was climbing again. Beyond the glass, New York glittered in winter light. Inside, the Board leaned forward, not to question Omnivista's survival, but to challenge its ambition.

Evelyn Grant, the Chair, spoke first. Her voice carried less edge than a year before, but no less weight.

"Chris, twelve months ago, this room asked whether Omnivista had a future. Today we have evidence. Revenues up nine percent. Costs reduced by nearly six percent. Valuation rebounding from $45 billion to $62 billion. Market share regained in three regions, with employee engagement up by double digits. Customer satisfaction is moving sharply in the right direction. These are not small achievements. This Board commends you and every member of your team for rebuilding relevance under AI's pressure."

She paused, then added: "And yet, the pressure only accelerates. In healthcare, AI copilots cleared radiology backlogs in Shanghai this year alone, weeks ahead of schedule. In California, startups are offering predictive diagnostics that cut misdiagnoses in half. In Europe, AI-driven care pathways are slashing waiting times by 30%. These curves are steepening. What is ingenuity today will be table stakes tomorrow."

Mei Lin nodded. "The adoption cycles are measured in quarters, not decades. The risk is not whether Omnivista can adapt once, but whether Omnivista can adapt continuously."

Tunde Adeyemi leaned forward. "You have restored momentum, Chris. But the question now is whether this becomes a habit. Can ORG6 and VISTA scale beyond the C-suite?"

Chris stood. "Let me show you what we built and what it produced. Then I will show you how it scales."

She began with VISTA.

"From February through June, we practiced five leadership choices. Each month, one choice. Each choice tested in the field, not on a whiteboard."

Vision. We replaced slogans with trade-off sentences. Budgets and calendars began to align with the North Star. Leaders learned to see before they act, and act in ways others can follow. The drift toward Void slowed because direction became legible.

"Intuition. We introduced premortems, red teams, and decision journals. Cycle time on judgment calls dropped. Leaders learned to move from overwhelm to orientation, trusting trained judgment rather than waiting for perfect data. The freeze of Inertia loosened because we designed habits for deciding under uncertainty.

"Synergy. We named handoffs, gave them owners, and wrote interface contracts at the seams where things used to break. Duplicate work dropped. Reuse rose. The retreat into Silos reversed because collaboration became visible and accountable.

"Trust. We built repair loops, fairness audits, and say-do ledgers. When idle-time tracking was removed from AI dashboards, stress dropped and engagement rose. The slide toward Tyranny stopped because safety, fairness, and repair became lived practices.

"Authenticity. We introduced congruence audits, walk-away rules, and result lines on every decision. Staff reported that for the first time, what leadership said matched what it did. The drift toward Apathy reversed because the say-do gap closed in daylight."

She paused, then turned to ORG6.

"From July through November, we redesigned six levers. Each month, one lever. Each lever tested with a pilot at every signal site.

"Talent. We replaced resume screens with micro-missions, surveillance dashboards with presence ledgers, badge collections with Friday experiments, and noise-based bonuses with networked contribution credits. We also defined the Chief People Officer for the Ingenuity Age and presented the charter to the Board. This is a different type of role than the Chief People Officers that exist today. It was an enterprise decision about who is accountable for the people who make ingenuity possible.

"Structure. We moved to ninety-day missions with expiry dates, decision ledgers with one-line trade-offs, shared backlogs with Merge Mondays, and edge voices with real decision-making power. Money followed evidence. Decisions lived at the edge. Flow replaced frozen charts.

"Operations. We protected maker time, cut meeting load, installed energy dashboards, added AI empathy prompts to clinical visits, redesigned workspaces around activity, and replaced slide theater with narrative memos. Operations became the daily truth instead of the daily grind.

"CEO Stewardship. This lever was mine. I spent a day with our Chair examining how I set clarity, carry presence, communicate purpose, sustain engagement, enforce accountability, nurture client relationships, catalyze innovation, and choreograph pace. That day also forced me to confront how I work with this Board: whether our time together makes Omnivista clearer and braver, or only busier. The hardest finding was that 70% of our airtime was devoted to reporting rather than deciding. I came back with commitments in every domain, starting with this room: fewer dashboards, more dilemmas, and meeting time spent on the choices that require collective judgment. The CEO role is not exempt from redesign. If anything, it is where redesign must be most visible.

"Leadership Everywhere. Teams learned to decide together instead of reporting in parallel. Middle managers were freed to act. Potential was tested in real dilemmas rather than rated on grids. Coaching became a daily practice rather than an annual event.

"Engaged Hearts, Minds & Bodies. We designed for the four causes of engagement: energy and well-being, recognition and belonging, purpose alignment, and passion for strategy, products, and customers. Say, Stay, and Strive rose because the system earned them."

She looked around the table. "Eleven dimensions. Eleven months of pilots. Results in every site. But the Board's question is the right one: can this scale? Tomorrow, we show you how."

Evelyn capped the meeting. "Then let us be clear. Omnivista has achieved a great deal in one year, and the market has taken notice. But the challenge ahead is steeper. AI is not pausing. This Board will hold you accountable not just for results, but for rhythm. Tomorrow, we look forward to seeing you prove that the system you have built can scale to the next hundred leaders and beyond."

The directors applauded briefly, a sound not heard in that room for years. The atmosphere had shifted. Omnivista was no longer fighting for survival; it was fighting for leadership.

One year earlier, this same room had been silent with dread, directors questioning whether Omnivista had a future at all, Evelyn warning that irrelevance was arriving faster than the company could respond. Now the silence was of a different kind: not fear, but focus. Instead of debating survival, the Board was pressing for scale. The contrast was unmistakable. Omnivista had moved from defending its relevance to proving it could lead, and the real challenge was no longer whether it would endure, but whether it would maintain its momentum.

17 December — NEW YORK

Top 100 Conference

Chris opened the day.

"Last night, in this same city, the Board reminded us of two truths.

"First, they commended what we have achieved. Revenues up. Costs down. Valuation climbing. Market share regained. Engagement and satisfaction rising. In twelve months, we proved that Omnivista is no longer on the edge of irrelevance. We are leading with ingenuity.

"Second, they challenged us. AI is not pausing. What is ingenuity today will be table stakes tomorrow. The risk is not whether we can adapt once, but whether we can adapt continuously.

"That is why we are here. The six levers of ORG6 rebuilt the mechanics of how we work. The five choices of VISTA reshaped who we become as leaders. Together, they gave us results. But now the Board has asked the harder question: can this rhythm scale beyond the executive team? Can it become the signature of Omnivista?

"Today, it passes to you. The Top 100. The stewards of our next year. You will take your teams through the same cadence we lived this year: one lever at a time, one choice at a time, one age at a time. And in December, you will stand where we stand now, with your own results to show.

"This is not a workshop. It is a rehearsal for the future. The Board, our people, and the market will be watching. The choice is still the same as it was one year ago: ingenuity or irrelevance. But this time, the responsibility belongs to all of us."

Chris looked around the room. "This year, we lived a rhythm.

"In January, we identified our inheritances, the habits of the Industrial Age and the Information Age that continue to shape us. February through June, we tested the five VISTA choices: Vision versus Void, Intuition versus Inertia, Synergy versus Silos, Trust versus Tyranny, and Authenticity versus Apathy.

"From July through November, we strengthened our six levers of ORG6: Talent, Structure, Operations, CEO Stewardship, Leadership Everywhere, and Engaged Hearts, Minds & Bodies.

"And we have now brought it all together with results. Not rhetoric, but results.

"Now it is your turn. Each month in the year ahead, you will run the same pattern with your teams. One lever at a time. One choice at a time. One age at a time. You will come back with proof, just as we did.

- "Yuki will lead you through Talent and through Vision.

- John through Structure and through Intuition.

- Maria through Operations and through Synergy.

- Sanjay through Leadership Everywhere and through Trust.

- Liam through Engagement and Authenticity.

- And I will be asking you to help me be the CEO Steward you need: to hold us to our purpose, our pace, and our promises, and to continue driving this organization toward the Ingenuity Age.

"This is how we cascade the work. This is how we keep the rhythm. One lever at a time. One leadership choice at a time."

Chris explained the process:

1. Name your team.

2. Assign one owner for each ORG6 lever: Talent, Structure, Operations, CEO Stewardship, Leadership Everywhere, and Engaged Hearts, Minds & Bodies.

3. Assign five people to hold the VISTA choices: Vision, Intuition, Synergy, Trust, and Authenticity.

4. Create your twelve-month cadence: each lever and each choice requires a month of focus and change.

5. Collect proof: for every month, log two or three visible results.

The executive team then shared one insight each from the VISTA choices they had practiced.

VISTA Leadership Choices: The Compass

Yuki on Vision:

"Vision only matters when it moves beyond the whiteboard and into daily decisions. What endures is the discipline of seeing, naming, and acting with consequence. That is how we prevent the drift into the Void."

John on Intuition:

"I spent my career trusting spreadsheets. This year I learned that the spreadsheet is the last step, not the first. Intuition is the trained judgment that tells you which question to ask before you open it. That is how we prevent the freeze of Inertia."

Maria on Synergy:

"Everyone talks about collaboration. Almost nobody designs it. This year we stopped talking and started drawing the seams. That is how we prevent the retreat into Silos."

Sanjay on Trust:

"I came into this year believing trust was soft. I was wrong. Trust is a system. You build it the way you build software: with architecture, testing, and repair cycles. That is how we prevent the slide into Tyranny."

Liam on Authenticity:

"Authenticity is the hardest one to teach because it cannot be performed. This year I learned the difference between telling a story and being one. That is how we prevent the drift into Apathy."

Chris let the VISTA insights settle, then shifted the room's attention.

"Those are the five leadership choices. They shape who we become. Now let me ask my team to share what they learned from the six levers that shape how we work. VISTA is the compass. ORG6 is the roadmap. You will need both."

ORG6 Levers: The Roadmap

Yuki on Talent:

"We learned that talent is not an HR cycle. It is a living system: sourcing, enabling, developing, and rewarding in continuous motion. When we replaced resume screens with micro-missions and linked recognition to networked contribution, people stopped waiting to be developed and started growing each other. The talent system either renews ingenuity or drains it. There is no neutral."

John on Structure:

"Structure is not a chart. It is a choice to freeze or to flow. When we moved to ninety-day missions with expiry dates, published decision ledgers, and gave edge voices real authority, money followed evidence and decisions lived where reality was richest. The lesson: if you cannot see your structure moving, it is already calcifying."

Maria on Operations:

"Operations is where strategy lives or dies. When we protected maker time, replaced slide theater with narrative memos, and installed energy dashboards that triggered reprioritization, the daily truth changed. Meetings shrank. Decisions sharpened. People stopped performing busyness and started doing work that mattered. Operations is the lever that whispers constantly. Listen to it."

Chris on CEO Stewardship:

"This lever belongs to every leader who sets tone and tempo for others. I examined how I carry presence, communicate purpose, and choreograph pace, including how I work with our Board and whether that relationship makes the organization braver or just busier. The lesson: your calendar is a public document of what you value. Your silence shapes as much as your speech. And if you are not willing to redesign your own leadership, you have no right to ask anyone else to redesign theirs."

Sanjay on Leadership Everywhere:

"We discovered that leadership was still tethered to title and hierarchy in half our sites. When we redesigned teams to decide together rather than report in parallel, freed middle managers to act, tested potential in real dilemmas rather than grids, and embedded coaching into daily work, the system accelerated. Leadership Everywhere is not a slogan. It is the difference between an organization that scales ingenuity and one that exhausts itself waiting for permission."

Liam on Engaged Hearts, Minds & Bodies:

"Engagement is not a survey score. It is what people Say about us, whether they Stay, and how hard they Strive. Those are outcomes. This year we designed the four causes: energy and well-being, recognition and belonging, purpose alignment, and passion for strategy, products, and customers. When we protected energy, people stayed. When we recognized contribution, people advocated. When we aligned purpose, people strove. When we channeled passion, all three compounded. Hearts, minds, and bodies are not resources to be consumed. They are renewable energy, if we choose to protect them."

Chris summarizing the year

Chris stepped forward. "What you have just heard is not a set of speeches. It is a living system. ORG6 provides the roadmap: the levers that drive the work. VISTA provides the compass: the choices that shape the direction. Together, they are how Omnivista will lead, not by reacting to the world, but by revealing what is possible within it.

"We began this year wondering if ingenuity could be rebuilt inside a company of our size. We now know it can. What we do next will decide whether it lasts. The roadmap shows us how to move lever by lever, proof by proof. The compass reminds us why: choice by choice, moment by moment.

"So take these with you. Teach them, test them, and translate them into your own teams. Let the rhythm we lived this year become the rhythm of how Omnivista learns. One lever at a time. One choice at a time. One age at a time."

CEO's Reflection, That Evening

The cab door thudded shut, and winter air met her face clean and cold. New York moved as it always does: steam rising from grates, a siren two avenues over, the quick rhythm of footsteps finding their way. Chris let herself into the apartment, set her bag by the door, and stood a moment at the window. The East River carried a thin ribbon of light; somewhere beyond it, the year she had just lived through began to take shape.

On the hallway table sat the small things she had kept from the road: a visitor badge from Shinjuku, a ferry stub from Sydney, a ward pass from São Paulo, a Whitefield metro card from Bangalore, a pressed clover from Dublin. Results, not trophies. Proof that the work had been done where it mattered: on the floor, in the lab, at the bedside, in the code.

She boiled water, poured tea, and opened the notebook that had traveled with her all year. The pages held the cadence of the months: ORG6 rebuilt, VISTA practiced, the roadmap and compass quickened, guardrails kept. They had reclaimed working wisdom from the Industrial and Information Ages and applied it with new tools. She read the lines she had written on hard days and smiled at how ordinary the right actions looked in ink: move the decision to the edge, name the trade-off, protect a rhythm, close a loop, tell the truth.

The year's final meetings replayed in brief images. The Board had acknowledged what shifted and asked for more. The Top 100 had taken the cadence as its own. Evelyn's insights still rang: clarity before complexity, voices at the edge, power pushed outward, operations telling the truth, energy treated as strategy, vision proven in trade-offs, intuition given design, synergy chosen over pride, trust built in loops, authenticity as congruence.

She wrote three sentences on a fresh page.

1. Keep the system human.

2. Keep the promises visible.

3. Keep the pace you can sustain.

She thought of AI, not as a tide to resist or a trick to perform, but as a force multiplier of whatever a leader makes real. In the space between stimulus and response, they had learned to work. It would not slow down. It would not choose for them. The choice remained theirs each day: Vision or Void, Intuition or Inertia, Synergy or Silos, Trust or Tyranny, Authenticity or Apathy. The aim was constant: let the tools amplify ingenuity, not irrelevance. The age they would inhabit would be the one they built.

Her phone buzzed with a last message from the team: a photo from the Top 100 workshop, sleeves rolled, walls marked with decisions and owners. She typed back only two words: "Begin again."

She closed the notebook and set it beside the year's results. Tomorrow she would thank the team, send a note to the whole company, and walk the floor at the clinic down the street. No speeches, just presence. Then, in January, the rhythm would start in other rooms, with other leaders, one lever, one choice at a time. Leader by leader, company by company, that discipline would earn the right to name the age ahead: the Ingenuity Age, where human wisdom works in concert with artificial intelligence.

Chris turned off the light and paused at the doorway. The city kept moving. So would they. In an age that can make organizations smaller or larger than themselves, this would be their signature: clarity without cruelty, pace without panic, technology without losing the human moment.

She let a quiet smile rise, the kind that comes when a plan becomes a discipline and a discipline becomes a way of being. The future was not waiting for permission. It was waiting for stewardship. And in the morning, they would choose it again, in that small, decisive space.

Outside, the city lights blurred into motion, each one a trace of human intent. Chris thought of the fingerprint, not fading, but deepening. Every decision, every repaired loop, every honest word left its ridge and whorl across the organization. It was never about permanence; it was about impression. What they had built this year was not an artifact but a signature, a living mark of ingenuity pressed into the age ahead.

Afterword

The Fingerprint, Indelible

An Invitation for You to Reflect

Before you read what follows, you may wish to turn to the scoreboards at the very back of this book. If you have completed the paired questions at the end of each chapter, your Foundation and AI Amplifier averages are ready to be plotted. Two matrices will show you where you stand: one for your leadership, one for your organization's culture. They may not be in the same place. That gap is where the most important work begins.

In closing

This book followed a fictional team through a real challenge. The frameworks are mine. The characters are not. But the convictions underneath both are as personal as anything I have written.

You may have noticed that a book about ingenuity in the age of artificial intelligence was itself written during that transition. Tools now exist that can assist writers with language and structure, drawing on patterns found across large bodies of human writing. Their presence changes the mechanics of writing, but not the responsibility for the ideas themselves.

The frameworks in this book were shaped long before such tools existed. They emerged from decades spent working with leadership teams, observing how organizations succeed, falter, and recover. They are the product of experience, reflection, and repeated testing in the real world of enterprise life.

If used wisely, intelligent tools can strengthen rather than diminish the human fingerprint behind the ideas. They can help ideas travel more clearly and more quickly. But the mark itself must still come from a human source. Ingenuity begins in the mind and conscience of the leader who chooses to exercise it.

I have spent thirty-five years inside and alongside leadership teams, asking one question: what does it take for people to bring their full ingenuity to work? The answer is not a model or a method. It is a stance.

Leadership is the disciplined union of four interdependent acts. Leadership of strategy: seeing context clearly, making choices, setting direction, and keeping a living narrative coherent as conditions change. Leadership in implementation: turning intent into action through mechanisms, milestones, and learning loops that deliver value. Leadership with others: empowering people, building trust, harmonizing diverse perspectives, and designing conditions in which initiative spreads. And leadership of self: the inner work that steadies judgment, keeps ego in its place, and aligns habits with purpose over time.

When these four acts are practiced together, leadership is not a role performed by a few but a property of the system. When any one is neglected, the others wobble. My short rule captures the essence: leadership without people is unstable; with people, strategy endures.

These four acts gave rise to the two frameworks in this book. VISTA, the leadership compass, names five choices that determine whether a leader amplifies ingenuity or drifts toward irrelevance: Vision, Intuition, Synergy, Trust, and Authenticity. ORG6, the organizational roadmap, names six levers through which culture becomes visible and operational: Talent, Structure, Operations, CEO Stewardship, Leadership Everywhere, and Engaged Hearts, Minds & Bodies. Leadership is the being. Culture is the doing. Neither holds without the other. The Chief People Officer for the Ingenuity Age is the leader accountable for the people who make ingenuity possible.

At its simplest, leadership is a conscious choice. Every day presents forks in the path: we can react from autopilot or respond from awareness. The practice begins with learning your triggers: how fear, pride, and scarcity show up in your body and your calendar. It continues with catching yourself in the moment when habit would typically take over. It strengthens as you build fitness to override survival reflexes: breath, perspective shifting, and curiosity under pressure. And it culminates in choosing the action that serves the whole: stakeholders now and in the future, people and performance, humans and the health of the system.

Leaders who make conscious choices repeatedly are not superhuman. They are students of attention. They use stories and symbols to remind themselves and others that there is always a wise action to follow, and then they take it. We become the roads we take, and the roads we take become our organizations.

The question posed at the beginning of this book still stands.
Will we build the Ingenuity Age through conscious leadership, or drift toward irrelevance in the presence of our own machines?

At the deepest level, leadership is a commitment to potential. It is the stance that people are not finished, that their capacity can grow faster than their circumstances. Three principles have anchored the way I teach potential to the leaders I coach.

The first is the power of *respicere*: "to look again." Respect means refusing to reduce anyone to an object of use. It is the discipline of seeing, again and again, the dignity and potential that might otherwise be missed.

The second is the Zulu greeting. Sawubona: "I see you, and I see your potential." Sikhona: "Because you see me and my potential, I exist and thrive." To be seen is to be called into being. Recognition precedes contribution.

The third is the Nelson Mandela rule. What if I met every person as if they were as fascinating as Mandela himself walking into the room? If I slowed down, summoned the curiosity to truly see their potential, then leading from behind and stepping forward in danger would not be a strategy but a natural act of humanity.

Taken together, these principles ignite performance: people risk ideas, learn quickly, and carry one another farther than any single leader could plan.

You have now walked with a team through a full year of this work. You have seen what ingenuity looks like when it is practiced, not just proclaimed. You have scored yourself honestly, and you know where your fingerprint is deepening and where it is at risk of fading.

The question that remains is not what you have learned. It is what you will do tomorrow morning, in the first meeting, the first decision, the first moment when autopilot would be easier than awareness. That is where the age you inhabit will be decided. Not in a boardroom. Not in a book. In that small, decisive space between stimulus and response.

I began this book with a question: how do we build enterprises where people are free to think, create, and matter? I end it with the same question, because it is never finished. It is renewed every day by every leader who chooses to see potential, name the truth, and act with both courage and care.

Katharine McLennan

SOURCES

The sources listed for each chapter are listed according to their appearance in that chapter. Each source appears once per chapter, at the point of its first reference.

PROLOGUE

Frost, Robert. "The Road Not Taken." In *Mountain Interval*. New York: Henry Holt, 1916.

Sasson, Steven. "Steven Sasson." *Encyclopaedia Britannica*. https://www.britannica.com/biography/Steven-Sasson

Kovach, Steve. "Netflix Offered to Sell to Blockbuster for $50 Million and Got Laughed Out of the Room." *Business Insider*, January 18, 2013.

Chen, Angela. "Nokia's Fall: A Case Study." *PCMag*, September 3, 2017.

Fubini, David. "Lessons from GE's Decline." *Harvard Business Review*, November 2018.

Gawdat, Mo. *Scary Smart: The Future of Artificial Intelligence and How You Can Save Our World*. London: Bluebird, 2021.

Ford, Martin. *Rise of the Robots: Technology and the Threat of a Jobless Future*. New York: Basic Books, 2015.

Harari, Yuval Noah. *Homo Deus: A Brief History of Tomorrow*. London: Harvill Secker, 2016.

Brynjolfsson, Erik, and Andrew McAfee. *The Second Machine Age: Work, Progress, and Prosperity in a Time of Brilliant Technologies*. New York: W.W. Norton, 2014.

Kurzweil, Ray. *The Singularity Is Nearer: When We Merge with AI*. New York: Viking, 2024.

Frankl, Viktor E. *Man's Search for Meaning*. Boston: Beacon Press, 1946. Reprint, 2006. (The quotation "Between stimulus and response, there is a space" is widely attributed to Frankl, notably through Stephen R. Covey's *The 7 Habits of Highly Effective People*. New York: Free Press, 1989, though it has not been located in Frankl's published works.)

Drucker, Peter F. *Management Challenges for the 21st Century*. New York: Harper Business, 1999.

Pfeffer, Jeffrey. *Dying for a Paycheck*. New York: HarperBusiness, 2018.

CHAPTER 1

Faulkner, William. *Requiem for a Nun*. New York: Random House, 1951.

Taylor, Frederick Winslow. *The Principles of Scientific Management*. New York: Harper & Brothers, 1911.

"Model T." Detroit Historical Society, *Encyclopedia of Detroit*.

"Ford's Assembly Line Starts Rolling." History.com, A+E Networks.

Fayol, Henri. *General and Industrial Management*. London: Pitman, 1949. (English translation of 1916 original.)

Weber, Max. *Economy and Society: An Outline of Interpretive Sociology*. Berkeley: University of California Press, 1978. (Originally published 1922.)

Serwer, Andy. "Manager of the Century." *Fortune*, November 22, 1999.

Drucker, Peter F. *The Practice of Management*. New York: Harper & Brothers, 1954.

McEwen, Bruce S. "Neurobiological and Systemic Effects of Chronic Stress." *Chronic Stress*, vol. 1, January 2017.

Pfeffer, Jeffrey. *Dying for a Paycheck*. New York: HarperBusiness, 2018.

"The Berlin Wall." Berlin.de, Official City of Berlin.

CHAPTER 2

Eliot, T.S. *The Rock*. London: Faber and Faber, 1934.

"Netscape's I.P.O. Opens." *The New York Times*, August 10, 1995.

Gates, Bill. *Business @ the Speed of Thought*. New York: Warner Books, 1999.

Friedman, Thomas L. *The World Is Flat: A Brief History of the Twenty-First Century*. New York: Farrar, Straus and Giroux, 2005.

Gerstner, Louis V., Jr. *Who Says Elephants Can't Dance? Leading a Great Enterprise through Dramatic Change*. New York: HarperBusiness, 2002.

Grove, Andrew S. *Only the Paranoid Survive*. New York: Doubleday, 1996.

Bezos, Jeff. *Invent and Wander: The Collected Writings of Jeff Bezos*. Boston: Harvard Business Review Press, 2020.

Dell, Michael. *Direct from Dell: Strategies That Revolutionized an Industry*. New York: HarperBusiness, 1999.

International Olympic Committee. "Sydney 2000: Facts and Figures." Olympics.com.

Michaels, Ed, Helen Handfield-Jones, and Beth Axelrod. *The War for Talent*. Boston: Harvard Business Press, 2001.

Goleman, Daniel. *Emotional Intelligence*. New York: Bantam, 1995.

Senge, Peter M. T*he Fifth Discipline: The Art and Practice of the Learning Organization*. New York: Doubleday, 1990.

Collins, Jim. *Good to Great: Why Some Companies Make the Leap and Others Don't*. New York: HarperBusiness, 2001.

Hamel, Gary. *The Future of Management*. Boston: Harvard Business School Press, 2007.

George, Bill. Authentic Leadership: *Rediscovering the Secrets to Creating Lasting Value*. San Francisco: Jossey-Bass, 2003.

Zohar, Danah, and Ian Marshall. *Spiritual Intelligence: The Ultimate Intelligence*. London: Bloomsbury, 2000.

Turkle, Sherry. Alone Together: *Why We Expect More from Technology and Less from Each Other*. New York: Basic Books, 2011.

McLennan, Katharine, host. *Stanford MBA: From Baby Boomer to Gen Z. Class of '95 Meets Class of '25*. YouTube podcast series, produced in 2025.

CHAPTER 3

Harari, Yuval Noah. *Homo Deus: A Brief History of Tomorrow*. New York: Harper, 2017.

Perrow, Charles. *Normal Accidents: Living with High-Risk Technologies*. Revised ed. Princeton: Princeton University Press, 1999.

Collins, Jim. *Good to Great: Why Some Companies Make the Leap and Others Don't*. New York: HarperBusiness, 2001.

Taylor, Frederick Winslow. T*he Principles of Scientific Management*. New York: Harper & Brothers, 1911.

Pfeffer, Jeffrey. *Dying for a Paycheck*. New York: HarperBusiness, 2018.

Turkle, Sherry. *Alone Together: Why We Expect More from Technology and Less from Each Other*. New York: Basic Books, 2011.

Davenport, Thomas H., and Rajeev Ronanki. "Artificial Intelligence for the Real World." *Harvard Business Review* 96, no. 1 (January-February 2018): 108-116.

Turing, A. M. "Computing Machinery and Intelligence." *Mind* 59, no. 236 (1950): 433-460.

Gawdat, Mo. *Scary Smart: The Future of Artificial Intelligence and How You Can Save Our World*. London: Pan Macmillan, 2021.

Ford, Martin. *Rise of the Robots: Technology and the Threat of a Jobless Future*. New York: Basic Books, 2015.

Brynjolfsson, Erik, and Andrew McAfee. *The Second Machine Age: Work, Progress, and Prosperity in a Time of Brilliant Technologies*. New York: W. W. Norton, 2014.

Goldman Sachs Global Investment Research. "Generative AI: Hype, or Truly Transformative?" *Top of Mind*, July 5, 2023.

PwC US. "PwC US Makes $1 Billion Investment to Expand and Scale AI Capabilities." Press release, April 26, 2023.

Microsoft. "What Is Microsoft 365 Copilot?" Product documentation.

GitHub. "Research: Quantifying GitHub Copilot's Impact on Developer Productivity and Happiness." GitHub Blog, September 7, 2022.

Amazon. "Amazon Introduces New Robotics Solutions; More Than 750,000 Robots Deployed." *About Amazon*, October 19, 2023.

Khan, Muhammad A., et al. "Artificial Intelligence in Robotic Surgery." *Cureus* 16, no. 1 (2024): e53116.

Waymo. "Safety Impact." Waymo.com.

Tesla. "Full Self-Driving (Supervised)." Tesla.com.

Google DeepMind. "RT-2: New Model

Delta Air Lines. "Delta Unveils AI-Powered Travel Journey." Delta Newsroom, January 7, 2025.

Ayers, John W., et al. "Comparing Physician and Artificial Intelligence Chatbot Responses to Patient Questions." *JAMA Internal Medicine* (April 28, 2023).

Khan Academy. "Khanmigo: AI-Powered Teaching Assistant." Khanmigo.ai.

Jumper, John, et al. "Highly Accurate Protein Structure Prediction with AlphaFold." *Nature* 596 (2021): 583-589.

CHAPTER 4

Keller, Helen. *The Open Door*. New York: Doubleday, 1957.

Cross, Rob, Brent Rebele, and Adam Grant. "Collaborative Overload." *Harvard Business Review* 94, no. 1-2 (2016): 74-79.

Apple. "Apple Reinvents the Phone with iPhone." Press release, January 9, 2007.

International Olympic Committee. "Test Events." Olympics.com.

Hastings, Reed, and Erin Meyer. *No Rules Rules: Netflix and the Culture of Reinvention*. New York: Penguin, 2020.

Clark, Graeme. *Sounds from Silence*. Sydney: Allen & Unwin, 2000.

Clark, Graeme. Cochlear Implants: *Fundamentals and Applications*. New York: Springer-Verlag, 2003.

Cochlear Limited. "About Us: Our Mission." Cochlear.com. Accessed 2025.

Bionics Institute. "Laureate Professor Graeme Clark AC." Bionicsinstitute.org. Accessed 2025.

Weil, Simone. *Gravity and Grace*. Translated by Emma Crawford. London: Routledge, 1952.

Baldwin, James. "The Creative Process." *In The Price of the Ticket: Collected Nonfiction 1948-1985*, 313-17. New York: St. Martin's/Marek, 1985.

Rilke, Rainer Maria. *Letters to a Young Poet*. Translated by Stephen Mitchell. New York: Vintage, 1984.

Butler, Octavia E. *Parable of the Sower*. New York: Four Walls Eight Windows, 1993.

Hadid, Zaha. *Complete Works*. London: Thames & Hudson, 2009.

Confucius. *The Analects*. Translated by Edward Slingerland. Indianapolis: Hackett, 2003.

"Akan Proverb (Ghana): 'The ruin of a nation begins in the homes of its people.'" Traditional proverb anthologies.

Raichle, Marcus E., et al. "A Default Mode of Brain Function." *Proceedings of the National Academy of Sciences* 98, no. 2 (2001): 676-82.

Kounios, John, and Mark Beeman. "The Aha! Moment: The Cognitive Neuroscience of Insight." *Current Directions in Psychological Science* 17, no. 6 (2008): 210-16.

Kahneman, Daniel. *Thinking, Fast and Slow*. New York: Farrar, Straus and Giroux, 2011.

Porges, Stephen W. *The Polyvagal Theory*. New York: W. W. Norton, 2011.

Zak, Paul J. "The Neuroscience of Trust." *Harvard Business Review*, January-February 2017.

Schultz, Wolfram, Peter Dayan, and P. Read Montague. "A Neural Substrate of Prediction and Reward." *Science* 275, no. 5306 (1997): 1593-99.

Keltner, Dacher, and Jonathan Haidt. "Approaching Awe, a Moral, Spiritual, and Aesthetic Emotion." *Cognition and Emotion* 17, no. 2 (2003): 297-314.

Dumas, Guillaume, et al. "Inter Brain Synchronization during Social Interaction." *PLOS ONE* 5, no. 8 (2010): e12166.

Wagner, Ullrich, et al. "Sleep Inspires Insight." *Nature* 427, no. 6972 (2004): 352-55.

Narayen, Shantanu. "Adobe's Creative Cloud Transition." Adobe Annual Reports, 2013-2023.

Nadella, Satya. *Hit Refresh*. New York: Harper Business, 2017.

Dweck, Carol S. *Mindset: The New Psychology of Success*. New York: Random House, 2006.

Polman, Paul, and Andrew Winston. *Net Positive*. Boston: Harvard Business Review Press, 2021.

Chouinard, Yvon. *Let My People Go Surfing*. New York: Penguin, 2016.

Siilasmaa, Risto. *Transforming Nokia*. New York: McGraw-Hill, 2019.

Wiedeman, Reeves. *Billion Dollar Loser: The Epic Rise and Spectacular Fall of Adam Neumann and WeWork*. New York: Little, Brown, 2020.

Isaacson, Walter. *Steve Jobs*. New York: Simon & Schuster, 2011.

Jumper, John, et al. "Highly Accurate Protein Structure Prediction with AlphaFold." *Nature* 596 (2021): 583-589.

McLennan, Katharine. "Leadership in Turbulent Times: A Neuroscientific Explanation." 2009. Available at katharinemclennan.com.

McLennan, Katharine. "Neuroleadership of Culture and Leadership." 2007. Available at katharinemclennan.com.

CHAPTER 5

Salk, Jonas. *Anatomy of Reality: Merging of Intuition and Reason*. New York: Columbia University Press, 1983.

Goodhart, C.A.E. "Problems of Monetary Management: The U.K. Experience." In *Monetary Theory and Practice*, 91-121. London: Macmillan, 1984.

Independent Directors of the Board of Wells Fargo & Company. *Sales Practices Investigation Report*. April 10, 2017.

Polanyi, Michael. *The Tacit Dimension*. Garden City, NY: Doubleday, 1966.

Pascal, Blaise. *Pensées*. Translated by Roger Ariew. Indianapolis: Hackett, 2005.

Pasteur, Louis. "Inaugural Lecture, University of Lille." December 7, 1854.

Nussbaum, Martha C. *Upheavals of Thought: The Intelligence of Emotions.* Cambridge: Cambridge University Press, 2001.

Laozi. *Tao Te Ching.* Translated by D. C. Lau. New York: Penguin, 1963.

Lorde, Audre. *Sister Outsider: Essays and Speeches.* Trumansburg, NY: Crossing Press, 1984.

Simon, Herbert A. *Models of Bounded Rationality.* Cambridge, MA: MIT Press, 1982.

Kahneman, Daniel. *Thinking, Fast and Slow.* New York: Farrar, Straus and Giroux, 2011.

Damasio, Antonio. *Descartes' Error: Emotion, Reason, and the Human Brain.* New York: Putnam, 1994.

Gigerenzer, Gerd. *Gut Feelings: The Intelligence of the Unconscious.* New York: Viking, 2007.

Klein, Gary. "Performing a Project Premortem." *Harvard Business Review,* September 2007.

Klein, Gary. *Sources of Power: How People Make Decisions.* Cambridge, MA: MIT Press, 1998.

Bezos, Jeff. "2016 Letter to Shareholders." Amazon.com, April 2017.

Duke, Annie. *Thinking in Bets: Making Smarter Decisions When You Don't Have All the Facts.* New York: Portfolio, 2018.

Gladwell, Malcolm. *Blink: The Power of Thinking Without Thinking.* New York: Little, Brown, 2005.

Berger, Eric. *Liftoff: Elon Musk and the Desperate Early Days That Launched SpaceX.* New York: William Morrow, 2021.

McNish, Jacquie, and Sean Silcoff. *Losing the Signal: The Untold Story Behind the Extraordinary Rise and Spectacular Fall of BlackBerry.* New York: Flatiron Books, 2015.

Carlson, Nicholas. *Marissa Mayer and the Fight to Save Yahoo!* New York: Hachette Books, 2015.

McLennan, Katharine. "Leadership in Turbulent Times: A Neuroscientific Explanation." 2009. Available at katharinemclennan.com.

McLennan, Katharine. "Neuroleadership of Culture and Leadership." 2007. Available at katharinemclennan.com.

CHAPTER 6

Meadows, Donella H. *Thinking in Systems: A Primer*. White River Junction, VT: Chelsea Green Publishing, 2008.

"African Proverb: 'If you want to go fast, go alone. If you want to go far, go together.'" Quote Investigator.

Aristotle. *Metaphysics*. Translated by W. D. Ross. In *The Complete Works of Aristotle*, edited by Jonathan Barnes, vol. 2. Princeton, NJ: Princeton University Press, 1984.

Confucius. *The Analects*. Translated by D. C. Lau. London: Penguin Classics, 1979.

Follett, Mary Parker. *Dynamic Administration: The Collected Papers of Mary Parker Follett*. Edited by Henry C. Metcalf and L. Urwick. New York: Harper & Brothers, 1941.

Ibn Khaldun. *The Muqaddimah: An Introduction to History*. Translated by Franz Rosenthal. Princeton, NJ: Princeton University Press, 1967.

Spinoza, Benedict de. *Ethics*. Translated by Edwin Curley. In *The Collected Works of Spinoza*, vol. 1. Princeton, NJ: Princeton University Press, 1985.

Beauvoir, Simone de. *The Ethics of Ambiguity*. Translated by Bernard Frechtman. New York: Citadel Press, 1948.

Buber, Martin. *I and Thou*. Translated by Walter Kaufmann. New York: Charles Scribner's Sons, 1970.

Habermas, Jurgen. *The Theory of Communicative Action*. Vol. 1. Translated by Thomas McCarthy. Boston: Beacon Press, 1984.

Tutu, Desmond. *No Future Without Forgiveness*. New York: Doubleday, 1999.

Fuller, R. Buckminster. *Synergetics: Explorations in the Geometry of Thinking*. New York: Macmillan, 1975.

Marcus Aurelius. *Meditations*. Translated by Gregory Hays. New York: Modern Library, 2002.

Hegel, G. W. F. *Phenomenology of Spirit*. Translated by A. V. Miller. Oxford: Oxford University Press, 1977.

Rizzolatti, Giacomo, and Laila Craighero. "The Mirror-Neuron System." *Annual Review of Neuroscience* 27 (2004): 169-192.

Wegner, Daniel M. "Transactive Memory: A Contemporary Analysis of the Group Mind." In *Theories of Group Behavior*, edited by Brian Mullen and George R. Goethals, 185-208. New York: Springer-Verlag, 1987.

De Dreu, Carsten K.W., et al. "The Neuropeptide Oxytocin Regulates Parochial Altruism in Intergroup Conflict Among Humans." *Science* 328, no. 5984 (2010): 1408-1411.

Cowan, Nelson. "The Magical Number 4 in Short-Term Memory." *Behavioral and Brain Sciences* 24, no. 1 (2001): 87-114.

Monsell, Stephen. "Task Switching." *Trends in Cognitive Sciences* 7, no. 3 (2003): 134-140.

Botvinick, Matthew M., Jonathan D. Cohen, and Cameron S. Carter. "Conflict Monitoring and Anterior Cingulate Cortex: An Update." *Trends in Cognitive Sciences* 8, no. 12 (2004): 539-546.

Harbaugh, William T., Ulrich Mayr, and Daniel R. Burghart. "Neural Responses to Taxation and Voluntary Giving Reveal Motives for Charitable Donations." *Science* 316, no. 5831 (2007): 1622-1625.

Mehta, Pranjal H., and Robert A. Josephs. "Testosterone and Cortisol Jointly Regulate Dominance." *Hormones and Behavior* 58, no. 5 (2010): 898-906.

Catmull, Ed, and Amy Wallace. *Creativity, Inc.* New York: Random House, 2014.

Zhang, Ruimin, and Bill Fischer. *Reinventing Giants: How Chinese Global Competitor Haier Has Changed the Way Big Companies Transform.* San Francisco: Jossey-Bass, 2013.

McLennan, Katharine. "Leadership in Turbulent Times: A Neuroscientific Explanation." 2009. Available at katharinemclennan.com.

McLennan, Katharine. "Neuroleadership of Culture and Leadership." 2007. Available at katharinemclennan.com.

CHAPTER 7

"Attributed to Ernest Hemingway." Quote Investigator.

Edmondson, Amy C. *The Fearless Organization.* Hoboken, NJ: Wiley, 2018.

Beyer, Betsy, Chris Jones, Jennifer Petoff, and Niall Richard Murphy, eds. *Site Reliability Engineering.* Sebastopol, CA: O'Reilly Media, 2016.

Beyer, Betsy, Niall Richard Murphy, David K. Rensin, Kent Kawahara, and Stephen Thorne, eds. *The Site Reliability Workbook.* Sebastopol, CA: O'Reilly Media, 2018.

Allspaw, John. "Blameless PostMortems and a Just Culture." Etsy Code as Craft, May 22, 2012.

Mitchell, Margaret, et al. "Model Cards for Model Reporting." arXiv, October 5, 2018.

Maister, David H., Charles H. Green, and Robert M. Galford. *The Trusted Advisor*. New York: Free Press, 2000.

Kets de Vries, Manfred F. R. "The Dangers of Narcissistic Leaders." *Harvard Business Review*, January 2004.

Collins, Jim. *Good to Great*. New York: HarperBusiness, 2001.

Goodhart, C.A.E. "Problems of Monetary Management: The U.K. Experience." In *Monetary Theory and Practice*, 91-121. London: Macmillan, 1984.

Hobbes, Thomas. *Leviathan*. Edited by Richard Tuck. Cambridge: Cambridge University Press, 1996.

Locke, John. *Two Treatises of Government*. Edited by Peter Laslett. Cambridge: Cambridge University Press, 1988.

Montesquieu. *The Spirit of the Laws*. Translated by Anne M. Cohler, Basia C. Miller, and Harold S. Stone. Cambridge: Cambridge University Press, 1989.

Madison, James. "Federalist No. 51." In *The Federalist Papers*, edited by Clinton Rossiter. New York: Signet Classics, 2003.

Kant, Immanuel. *Groundwork of the Metaphysics of Morals*. Translated by Mary Gregor and Jens Timmermann. Cambridge: Cambridge University Press, 2012.

Machiavelli, Niccolo. *The Prince*. Translated by Harvey C. Mansfield. Chicago: University of Chicago Press, 1998.

Bok, Sissela. *Lying: Moral Choice in Public and Private Life*. New York: Pantheon Books, 1978.

O'Neill, Onora. *A Question of Trust: The BBC Reith Lectures 2002*. Cambridge: Cambridge University Press, 2002.

Berlin, Isaiah. *The Crooked Timber of Humanity*. Edited by Henry Hardy. Princeton, NJ: Princeton University Press, 1990.

Popper, Karl R. *The Open Society and Its Enemies*. Vol. 1. Princeton, NJ: Princeton University Press, 1966.

Havel, Vaclav. "The Power of the Powerless." In *Living in Truth*, edited by Jan Vladislav, 36-122. London: Faber and Faber, 1986.

Goleman, Daniel. *Emotional Intelligence*. New York: Bantam Books, 1995.

Porath, Christine, and Christine Pearson. "The Price of Incivility." *Harvard Business Review*, January-February 2013.

Zak, Paul J. "The Neuroscience of Trust." *Harvard Business Review*, January-February 2017.

O'Neill, Paul H. Testimony before the U.S. Senate Committee on Health, *Education, Labor, and Pensions*, March 23, 2001.

McLean, Bethany, and Peter Elkind. *The Smartest Guys in the Room*. New York: Portfolio, 2003.

Watkins, Sherron. Testimony before the U.S. House Committee on Energy and Commerce, February 14, 2002.

Carreyrou, John. *Bad Blood: Secrets and Lies in a Silicon Valley Startup*. New York: Knopf, 2018.

McLennan, Katharine. "Leadership in Turbulent Times: A Neuroscientific Explanation." 2009. Available at katharinemclennan.com.

McLennan, Katharine. "Neuroleadership of Culture and Leadership." 2007. Available at katharinemclennan.com.

McLennan, Katharine. "How Trustworthy Are You, Really? The Neuroscientific and Business Argument for Trust." 2017. Available at katharinemclennan.com..

CHAPTER 8

Cummings, E. E. *A Miscellany Revised*. Edited by George J. Firmage. New York: October House, 1965.

Nietzsche, Friedrich. *The Gay Science*. Translated by Walter Kaufmann. New York: Vintage Books, 1974.

Kierkegaard, Soren. *The Point of View*. Translated by Howard V. Hong and Edna H. Hong. Princeton, NJ: Princeton University Press, 1998.

Sartre, Jean-Paul. *Existentialism Is a Humanism*. Translated by Carol Macomber. New Haven, CT: Yale University Press, 2007.

Camus, Albert. *The Rebel*. Translated by Anthony Bower. New York: Vintage Books, 1956.

Heidegger, Martin. *Being and Time*. Translated by John Macquarrie and Edward Robinson. New York: Harper & Row, 1962.

Taylor, Charles. *The Ethics of Authenticity*. Cambridge, MA: Harvard University Press, 1991.

Frankl, Viktor E. *Man's Search for Meaning*. Boston: Beacon Press, 2006.

Diogenes Laertius. *Lives of Eminent Philosophers*. Translated by R. D. Hicks. 2 vols. Loeb Classical Library 184-185. Cambridge, MA: Harvard University Press, 1925.

Epictetus. *Discourses and Selected Writings*. Translated by Robert Dobbin. New York: Penguin Classics, 2008.

Thoreau, Henry David. *Walden*. Edited by J. Lyndon Shanley. Princeton, NJ: Princeton University Press, 2004.

Ortega y Gasset, Jose. *Meditations on Quixote*. Translated by Evelyn Rugg and Diego Marin. Urbana: University of Illinois Press, 2000.

Baldwin, James. *No Name in the Street*. New York: Dial Press, 1972.

May, Rollo. *Man's Search for Himself*. New York: W. W. Norton, 1953.

Zak, Paul J. "The Neuroscience of Trust." *Harvard Business Review*, January-February 2017.

REI Co-op. "REI Closing Its Doors on Black Friday." Press release, October 27, 2015.

"REI #OptOutside Campaign Results Show Power of Sincerity Plus Engagement." *Retail TouchPoints*, March 21, 2016.

CVS Health. "CVS Health Completes Removal of Tobacco from All Store Locations." Press release, September 3, 2014.

Brennan, Troyen A., and Thomas H. Lee. "Allergic to Nonsense: How CVS Stripped Away Tobacco." *New England Journal of Medicine* 371 (2014): 1469-1471.

Sturchio, Jeffrey L. "The Case of Ivermectin: Lessons and Implications for Improving Access to Care and Treatment in Developing Countries." *Community Eye Health* 14, no. 38 (2001): 22-23.

Chesky, Brian. "A Message from Co-Founder and CEO Brian Chesky." Airbnb Newsroom, May 5, 2020.

Keefe, Patrick Radden. *Empire of Pain: The Secret History of the Sackler Dynasty*. New York: Doubleday, 2021.

Confessore, Nicholas. "The Unlikely Activists Who Took On Silicon Valley and Won." *New York Times*, August 14, 2018.

Federal Trade Commission. "FTC Imposes $5 Billion Penalty and Sweeping New Privacy Restrictions on Facebook." Press release, July 24, 2019.

Victor, Daniel. "Pepsi Pulls Ad Accused of Trivializing Black Lives Matter." *New York Times*, April 5, 2017.

McCrum, Dan. *Money Men: A Hot Startup, a Billion Dollar Fraud, a Fight for the Truth*. London: Bantam Press, 2022.

McLennan, Katharine. "Leadership in Turbulent Times: A Neuroscientific Explanation." 2009. Available at katharinemclennan.com.

McLennan, Katharine. "Neuroleadership of Culture and Leadership." 2007. Available at katharinemclennan.com.

CHAPTER 9

Charan, Ram, Dominic Barton, and Dennis Carey. *Talent Wins: The New Playbook for Putting People First*. Boston: Harvard Business Review Press, 2018.

Pfeffer, Jeffrey. *Dying for a Paycheck*. New York: HarperBusiness, 2018.

Brynjolfsson, Erik. "The Turing Trap: The Promise and Peril of Human-Like Artificial Intelligence." *MIT Initiative on the Digital Economy*, 2021.

Gallwey, W. Timothy. *The Inner Game of Tennis*. New York: Random House, 1974.

Zander, Rosamund Stone, and Benjamin Zander. *The Art of Possibility*. Boston: Harvard Business School Press, 2000.

Hern, Alex. "Unilever Saves on Recruiters by Using AI to Assess Job Interviews." *The Guardian*, October 25, 2019.

World Business Council for Sustainable Development. "Unilever: Transforming Early Careers Recruitment Through AI." 2021.

Schneider Electric. "Open Talent Market: What We Learned." Schneider Electric Blog, 2021.

Gloat. "Schneider Electric Case Study: Launching an AI-Powered Open Talent Market." 2020.

GitHub. "Copilot Research: Measuring the Impact of GitHub Copilot." GitHub Blog, 2023.

Nuance Communications. "Dragon Ambient eXperience (DAX Copilot)." Nuance Healthcare.

Qin, Fan, and Thomas A. Kochan. "The Learning System at IBM: A Case Study." MIT Sloan Working Paper, 2020.

Bersin, Josh. "IBM Your Learning: A Case Study in the New World of Learning." *MIT Sloan Management Review*, 2018.

Donovan, John, and Cathy Benko. "Inside AT&T's Radical Talent Overhaul." *Harvard Business Review*, October 2016.

Cappelli, Peter, and Anna Tavis. "HR Goes Agile." *Harvard Business Review* 96, no. 2 (2018): 46-52.

Syndio. "How Salesforce Uses Syndio to Advance Pay Equity." 2022.

Salesforce. "Equality at Salesforce: Pay Equity." Salesforce Equality Update, 2023.

Workhuman. "Cisco Case Study: Connected Recognition at Global Scale." 2020.

McGregor, Jena. "Shopify Is Canceling All Meetings with More Than Two People." *Forbes*, January 3, 2023.

Atlassian. Workplace and Meetings Blog.

Microsoft. "Viva Insights: Introduction." Microsoft Documentation.

Asana. "Anatomy of Work Index." Asana Resources.

McLennan, Katharine. "The CEO and CPO We Need for the AI Age." 2023. Available at katharinemclennan.com.

CHAPTER 10

Deming, W. Edwards. *The New Economics for Industry, Government, Education*. Cambridge, MA: MIT Press, 1994.

Jaques, Elliott. *Requisite Organization: A Total System for Effective Managerial Organization and Managerial Leadership for the 21st Century*. Arlington, VA: Cason Hall, 1996.

Chandler, Alfred D. Jr. *The Visible Hand: The Managerial Revolution in American Business*. Cambridge, MA: Harvard University Press, 1977.

Sloan, Alfred P. Jr. *My Years with General Motors*. New York: Doubleday, 1963.

Weber, Max. *Economy and Society: An Outline of Interpretive Sociology*. Berkeley: University of California Press, 1978.

Laloux, Frederic. *Reinventing Organizations*. Brussels: Nelson Parker, 2014.

Haier Group. "Rendanheyi Model." Haier Global.

Panzarino, Matthew. "Supercell's Secret Sauce." *TechCrunch*, October 15, 2013.

Berkun, Scott. *The Year Without Pants: WordPress.com and the Future of Work*. San Francisco: Jossey-Bass, 2013.

Jacobs, Peter, and Bart Schlatmann. "ING's Agile Transformation." *McKinsey Quarterly*, January 2017.

Valve Corporation. *Handbook for New Employees*. Bellevue, WA: Valve Press, 2012.

Dalio, Ray. *Principles: Life and Work*. New York: Simon & Schuster, 2017.

Lindsay, Niels. *The Handelsbanken Way*. London: Kogan Page, 2021.

Ferdows, Kasra, Michael A. Lewis, and Jose A.D. Machuca. "Rapid-Fire Fulfillment." *Harvard Business Review*, November 2004.

Kniberg, Henrik, and Anders Ivarsson. "Scaling Agile at Spotify with Tribes, Squads, Chapters & Guilds." Spotify Engineering White Paper, 2012.

GitLab. "The GitLab Handbook." Accessed 2025.

Buterin, Vitalik. "DAOs, DACs, DAs and More: An Incomplete Terminology Guide." Ethereum Blog, 2014.

Buurtzorg. "About Buurtzorg." Accessed 2025.

W. L. Gore & Associates. "Culture and Lattice Organization." Accessed 2025.

Catmull, Ed, and Amy Wallace. *Creativity, Inc.* New York: Random House, 2014.

Folding@home. "About." Accessed 2025.

Dastin, Jeffrey. "Amazon Scraps Secret AI Recruiting Tool That Showed Bias against Women." *Reuters*, October 10, 2018.

Narasimhan, Vas. "Reimagining Medicine at Novartis." Presentation at J.P. Morgan Healthcare Conference, January 2020.

Microsoft. "Viva Insights and Glint: Employee Listening and ONA." Microsoft, 2025.

Haier Group. "COSMOPlat Industrial Internet Platform." Accessed 2025.

Airbus. "Skywise." Accessed 2025.

Syndio. "Salesforce Scales Pay Equity Using Syndio." Case study.

Schneider Electric. "Open Talent Market: What We Learned." Schneider Electric Blog, 2021.

Gloat. "Schneider Electric Case Study." 2020.

Bezos, Jeff. "2015 Letter to Shareholders." Amazon.com.

CHAPTER 11

Einstein, Albert. Relativity: The Special and the General Theory. Translated by Robert W. Lawson. New York: Crown, 1961. (Originally published 1916.)

Isaacson, Walter. Einstein: His Life and Universe. New York: Simon & Schuster, 2007.

Womack, James P., and Daniel T. Jones. Lean Thinking. Revised ed. New York: Simon & Schuster, 2003.

Womack, James P., and Daniel T. Jones. *Lean Thinking.* Revised ed. New York: Simon & Schuster, 2003.

Ohno, Taiichi. *Toyota Production System: Beyond Large Scale Production*. Portland, OR: Productivity Press, 1988.

Spear, Steven, and H. Kent Bowen. "Decoding the DNA of the Toyota Production System." *Harvard Business Review* 77, no. 5 (1999): 96-106.

Forsgren, Nicole, Jez Humble, and Gene Kim. *Accelerate: The Science of Lean Software and DevOps*. Portland, OR: IT Revolution Press, 2018.

Beyer, Betsy, Chris Jones, Jennifer Petoff, and Niall Richard Murphy, eds. *Site Reliability Engineering*. Sebastopol, CA: O'Reilly, 2016.

Graham, Paul. "Maker's Schedule, Manager's Schedule." Essay, July 2009.

Newport, Cal. *Deep Work*. New York: Grand Central Publishing, 2016.

Schmidt, Christina, et al. "Circadian Rhythms and Cognitive Performance." *Nature Reviews Neuroscience* 8, no. 7 (2007): 547-558.

Gallup. "Employee Burnout: Causes and Cures." Research report, 2020.

Atlassian. "No Meeting Days and Team Playbook." Accessed 2025.

Bezos, Jeff. Invent and Wander: *The Collected Writings of Jeff Bezos*. Boston: Harvard Business Review Press, 2020.

Bryar, Colin, and Bill Carr. *Working Backwards*. New York: St. Martin's Press, 2021.

Kohavi, Ron, Diane Tang, and Ya Xu. T*rustworthy Online Controlled Experiments*. Cambridge: Cambridge University Press, 2020.

Microsoft Japan. "Work Life Choice Challenge 2019 Summer." Microsoft Japan News Center, 2019.

Michelli, Joseph A. *The New Gold Standard*. New York: McGraw-Hill, 2008.

Gallup. *State of the Global Workplace: 2023 Report*. Washington, DC: Gallup Press, 2023.

Roche. *Annual Report 2022*. Basel: Roche Holding AG, 2023.

Dropbox. "Virtual First: How We're Designing the Future of Work." Dropbox Blog, October 13, 2020.

Unilever. "U-Work: A New Way of Working at Unilever." Press release, 2019.

Gratton, Lynda. *Redesigning Work*. London: Penguin Business, 2022.

Siemens AG. "Siemens Industrial Copilot." Press release, October 2023.

USAA. "Life Events and Member Support." Accessed 2025.

Berkun, Scott. *The Year Without Pants*. San Francisco: Jossey-Bass, 2013.

Singer, Ryan. *Shape Up: Stop Running in Circles and Ship Work that Matters*. Basecamp, 2019.

Potvin, Rachel, and Josh Levenberg. "Why Google Stores Billions of Lines of Code in a Single Repository." *Communications of the ACM* 59, no. 7 (2016): 78-87.

Salihefendic, Amir. "The Async-First Company." Doist Blog, 2021.

Dalio, Ray. *Principles: Life and Work*. New York: Simon & Schuster, 2017.

"How Notion Uses Notion." First Round Review, 2022.

LEGO Group. "LEGO Ideas: How It Works." LEGO.com.

Blissfully. *SaaS Trends Report 2020*. 2020.

Slack. "New AI Features to Reduce Collaboration Overload." Slack Blog, 2023.

GitHub. "Introducing GitHub Copilot." 2021.

Salesforce. "Ohana Culture and All Hands Meetings." 2022.

McGregor, Jena. "Shopify Is Canceling All Meetings with More Than Two People." Forbes, January 3, 2023.

CHAPTER 12

Block, Peter. *Stewardship: Choosing Service Over Self Interest*. 2nd ed. San Francisco: Berrett-Koehler, 2013.

Taylor, Frederick Winslow. *The Principles of Scientific Management*. New York: Harper & Brothers, 1911.

Ford, Henry, with Samuel Crowther. *My Life and Work*. New York: Doubleday, 1922.

Sloan, Alfred P. Jr. *My Years with General Motors*. New York: Doubleday, 1963.

Chandler, Alfred D. Jr. *The Visible Hand*. Cambridge, MA: Harvard University Press, 1977.

Grove, Andrew S. *Only the Paranoid Survive*. New York: Doubleday, 1996.

Gerstner, Louis V. Jr. *Who Says Elephants Can't Dance?* New York: HarperBusiness, 2002.

Nadella, Satya. *Hit Refresh*. New York: Harper Business, 2017.

Cohen, Adam. *The Perfect Store: Inside eBay*. New York: Little, Brown, 2002.

Clark, Don. "How Lisa Su Rescued AMD." *Wall Street Journal*, June 2022.

Colvin, Geoff. "Mary Barra's Extraordinary Gamble." *Fortune*, October 2021.

Vlasic, Bill. "G.M. Chief's Bet on Electric Vehicles." *New York Times*, January 2021.

Ignatius, Adi. "How Indra Nooyi Turned Design Thinking into Strategy." *Harvard Business Review*, September 2015.

Catmull, Ed, with Amy Wallace. *Creativity, Inc*. New York: Random House, 2014.

Polman, Paul, and Andrew Winston. *Net Positive*. Boston: Harvard Business Review Press, 2021.

Gapper, John. "Danone and the Costs of Activist Capitalism." *Financial Times*, March 2021.

Gelles, David. "Billionaire No More: Patagonia Founder Gives Away the Company." *New York Times*, September 2022.

Chouinard, Yvon. *Let My People Go Surfing*. New York: Penguin, 2006.

Edmondson, Amy C. *The Fearless Organization*. Hoboken, NJ: Wiley, 2019.

Amabile, Teresa M., and Steven J. Kramer. *The Progress Principle*. Boston: Harvard Business Review Press, 2011.

CHAPTER 13

Lao Tzu. *Tao Te Ching*. Translated by Stephen Mitchell. New York: Harper Perennial, 1988.

Collins, Jim. *Good to Great*. New York: HarperBusiness, 2001.

Goleman, Daniel. *Emotional Intelligence*. New York: Bantam Books, 1995.

Kerr, James. *Legacy: What the All Blacks Can Teach Us About the Business of Life*. London: Constable, 2013.

Garvin, David A. "How Google Sold Its Engineers on Management." *Harvard Business Review*, December 2013.

"Developing a Coaching Culture at Standard Chartered." International Coaching Federation case study, 2018.

Hunt, James M., and Joseph R. Weintraub. *The Coaching Manager*. Thousand Oaks: Sage, 2016.

Lashinsky, Adam. *Inside Apple*. New York: Business Plus, 2012.

Mickle, Tripp. *After Steve*. New York: William Morrow, 2022.

Lafley, A.G., and Ram Charan. "The Art and Science of Finding the Right CEO." *Harvard Business Review*, October 2011.

Charan, Ram. *Leaders at All Levels*. San Francisco: Jossey-Bass, 2007.

Nayar, Vineet. *Employees First, Customers Second*. Boston: Harvard Business Press, 2010.

Hamel, Gary, and Michele Zanini. *Humanocracy*. Boston: Harvard Business Review Press, 2020.

Zhang, Ruimin, and Bill Fischer. *Reinventing Giants*. San Francisco: Jossey-Bass, 2013.

Gore, Robert. T*he Lattice Organization*. Newark, DE: W. L. Gore & Associates, 1992.

De Blok, Jos. Buurtzorg: *Humanity above Bureaucracy*. Utrecht: Buurtzorg Foundation, 2010.

Kniberg, Henrik, and Anders Ivarsson. "Scaling Agile at Spotify." Spotify Engineering White Paper, 2012.

Catmull, Ed, with Amy Wallace. *Creativity, Inc.* New York: Random House, 2014.

Nadella, Satya. *Hit Refresh*. New York: Harper Business, 2017.

McCord, Patty. *Powerful: Building a Culture of Freedom and Responsibility*. Silicon Guild, 2018.

Doerr, John. *Measure What Matters*. New York: Portfolio, 2018.

Edmondson, Amy C. *The Fearless Organization*. Hoboken, NJ: Wiley, 2018.

Edmondson, Amy C. *Teaming*. San Francisco: Jossey-Bass, 2012.

Bryar, Colin, and Bill Carr. *Working Backwards*. New York: St. Martin's Press, 2021.

CHAPTER 14

Kahn, William A. "Psychological Conditions of Personal Engagement and Disengagement at Work." *Academy of Management Journa*l 33, no. 4 (1990): 692-724.

Chapman, Bob, and Raj Sisodia. *Everybody Matters*. New York: Portfolio/Penguin, 2015.

Bertolini, Mark. "How Aetna's CEO Used Mindfulness and Yoga to Slash Health Care Costs." *Harvard Business Review*, March 2015.

Gittell, Jody Hoffer. *The Southwest Airlines Way*. New York: McGraw-Hill, 2003.

Frei, Frances X., and Anne Morriss. "The Culture Factor." *Harvard Business Review*, January-February 2020.

Cascio, Wayne F. "The High Cost of Low Wages." *Harvard Business Review*, December 2006.

Ton, Zeynep. *The Good Jobs Strategy*. Boston: New Harvest, 2014.

Novo Nordisk. Annual Report and Triple Bottom Line Reporting, 2023. Copenhagen: Novo Nordisk A/S.

Thomke, Stefan, and Barbara Feinberg. "IKEA: Design and Pricing." Harvard Business School Case 9-618-070, 2018.

Robertson, David C., with Bill Breen. *Brick by Brick*. New York: Crown Business, 2013.

Friedman, Vanessa. "The Philosopher King of Italian Fashion." *New York Times*, September 2018.

Spector, Robert, and Patrick D. McCarthy. *The Nordstrom Way to Customer Experience Excellence*. Hoboken: Wiley, 2017.

Kowitt, Beth. "Inside Trader Joe's." *Fortune*, August 23, 2010.

Gardiner, Bryan. "Why Trader Joe's Stands Out from All the Rest." *The Atlantic*, November 2019.

World Health Organization and International Labour Organization. *Mental Health at Work: Policy Brief*. Geneva: WHO/ILO, 2022.

Pfeffer, Jeffrey. *Dying for a Paycheck*. New York: HarperBusiness, 2018.

Gratton, Lynda, and Andrew Scott. *The 100-Year Life: Living and Working in an Age of Longevity*. London: Bloomsbury, 2016.

Gratton, Lynda. *Redesigning Work*. London: Penguin Business, 2022.

EPILOGUE

Schaar, John H. *Legitimacy in the Modern State*. New Brunswick, NJ: Transaction Publishers, 1981.

National Health Service (England). "NHS AI Expansion to Help Tackle Missed Appointments and Improve Waiting Times." March 14, 2024.

Davis, Caroline. "First NHS AI Run Physio Clinic in England Halves Back Pain Waiting List." *The Guardian*, July 31, 2025.

Ang, Adam. "Shanghai's Model Hospital of the Future." *Healthcare IT News*, July 22, 2025.

"Shanghai Releases the 'Work Plan for Developing Medical Artificial Intelligence (2025-2027).'" *CACLP Industry News*, December 25, 2024.

Selected Works by the Author

Written Works:

See all on katharinemclennan.com
- The CEO and CPO we need for the AI Age. (2023).
- The Neuroscience of Coaching. (2023).
- Building Leaders for the Imagination Age (2016).
- The Neuroscience of Leadership in Turbulent Times. (2008).
- The Neuroscience of Leadership and Culture. (2007).
- The Neuroscience of Trust. (2017).

Podcasts

See go.katharinemclennan.com/stanfordMBA
- Stanford MBA: From Baby Boomer to Gen Z | Class of '95 Meets Class of '25.

Videocast Set

See vimeo.com/showcase/8323583
- Katharine conducts 26 interviews of Olympics Executives for the 20th anniversary of the 2000 Sydney Olympic Games.

Videos of Keynote Speeches

See all speeches on youtube.com/@speakerkatharine
- Introduction to Katharine McLennan (2025)
- TEDx Talk: Katharine McLennan, Creating a Brain-Friendly Culture (2024)
- How to Attract, Develop, and Retain Talent in the Age of AI and Anxiety (2025)
- Video Summary of Podcast "Stanford MBA: From Baby Boomer to GenZ (2025)
- Class of '95 Meets Class of '25." (2025)
- Fearless Leadership: A Neuroscience Explanation. (2016)

Courses

Contact kath@katharinemclennan.com for more details

For those who coach - or aspire to coach- CEOs and their teams

Coach the C-Suite

Five Masterclass Series

Series One:
Orchestrating CEO Succession

Series Two:
Coaching a C-Suite Team

Series Three:
Designing Culture to Deliver Ingenuity

Series Four:
Coaching a CEO

Series Five:
Becoming and Evolving as a Chief People Officer

Designed for

- Consultants and coaches in leadership, assessment, strategy, executive search
- Chief People Officers and other HR Professionals
- Board Directors who oversee talent, culture, and succession
- Private-equity or family-owners assessing culture or determining leaders for their companies

Invitation to Self-Assess Your

Ingenuity Readiness in Leadership and Culture

You have now completed the paired questions at the end of each chapter. The two scoreboards on the following pages bring your Foundation and AI Amplifier averages together in one place: one for your leadership (VISTA) and one for your organization's culture (ORG6).

Transfer your end-of-chapter averages to the scoreboard rows if you have not already done so. Then calculate your overall averages for each dimension and plot your position on the two matrices. You will have two positions. They may not be in the same quadrant.

Once you can see both plots, sit with these questions:

1. Where is my biggest gap between Foundation and AI Amplifier? What does that reveal about where I am investing my attention?

2. Am I in the Outpaced quadrant anywhere, deploying AI faster than my foundations can support?

3. Where is my greatest untapped potential: strong foundations that AI could amplify further?

4. Where is the gap between my personal leadership (VISTA) and my organization (ORG6)? Am I leading beyond what my organization can follow, or is my organization outpacing my own development?

5. If I could move one score by one point in the next ninety days, which would create the most ripple?

6. What is one Foundation commitment and one AI Amplifier deployment I will begin this quarter?

The choice was never between technology and humanity. It was always between what AI amplifies in us. You now have a map of exactly where you stand.

For more information on interpretation, a more detailed assessment, or assistance with an action plan for achieving ingenuity rather than falling into irrelevance in the AI Era, please contact me at kath@katharinemclennan.com.

Transcribe your scores from the end of each chapter

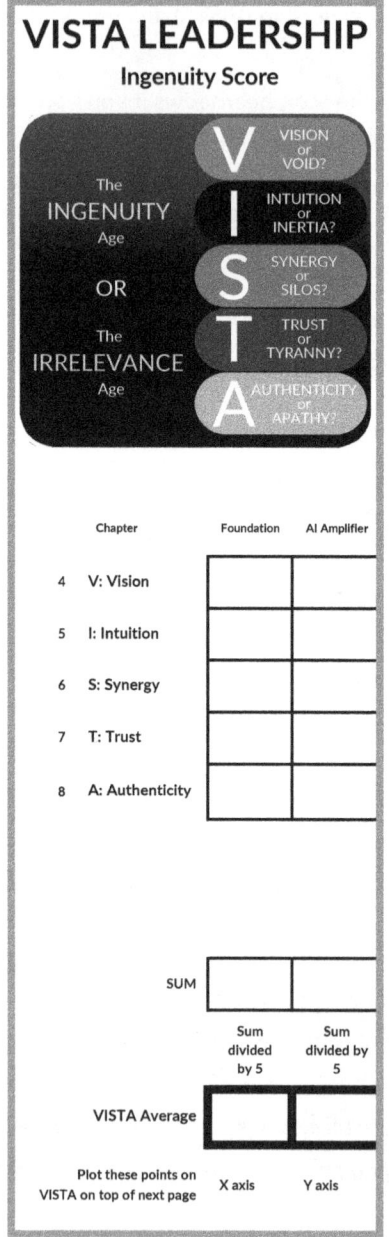

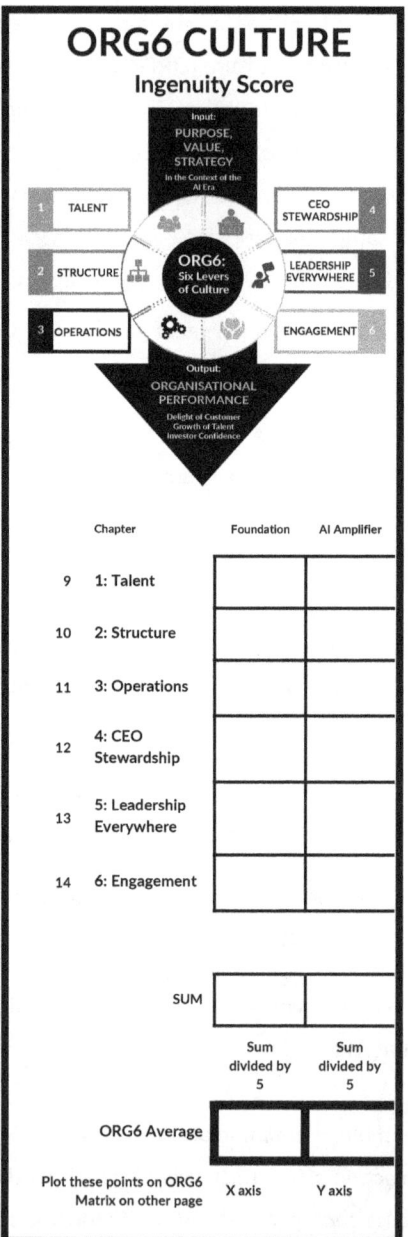

Plot your scores from the page before

About the Author

Katharine McLennan is an acclaimed keynote speaker and leadership strategist who has spent thirty-five years both inside and alongside the C-suite, alternating between executive leadership roles and external advisory work in leadership and culture. She has advised, coached, and facilitated over 200 boards and executive teams across industries and sectors, and held senior enterprise-wide positions as Global Vice President of People & Culture at Cochlear, the most senior HR executive at the Commonwealth Bank of Australia, Founder of the Global Leadership Academy at QBE, and Head of Operational Planning during the four years of preparation for the Sydney 2000 Olympics and Paralympics.

Katharine combines practical executive experience with deep academic grounding. She holds a B.S. in Biology (Neuroscience) and History from Duke University, an M.A. in Political Science from UNSW, and an MBA from Stanford University, where she studied at the dawn of the Internet Age, graduating in 1995. She is also an accredited psychotherapist, integrating insights from neuroscience, psychology, operations, culture, and strategy to help leaders design workplaces where people can think, create, and matter. Her insights draw as much from older wisdom traditions and a long-standing contemplative practice in nature as from her organizational life and research.

Her work centers on helping CEOs and their teams unite AI and human wisdom into purposeful action. She is the creator of the Coach the C-Suite masterclass series and the host of the **podcast Stanford MBA: From Baby Boomer to Gen Z**. In each episode, she facilitates a conversation between two Stanford MBA alumni, one from an earlier generation and one from a more recent class, each bringing equal wisdom to share. In 2026, the podcast is expanding to include graduates from the 1960s through the 1990s alongside graduates from the 2000s onward, widening the generational range and deepening the conversations across an entire arc of leadership experience.

To book Katharine as a keynote speaker or to inquire about her masterclass series, please contact kath@katharinemclennan.com.

katharinemclennan.com

kath@katharinemclennan.com

youtube.com/@speakerkatharine

linkedin.com/in/katharinemclennan/

www.ingramcontent.com/pod-product-compliance
Lightning Source LLC
Chambersburg PA
CBHW020405040426
42333CB00055B/403